PURCHASED FROM
MULTNOMAH COUNTY LIBRARY
TITLE WAVE BOOKSTORE

RIGHT FACE

Niels Bjerre-Poulsen

RIGHT FACE

Organizing the American Conservative Movement
1945-65

Museum Tusculanum Press
University of Copenhagen
2002

Niels Bjerre-Poulsen: Right Face
© by Museum Tusculanum Press 2002

Cover design by Sysser Bengtsson
All rights reserved
Printed in Denmark by Narayana Press

ISBN 87 7289 720 1 (hardcover edn.)
ISBN 87 7289 809 7 (paperback edn.)

Published with the support of:
Statens Humanistiske Forskningsråd
(The Danish Research Council for the Humanities)
Nordea Danmark Fonden

Cover photo: Ronald Reagan,
an alternate delegate to the GOP
convention shows his Goldwater
ribbon as second session of the
convention gets under way.
San Francisco, California, USA
Date of photo, July 13, 1964
© Bettmann/CORBIS

Museum Tusculanum Press
University of Copenhagen
Njalsgade 92
DK-2300 Copenhagen S
Denmark

www.mtp.dk

Contents

Acknowledgements   7

Introduction   11

1   The Revolt against Liberalism   21
2   Fusing Ice and Fire   39
3   McCarthyism and the Conservative Quest for a Public Orthodoxy   55
4   Out of Isolation   79
5   Finding a Voice: the National Review   115
6   Third-Party Probings: The Case of the New York Conservative Party   141
7   Preparing the Next Generation: Conservatism on Campus   163
8   The Respectable- and the Not-so-respectable Right   185
9   The Reluctant Crusader   209
10   Conquering the GOP   233
11   The Anatomy of a Landslide   261
12   Epilogue   291

Bibliography   309

Index   329

Acknowledgements

I WOULD LIKE to express my gratitude to the mentors, colleagues and friends, in Denmark, the United States, and elsewhere, who have helped me through the undertaking of writing this book. They deserve much of the credit and none of the blame.

My mentor at the University of Copenhagen, Professor Inga Floto, inspired me to want to spend the rest of my professional life on the study of American history. Throughout the years she has helped and encouraged me far beyond the call of duty.

I am sorry that I can no longer extend my gratitude directly to two people who have also contributed generously to this project. It was my great fortune to have Professor Robert L. Kelley as my Ph.D. advisor at University of California, Santa Barbara until he passed away in 1993. Niels Thorsen, my teacher and friend at the University of Copenhagen University, passed away in 2000. Both inspired and guided me with their tremendous insight into American political culture. I could not have undertaken or completed a project like this one without their training and support, and I feel very privileged to have known them.

Professor Otis Graham became my Ph.D. advisor in 1993 and has helped and encouraged me ever since. He has read my manuscript at different stages and provided substantive suggestions. I have profited enormously from his insight and wise counsel.

Among the American studies scholars in Denmark I would particularly like to thank Regin Schmidt from University of Copenhagen, Peter Kurrild Klitgaard from University of Southern Denmark, and my colleague at the Copenhagen Business School, Eric Guthey. They have all read parts of my manuscript at different stages and provided thoughtful comments and suggestions. Likewise, I am indebted to Professor Erik Åsard from the Swedish Institute for North American Studies at Uppsala University and Professor Keith Olson from University of Maryland at College Park for their comments and suggestions. Professor James T. Patterson of Brown University and Professor Ted McAllister of Pepperdine University both found time in their busy schedules to read and comment on the final manuscript. I am most grateful for their generous help.

Given the nature of this study, a crucial source has been provided by correspondence between principal organizers and other leading figures of the conservative movement. I would like to thank William F. Buckley, Jr., William A. Rusher, and F. Clifton White for granting me permission to use their papers, and Dean Burch for granting me access to the papers of the Republican National Committee.

In the first years of my research, before there was much of interest to find on the Internet, the staff at the Library of the American Embassy in Copenhagen was a lifeline for everyone doing American studies in Denmark. I am particularly indebted to librarians Karen Kirk-Sørensen and Inge Glud for all their help in those years.

On my journeys to do archival research in the United States, I have received generous help from librarians at the Hoover Institution Archives at Stanford University, the Olin Library at Cornell University, Herbert Hoover Presidential Library, West Branch, Iowa, the Manuscript and Archives Department, Yale University, the "Right Wing Collection" at Iowa University, the Arizona Historical Foundation, Arizona State University, the Lyndon B. Johnson Library in Austin, Texas, the Chicago Historical Society, the Center for American History, University of Texas, the John F. Kennedy Presidential Library in Boston, and the Library of Congress in Washington, D.C. I sincerely thank all the librarians who have guided me safely through the collections at these splendid libraries.

My thanks also to Joyce Kling of The Language Center, Copenhagen Business School for her meticulous proof-reading and to the effective publishing team at Museum Tusculanum Press for seeing the manuscript through production.

The publication of this book was made possible by a grant from the Danish Research Council for the Humanities, as well as by the generous support that I have enjoyed over the years from my department at the Copenhagen Business School. I also owe much to the Fulbright Committee and the Denmark-America Foundation, who made my study of the American conservative movement possible in the first place through grants which enabled me to enter the Ph.D. Program at the Department of History at University of California, Santa Barbara. I am truly grateful to everyone who made my years in Santa Barbara so happy and rewarding.

Last but certainly not least, I would like to thank my wife, Sysser, and my children for almost everything in my life except the contents of this book. They have rejuvenated me whenever I was growing just a little bit tired of the American conservative movement.

Copenhagen, May 2002

Introduction

> In reality, there is no One Big Idea, or One Infallible Platform, which can unite the disparate conservative elements in the United States. No simple formula can join inseparably the Northerners and the Southerners, the rural interests and the urban interests, the religious conservatives and the utilitarian old-fangled liberals, the anti-Soviet people and the isolationists—not to mention the anti-flouridationists, the "philosophical" anarchists, and the protectionists. All that can be hoped for, so far as the immediate future is concerned, is a series of leagues and coalitions of anti-collectivist elements against the collectivist tendency of the times.
>
> Russell Kirk[1]

"Why Is There So Much Conservatism in the United States and Why Do So Few Historians Know Anything About It?" So asked historians Alan Brinkley and Leo Ribuffo in the April 1994-issue of *American Historical Review*.[2] They argued that despite the profound impact that conservative forces since the late 1970s had had on the political discourse in America, the conservative movement remained an orphan in historical scholarship. Thus, this book has been written in an attempt to help remedy that situation.

The central theme of this book is not the social psychology of American conservatives, but their political mobilization. I am less concerned with how and why they became conservative than I am with how they attempted to translate their views into political action. I argue that conservatives in the postwar years made a deliberate attempt to move from the sidelines of American politics to center stage through the creation of a

---

1 Russell Kirk, "The Seventh Congress of Freedom," *National Review* (May 3, 1958), p. 418.
2 It was Alan Brinkley who opened the discussion about conservatism as an neglected issue in American history in "The Problem of American Conservatism," *American Historical Review* (April 1994), pp. 409-429. The actual question was the title of Ribuffo's response in the same issue, pp. 438-449.

counterpart to the "liberal establishment" they so resented. During the 1950s, the movement evolved from a small gathering of scattered voices, decrying the prevailing New Deal order, to a loosely knit network of local and national organizations, determined to take back what they considered their historic home: the Republican Party. In other words, this is a study of a would-be political elite.

The connection between this elite and those at the receiving end is only addressed sporadically. Although this is mostly a deliberate choice, the lack of usable quantitative material had also played its part. There is still a scarcity of surveys, oral histories, studies of voting behavior, etc., which might shed light on the political motivation of rank and file conservatives, at least on the national level.[3]

Although the organizational aspects of the postwar conservative movement is my main concern in this book, these aspects have to a large extent been shaped by tactical and intellectual disagreements among conservatives themselves. The movement remained an uneasy alliance against a common enemy rather than a real fusion of different intellectual strains. Accordingly, the story of how it was organized can not be told without reference to the ideological struggles that shaped conservative thought in postwar America.[4]

---

3 See William B. Hixon, Jr.'s comprehensive survey *Search for the American Right Wing; an Analysis of the Social Science Record, 1955-1987* (Princeton: Princeton University Press, 1992), p. xix. A number of regional studies of the conservative movement at grass-roots level have filled in some of the gaps. Among the best are Jonathan Rieder's *Canarsie: The Jews and Italians of Brooklyn Against Liberalism* (Cambridge: Harvard University Press, 1987), Rebecca E. Klatch's study of SDS and YAF, *A Generation Divided; The New Left, the New Right, and the 1960s* (Berkeley: University of California Press, 1999), and Lisa McGirr's study of the conservative movement in Orange County, *Suburban Warriors; The Origins of the New American Right* (Princeton: Princeton University Press, 2001).
4 The best account of the intellectual development of postwar conservatism is still George H. Nash's *The Conservative Intellectual Movement in America Since 1945.* (New York: Basic Books, Inc., 1979 [1976]). Other works of interest include Godfrey Hodgson, *The World Turned Right Side Up: A History of the Conservative Ascendancy in America* (Boston: Houghton Mifflin Company, 1996), Rick Perlstein, *Before the Storm; Barry Goldwater and the Unmaking of the American Consensus* (New York: Hill and Wang, 2001), John P. Diggins, *Up From Communism* (New York: Harper & Row, 1975), Ronald Lora, *Conservative Minds in America* (Chicago: Rand McNally & Company, 1971), John P. East, *The American Conservative Movement: The Philosophical Foundations* (Chicago: Regnery Books, 1986), Dunn, Charles W. & J. David Woodard, *American Conservatism From Burke to Bush* (Lanham: Madison Books, 1991), and Gottfried, Paul & T Fleming, *The Conservative Movement* (Boston: Twayne Publishers, 1988).

My own interest in the history of American conservatism was first awakened under the impression of the conservative tide that apparently swept the United States in 1980 and carried Ronald Reagan to the White House. The network of organizations which had become known to the public as "the New Right" took a great deal of the credit for this alleged conservative revolution and self-confidently announced that they were now "ready to lead."[5].

The "New Right" label encouraged me to look beyond the hype and attempt to place this proclaimed conservative groundswell in a larger historical context. I soon realized that the New Right of the 1980s was simply one among several "New Rights" in postwar America. (In fact "the New New New Right" would have been a more appropriate label for it). I began to look for the continuity between these phenomena and found something I think can be fairly described as a movement.

Just as the term "conservative" is slippery, the description of conservatism as a "movement" is problematic as well. Skeptics may rightly question this notion and argue that there is little to the claim, apart from the fact that at any given time since the late 1940s a certain number of right-wing organizations have been in existence. However, as I hope this study will show, these various organizations have demonstrated continuity, a will to cohere, and a deliberate intent to counter most parts of the alleged liberal establishment with "parallel organizations."[6] In order to gain political representation, conservatives have recruited activists and mobilized voters, both at local and national levels. They have organized vertically as well – within specific religious denominations and/or within specific professions. They have established outlets for conservative ideas and channels for fundraising. In short, American conservatives have made deliberate efforts to institutionalize their political ideas.

---

5   See Richard Viguerie, *The New Right: We're Ready to Lead* (Falls Church, Va., 1981).
6   To mention just a few examples, The New York Conservative Party was organized to counter the Liberal Party of New York; Young Americans for Freedom (YAF) was organized to counter the National Student Organization (NSA); Americans for Constitutional Action (ACA) was intended as a counterpart to Americans for Democratic Action (ADA). Likewise, journals such as *Human Events* and *National Review* were intended as rivals to *The Nation* and *The New Republic*, and conservative think tanks such as the American Enterprise Institute and the Hoover Institution were intended as counterparts to the Brookings Institution.

Before we embark on the history of postwar conservatism, it might be useful to briefly address some problems concerning terminology. I use the term "conservatism" rather freely in this book. I do not contribute to the list of attempts to define the true meaning of the concept.[7] It is not my aim to write anybody into the conservative movement or out of it. My purpose, in brief, is simply to describe the movement which, rightly or wrongly, called itself "conservative," rather than proceeding in the opposite fashion, which has produced so much confusion: "defining" the term and then examining those who fit that description.[8]

Of course this does not imply that the struggle over the meaning of the conservative label is irrelevant. Far from it. One may question the attempt to define American conservatism as an ideology with a core of shared ideas. Yet, the very quest for such a definition has itself been a crucial factor in the shaping of the movement – for its political organization, as well as for its development of ideas.

It might be argued that given my inability to give a closer definition of the term "conservative," I should rather avoid it altogether and simply use the neutral and inclusive term "right wing," or stick to the more specific terms such as "traditionalist," "libertarian," and "anticommunist." I have used these more specific terms when necessary, such as in the obvious case

---

7   Over the last four decades, numerous attempts at a definition of modern American conservatism have been made. An outline of its taxonomy can be found in Clinton Rossiter, *Conservatism in America; The Thankless Persuasion* (New York: Alfred A. Knopf, 1962 [1955]), pp. 3-20. Recent attempts at a definition of conservatism include Robert Nisbet, *Conservatism: Dream and Reality* (Minneapolis: University of Minnesota Press, 1986) and Melvin J. Thorne, *American Conservative Thought since World War Two* (New York: Greenwood Press, 1990). The latter includes an attempt to explain why all previous definitions of American conservatism so far have been inadequate, as well as the author's own attempt at a definition (courageous as it might be, Thorne's definition does not leave one convinced that his own foot fits the shoe any better than any of his predecessors). Among the right's own attempts to define the bounds of conservatism is Frank S. Meyer, *What is Conservatism?* (New York: Holt, Rinehart and Winston, 1964). The diversity of postwar conservative thought is well demonstrated by William F. Buckley, Jr. (ed.), *Keeping the Tablets* (New York: Harper & Row, 1988).
8   For an example of this strategy, see Samuel P. Huntington, "Conservatism as an Ideology," *The American Political Science Review*, Vol. LI, No. 2 (June 1957), pp. 454-473. Huntington ascribes to a situational definition of conservatism, which somewhat simplified brings him to the conclusion that liberals defending the political order in America against Communism are the true conservatives, while the self-proclaimed conservatives are in fact radical reactionaries. Particularly the traditionalists, with their belief in transcendent moral principles, were according to Huntington's definition non-conservatives.

of conflicts within the movement, but I do feel that there are compelling reasons for using the term "conservative," despite the confusion that it might result in. Most of all, it is the term that the people and organizations in question here most frequently used about themselves, and for that reason alone avoiding it would only add to the confusion.

According to *Webster's Encyclopedic Unabridged Dictionary of the English Language*, conservatism is "the disposition to preserve what is established and to promote gradual development rather than abrupt change."[9] Such a temperamental definition of conservatism is also found in political philosopher Michael Oakeshott's classical essay "On Being Conservative" (1956):

> To be conservative, then, is to prefer the familiar to the unknown, to prefer the tried to the untried, fact to mystery, the actual to the possible, the limited to the unbounded, the near to the distant, the sufficient to the superabundant, the convenient to the perfect, present laughter to utopian bliss.[10]

Oakeshott's view of conservatism was largely shared by American historian Clinton Rossiter, who in his book *Conservatism in America* contended that "'creeping conservatism' rather than 'creeping socialism' was the grand trend of the 1950s. By the middle of the decade we were, as much as restless America ever can be, a conservative country."[11] His concept of conservatism falls in line with the common description of the Eisenhower-era as "conservative," and gives associations to words such as "complacency" and "conformity." Rossiter is concerned with a general shift in the public mood, an inclination or a *zeitgeist* rather than an ideology.

Oakeshott and Rossiter's use of the conservative label is evidently different from the way in which it is used in this book. Only a few of the people and organizations in question would probably qualify as conservatives in their terminology. Most of them would be more aptly labeled as "reactionaries," "right wing radicals," or – to use the term preferred by many of

---

9 (New York: Gramercy Books, 1989), p. 312.
10 Reprinted in Michael Oakeshott, *Rationalism in politics and other essays* (Indianapolis: Liberty Press 1991), p. 408
11 Clinton Rossiter, *Conservatism in America; the Thankless Persuasion* (New York: Alfred A. Knopf, 1962 [1955]), p. 4.

the leading voices of consensus-liberalism at the time – "pseudo-conservatives."[12]

The concern of those in question here was not to conserve the best elements of the existing political order, but to overthrow it. In their own understanding, they were trying to take the country back. Most longed to return to the era before the New Deal, although a few did dream of rolling government back all the way to the Articles of Confederation.[13]

The terms "conservatism," "the American Right," and "the right wing" are often used interchangeably in this book, but it is important to note that there have always been groups and organizations further to the right of those concerned here. However, the line between the "respectable" conservatives and "the Radical Right" represented by organizations such as the John Birch Society, Christian Crusade, and the Liberty Lobby has often been difficult to draw. On many issues they have been on common ground, just as there have always been personal ties between both sponsors and leading political figures of the conservative movement and the Radical Right. Despite the temptation of a "guilt by association" approach, it is nevertheless important to note the distinctions. It does not make any sense to refer to everyone from the American Nazi Party to Nelson Rockefeller as simply "members of the New Right," as some scholarly works on the subject have done.[14]

The conservative movement can probably be most immediately understood as a political coalition of widely different ideological strains which in the classic fashion, in politics, became united in their common antagonism to a common enemy: the liberal political order which had been established with the New Deal. These ideological strains can be divided into three major directions usually referred to as "traditionalism," "libertarianism," and "anti-communism." While they were not necessarily sharply separated, they were, on the other hand, never blended convincingly into a common credo.[15] For all practical purposes, the essential ideological glue

---

12 See Daniel Bell, *The Radical Right* (New York: Doubleday & Company, 1963).
13 See Murray N. Rothbard, "A Strategy for the Right; Presidential Address to the Randolph Club, Herndon, Virginia, January 18, 1992," (www.lewrockwell.com/rothbard/ir/Ch1.html)
14 For an example, see Jonathan Martin Kolkey, *The New Right, 1960-1968 With Epilogue, 1969-1980* (Washington, D.C.: University Press of America, 1983).
15 A representative example is Frank S. Meyer, *What is Conservatism* (New York: Holt, Rinehart and Winston, 1964).

that would hold the new conservative coalition together was provided by the new aggressive brand of anti-communism that evolved in postwar America as the conflict with the Soviet Union and its allies escalated. Indeed, it remains an open question whether a conservative movement could have evolved as a national political force without the emergence of the Cold War.

To describe the American conservative movement as a post World War II phenomenon is not to imply that there were no conservative individuals and organizations prior to that. Only that there was no movement. Indeed, one might argue that conservative views on the proper role of the state had rather been so widespread that there had not been any strong need to articulate them, nor any urgency to mobilize conservatives nationally. By nature, American conservatism was largely parochial. All this changed with the emergence of the Great Depression and with the new interventionist role of the federal government, which became the liberal response to it.

Throughout the 1930s, there were scattered attempts to challenge the policies of the New Deal. In 1934 a group of businessmen founded the American Liberty League with the explicit purpose of promoting opposition to the New Deal. At the height of its popularity the League had almost 125,000 members.[16] The organization, however, did not represent any serious attempt to spell out an alternative political vision, let alone a serious effort to mobilize conservative "grassroots" in the country. To the majority of Americans it looked more like a club of greedy businessmen attempting to rationalize their self-interest. So common was this perception that the Republican National Committee in the election of 1936 asked the league to refrain from endorsing the GOP presidential candidate Alf Landon.[17]

The New Deal met a more serious challenge when the election of 1938 brought a new breed of conservatives to Capitol Hill. For all practical pur-

---

16 For the history of the American Liberty League, see George Wolfskill, *The Revolt of the Conservatives: A History of the American Liberty League, 1934-1940* (Boston: Houghton Mifflin Company, 1962).

17 William E. Leuchtenburg, *Franklin D. Roosevelt and the New Deal, 1932-1940* (New York: Harper & Row, Publishers, 1963), p. 179.

poses, President Roosevelt's reform program was stopped dead in its tracks that year.[18] However, America's involvement in World War II delayed any further organizing of this opposition, as FDR changed his title from "Dr. New Deal" to "Dr. Win-the-War." Thus, if the seeds of discontent had been sown by the dramatic social and political changes of the 1930s, it was not until the late 1940s that the label of conservatism, which for many years had been out of use except as an occasional smear, found its way back into the nation's political vocabulary.[19]

The new movement which now described itself as "conservative" was at first mainly intellectual in nature. Its aim was to provide a philosophical framework for opposition to the reigning liberal order. The movement's political aspirations were nevertheless clear from the beginning. Although it would take many years before conservative intellectuals truly took the plunge into practical politics, they were soon busy providing ammunition for right-wing politicians within the established political system. Likewise, the quest for appropriate conservative forums in the form of journals, newsletters, conferences, and seminars also became a natural corollary to the search for a philosophical framework.

Although conservatives generally had closer ties to the Republican Party than to the Democrats, it was to a large extent the growing sense of homelessness that some felt within the Republican Party, which helped forge the movement. With the claim that the "me-too Republicans" had taken over the party and displaced it from its natural role as a conservative counterpart to the Democratic Party, the right created an independent organizational network. This network could either help regain control of the GOP, or create a genuinely conservative alternative.

This book traces the evolution of the conservative network. The first part is mainly concerned with the anatomy of the movement: what (and who) it was, and, perhaps equally important, what it was not. It is my hope that this part will provide a conceptual framework for understanding postwar conservatism in the absence of a strict definition. Chapter 1 describes how conservatives attempted to define their own political identity in relation to the reigning New Deal liberalism. Chapter 2 describes the at-

---

18 See James T. Patterson, *Congressional Conservatism and the New Deal* (Lexington: University of Kentucky Press, 1967).

19 As a matter of fact, Peter Viereck's *Conservatism Revisited* (New York: Collier Books, 1962), initially published in 1949, was the first book in the postwar years where the word "conservatism" was used in the title.

tempt to find common ground among the widely different ideological strains which existed on the right, while Chapter 3 analyzes the impact of McCarthyism on the emerging conservative movement.

Chapters 4 and 5 concern the struggle to create appropriate outlets for conservative opinion. The role of journals such as *Human Events, the Freeman*, and *National Review* went far beyond the effort to spread the gospel of conservatism to the hinterlands. They became nerve centers in a growing political network. The story of these journals also provides an excellent opportunity to analyze some major events in the shaping of the conservative movement. The internal struggles as well as the strategic considerations that took place in the editorial offices aptly reflected the major transformations that the movement underwent in the two decades covered herein. They also illustrate the extent to which ideas really did have consequences for the organizing of the right (also evidenced by the fact that internal disagreements on conservative principles in several cases proved to be fatal for the journals involved). Studying the conservative media, in other words, gives a valuable insight into the efforts to translate into political action the ideas that were generated by the growing counter-intelligentsia.

Chapter 4 specifically analyzes the transformation in the conservative view of foreign policy, from isolationism to Cold War interventionism, while Chapter 5 deals with the seminal role of William F. Buckley, Jr. and the crowd he gathered around his journal *National Review*. While the journal became the leading voice of the conservative movement, the contributors assumed the role as the gatekeepers of "responsible" conservatism.

Chapters 6 through 11 deal with the conservative movement's plunge into national politics, beginning in the late 1950s. Especially after the election of 1960, which sent a liberal Democrat to the White House, right-wing organizations apparently began to mushroom all over the country. On campuses across the nation, the next generation of conservatives began to organize under the banners of Young Americans for Freedom (Chapter 6). In New York a group of conservative Republicans founded their own independent party in the hope of defeating the liberal Republican leadership in that state (Chapter 7). The chapter describes the problems that conservatives faced when they attempted to change the Republican Party from the outside.

Other right-wing activists were at work inside the GOP. They wanted to pave the way for a dedicated conservative as the next Republican presidential candidate. However, in the early 1960s, a new national attention on "the Radical Right" and right wing "extremism" marked the political debate. "Extremism" also became a major issue in the Goldwater campaign. This confronted the conservative movement with a dilemma. In their quest for intellectual respectability many now felt compelled to shut out potential allies from the movement, among them well-organized and well-funded organizations such as the John Birch Society. Chapter 8 deals with this struggle to define the limits of "responsible conservatism."

During the primaries of 1960, the conservative movement had for the first time in many years found a national leading figure in Senator Barry Goldwater of Arizona. Before long, a small group of right-wing Republicans set out to organize the conservative grass roots across the country in the "Draft Goldwater movement." Their efforts are described in Chapter 9. Chapters 10 and 11 deal with the fate of Barry Goldwater and the conservative movement in the 1964 presidential election – an election which eventually buried Goldwater in a landslide. It also describes the often strained relationship between the candidate and his "Arizona Mafia" on the one side, and the conservative movement on the other.

Was the nomination of Goldwater a tragic blunder? Many liberal and moderate Republicans chose to see it that way. They pointed to the irony in the fact that the uncompromising Goldwater and his zealous supporters had actually paved the way for a new wave of social reform by helping re-elect Lyndon B. Johnson. The nomination of Goldwater had indeed polarized the Republican Party, or at least brought the existing conflicts out into the open. It had also given LBJ a very strong mandate for reform.

Nevertheless, the Goldwater campaign became a watershed in the history of American conservatism, the movement's baptism of fire. The following years would make it evident that President Johnson's landslide victory had not been the last nail in the coffin of the conservative movement, as many liberal observers had believed in the wake of the election. Rather, it had been the beginning of a new phase in the organizing of the American Right. In the following decades, the institutionalization of the conservative movement amid the major social upheavals of the time and the exhaustion of liberalism would pave the way for a dedicated conservative president in the White House. The Epilogue of the book traces the remarkable development of the movement, from the ashes of Goldwater's defeat to the Reagan-years and beyond. Furthermore, it attempts to assess the actual strength of American conservatism at the dawn of the 21st century.

Chapter 1

The Revolt against Liberalism

> What holds us under one tent — to use the current popular image — is our common loathing for what liberalism has done to the American ethos.
> MIDGE DECTER[1]

IF THE VARIOUS strains of postwar American conservatism were first of all integrated by their common opposition to New Deal liberalism, then one way of getting closer to an understanding of who the conservatives were and how they defined their own political role is to look at how they perceived their liberal counterpart.

Right-wingers objected to New Deal liberalism on a range of different levels. From matters of economic and political theory to moral and spiritual objections, they blamed modern liberalism and the "ethical relativism" that it represented for the impending "Suicide of the West."[2] Although several of these types of objections were usually clustered together, it nevertheless makes sense to separate them for analytical purposes. First, a brief look at how the connotations of the word "liberal" changed with the New Deal.

The Transformation of Liberalism

Liberalism, conservatives of the 1940s and 1950s were frequently told, was not only the dominant but also the sole political tradition in America.[3]

---

1 "On the Future of Conservatism; A Symposium", *Commentary,* February 1997.
2 The expression is taken from James Burnham, *Suicide of the West* (New York: The John Day Company, 1964).
3 The most important expression of this view was probably Louis Hartz, *The Liberal Tradition in America* (New York: Harcourt, Brace & World, 1955).

This idea did not necessarily trigger strong objections. A great many of those who for lack of a better word had adopted the conservative label felt that they were indeed the true inheritors of the American liberal tradition in the laissez-faire sense of devotion to free enterprise capitalism. In their view, it was the adherents to the New Deal who represented a radical departure from that tradition.

In contrast to FDR, who acquired status as the chief villain, his immediate predecessor in the White House, Herbert Hoover, in retrospect acquired a position in the conservative pantheon as the last liberal champion of free enterprise. As studies of the Hoover presidency by Murray S. Rothbard, Joan Hoff Wilson and others have pointed out, the decades before the New Deal were not a golden era of free enterprise.[4] From its founding in the 1850s, the Republican Party, inheriting the ideas of its Federalist and Whig predecessors, had consistently advocated, and put into public policy, the idea that government should so far avoid laissez-faire as to intervene actively and continuously in the economy. Its purpose, however, was in their view to provide powerful aids to entrepreneurs (as in protective tariffs) rather than to serve as a stern socially conscious watchdog and regulator, in the style of the New Deal, anxious to eliminate special privilege and insure social justice.[5] In other words, it was not so much the question of *whether* the government should intervene in the economy as it was the question of *how* the government should intervene, that separated Roosevelt's policies from those of his predecessor.[6]

The myth of FDR's alleged betrayal of the American liberal tradition of laissez-faire nevertheless became a crucial element in the *weltanschauung* of

---

4   Ronald Radosh & Murray Rothbard, *A New History of Leviathan* (New York, E.P. Dutton & Co., Inc., 1972); Joan Hoff Wilson, *Herbert Hoover: Forgotten Progressive* (Boston: Little, Brown, 1975).

5   FDR himself pointed out this ambiguous view of government intervention in his 1932 address to the Commonwealth Club: "Republican administrations for business urgently to ask the government to put at private disposal all kinds of government assistance. The same man who tells you that he does not want to see the government interfere in business – and he means it, and has plenty of good reasons for saying so – is the first to go to Washington and ask the government for a prohibitory tariff on his product." Quoted from Michael Kammen, *People of Paradox* (New York: Alfred A. Knopf, Inc., 1972), p. 274.

6   Adam Smith himself warned of the entrepreneur's appetite for monopoly, Smith's true *bete noire*, of the business community's constant urge to overcharge the public and exploit labor, and of the dangerous power of bankers.

the Right.⁷ Considering the fact that one of the most common objections to liberals was their "relativism," their alleged lack of belief in an objective moral order, there was a certain irony in the fact that conservatives usually treated liberalism as if it were an absolute. They largely neglected the fact that what went under the label of modern liberalism actually covered a wide spectrum of opinions which had evolved considerably since the early days of the New Deal. Especially in the paramount field of foreign policy, liberalism in the first Cold War years had actually moved significantly to the right — to the kind of militaristic balance-of-power foreign policy "realism" advocated by such presidents as Theodore Roosevelt. Power (Soviet) must be matched by power (American), said those two towering figures of postwar Democratic foreign policy thought Reinhold Niebuhr and George Kennan. After the election of 1948, the Henry Wallace type of anti-militaristic, trusting-of-the-Soviets progressive liberalism that came closest to the stereotype promoted by conservatives was virtually dead. It had not been killed by the conservatives, but by the new brand of Cold War liberalism which characterized the Truman-administration, as well as organizations such as Americans for Democratic Action.⁸

Regardless of this transformation, there were also disenchanted liberals who maintained their focus on domestic issues and saw the continuous attempts to expand the role of the state in social welfare as a betrayal of the liberal tradition. A minor but nevertheless significant part of the postwar conservative movement was made up of such former liberals.

Two illustrative examples of people who for all practical purposes had become part of the conservative camp by the 1940s, but who nevertheless insisted they were the true liberals or "progressives" were a former member of FDR's Brain Trust Raymond Moley and a former chief counsel in FDR's National Recovery Administration Donald R. Richberg. Both

---

7   One notable exception, a person who did not share the common detestation of FDR was Ronald Reagan. While attempting to carry out the political mission of ending the era initiated by John Kennedy and Lyndon Johnson and their reforms, Reagan throughout his political career maintained a strong personal admiration of FDR. As William E. Leuchtenburg has pointed out, there is a certain irony in the fact that the president who allegedly set out to reverse the legacy of FDR also was the successor who most openly emulated his political style and rhetoric. See William E. Leuchtenburg, *In the Shadow of FDR; From Harry Truman to Ronald Reagan* (Ithaca: Cornell University Press, 1983), pp. 209-235.

8   See Norman D. Markowitz, *Rise and Fall of the People's Century: Henry A. Wallace and American Liberalism, 1941-1948* (1974).

would even maintain, long after having become celebrated figures on the Right, that they had remained faithful to what they saw as the original intentions of the New Deal, namely to "save capitalism" through cooperation between government and business.

However, even while they were still involved in New Deal legislation, the sympathies of Richberg and Moley had clearly been on the side of the business community. In their views, the original intentions behind the National Industrial Recovery Act of 1933 (which created the National Recovery Administration) was never to impose some kind of federal regulation of business, but rather to minimize social conflict by getting all economic interests working together within the NRA to create "fair competition." The government's purpose was first of all to serve as an honest broker, in order to optimize the free enterprise system.[9]

As they saw it, the New Deal had betrayed these original intentions. Moley and Richberg became increasingly disenchanted with the policies of the Roosevelt-administration in the early 1940s and vigorously opposed any measure which could be regarded as a step in the direction of a paternalistic welfare state. To Richberg, the calls by FDR's successor Harry Truman for a national health insurance, higher minimum wages, higher unemployment compensation, and similar measures, was "nothing but Communism watered down for amateur consumption."[10]

"The Road to Serfdom"

Although former liberals such as Moley and Richberg remained faithful to what they saw as the New Deal's original intentions of cooperation between government and business, the majority of postwar conservatives were brought up to think differently. To them the very idea of "planning," as embodied in the NRA and other new deal programs, was the Original Sin and all the alleged evils of "collectivism" were bound to follow sooner or later. The most influential presentation of this argument was found in

---

9 See William E. Leuchtenburg, *Franklin D. Roosevelt and the New Deal 1932-1940* (New York: Harper & Row, Publishers, 1963), and Frank Annunziata, "Donald R. Richberg and American Liberalism; An Illinois Progressive's Critique of the New Deal and Welfare State," *Journal of the Illinois State Historical Society* (November, 1974), pp. 531-547.
10 Quoted from Frank Annunziata, *Donald R. Richberg...*, p. 544.

a little foreign book, which appeared in 1944 and became an overnight success in wartime America. The title was *The Road to Serfdom*, and the author was F.A. Hayek, an Austrian émigré teaching at the London School of Economics.[11] Having stirred a lot of intellectual controversy, the book was soon reprinted by *Readers Digest* and distributed in more than a million copies in the United States.[12]

Despite the catchy title, the book had never been intended for popular consumption, and its commercial success was a major surprise, not least to Hayek himself. The book was scholarly and dispassionate in style, yet its message was uncompromising: any attempt at economic "planning" would ultimately change the social and moral values of the nation and lead it down the road to "totalitarianism." Planning was an absolute. There was no middle ground between that and unconditional faith in the virtues of the free market. The latter was the only choice that in the long run was compatible with democracy.[13]

Evil conspiracies did not play any part in Hayek's book. One of his main points was that countries such as Britain and the USA were most likely to be taken down the unforeseen road to "totalitarianism" by well-meaning democratic "socialists,"[14] who adopted "planning" in their attempt to promote the general welfare of the nation.[15] So why did Hayek's book become so popular in America? The question is worth pondering for

---

11 F.A. Hayek, *The Road to Serfdom* (Chicago: The University of Chicago Press, 1972 [1944]).

12 For further details on the reception of Hayek's book in America, see George H. Nash, *The Conservative Intellectual Movement...*, pp. 5-8.

13 While Hayek may justly be classified as a "libertarian" (although he personally has preferred to be labeled a "whig,") he was not a radical anti-statist. The state had an important role to play in his model society (as in Adam Smith's), creating and enforcing a legal framework in order to keep competition free. This viewpoint actually brought him at odds with more radical American libertarians such as Frank Chodorov and, later, Murray N. Rothbard, who found that Hayek's argument was self-contradictory (not to mention Ayn Rand and her followers, for whom "the road to serfdom" did not begin with social planning, but with altruism).

14 The book was dedicated to "socialists of all parties." Hayek did not use the word "liberal" in its modern American sense, but with its nineteenth century connotations (i.e. *laissez-faire* liberalism).

15 For the record, it should be mentioned what Hayek did **not** say (or at least what he later claimed he did not intend to say): "Planning" would not inevitably lead directly to the rise of a totalitarian regime, but result in an "alteration in the character of the people" that would create the social and moral climate for a totalitarian state. *Serfdom,* p. xi ff.

at least two reasons. First, the reaction to it is often mentioned as one of the first signs of the birth (or rebirth) of libertarian conservatism in post-New Deal America. Several conservative intellectuals would later refer to their reading of it as a crucial event in their political awakening.[16] Second, the strong promotion of the book, as well as the passionate reactions that it triggered, say a lot about the intellectual climate from which the postwar conservative movement emerged.[17]

One of the reasons for Hayek's success is probably to be found in his status as an economist (though his basic argument in fact had little, if anything, to do with economic theory). While the central idea of his book had been expressed repeatedly since the early years of the New Deal by Robert Taft, Alfred M. Landon and other of its conservative opponents, it had usually been in the form of more or less impressionistic statements.[18] Hayek's elaborate style appeared to raise the idea above the political fray and give it a "scientific" quality. He provided the glide down the "slippery slope" to serfdom with inevitability as if caused by the pull of gravity.

The most important reason for the waves created by Hayek's book, however, was probably the timing of its publication. Just a few years earlier, when the American economy was still in the grip of the Depression,

---

16 See Nash, op.cit, p. 12 ff. F.A. Hayek was not the only foreign economist who was "adopted" by the American Right. His mentor, Ludwig von Mises, became another prominent figure, whose disciples included Professor Gottfried von Haberler of Harvard University and Professor Fritz Machlup of Johns Hopkins University. Like Hayek, Mises also had a profound influence on the so-called "Chicago school," led by Professor Frank H. Knight at the University of Chicago. There is much to the claim that it was the seeds planted in the early 1940s by Hayek, Von Mises and their American disciples which were harvested in the revival of libertarian conservatism in the late 1970s and early 1980s.

17 The highly emotional nature of the controversy is well illustrated by Professor Herman Finer's book *The Road to Reaction* (Boston: Little, Brown and Company, 1946), which was written in direct response to Hayek's book.

18 In the 1936 campaign, Alfred M. Landon had warned his voters that there was "no halfway house" between free enterprise and "a system under which the minutest doings of every citizen are scrutinized and regulated." (*New York Times*, September 13, 1936). Just a year before the publication of Hayek's book, Albert Jay Nock had noted in his *Memoirs of A Superfluous Man*, that "the idea of self-limiting or temporary collectivism impresses me as too absurd to be seriously discussed. As long as Newton's law remains in force, no one can fall out of a forty-storey window and stop at the twentieth storey." (New York: Harper & Brothers, 1943), p. 319.

many of those who now reacted fiercely would probably have found his advocacy of a turn to laissez-faire liberalism too far-fetched to even comment on. By 1944, however, a new optimism created by the booming wartime economy had begun to improve the bruised image of American business, and with the prospects of a forthcoming end to the war, the debate about the nature of the future economy had already begun. Hayek's book appealed to the deep-rooted American penchant, fixed in place since the American Revolution, for "anti-statism." Many saw Hayek's vision of society as a return to a genuine American tradition of Jeffersonian democracy, where liberty first of all meant liberty from government.

However, for American liberals, who had come to embrace Keynesian economics and to recognize a permanent role for the state in the attempt to optimize the economy and make up for the inherent flaws in the system of the free market, it bordered on reckless demagoguery when Hayek and other libertarians claimed that there were no such flaws. They rejected the idea that recession, large-scale unemployment, the rise of monopolies, and related problems actually were the results of government intervention – or at least only became serious problems because of that intervention.

For those who had continued to regard Herbert Hoover as a patron saint, and the New Deal as an aberration from "the American Way," Hayek's message naturally sounded like sweet music. He made it possible for conservatives to react against a fixed image of "New Deal liberalism." By the time his book was published, ideas about extensive government regulation of industry, which had been prevalent in the early New Deal years, had largely been abandoned in favor of more subtle fiscal and monetary instruments. This did not make any real difference according to Hayek's line of thought.[19] Most important, perhaps, his book provided conservatives with a moral rationale for linking New Deal liberalism to communism, as basically two different degrees of the same "collectivist" disease. The virtue of laissez-faire was no longer simply economic efficiency. Democracy was at stake.[20]

---

19 See Alan Brinkley, "The New Deal and the Idea of the State" in Steve Fraser & Gary Gerstle, *The Rise and Fall of the New Deal Order, 1930-1980* (Princeton: Princeton University Press, 1989), p. 85-122.

20 In 1947, Hayek cofounded the Mont Pelerin Society, a transatlantic gathering of advocates of classic liberalism. The society provided a forum for both economists and politicians with a firm belief in the virtues of a free market. Over the years the membership included →

"Suicide of the West"

Not just on the level of economic theory, but politically, morally and spiritually as well, the most common charges against liberalism were variations on the theme that liberals were "soft on communism." However, the charges went in two different, sometimes contradictory, directions. According to the first line of reasoning, liberals were soft on communism because they largely shared the same view of human nature, and the same set of political abstractions. Communists were basically just "liberals with guts." In a typical expression of this attitude *Freeman*- editor Forrest Davis asked his readers:

> Is it not the prevailing political 'liberalism' of the midcentury, that potpourri of indiscriminate do-goodism trending into statism and Marxism and blending so indistinguishably with treason, that is the deepest enemy of the traditional America and the West?[21]

Whittaker Chambers for his part was also convinced that his charges against Alger Hiss had caused such an outcry among liberals because they instinctively felt a natural kinship to communism. In his best-selling book *Witness* he wrote about the Hiss case:

> The simple fact is that when I took up my little sling and aimed at Communism, I also hit something else. What I hit was the forces of that great socialist revolution, which, in the name of liberalism, spasmodically, incompletely, somewhat formlessly, but always in the same direction, has been inching its ice cap over the nation for two decades."[22]

The second string of conservative arguments concerning the relationship between liberalism and communism did not focus on the similarities but

---

← both leading economists such as Milton Friedman, Frank Knight, Ludwig von Mises, Wilhelm Roepke, and James Buchanan, and leading politicians such as German Chancellor Ludwig Erhardt, French Minister of Finance Jaques Rueff., Ed. Giscard d'Estaing, and Sir Geoffrey Howe of Great Britain: It also included a contingent of American conservative intellectuals such as William Henry Chamberlin, Henry Hazlitt, and Felix Morley.

21 Forrest Davis, "The Treason of 'Liberalism'," the *Freeman*, Vol. 1, No.10 (February 12, 1951), p. 305.

22 Whittaker Chambers, *Witness* (London: Andre Deutch, 1953), p.566.

on the differences between the two. Liberals were unable to stem the tide of communism because they, unlike the conservatives, lacked what the communists had: commitment, dedication and a sense of mission. According to several conservative intellectuals, the reason for the alleged weakness of the West in its struggle with communism was that the tone of contemporary Western thought was set by liberalism, which was not a redemptive creed, but a secular ideology. Communism might be secular as well, but it was nevertheless eschatological in nature. It had a set of clear political objectives such as the elimination of poverty and inequality. In other words, it had a vision of "the Good Society" and a strategy for how to get there. The liberals, on the other hand, had lost their sense of mission because they had lost their belief in an objective moral order.

The view of modern liberalism as an advanced stage in the process of secularization was presented in one of the first important conservative books published in postwar America, Richard Weaver's *Ideas Have Consequences*.[23] Weaver found a tragic irony in the fact that "Soviet communism, despite its ostensible commitment to materialism, has generated a body of ideas with a terrifying power to spread ... while the United States, which supposedly has the heritage of values and ideals, frantically throws up barricades of money around the globe."[24]

As the reigning philosophy of the West, modern liberalism could be held responsible for this alleged paradox. Yet, it was more likely a symptom than the root of the impending defeat to communism. Weaver saw New Deal liberalism as the final step in a decline of Western civilization which had been in progress since William of Occam's nominalist philosophy in the fourteenth century (!) made Western man abandon his belief in transcendental values and drift into moral relativism.

The claim that this alleged decline had been initiated some five hundred years ago gave the whole process a quality of historical inevitability, which made the passionate antagonism towards New Deal liberalism a little hard to understand. Yet, if Weaver was a pessimist regarding the survival of Western culture, he was not, after all, a fatalist. The battle could still be won if the "spoiled-child psychology" of contemporary liberalism was overcome. Only a conservative leadership could, in Weaver's view, mo-

---

23 Richard Weaver, *Ideas Have Consequences* (Chicago: University of Chicago Press, 1948).
24 Weaver, p. 122.

bilize the ideological strength and sufficient discipline to counter the forces of communism.[25]

The idea that the Cold War first of all was a spiritual struggle between atheism and religion, and thus a struggle that liberals were unfit to be in charge of, was also the central theme in Whittaker Chambers' book *Witness*. Communism, Chambers argued, was first of all a modern expression of "the great alternative faith of mankind ... the vision of Man without God."[26]

> The crisis of the Western World exists to the degree in which it is indifferent to God. It exists to the degree in which the Western World actually shares Communism's materialist vision, is so dazzled by the logic of the materialist interpretation of history, politics and economics, that it fails to grasp that, for it, the only possible answer to the Communist challenge: Faith in God or Faith in Man? is the challenge: Faith in God.[27]

In practical politics, conservatives claimed the liberals' moral relativism and their sneaking sympathy for much of what communism said it was trying to do resulted in permissiveness, compromise and appeasement. James Burnham, the Right's leading guru of power politics, saw the Cold War as a geopolitical struggle with a powerful and clearly recognizable external enemy: the Soviet Union. Yet he spoke of the "suicide of the West," because in his view it was the softness of the liberals at home that made the threat mortal.[28]

In the view of many conservatives, liberals compensated for their lack of transcendent values by devoting themselves to a set of abstract political goals. In a particularly bold pronouncement, which rejected root and

---

25 Weaver, p. 124.
26 Chambers, *Witness*, p. 9.
27 Chambers., p. 17.
28 Like many others on the American Right, Burnham was most likely influenced by yet another Austrian social scientist, Joseph Schumpeter. Schumpeter's thesis in his *Capitalism, Socialism and Democracy* (1942) was that capitalism so to speak carried the seeds of its own destruction, and fell victim to its own success by creating a class of critical intellectuals, whose persistent criticism of private property and bourgeois values helped create a political atmosphere that ultimately undermined the social framework of capitalism itself.

branch ideas, which for millions were at the core of the American system, William F. Buckley, Jr. found that the liberal credo could simply be summed up as:

> A loose agglutination of methodological principles that have denied metaphysics, that rely primarily on positivism and pragmatism, and that suggest the emptiness, with which so much of the West faces its current problems.[29]

Liberals, Buckley claimed, compensated for their lack of true convictions by "making fetishes" out of notions such as "academic freedom," "democracy" (which in his political thought was not even a basic political principle, but merely "a procedural device aimed at institutionalizing political liberty") and "civil rights." [30]

Regarding the latter, Buckley found it natural that "a conservative feels a sympathy for the Southern position which the liberal, applying his ideological abstractions ruthlessly, cannot feel." Most conservatives understood, in his view, that it was "more important for a community, wherever situated geographically, to affirm and live by civilized standards than to labor at the job of swelling the voting lists."[31]

For American conservatives – not least the significant group of ex-communists who had crossed the political spectrum without any stop at Arthur M. Schlesinger, Jr.'s "Vital Center" – loathing of liberalism seemed to be the one constant in their political vision. Back in 1932, when future editor of the right-wing journal the *Freeman*, John Chamberlain, was still a socialist and voted for Norman Thomas, he had contended that "only conservatives and radicals know how capitalism works: it is only the liberal, who has mistaken an adjective for a credo, that is deluded."[32] As a conservative he would probably still agree twenty years later.

---

29 Transcript of William F. Buckley's appearance in "Cross Exam," January 8, 1962. The Buckley Papers.
30 William F. Buckley, Jr., *Up From Liberalism* (New York: McDowell, Obolensky, 1959), p. 115.
31 Buckley, Jr., *Up From Liberalism*, p. 158.
32 John Chamberlain, *Farewell to Reform: Being A History of the Rise, Life and Decay of the Progressive Mind in America* (New York, 1932), p. viii.

Conservatism and Corporate America

What most of all set the majority of American conservatives apart from their European counterparts was an outspoken anti-statism. They were Lockean liberals rather than Tories. Concern about capitalism's subversive effects on traditional social structures and values – or the environment for that matter – was never particularly outspoken. American conservatives were not engaged in the saving of spotted owls and similar victims of material progress.

However, most of them maintained a veneration for the small independent businessman, and many harbored a profound distrust of large corporations. The breeds of conservatives who formed the core of the postwar right were clearly not mouthpieces of "big business," as it was sometimes alleged from the left. On the contrary, they often appeared to be fueled as much by distrust of corporate America as by their antagonism towards New Deal liberals. Particularly traditionalist conservatives deplored the process which James Burnham had labeled the "managerial revolution."[32a]

As individually owned companies were replaced by corporations where legal ownership and administrative control were separated, business America was increasingly ruled by a new managerial class. Often right wingers would resort to a vocabulary that was strikingly close to that of their counterparts on the left when they described this new "power elite" ruling the country against the will of "the people."[33]

"Big business" seemingly went hand in hand with "big government." Conservatives were frustrated by corporate America's general acceptance of government intervention in the economy and the widespread support it offered for permanent welfare measures. The social revolution, which the New Deal according to the conservatives represented, had been *de facto* legitimized as bipartisan doctrine by the Eisenhower administration under the banner of "enlightened Republicanism." The dominant part of

---

32a James Burnhans, *The Managerial Revolutions: or, what is happening in the world now* (New York: The John Day Company, 1941).

33 In his book *The Higher Circles, The Governing Class in America* (New York: Random House, 1970), G. William Domhoff describes both the similarities and the notable differences between the common rightwing view of the "establishment" in America, and the one represented by himself and his mentor C. Wright Mills. pp. 279-308.

the business community had seemingly swallowed this social revolution, and now praised the alleged advantages of a managed economy.

Particularly on the far right there was also a deep-seated suspicion of many of the organizations which provided connections between the government and the corporate business community. Organizations such as the Council on Foreign Relations and the Committee for Economic Development were frequently bundled together with the Alger Hisses, the Rockefellers, the Wall Street financiers, the "secret kingmakers" of the Republican Party, and other villains from the "Eastern establishment."[34]

There were of course also several larger corporations among the major sponsors of the conservative movement, among them Deering Milliken, McGraw-Edison, General Electric and Sun Oil, but most of the large corporations had a vital interest in keeping good relations with both political parties and to a certain extent also with the labor movement. A focus on narrow goals rather than on long-term changes in the ideological assumptions shaping public policy made corporations acknowledge the advantages of a trade-off with liberal policies in such areas as labor-management relations and social insurance programs.

Another common right-wing charge was that big business, like the federal government, worked against the national interest by trading with the Soviet Union and its satellites in Eastern Europe and elsewhere, thus legitimizing communist regimes and sustaining the life of an otherwise bankrupt economic system. Conservative intellectuals lamented that only a tiny fraction of American businessmen seemingly were concerned about the defense of freedom. Greed and indifference to moral principles in

---

34 During the Goldwater-campaign in 1964, Phyllis Schlafly's book *A Choice Not an Echo* (Alton, Ill.: Pere Marquette Press, 1964) became a bestseller on the American Right. One of its chapters was devoted to the uncovering of a major gathering of "secret kingmakers," the so-called Bilderberg group, which Schlafly claimed she had accidentally stumbled on. The group was most certainly a real one. Since its first meeting organized by Prince Bernhard of the Netherlands (at Hotel de Bilderberg) in 1954, it had provided a forum for industrialists, public officials, economists and labor-leaders from both sides of the Atlantic. These meetings were informal, but as G. William Domhoff has pointed out, there was nothing secret about them. Despite Schlafly's claim that there had not been a word in the American press about these meetings, Domhoff refers to several reports in the *New York Times* as far back as 1954. *The Higher Circles*, p. 302 ff. Yet, it was the idea of secrecy that made the idea of "the Bilderbergers" an attractive expression of the anti-big business sentiments that many on the American right shared.

their view largely characterized the business community. As William F. Buckley, Jr. would later express it, the American businessman most often appeared to be an "inarticulate, self-conscious, bumbling mechanic of the private sector ... fleeing into the protective arms of government at the least hint of commercial difficulty."[35] This conflict between their own entrepreneurial ideals and the realities of American business, frequently presented right-wing intellectuals with the dilemma of how to embrace the system of capitalism without embracing the capitalists.

It was not until the 1970s that a crucial change occurred in the political behavior of the business community and engaged it seriously in the financing of a conservative counterintelligentsia. When it did happen, it was more likely the conservative think tanks and the many new PACs that would benefit than the more conventional political organizations.[36] Rather than to the large corporations, most right-wing organizations had to direct their financial requests toward dedicated sponsors such as the J. Howard Pew Freedom Trust, the Smith Richardson Foundation, the Scaife Foundation, the John M. Olin Foundation, and the Volker Fund.

From "Moral Minority" to "Hidden Majority"

If American conservatism in the early postwar years was inhibited by its lack of an intellectual and organizational base, it was also to a certain extent inhibited by its own latent disgust for majoritarian politics. Conservative intellectuals were oscillating between two conflicting self-perceptions: One was the ancient elitist notion of the conservative "remnant": the perception of conservatives as the scattered keepers of the cultural treasures of Western civilization in a society which had succumbed to the vulgarity of "the masses." The other was the perception of conservatives as

---

35 William F. Buckley, Jr., "The Road to Serfdom: The Intellectuals and Socialism," in Fritz Machlup (ed.) *Essays on Hayek* (New York: New York University Press, 1976), p. 102.

36 On the explosive growth in the funding of conservative think tanks during the 1970s, see James Allen Smith, *The Idea Brokers; Think Tanks and the Rise of the New Policy Elite* (New York: The Free Press, 1991), Sidney Blumenthal, *The Rise of the Counter-Establishment; From Conservative Ideology to Political Power* (New York: Times Books, 1986), pp. 32-54, and Niels Bjerre-Poulsen, "The Heritage Foundation: A Second Generation Think Tank," *Journal of Policy History*, Vol. 3, No. 2, 1991, pp. 152-172.

the genuine spokesmen of a "silent majority" which was being held hostage by an overpowering liberal elite.

The notion of "the Remnant" had been given its most famous expression by Albert Jay Nock, whom many saw as a father of postwar intellectual conservatism in America. Many conservatives cherished his *Memoirs of a Superfluous Man*, not just for its style of prose but also for its unabashed elitism. Likewise, his editorship of *The Freeman* in the early 1920s had made it a model for several postwar conservative journals.

Like many leading conservative intellectuals of the postwar era, Nock was heavily inspired by the cultural pessimism of books such as Oswald Spengler's *The Decline of the West*, and Jose Ortega Y Gasset's *The Revolt of the Masses*.[37] Both Spengler's fatalistic worldview and Ortega Y Gasset's elitist disdain for "mass man" were reflected in Nock's essay "Isaiah's Job."[38] In his terminology, the line of differentiation between *the masses* and the Remnant was set by quality, not by circumstance. The masses did not refer to poor, unprivileged, laboring people, but simply to the majority of people, "who has neither the force of intellect to apprehend the principles issuing in what we know as the humane life, nor the force of character to adhere to those principles steadily and strictly as laws of conduct."[39] In contrast, "the Remnant" was the minority in society with the ability to apprehend these principles and to cleave to them under the pressure of mass culture.

In terms of political organization, the implications were clear. The conservative task ahead, according to Nock, was not to win over the masses for the conservative cause, but to stimulate and encourage "the Remnant" whose responsibility if would be to build up a new society "when everything has gone completely to the dogs."[40] Job one was to create a conservative "counter-establishment" that in time would be ready to displace the ruling liberal establishment.

---

37 Oswald Spengler, *The Decline of the West* (New York: A.A. Knopf, 1926); Jose Ortega Y Gasset, *The Revolt of the Masses* (New York: W.W. Norton & Company, Inc., 1932).

38 From Albert J. Nock, *Free Speech and Plain Language* (New York: William Morrow, 1937), pp248-265. Reprinted in William F. Buckley, Jr. & Charles R. Kesler (eds.), *Keeping the Tablets; Modern American Conservative Thought* (New York: Harper & Row, 1988), pp. 431-442.

39 Nock, pp. 431-442.

40 Buckley, Jr., *Keeping the Tablets*, pp. 431-442.

For conservatives who lamented the lack in popularity of conservative principles there was also comfort in Richard Weaver's explanation of how the "spoilt child psychology" of the masses made them march to the seductive tones of modern liberalism, rather than to those of personally demanding conservative principles:

> The spoiled children perceive correctly that the superior person is certain, sooner or later, to demand superior things of them, and this interferes with consumption and, above all, with thoughtlessness.[41]

The same disdain for "the common man" was also reflected in the working title for the book on conservative thought that William F. Buckley, Jr. planned for years, but never got to write: *The Revolt Against the Masses.*[42]

Along with the striking elitist cultural pessimism that so often characterized the writings of the postwar intellectual right, there was, however, also a conflicting notion. It presented conservatives as spokesmen for a "silent majority" of Americans, with whom the liberal establishment had lost touch, both morally and politically. The anticommunist crusades of the late 1940s, and later the widespread public support which seemingly existed for Senator Joe McCarthy's endless attempts to link New Deal liberalism to communism and treason, were important factors in encouraging the belief among right-wing intellectuals that the basic political instincts of the masses were perhaps conservative after all. Also, many of the ex-communists who drifted into the conservative camp in these years brought with them a more positive view of "the masses."

Whittaker Chambers, who had secured himself a place in the conservative pantheon after his testimony against Alger Hiss, is a good example. When William F. Buckley, Jr. and Willi Schlamm founded the leading right-wing magazine *National Review* in 1955, Chambers ranked highest on the list of potential editors to whom they catered. Chambers, however, declined the offer to join the magazine due to the important differences he saw between Buckley's reactionary positions and his own Disraelian

---

41 Richard Weaver, *Ideas Have Consequences*, p. 126.
42 See John B. Judis, *William F. Buckley, Jr.; Patron Saint of the Conservatives* (New York: Simon and Schuster, 1988), pp. 213-219.43   Whittaker Chambers, Odyssey of a Friend:

visions of an organic pro-limited social reform conservatism. (Chambers did eventually join the staff of *National Review* in 1957.) In a letter to Buckley and Schlamm, he explained that his differing views on the social needs and political instincts of "the common man" had been crucial for his decision:

> I remain a dialectician, and history tells me that the rockcore of the Conservative Position ... can be held realistically only if conservatism will accommodate itself to the needs and hopes of the masses.[43]

Whittaker Chambers' explanation highlights the inherent tension between elitist and populist strains within American conservatism. This tension would persist, and from time to time it would break out in the open, as in the conflict between "neoconservatives" and "paleoconservatives" in the 1990s. This, however, was neither the only, nor the worst obstacle that conservatives faced in their struggle to find common ground. The following chapter deals with some of the other ideological gaps that the movement felt compelled to bridge.

---

43 Whittaker Chambers, *Odyssey of a Friend*: Whittaker Chambers' Letters to William F. Buckley, Jr. (New York: G.P. Putnam's Sons, 1969), p.79.

Chapter 2

Fusing Ice and Fire

> [Conservatives and libertarians] share a detestation of collectivism. They set their faces against the totalist state and the heavy hand of bureaucracy. That much is obvious enough. What else do conservatives and libertarians profess in common? The answer to that question is simple: Nothing. Nor will they ever have. To talk of forming a league or coalition between these two is like advocating a union of ice and fire.
>
> Russell Kirk[1]

Postwar American conservatism did not emerge as a coherent body of beliefs, but rather as a set of separate strains of thought, aligned for practical purposes by their anticommunism and their opposition to New Deal liberalism. The perception of a common enemy served as the ideological glue within the movement, but just how far could conservatives go without attempting to formulate a shared vision of "the good society"?

Although a fairly wide spectrum of beliefs could be found within the movement, the most evident division was the one between traditionalist and libertarian views. One of the major intellectual tasks facing conservatives would be to sort out the relationship between these two bodies of ideas. Were they, as Robert Nisbet suggested, "uneasy cousins"? —offspring of the same political tradition with different emphases—or were they, regardless of the attempts to make them pull in the same political direction, inherently contradictory on the intellectual level - reflecting different views on the state, on freedom, on authority, on reason, and on human nature?

---

1 Russell Kirk, "Libertarians: The Chirping Sectaries," in George W. Carey (ed.), *Freedom and Virtue: The Conservative/Libertarian Debate* (Lanham: University Press of America, 1984), p. 113.

If so, how important, then, was this lack of coherence? Would it have any practical consequences for the organization and activity of the American Right, so long as all parties could agree on identifying a common enemy? Such questions remained pertinent and had a profound influence on the organizational development of the movement.

Any attempt to summarize the basic differences between the two strains of thought is obviously made at the risk of oversimplification. Both actually covered a wide spectrum of opinions. Libertarian beliefs ranged all the way from F.A. Hayek's advocacy of laissez-faire capitalism governed by the "Rule of Law," through Frank Chodorov and Murray N. Rothbart's radical libertarianism where government was inherently criminal and immoral, to Rand's Nietzschean "objectivism" where selfishness was the primary virtue and altruism the root of all evil.[2] Among the traditionalists, it was also a fairly long shot from authors such as Peter Viereck and Clinton Rossiter, who both saw the New Deal as the savior of capitalism and as a part of the American political tradition to be conserved, to Russell Kirk's brand of traditionalism which took the form of a frontal attack on modernity and a pledge for a return to a simpler lifestyle.[3] While Rossiter would generally welcome the fruits of industrialization, even the automobile was a "mechanical Jacobin" in Kirk's universe.[4] Despite this actual fluidity of opinions, it nevertheless seems justified to make the separation into two major camps by pointing to a basic consensus within each on such crucial core issues as freedom, authority, and human nature.

---

[2] For an account of the libertarian spectrum, see Stephen L. Newman, *Liberalism at Wit's End* (Ithaca: Cornell University Press, 1984).

[3] His Northern ancestry notwithstanding, Kirk could in this respect be seen as a descendent of the so-called "Southern agrarians." The views of this group of intellectuals, which included people such as Robert Penn Warren, Donald Davidson and John Crowe Ransom, found its most famous expression in the manifesto *I'll Take My Stand* (1930). The influence from this group was even clearer in the case of another postwar traditionalist, Richard M. Weaver, who became the leading spokesman for the argument that Southern culture, with its feudal and anti-industrial traits, represented a genuine American conservative tradition.

[4] Russell Kirk, *The Conservative Mind: From Burke to Santayana* (Chicago: Henry Regnery Company, 1953), p. 325.

The Traditionalist Vision

Traditionalist conservatism – or the New Conservatism as it was sometimes called – was in a sense an attempt to tap into the tradition of European conservatism which had evolved since the days of the French Revolution. A conservative tradition whose basic belief in modest reform and "organic" growth, rather than radical change, had found its most famous expression in Edmund Burke's *Reflections on the Revolution in France*.[5]

In the traditionalist view, political change could only take place in accordance with the accumulated wisdom of the culture; or as Burke's most notable postwar American disciple Russell Kirk expressed it, in accordance with "received opinions, convictions religious and moral and political and aesthetic passed down from generation to generation, so that they are accepted by most men as a matter of course."[6] In other words, politics and culture would have to evolve within a moral framework which, most traditionalists would contend, was to be found in religion or in a system of laws derivative from religious beliefs (which to most traditionalists implied Judeo-Christian beliefs).[7]

The traditionalist vision of society was in a sense that of the patriarchal family, where every member knew his or her place in the hierarchy and happily accepted it. Order and social harmony were in this view the primary goals of society, as well as the necessary preconditions for any meaningful pursuit of liberty and justice. The value of the individual derived primarily from his contribution to the community.[8] The notion of equality – in any other sense than "equality of opportunity" – was to the traditionalist an artificial product of the Enlightenment that was incom-

---

[5] Edmund Burke (1729-1797) is widely acclaimed as the father of modern conservative thought. His *Reflections on the Revolution in France* (1790) ed. Conor Cruise O'Brien (Harmonsworth: Penguin Books, 1968) made him the leading exponent of the conservative reaction to the French revolution. Throughout the 19th and 20th centuries he has maintained his position as the leading advocate of a social development based on experience and tradition rather than on rational abstractions such as the ideas of "natural rights" and the "social contract."

[6] Russell Kirk, "Prescription, Authority, and Ordered Freedom." In Frank S. Meyer (ed.), *What is Conservatism?* (New York: Holt, Rinehart and Winston, 1964), p. 27.

[7] For an example of this argument, see Edward B. McLean, "Libertarianism as the Philosophy of Moral Freedom – A Response." In George W. Carey, *Freedom and Virtue.*, pp. 147-154.

[8] Edward B. McLean, p. 147-154.

patible with true liberty. The key to social harmony, traditionalists would argue, was not to abolish classes, but to reconcile them.

In accordance with the traditionalist preoccupation with order, the least government was not necessarily considered the best. Traditionalists would, at least in principle, claim the primacy of preserving the social fabric of the community over individual freedom. If necessary, that might entail support for a limited welfare state which, in the words of George Will, could "reconcile the masses to the vicissitudes and hazards of a dynamic and hierarchial industrial economy."[9] Thus, the notion of freedom could not be separated from self-restraint, responsibility, submission, and a sense of duty towards the general interest of society. In accordance with John Winthrop's puritan concept, the true purpose of freedom was to confer the ability to pursue virtue by acknowledging and submitting to the divine intentions of an absolute moral authority. True freedom, Kirk asserted, derived from the sense of being part of a larger whole, and it required "order within the soul and order within the state."[10]

In accordance with this reading of what constituted freedom, conservative traditionalists generally opposed John Locke's notion of society as simply a "social contract," as well as the notion of liberty based on a set of these "natural rights" which since the Enlightenment had become core elements in liberal thought. Most traditionalists would subscribe to Edmund Burke's famous notion that society could not be a contract in the Lockean sense, inasmuch as the state was not a "partnership agreement in a trade of pepper and coffee ..." but

> a partnership not only between those who are living, but between those who are living, those who are dead, and those who are to be born. Each contract of each particular state is but a clause in the great primeval contract of eternal society, linking the lower with the higher natures, connecting the visible and invisible world, according to a fixed compact sanctioned by the inviolable oath which holds all physical and all moral natures, each in their appointed place.[11]

---

9 George Will, *Statecraft as Soulcraft* (New York: Simon & Schuster, 1983), p. 126.
10 In Frank S. Meyer (ed.), *What is Conservatism?* (New York: Holt, Rinehart & Winston, 1964), p. 24.
11 Edmund Burke, *Reflections on the Revolution in France*, pp. 194-195.

Libertarianism and the Virtues of the Market

Unlike the traditionalists in the conservative movement, the libertarians had little use for Edmund Burke. Their philosophy was in its purest form best described as a modern version of Spencerian social Darwinism based in a rigorous belief in survival of the fittest. In contrast to the traditionalist emphasis on the community and the institutional framework of society, the basic concept of libertarian thought was the absolute autonomy of the individual, working out a destiny among the unrestrained forces of the free market.

Like liberalism, libertarianism was rooted in a severely rationalist view of human nature, as well as in a Lockean notion of society as a "social contract" between free individuals. To the extent that there was a quest for virtue in libertarian theory, it was grounded in a scientific morality rather than in a commitment to the moral values of the Judeo-Christian tradition. To the libertarian, the free market was the supreme instrument of virtue exactly because of its efficiency and its potential for social change, not in spite of it.

Like traditionalist conservatives, libertarians would detest egalitarianism as an artificial construct, and acknowledge the necessity and desirability of a social hierarchy. But whereas the traditionalist in theory favored a more or less fixed social order under the presumption that it took more than one generation to cultivate a qualified elite, the libertarian would rather see the social hierarchies as freely and perhaps swiftly rising and falling as an inevitable result of the dynamics of free market capitalism. Accordingly, he did not consider lively social mobility a threat to social harmony. Rather, it proved the efficiency of laissez-faire capitalism as an allocator of burdens and benefits. The market was the sublime selector of a "natural aristocracy" to lead society forward; it guaranteed that the best would get on top.

Having it Both Ways: "Fusionism"

If traditionalists and libertarians did not clash as often as one might have expected, it was to a large degree because their differing views on the road to a virtuous society tended to direct their attentions in separate directions.[12] While libertarians were preoccupied with economic issues, traditionalists would mostly direct their attention towards social and cultural issues. It was also, however, because leading voices within the conservative movement persistently attempted to fuse the two strains of political thought.

Without denying the profound ideological differences, William F. Buckley, Jr. would point to how well the conservative movement regardless had managed to organize. His own journal, National Review, was in his opinion a showcase for the success of conservative ecumenicism in America.[13] Neither did Buckley's mentor, Willmoore Kendall, find intellectual coherence to be a crucial issue for the movement.

> What is more important by far than the meaning we assign to "conservative," is: who are the anti-Conservatives, and what are their supreme values? ... the conservatives in the modern period are simply those who resist the revolutionary program Burke identified and opposed in the Reflections, ... the question is not whether [conservatives] have a program and can carry it out but whether they can continue to frustrate the Machiavellians.[14]

Others would go even further and maintain that ideological incoherence had to be an essential and unavoidable feature of conservatism. Since, as traditionalists claimed, its core was to be found in the belief that humanity is inherently sinful and its reasoning powers limited, so that the world is not perfectible, it also followed that any rationalist reform program based on abstract and allegedly universal principles and aimed at the perfection of society would be futile at best. Conservatism could by definition never become an ideology in the sense of a consistent set of ideas – and luckily so, most traditionalists would add.[15]

---

12 Interestingly enough, the social status of libertarianism and traditionalism also seemed to differ significantly, at least in the 1950s. The former still had an "underground" character, a certain furtiveness as a voice for unrestrained greed and a lack of social cachet, whereas most of the traditionalists held academic positions and mostly published in scholarly journals.
13 See William F. Buckley, Jr., "Notes Towards an Empirical Definition of Conservatism," Meyer, *What is Conservatism?* pp. 211-226.
14 Willmoore Kendall, *The Conservative Affirmation* (Chicago: Henry Regnery Company, 1963), p. 142.
15 For an example of this traditionalist argument, see Russell Kirk, *A Program for Conservatives* (Chicago: Henry Regnery Company, 1954), pp. 1-19.

It can be argued, of course, that the coexistence of traditionalist and libertarian beliefs simply provided conservatives with an opportunity to have their cake and eat it too. In economic matters they could argue according to libertarian principles; in moral and social matters they could maintain traditionalist views on the need for authority and coercion.

Even Russell Kirk occasionally appeared willing to dispense with the larger principles of his own political visions when it came to positions on actual policy issues. As several liberal critics delightfully noted, his attacks on the school lunch program as a "vehicle of totalitarianism" was completely out of line with the aristocratic sense of noblesse oblige he cherished in theory.[16]

However, the fact that many conservatives felt quite comfortable picking and choosing from both libertarian and traditionalist ideas did not diminish or remove the tensions between the two strains of thought. Rather, as Garry Wills has noted, it merely made the contradictions "go philosophically 'underground' and play funny games there."[17] Thus, when conservatives moved beyond denouncing the enemy, and set out to tear his house down, they frequently discovered the urgency of fixing their own house first. The attempt to do this by reconciling traditionalism and libertarianism philosophically became known as "fusionism."

Fusionists would generally insist that the two camps shared a set of basic beliefs and a common vision of "the good society." Both believed in private property and limited government, and both resisted "planning" and all "collectivist" attempts at social leveling. They could also agree on the desirability of a hierarchical society, although their opinions about the proper basis for such a hierarchy might differ. The conflict, fusionists would hold, was mostly a matter of different priorities. As Frank S. Meyer – usually recognized as the fusionist par excellence – would repeatedly claim, the conflict resulted from "differences of emphasis, not of underlying opposition."[18] In short, the argument would go, all conservatives re-

---

16 See Arthur M. Schlesinger, Jr., "The New Conservatism: Politics of Nostalgia" *The Reporter* (June 16, 1955), p. 11.
17 Garry Wills, *Confessions of a Conservative* (Garden City, New York: Doubleday & Company, Inc., 1979), p. 55.
18 Frank S. Meyer, *What is Conservatism?* p. 19. Later in the book Meyer elaborated, claiming that "the divergences can be simply summarized as the degree of emphasis placed ... upon the relative importance for the good society of moral tradition and freedom; upon the extent to which, on the one hand, the sanctions of state and community or, on the other hand, *peitho*, the persuasion of moral and intellectual authority functioning through free individual persons, should be emphasized." (p. 232)

cognized the need for both "freedom" and "authority," the libertarians just wanted more freedom, and the traditionalists more authority.

The crucial assumption underlying this argument was of course that both groups put the same connotations to these concepts. This was not, in reality, the case. As for the question of authority, the differences were not easily brushed aside as matters of degree. The crucial issue, many critics of fusionism would claim, was not how much authority, but what kind of authority a virtuous society would require. Likewise, it was indeed a difficult task to convince skeptics that the concept of individual freedom outlined by John Stuart Mill as absence of coercion (as long as the freedom of one individual did not pose a threat to the freedom of others) was by and large identical to the theocratic concept that most traditionalists adhered to, where true freedom was the ability to recognize virtue, as determined by an objective moral order, and act in accordance with it. From the libertarian perspective, the traditionalists were simply seizing the concept of freedom as their own while at the same time rendering it meaningless. Considering his status as a leading exponent of fusionism, it is worth noting that Frank S. Meyer was clearly on the libertarian side on this crucial issue:

> Freedom means freedom: not necessity, but choice; not responsibility, but the choice between responsibility and irresponsibility; not duty, but the choice between accepting and rejecting duty; not virtue, but the choice between virtue and vice.[19]

Traditionalists in Search of a Tradition

Another key issue in the traditionalist/libertarian controversy concerned the alleged conflict between reason on the one side and experience and tradition on the other. If libertarians generally favored political solutions based on rational reasoning, traditionalists tended to advocate experience as a superior foundation. With Edmund Burke as patron saint, they would hold a reverence for tradition and the wisdom passed on from previous generations as the proper basis for a slow, organic development of society.

---

19 Frank S. Meyer, *In Defense of Freedom: A Conservative Credo* (Chicago: Henry Regnery Company, 1962), p. 53.

But what if the American tradition was not conservative? What if liberalism was the sole tradition upon which the American polity was built, as Louis Hartz among others had argued?[20] What then were conservatives supposed to conserve?

Even if this interpretation was not accepted, it was still obvious that there was not one political tradition, but a plurality of traditions which conservatives – like others attempting to sustain their positions by drawing on historical experience – would have to pick from. How would they go about that if not by rational choice? An obvious illustration of the dilemma was the fact that very few conservatives would agree with Rossiter and Viereck's aforementioned view of the New Deal as a part of the political tradition to be conserved.[21] Rather, they would hold it was an aberration to this tradition. As M. Stanton Evans noted, the very idea of conserving it would in effect empty conservatism of all value content and reduce it to simply a political technique.[22]

A number of conservative intellectuals defied the dominant Hartzean interpretation and maintained that the American political tradition was indeed an expression of true conservative principles. Others chose to enlarge the scope and claim that the tradition to be conserved was not simply the American political tradition, but the consensus of "the Great Tradition" of Western civilization. With the ability to draw upon everything from Plato through Thomas Aquinas to Edmund Burke, the task of finding a common thread became somehow easier. Frank S. Meyer shared this view of conservatives as guardians of a greater tradition, which did not necessarily have to be reflected in the political issues of the day:

> What the conservative is committed to conserve is not simply whatever happens to be established conditions of a few years or a few decades, but

---

20 Louis Hartz, *The Liberal Tradition in America* (New York: Harcourt, Brace & World, 1955). See also Arthur Schlesinger, Jr., "The New Conservatism in America: A Liberal Comment," *Confluence* (December 1953), pp. 61-71, Allen Guttmann, *The Conservative Tradition in America* (New York: Oxford University Press, 1967).

21 While both Viereck and Rossiter were often praised by many American liberals as being among the few voices of "responsible" conservatism in America, they remained largely alienated from other conservative intellectuals, who tended to view them as "closet liberals," who under the guise of "responsible opposition" helped legitimize the liberal order of society.

22 M. Stanton Evans, "A Conservative Case for Freedom." In Frank S. Meyer, *What is Conservatism?* p. 70.

the consensus of his civilization, of his country, as that consensus over the centuries has reflected truth derived from the very constitution of being.[23]

Thus, in the view of conservatives such as Evans and Meyer there was nothing philosophically contradictory about their role as dissenters to the present New Deal order. The postwar national consensus had simply strayed so far away from the alleged path of tradition that conservatives were required to temporarily step out of their mold and become radicals until order had been restored.

Still, such reasoning did not get traditionalist conservatives off the hook. If New Deal liberalism was an aberration to the American political tradition – a "European" solution to social problems, without any roots in the American polity – then the same could be said of the traditionalists' own alternative vision of society. Liberal critics touched a sore spot when they pointed out that the European form of conservatism that the traditionalists emulated was the product of a feudal past, which – with the possible exception of the South – was alien to the American experience. There had never been, they said, a benevolent aristocracy in America with the sense of *noblesse oblige* required by the traditionalist vision. The belief that an aristocratic mind took more than one generation to cultivate faced hard odds in a society that worshipped the notion of the self-made man.

Rather, the natural carriers of an American conservative tradition would be the business community, which traditionally had represented an entirely different set of values, stressing rugged individualism, self-reliance, and progress. As one of the leading liberal historians Arthur M. Schlesinger, Jr. pointed out,

> Liberals, heaven knows, have been foolishly romantic, but few have recently been so romantic as to suppose that American businessmen, after reading a few edifying tracts, are going to start behaving like the British landed gentry.[24]

Most conservative intellectuals acknowledged this, according to Schlesinger, Jr., even if they were unwilling to admit it in rhetorical exchanges. When it came to actual political issues, the American situation would lead most of them to "leap from Tory fantasy into Republican reality."[25]

---

23 Frank S. Meyer, *What is Conservatism?* p. 10 ff.
24 Arthur M. Schlesinger, Jr., "The Politics of Nostalgia," p. 76.
25 Arthur M. Schlesinger, Jr., p. 76.

The vulnerability of giving a claim to tradition rather than to reason in the political context of the United States was also evident in the case of Russell Kirk's book *The Conservative Mind*, which to some marked the beginning of the conservative intellectual movement in postwar America.[26] Libertarians could join liberal critics in asking what Kirk's American conservative tradition consisted of other than a exclusive selection of individuals such as John Adams, John C. Calhoun, Randolph of Roanoke, William Graham Sumner, Paul Elmer Moore, Irvin Babitt, and George Santayana; people who in many cases had been isolated from the intellectual mainstream of their own times.

Even if Kirk's conservative genealogy was accepted, it was still Burke who remained the central figure in his book. Kirk maintained that American conservatism as well as British conservatism had largely been Burkean. Several prominent conservatives would disagree.[27] Some would, despite their general admiration for Kirk's book, concede that his claim to a tradition of Burkean conservatism in America was wishful thinking.

Clinton Rossiter praised the book, but found that the author had been "born one hundred and fifty years too late and in the wrong country."[28] Peter Viereck likewise felt that Kirk often neglected the main currents of the American political tradition to an extent that made his conception of conservatism "a traditionless worship of tradition," or an "unhistorical appeal to history."[29]

The discussion of Kirk's book illuminated an apparent paradox in the traditionalist/libertarian debate. On the one hand the libertarians, to whom loyalty to tradition and acknowledgement of the wisdom of the forefathers were not serious political concerns, had few problems giving claim to the principles of nineteenth century laissez-faire capitalism which more than anything had become associated with "the American Way." On the other hand the traditionalists, who considered the claim to

---

26 For an example, see Henry S. Regnery, *Memoirs of a Dissident Publisher* (New York: Hartcourt, Brace, Jovanovich, 1979). Whittaker Chambers went so far as to call it the most important book of the twentieth century (George H. Nash, *The Conservative Intellectual Movement in America*, p. 74).
27 For some conservative reservations about Kirk's book, see Nash, *The Conservative Intellectual Movement in America since 1945*, p. 197.
28 *Conservatism in America*, Op.Cit. p. 222.
29 Peter Viereck, "The Philosophical 'New Conservatism,'" in Daniel Bell (ed.), *The Radical Right* (New York: Doubleday & Company, Inc., 1963), p. 188.

tradition an essential part of their political legitimacy, time and again had to invoke the Englishman Burke in their attempt to construct a usable past. Why? Because part of the problem that traditionalists of Kirk's persuasion faced stemmed from their ambivalent feelings towards the very phenomenon libertarianism celebrated: Industrial capitalism.

Freedom to Do What?

While traditionalists would usually second the libertarian advocacy of free market capitalism, there were important differences in their commitment. Libertarians would hold that the very key to "the good society" was to be found in a free-market economy. Traditionalists, on the other hand, would generally not find anything inherently virtuous about it. Although they would mostly welcome its efficiency, many traditionalists also recognized the contradictions – at least on the philosophical level – between capitalism and the traditionalist vision of society.

Where capitalism encouraged change, growth and social mobility, traditionalism cherished continuity, stability, local attachment, and the existence of social hierarchy. The gospel of rugged individualism, and the common perception of America as "land of new beginnings" were clearly at odds with the traditionalist vision. The notion that private property (and best of all, landed property) was not only a basic human right, but also the key to social stability, since it provided "a stake in society," was also somehow at odds with the complex, amorphous and often multi-national nature of ownership that characterized modern corporate capitalism. In the light of such contradictions, many libertarians regarded the traditionalist commitment to the principles of laissez-faire capitalism as half-hearted at best.

This view found famous expression in F.A. Hayek's essay "Why I Am Not a Conservative," which appeared as a postscript to his book *The Constitution of Liberty*.[30] Although conservatives and libertarians in modern times had often found common ground in their resistance to "collectivism," Hayek found widely different political motivations below the sur-

---

30 "Why I Am Not a Conservative," in *The Constitution of Liberty* (London: Routledge & Kegan Paul, 1960), pp. 397-411.

face. Conservatives, who in Hayek's use of the word obviously meant traditionalists, resisted change on habitual rather than rational grounds.

Thus, when conservatives defended laissez-faire liberalism, their defense of it was not necessarily grounded in a deep commitment to individual liberty. Rather, they might just as likely root their position in the historical fact that this sort of liberalism happened to be the tradition on which the American polity was built, and thus for this reason should be defended. The traditionalist was a prisoner of tradition, unable to provide fresh alternatives. He could only affect the speed of political development, not the direction.

As Hayek saw it, the conservative's almost instinctive fear of social change was closely related to a "fondness for authority and ... lack of understanding of economic forces."[31] The conservative was more interested in controlling government than in limiting it, and would not as a matter of principle shy away from the use of protectionism and other means of government interference in the economy.

This, in Hayek's view, constituted the basic conflict between the traditionalist and the libertarian. Yet he was not blind to the importance of tradition, since, as he noted,

> There probably never has existed a genuine belief in freedom, and there has certainly been no successful attempt to operate a free society, without a genuine reverence for grown institutions, for customs and habits and "all those securities of liberty which arise from regulation of long prescription and ancient ways." Paradoxical as it may appear, it is probably true that a successful free society will always in a large measure be a tradition-bound society.[32]

If Hayek and other libertarians resented being labeled as "conservatives," then many traditionalists on the side also resented to be labeled together with the libertarians. To Russell Kirk – one of the most truculent opponents of such an alliance – the very notion of a "libertarian conservative" was an oxymoron comparable to a "Muslim Christian" or a "Jewish

---

31 F. A. Hayek, p. 400.
32 F. A. Hayek, *The Constitution of Liberty*, p. 61.

Nazi."[33] The idea of liberty as a goal in itself, which he saw as the primary feature of libertarianism, simply seemed absurd to him.

With an image borrowed from C.K. Chesterton, Kirk compared it to liberating goldfish by smashing their bowl.[34] Just as liberty was a useless privilege for the goldfish without the water, it was equally useless for human beings if it was not used within a framework of transcendental moral values.

The libertarian notion of freedom, which sanctioned the moral choice between vice and virtue, as well as between responsibility and irresponsibility, was obviously anathema to Kirk and other traditionalists. It frequently led them to charge that libertarians were simply agnostics, if not nihilists, in pursuit of nothing but material goods and cool cash. According to the libertarian economist Murray N. Rothbard, this image was a mere caricature, which missed the essential point. Libertarians, he noted, might very well share the Christian sense of moral virtue, indeed they were very likely to do so. The point was that they did not have to, since morality was simply beyond the scope of libertarianism.

In contrast to traditionalist conservatism, which embodied a belief in an objective moral order and a set of social ethics, libertarianism was a strictly political philosophy, which did not consider morality to be a public matter. While politics and morality from the traditionalist perspective were inseparable, libertarians would hold that they by definition belonged to two different spheres, although freedom was a necessary precondition for the pursuit of virtue.

Thus, while virtue might be humanity's primary objective, freedom was its most important political goal, and the distinction, to libertarians, was crucial. True moral virtue could not be installed by coercion, whether by the state or by religious authorities, since, as Frank Meyer put it, "virtue is the fruit of well-used freedom."[35] Radical libertarians such as Murray Rothbard would even hold that the state itself was an immoral expression of organized theft and violence, and accordingly the greatest obstacle to a virtuous society.[36] The state could best contribute to the moral education of the individual by ceasing to exist:

---

33 Russell Kirk, "Libertarians: The Chirping Sectaries," in *Freedom and Virtue; the Conservative/Libertarian Debate* (Lanham, MD: University Press of America, 1984), pp. 119-120.
34 Russell Kirk, "Libertarians: The Chirping Sectaries," p. 118.
35 Meyer, *In Defense of Freedom,* p. 66.
36 See Murray N. Rothbard, "Myth and Truth About Libertarianism," *Modern Age* (winter 1980), pp. 9-15.

> A free society, by not establishing such a legitimated channel for theft and tyranny, discourages the criminal tendencies of human nature and encourages the peaceful and the voluntary. Liberty and the free market discourage aggression and compulsion, and encourage the harmony and mutual benefit of voluntary interpersonal exchanges, economic, social, and cultural.[37]

Moreover, many libertarians would assert, people had to be morally prepared for freedom through education and persuasion. The task was to promote belief in a set of natural rights for every individual, and the existence of a universal human ethic with which every human being behaving rationally would be compelled to comply.[38]

To most traditionalists, the libertarian alternatives to state coercion, and the view of the intrinsic goodness of human nature which they reflected were not only overtly optimistic, they were pathetically naive. In short, any idea based on encouraging the good sides of human nature, rather than restraining the evil aspects of it, would only allow "the worst to get on top."[39]

Once again, the fusionists would attempt to find a middle course between these two positions. Frank Meyer, while agreeing with the libertarian position that freedom was the primary political priority, maintained that the state could play a positive, even necessary, role in this struggle.

> Rights, rather, are obligations upon the state to respect the inherent nature of individual human beings and to guarantee to them conditions in which they can live as human beings, that is, in which they can exercise the freedom which is their innate essence. The paradox that to achieve this it is necessary in practice to restrain the freedom of individuals to interfere with other individuals, is the reason for the state's existence.[40]

Foreign policy was another field where disagreements between the two camps were bound to occur. Obviously, it was hard for most libertarians

---

37 Rothbard, "Myth and Truth About Libertarianism," pp. 9-15.
38 For an example of this argument, see Tibor R. Machan, "Libertarianism: the Principle of Liberty," in *Freedom and Virtue*, pp. 35-58.
39 The phrase is borrowed from Hayek's almost opposite argument in *The Road to Serfdom* that government interference in the economy paves the way for a take-over by the worst elements in society.
40 Meyer, *In Defense of Freedom*, p. 75.

to swallow the idea of huge sums of federal money being spent on large-scale military build-ups, research and development of new weapon technology, and the retaining of a large number of military bases all over the globe. Not to speak of the idea of involuntary military service. Although many libertarians would argue that statism in the form of large-scale military spending was an exception to sound principles, dictated by the political necessity of defending free market capitalism against communism, more radical libertarians such as Murray N. Rothbard would stick to the isolationist principles of the Old Right. In time this would place them seriously at odds with the rest of the conservative movement.[41]

The Failure of Fusionism

To what extent was the attempted fusion of "ice and fire" – of libertarian and traditionalist beliefs – a success? The question comes close to asking whether a cup is half empty or half full. As mentioned above, many conservatives of the fusionist blend would claim that the coalition actually worked on the practical level, and it is probably true that differences of opinion tended to be more fluid on actual issues than in the intellectual battles over political theory. However, it is also clear in retrospect that no real fusion ever took place, and that the coalition remained a shotgun marriage based almost entirely on hatred of the common enemy: New Deal liberalism. By the 1970s, libertarianism and traditionalism would increasingly separate into two movements, with separate institutional frameworks in the form of think tanks, political action committees, journals, and the like. The quest for unity and ideological coherence no longer seemed imperative, as the vision of an almighty liberal establishment was by these years rapidly fading.

---

41 By the late 1960s, resistance to the American involvement in Vietnam, and especially the draft issue, had led several radical libertarians such as Murray Rothbard, and Barry Goldwater's former speechwriter Karl Hess, to establish closer connections with the New left. Rothbard, for one, had come to view the Students for a Democratic Society as a more congenial and responsive forum than conservative organizations of the *National Review* brand.

Chapter 3

McCarthyism and the Conservative Quest for a Public Orthodoxy

> It seems to be almost a law of human nature that it is easier for people to agree on a negative program – on the hatred of an enemy, on the envy of those better off – than on any positive task. The contrast between the "we" and the "they," the common fight against those outside the group, seems to be an essential ingredient in any creed which will solidly knit together a group for common action.
>
> F.A. HAYEK[1]

Partisan Struggle and the Loyalty Issue at Mid-century

WHILE THE SCATTERED forces of American conservatism were struggling to find a voice of their own in the early 1950s, the country was swept by the political phenomenon which became known as "McCarthyism." For conservatives sharing the passionate anti-communism and the dislike and distrust of New Deal liberalism which Senator Joseph McCarthy so clearly catered to, it was obviously a strong temptation to hitch their emerging political movement to his bandwagon. How exactly did this rise – and ultimately the fall – of Joe McCarthy and his witch hunt for "subversive elements" affect the political and intellectual aspirations of the conservative movement? How did it affect the efforts to mobilize conservatives as an independent political movement? The following is an attempt to throw light on these questions.

---

1   Hayek, *The Road to Serfdom* (Chicago: The University of Chicago Press, 1976 [1944]), p. 139.

In the years from his famous 1950 speech in Wheeling, West Virginia to his political suicide during the Army-McCarthy hearings in the summer of 1954, McCarthy was a powerful figure in American politics.[2] Almost overnight, McCarthy had become a focal point in the hunt for subversive elements, though obviously, he was by no means the progenitor of this hunt. "Red Scare" had already become part and parcel of the partisan battle by the time McCarthy caught the nation's attention.

Political abuse of the loyalty issue was not even a new weapon in McCarthy's own tactical arsenal. As his biographer David M. Oshinsky has pointed out, it is a myth that the Wisconsin senator accidentally stumbled over it during his campaign for reelection.[3] As early as in his 1946 senatorial campaign, McCarthy had – like several other Old Guard Republican candidates that year – done his best to link his opponent, as well as the New Deal and the Democratic Party in general, to communism. When the Democratic candidate Howard McMurray received a public endorsement from the Wisconsin Communist Party, McCarthy had quickly seized the opportunity to refer to him as "Communistically inclined."[4]

The method had also been employed by others from the new breed of conservative Republicans who were elected for Congress that year. Among them were Richard Nixon and William Knowland (California), William Jenner (Indiana), John Bricker (Ohio), and Harry Cain (Washington), who had all relentlessly hammered away on the New Deal and promised to rid Washington of the numerous communists who supposedly worked for the federal government. Several older members of Congress, such as GOP National Chairman B. Carroll Reece, had likewise presented the election as a choice between "Communism and Republicanism."

---

2 On February 9, 1950, Senator Joseph McCarthy of Wisconsin was the featured speaker at a meeting of the Republican Women's Club in Wheeling, West Virginia. The high point of the senator's speech, was his claim of being in possession of "a list of 205 (the number was later changed several times – in the transcript of his speech in *Congressional Record*, McCarthy wrote 57) names that were made known to the Secretary of State as being members of the Communist Party and who nevertheless are still working and shaping policy in the State department." The national media were quick to pick up the story, and within weeks, McCarthy had become the most controversial political figure in the country.

3 David M. Oshinsky, *A Conspiracy So Immense; The World of Joe McCarthy* (New York: The Free Press, 1983), pp. 49-52.

4 Quoted from Oshinsky, *A Conspiracy So Immense*, pp. 49-50.

What gave McCarthy's speech in Wheeling such a tremendous impact, then, was not the issue, but the timing. The road had among other things been paved by the Communist victory in China in August 1949, the announcement of a successful nuclear explosion by the Soviet Union in the following month and the case against Alger Hiss, which occupied the minds of so many Americans throughout that year.

Was Senator Joseph McCarthy a dedicated conservative? Hardly. Although he could probably best be placed on the right wing of the Republican Party, domestic communist subversion seemed to be the only issue he really cared about. He rarely addressed other political issues, and he never attempted to develop anything resembling a conservative political program.[5] Still, while anticommunism was only one aspect of conservatism, it was without doubt the most important in terms of publicity and public support. More generalized arguments about the virtues of laissez-faire capitalism, and the inherent evil of the welfare state, were somehow harder to sell in a time of economic boom and unprecedented prosperity.

Regardless of the nature of his commitment to conservative principles, McCarthy could count on unflinching support from the Republican right in Congress. Most of his more moderate Republican colleagues had also come to realize that he served as a very effective spoiler for the party, even if they were privately appalled by his conduct. Besides, McCarthy had acquired the reputation of a political survivor. Nobody knew just how influential he actually was, or for how long he would be around, but most of his colleagues considered it wise to stay on friendly terms with him.[6]

"Mr. Republican," Senator Robert Taft, was no exception. While he attempted to keep some distance from McCarthy in order to maintain his image as a politician above the mud-slinging level, Taft nevertheless encouraged him to "keep talking and if one case doesn't work out, bring up another."[7] When McCarthy launched a vicious attack on General Marshall

---

[5] The true nature of Senator McCarthy's political commitment and the sources of "McCarthyism" have been the subjects of a lively historiographical debate since the early 1950s. For an introduction to this debate, see William B. Hixson, Jr., *Search for the American Right Wing; an Analysis of the Social Science Record, 1955-1987* (Princeton: Princeton University Press, 1992), pp. 1-49.

[6] McCarthy's reputation was partly built on the popular myth that he had been instrumental in the defeat of a number of candidates in the 1950 election, first of all Senator Millard Tydings of Maryland.

[7] Quoted from Oshinsky, *A Conspiracy So immense*, p 133.

in June of 1951, Taft initially labeled his accusations as "extreme," but after a flood of indignant letters, he soon muffled his criticism and declared that "broadly speaking, I approve of Senator McCarthy's program," although he maintained that as for his charges, some of them were justified "and others perhaps not."[8]

Senator Taft, as well as other leading Republicans who cheered McCarthy's relentless attacks on the Truman administration, believed that he could be controlled in time. With a Republican in the White House, McCarthy was to be placed "where he can't do any harm."[9] As it turned out, however, McCarthy apparently intended to stick to his success formula of wild charges of treason in high offices, despite the change of guard in the White House.

This suited many on the right just fine. There was still a widespread bitterness after Senator Taft's defeat at the Republican national convention, and it was further increased once right-wing Republicans realized that the Eisenhower administration under the banner of "modern Republicanism" had set out to create what Barry Goldwater labeled "a dimestore New Deal." Through a continued, albeit slower, expansion of the welfare state, the Eisenhower-administration in fact legitimized New Deal policies in several crucial areas.[10] In consequence an many conservatives felt homeless in the party, which in their view had been taken over by corporate managerial types, representing the Northeastern brand of "me-too-Republicanism."

Senator McCarthy and the Conservative Intellectuals

Both inside and outside of Congress, the right wing became invariably linked to McCarthy for better or worse. In private, however, many conservatives expressed fears that the senator's wild charges and reckless per-

---

8   Oshinsky, *A Conspiracy So immense*, p. 202.
9   In early 1953, the Republican leadership decided to transfer the responsibility on the Communist issue to the Internal Security Committee headed by Senator William Jenner. McCarthy in turn was expected to investigate government corruption as chairman of Committee of Government Operations.
10 The coverage of social security was broadened under Eisenhower, adding some 10 million Americans to the number of eligible recipients. Likewise, federal aid to the schools was increased, as was the minimum wage, and Eisenhower furthermore approved the creation of the Department of Health, Education, and Welfare.

formance could eventually derail the movement, which after all had other goals than political publicity to pursue. Many conservatives felt that respectability and intellectual credibility were equally, if not more important at this stage, and these were hardly qualities that McCarthy could provide.

Among the conservative intellectuals who addressed this dilemma was Whittaker Chambers. In a private letter to McCarthy's personal friend and ardent defender William F. Buckley, Jr., Chambers wrote:

> McCarthy divides the ranks of the Right ... He is a man fighting almost wholly by instinct and intuition, against forces for the most part coldly conscious of their ways, means, and ends. In other words, he scarcely knows what he is doing. He simply knows that somebody threw a tomato and the general direction from which it came.[11]

Despite such reservations, Chambers conceded that "the Senator represents the one force that all shades of the Left really fear," and he felt that criticizing McCarthy and his methods in public was an unaffordable luxury, given the polarized political debate of the time.[12]

Anticommunist scholars such as James Burnham and Max Eastman shared this opinion. Burnham, who had never endorsed the senator, labeled himself an "anti-anti-McCarthyite," and denounced as "a trap" the calls for "responsible" conservatives to repudiate the senator.[13] Max Eastman, who privately described McCarthy as "a misbehaving and sloppy-minded person functioning in a place where the prime demand was for a well-behaved and extremely accurate and exact mind," nevertheless concluded that after all the senator was doing "a job that had to be done."[14]

The evident impact of McCarthy's recklessness led many conservative intellectuals to, in the words of Ralph De Toledano, "shut their eyes to the essential nature of Joe McCarthy's political roots, drowning their doubts in the emotion of the moment. McCarthy was under attack from the lib-

---

11 Whittaker Chambers to William F. Buckley, Jr., April 6, 1954, printed in William F. Buckley, Jr. (ed.), *Odyssey of a Friend; Whittaker Chambers' Letters to William F. Buckley, Jr. 1954-1961* (New York, 1969), p. 56 ff.
12 Buckley, Jr., *Odyssey of a Friend*, p. 56 ff.
13 James Burnham's letter of resignation to the American Committee For Cultural Freedom, cited in John Diggins, *Up From Communism* (New York, 1975), p. 329.
14 John P. Diggins, *Up from Communism; Conservative Odysseys in American Intellectual History* (New York, 1975), p. 217.

erals, and this sufficed."[15] One result of this attitude was further intellectual polarization between on the one side liberal anti-Communists such as Arthur S. Schlesinger and Richard Rovere, who tenaciously opposed McCarthy, and on the other side ex-radical anti-Communists such as James Burnham and Max Eastman, whose defense of the senator now placed them firmly in the conservative camp.

There were some conservatives who openly repudiated McCarthy, and warned that eventually he could discredit the entire movement. In their view, the senator's majoritarian politics were fundamentally at odds with conservative principles of authority. According to the sociologist and later contributor to *National Review* Will Herberg, it was exactly this form of "government by rabble-rousing" that the Constitution had been intended to prevent.[16] Poet and historian Peter Viereck expressed similar views. To him McCarthyism was nothing more than "the same old isolationist, Anglophobe, Germanophile revolt of radical Populist lunatic-fringers against the eastern, educated Anglicized elite."[17] Nevertheless, the contempt for McCarthy's brand of "populist" democracy that Herberg and Viereck so openly expressed was clearly a minority opinion among conservatives.

Liberal counter-attacks on McCarthy and "McCarthyism" stimulated a siege mentality on the right, which caused a great deal of animosity against alleged defectors such as Viereck.[18] The young rising star on the conservative scene, William F. Buckley, Jr., who otherwise shared the elitist distaste of mass politics, was among those who claimed that the ends justified the means in McCarthy's case. He too, however, realized the threat that the senator's appearance and reckless methods posed to the conservative quest for respectability, but while Viereck and Herberg responded to the senator by repudiating him, William F. Buckley, Jr. set out to save McCarthyism from McCarthy.

---

15 Diggins, *Up from Communism*, p. 177.
16 Will Herberg, "Government by Rabble-Rousing," *New Leader* 37 (January 18, 1954).
17 "The Revolt Against the Elite" (1955), in Daniel Bell (ed.), *The Radical Right* (New York, 1963), p. 164.
18 In Viereck's case, the open repudiation of McCarthy reinforced his high standing with many Liberals as a "responsible" opponent, but it also confirmed many conservatives in their opinion of him as a liberal in disguise, who harmed attempts to create a consensus within the movement by his constant shooting in all directions. Among the other factors which made many conservatives suspicious of Viereck's conservative commitment were his advocacy of conservative cooperation with liberal anti-Communists such as Arthur M. Schlesinger, Jr., his endorsement of the New Deal, and his support for Adlai E. Stevenson.

The Attack on Academic Freedom

The first target Buckley picked in his crusade for McCarthy was the notion of "academic freedom." Fresh out of university, he had acquired his reputation as the *enfant terrible* of American conservatism with the publication of *God and Man at Yale* in 1951.[19] The book, which would later become quintessential reading for the growing new breed of right wing radicals on colleges and universities across the nation, was a frontal attack on his *Alma Mater*, and a defense of the McCarthyite witch hunt among university professors in general. It was, as John P. Diggins has noted, "one of the few documents in American intellectual history in which youth attacks age for its liberal permissiveness."[20]

According to Buckley, what went for "academic freedom" was in reality little more than a subtle way to pressurize students to accept a hegemonic liberal consensus based on atheism and "collectivism." The concept of the university as a free marketplace of ideas ought in his view to be replaced by the economic forces of the free market. As in a regular service industry, the teaching should loyally reflect and inculcate the values desired by the consumers, which first of all meant the parents who paid for their children's education. With a venture in rhetorical cross-dressing, Buckley attempted to redefine the notion of academic freedom as "the freedom of men and women to supervise the educational activities and aims of the schools they oversee and support."[21]

In the true spirit of the time, Buckley also named names, and called for a number of teachers to be fired. Concerning John Smith, a professor in the economics department at Yale, he wrote: "Let us bar him from teaching because he is inculcating values that the governing board at Yale considers to be against the public welfare."[22]

Buckley did recognize the intellectual need to challenge established ideas, just as he acknowledged that without this crucial role of the university in the generation of new ideas, the Copernican system would probably still be considered a heresy. His only answer to this dilemma was

---

19 William F. Buckley, Jr, *God and Man at Yale: The Superstitions of "Academic Freedom"* (Chicago, 1951).
20 John P. Diggins, *Up from Communism*, p. 403.
21 Buckley, Jr., *God and Man at Yale*, p.190.
22 Buckley, Jr., *God and Man at Yale*, p. 186.

to separate teaching and research. Thus, new ideas could be tested in remote chambers of the ivory tower, but as far as teaching was concerned, an academic institution was not an arena where ideas were supposed to compete on equal terms. Rather, Buckley claimed, it was comparable to:

> The practice field on which the gladiators of the future are taught to use their weapons, are briefed in the wiles and stratagems of the enemy, and are inspired with the virtue of their cause in anticipation of the day when they will step forward and join the struggle against error.[23]

He took the Gladiator analogy even further and contended that dissent ought to be an act of bravery anyway. Thus, the dissenter should be prepared to take the consequences of his opinions: "If the professor chooses to defy the will of the society, and of the community, and of the private institution, let him do so and let him be prepared to seek employment elsewhere."[24]

Buckley did not limit his efforts in making McCarthyism respectable to the issue of academic freedom. Together with his brother-in-law, L. Brent Bozell (who also became McCarthy's legislative assistant and leading speechwriter), he went on to answer the Wisconsin senator's critics with a book entitled *McCarthy and His Enemies*.[25]

The two young authors did make certain concessions to the senator's critics, and admitted that in several cases he had stepped over the line or been guilty of "exaggerations," "inaccuracies" and "temperamental failures." However, they argued, it was mainly a result of McCarthy's zealous patriotism, just as his political and rhetorical style largely was justified as an attempt to get the message across to "the non-university crowd."[26]

---

23 Buckley, Jr., *God and Man at Yale*, p. 157.
24 Excerpts from William F. Buckley's appearance on "Cross Exam," Indianapolis, January 8, 1962, p. 5. The Buckley papers.
25 William F. Buckley, Jr. and L. Brent Bozell, *McCarthy and His Enemies; the record and its meaning* (Chicago: Henry Regnery Company, 1954).
26 This idea made the critic Dwight MacDonald denounce *McCarthy and His Enemies* in the *Partisan Review* as "a remarkably silly book." According to MacDonald, the book defended "a coarse demagogue in an elegantly academic style replete with nice discriminations and pedantic hair-splittings, giving the general effect of a brief by Cadwalader, Wickersham & Taft on behalf of a pickpocket arrested in a subway men's room." MacDonald's review, "McCarthy and His Apologists," is reprinted in Phillips & Rahv, *The Partisan Review Anthology* (New York: Holt, Rinehart and Winston, 1962), pp. 447-452.

Although the mildly critical passages in the book gave it an air of scholarship, they could not remove the general impression of a tailor-made piece of propaganda for the senator, who the authors saw as a powerful "weapon in the American arsenal."[27] Indeed, they concluded that "on McCarthyism hang the hopes of America for effective resistance to communist infiltration."[28]

In Search of a Public Orthodoxy

What *McCarthy and His Enemies* in a sense attempted to do was to expand the concept and purpose of McCarthyism beyond McCarthy's crusade against alleged threats to the national security. It was not enough, the authors argued to get rid of those who were disloyal and "with wicked intent" harmed national security. It was equally important to get rid of those who *without* wicked intent frustrated "the advancement of American interests."[29] In other words, the true purpose of McCarthyism was more than just to get rid of alleged traitors and security leaks: it was to ensure a "public orthodoxy" that served the national interest as Buckley and Bozell saw it.[30]

The intellectual strait-jacket of conformity that McCarthy's hunt for "subversive elements" had imposed on the nation, was thus not a regrettable side effect, but rather the essential purpose of McCarthyism.

---

27 According to Buckley's biographer, John B. Judis, the criticism of McCarthy in the book was further softened before its publication. In order to promote the book, the authors wanted an official endorsement from the senator, and in December 1953, they sent the manuscript to McCarthy in order to get his approval. The senator was by then so steeped in alcoholism that he was virtually unable to read the manuscript. The criticisms, however, made McCarthy's wife furious, and she advised the senator not to endorse the book. Buckley and Bozell finally agreed to rewrite the passages that the senator found "too stridently anti-McCarthy." The changes were not radical enough for McCarthy's wife, and the book never got the senator's official endorsement, but he did agree to participate in the celebration of the book's publication. For a full account of the incident, see John B. Judis, *William F. Buckley, Jr.; Patron Saint of the Conservatives* (New York, 1988), pp. 107-109.

28 Buckley, Jr. & Bozell, *McCarthy and His Enemies*, pp. 335, 340.

29 Buckley, Jr. & Bozell, *McCarthy and His Enemies*, p. 252.

30 According to the authors, most of McCarthy's excesses were justified by the fact that McCarthyism represented "an orthodoxy still-in-the-making; and therefore, as with all imperfect conformities, some coercive sanctions are being exercised in its behalf." (*McCarthy and His Enemies*, p. 318.)

Thus, by making it an attack on the very notion of "the open society," McCarthyism was placed at the central core of the conflict between liberals and conservatives in America.

The view of McCarthyism's ultimate purpose expressed by Buckley and Bozell was shared by most of what would later become known as the *National Review* crowd. After the death of McCarthy, James Burnham contended that the real issue "in the whole McCarthy business ... was philosophical, metaphysical: what kind of community are we?"[31] Statements on the need for public orthodoxy reflected the profound influence that the ideas of political philosopher Leo Strauss on the emerging group of conservative intellectuals in America.[32] The "Straussian" notion of public orthodoxy found its most extreme expression in the writings of Buckley's co-editor and former mentor at Yale, Willmoore Kendall.

Kendall clearly rejected the notion of a conservative "remnant." As a key exponent of majoritarian conservatism, he did not find that the suppression of communist ideas had to be justified by arguing that they were a danger to society. Rather, he claimed, the issue was that society only made sense as long as its members used "Public policy as an instrument for creating the kind of society their values call for."[33] The Bill of Rights was not Kendall's cup of tea. Accordingly, he resented the fact that many of those who defended the activities of the House Un-American Activities Committee were defensive about it.

Kendall rejected the axiom that America according to the Constitution was intended as an "open society" with freedom of thought and freedom

---

31 James Burnham, "Re-Legitimization," *National review* (June 1, 1957), p. 518.
32 Leo Strauss (1899-1973) emigrated to the United States in 1938 and served as a professor of political science at New School for Social Research, New York City, and later the University of Chicago. Admittedly, both the nature and the extent of his influence on American conservatism are subjects of heated debate. See Ted V. McAllister, *Revolt Against Modernity: Leo Strauss, Eric Voegelin and the Search for a Postliberal Order* (Lawrence: University Press of Kansas, 1996); Kenneth L. Deutsch and John A. Murley (eds.) *Leo Strauss, the Straussians, and the American Regime* (Lanham, MD: Rowman and Littlefield, 1999); and Shadia B. Drury's controversial *Leo Strauss and the American Right* (London: MacMillan Press, 1997).
33 Willmoore Kendall to the editor, *Yale Daily News*, April 28, 1950. Quoted from George H. Nash, *The Conservative Intellectual Movement*, p. 121. Buckley and Bozell's view of McCarthyism as a new public orthodoxy was clearly inspired by Kendall, who had read and revised the manuscript for *McCarthy and His Enemies* prior to its publication. For an account of his views on the meaning and purpose of McCarthyism, see: Willmoore Kendall, "McCarthyism: The Pons Asinorum of Contemporary Conservatism" in *The Conservative Affirmation* (Chicago, 1963), pp. 50-76.

of opinion as basic rights. In response to the central question of whether a free society could use the powers of government in order to strike at a minority "whose beliefs and intentions we deem utterly objectionable," Kendall's answer was that "We are not only entitled to strike at such a minority; it is our solemn duty to do so."[34] Yet, he claimed,

> The defenders of the loyalty-security program, as also of the investigating committees, forgot they were proscribing a minority, forgot that they were affirming an American political orthodoxy, and fell into the habit of describing what they were doing as merely an attempt to forestall the violent overthrow of the United States government.[35]

Through a complex semantic discourse, Kendall came to the conclusion that while "freedom of speech" was guaranteed by the constitution, "freedom of thought" was not. He also found that "a restraint of the freedom of speech of certain individuals may be not an abridgement but a protection of freedom of speech in general."[36] Such suggestions were evidently far from the libertarian view on academic freedom, which F.A. Hayek had expressed in the *Road to Serfdom*:

> [The] interaction of individuals, possessing different knowledge and different views, is what constitutes the life of thought. The growth of reason is a social process based on the existence of such differences. It is of its essence that its results cannot be predicted, that we cannot know which views will assist this growth and which will not – in short, that the growth cannot be governed by any views which we now possess without at the same time limiting it.[37]

The views on public orthodoxy presented by Buckley and Kendall were not only at odds with the libertarian principles which Hayek represented, but also with Albert J. Nock's elitist notion of a conservative "remnant," to whom academic freedom provided a breathing space from the vulgar ideas of the masses. The "remnant" had in the writings of Buckley and Kendall

---

34 Willmoore Kendall, "Do We Want an "Open Society?" *National Review* (January 31, 1959), p. 491.
35 Kendall, "Do We Want an Open Society?," p. 492.
36 Kendall, "Do We Want an Open Society?," p. 492.
37 Hayek, *The Road to Serfdom*, p. 165.

been replaced by the communitarian notion of a dispossessed conservative majority, which was held hostage by a liberal elite in the bureaucracy and the university faculties.[38] Behind their calls for a public orthodoxy was the implicit assumption that such orthodoxy would naturally be conservative rather than liberal in nature.

Conservatism and Catholicism

Senator Joseph McCarthy's appearance on the national stage further strengthened a new public attention to the anticommunist politics of the American Catholic Church. It had become a common assumption that McCarthy, as it was expressed in the *New Republic*, "had a tremendous gravitational pull on [the] Catholic masses."[39] This assumption, combined with the emergence of a substantial number of outspoken conservative intellectuals of Catholic faith – among them the young William F. Buckley, Jr., L. Brent Bozell, Willmoore Kendall, and Russell Kirk – helped promote the notion that Catholicism was a cornerstone of the postwar American Right.

What role did Catholicism actually play in postwar conservatism? Obviously Catholics and conservatives shared common ground in their views on communism and the need to fight alleged domestic subversion, but were Catholics otherwise more inclined to conservative views than other

---

38 The attack on the notion of academic freedom in *God and Man at Yale* triggered responses from Sidney Hook, as well as from Russell Kirk. Despite the fact that Kirk largely shared Buckley's view on McCarthyism as a desirable effort to enforce a public orthodoxy, he nevertheless kindly but firmly rejected Buckley's communitarian view of higher education. The researchers loyalty, he contended, was not to the community, but to truth, and academic freedom was the researchers reward of risk: "The risk which the scholar and the teacher run is the risk of being reprimanded or discharged by persons intolerant of frank expression. To compensate the entrepreneur for the risk of financial loss, profit exists; to compensate the clerisy for the risk of security, academic freedom exists." Sidney Hook, *Heresy, Yes Conspiracy, No* (New York: The John Day Company, 1953). Russell Kirk, *Academic Freedom; an Essay in Definition* (Henry Regnery Company: Chicago, 1955), p. 119.

39 TRB, "Washington Wire," the *New Republic*, Vol.130 (January 11, 1954), p. 2. For a full exploration of the relationship between "McCarthyism" and the American Catholic Church, see Donald F. Crosby, S.J., *God, Church, and Flag; Senator Joseph R. McCarthy and the Catholic Church 1950-1957* (Chapel Hill: The University of North Carolina Press, 1978). See also, Vincent P De Santis, "American Catholics and McCarthyism," *The Catholic Historical Review*, Vol. LI (April, 1965), pp. 1-30.

religious groups? Did the allegedly strong support for Senator McCarthy lead large numbers of Catholics into the conservative camp?[40]

Catholic conservative intellectuals frequently expressed the notion that there was a natural kinship between Catholicism and traditionalist conservative ideology. In his *Conservatism in America*, Professor Clinton Rossiter concluded that regardless of the widely different political opinions held by American Catholics, "the political theory of Catholicism, even as shaped by the realities of American life and dictates of the American tradition, remains an essentially Conservative body of principles."[41] According to Rossiter, the true guardians of Burkean conservatism in America were to be found in the Catholic colleges and universities.[42]

What Rossiter, along with Frederick D. Wilhelmsen, John Flynn, William F. Buckley, Jr., Willmoore Kendall and other conservative intellectuals pointed to in Roman Catholicism was first of all its authoritarian and hierarchical structure and its strong sense of tradition. Likewise, they found a close kinship between the religious belief in original sin and the rather somber view of human nature, which they considered a basic feature of traditional conservatism. To Peter Viereck, conservatism could be seen as "the political secularization of the doctrine of original sin."[43]

In their rejection of the alleged philosophical relativism of American liberalism, conservative Catholics would also point to the idea of a divine "natural law" which provided the fundamental principles for the moral order of society. This view separated them from the rationalist belief in

---

40 This assumption has been expressed by Seymour Martin Lipset among others, who in his 1955-essay, "The Sources of the 'Radical Right', concluded that "the radical right, stressing the anti-Communist issue, is able to advance other parts of its program. The radical right uses the anti-Communist issue to create or sustain hostility among the Catholics against the New Deal, against social reform, at the same time identifying liberalism with Communism." In Daniel Bell (ed.), *The Radical Right* (Garden City, N.Y.: Doubleday & Company, Inc., 1964 [1955]), p. 355.

41 Clinton Rossiter, *Conservatism in America; the Thankless Persuasion* (New York: Vintage Books, 1962 [1955]), p. 234. The most comprehensive study of the profound influence of Catholic intellectuals in the conservative movement is Patrick Allitt, *Catholic Intellectuals and Conservative Politics in America, 1950-1985* (Ithaca: Cornell University Press, 1993).

42 Rossiter, *Conservatism in America*, p. 234.

43 Peter Viereck, *Conservatism Revisited* (New York: Collier Books, 1962 [1949]), p. 47.

"natural rights," which liberalism had inherited from Hobbes, Locke, and Rousseau.⁴⁴

If the authoritarian structure of Catholicism supposedly provided an especially suitable moral framework for traditionalist conservatives, then the same appeared to be true for a number of ex-communists, who, often in well publicized cases, completed their exodus from Marxism by converting (or returning) to Catholicism. The list included among others Elizabeth Bentley, Louis Budenz, Freda Utley, and William Henry Chamberlin. Elizabeth Bentley explained her own conversion to Catholicism with the need to replace the absolutist framework, which Communism had previously supplied: "People, who are genuine Communists, as I was, aren't the lukewarm type. They can't go into a vacuum if they give up Communism. They must have something to tie to."⁴⁵

As described above, several elements of Catholic church teachings could give conservative Catholics a gratifying sense of harmony between their political views and their religious beliefs. Yet, it required a selective view of the political theory of the Church to claim that Catholics would be more predisposed to gravitate towards conservative political views. Actually, it is hard to think of any other faith capable of harboring such widely different views on social issues within its dogmatic framework.

If conservatives could pick the doctrines of original sin and natural law to sustain their positions, liberal Catholics could pick the idea of social justice, which had been part of the social philosophy of Catholicism since the papal *De Rerum Novarum* in 1891. The Church, which traditionally had a major part of its constituency in the lower social classes, had also maintained strong ties with the labor movement, and was generally supportive of pro-labor legislation. Just how selective the conservative use of Catholic doctrine was would become evident when William F. Buckley, Jr. and other Catholic conservatives at the *National Review* denounced the social philos-

---

44 The conflict between natural law and natural rights is basically a conflict between a "descending" and an "ascending" principle of authority. The idea of natural rights is egalitarian in the sense that every man is considered to be born with the same set of inalienable rights, and should only be submitted to the political authority of others by his own consent. For further exploration of the concepts and their political implications, see J.M. Finnis, *Natural Law and Natural Rights* (Oxford: Oxford University Press, 1980).

45 *Time* (November 29, 1948), p. 46.

ophy of Pope John XXIII's encyclical *Mater et Magistra* as "a venture in triviality."[46]

The Catholic Anticommunist Tradition

More than in religious beliefs, the explanation for the strong Catholic profile among conservative intellectuals and organizers in the 1950s was probably first of all to be found in the anticommunist policies of the Catholic Church. There was a certain parallel between the political outsider-status of American conservatism and the religious and cultural outsider-status of American Catholicism prior to the 1950s.

The emergence of the second Red Scare and the forging of a near anticommunist consensus pulled American conservatism in a more majoritarian direction and gave it a political credibility it had not enjoyed in previous decades. Likewise, the fierce anticommunist politics of the American Catholic Church probably more than anything eased its way into the religious and cultural mainstream of the country. For Catholics, who throughout American history had been confronted with accusations of "dual loyalty," anticommunism provided a chance to demonstrate that allegiance to the Pope was fully compatible with "Americanism."

Actually the American Catholic Church had been combating communism since the 1870s and 1880s, when conservative Catholics accused the Knights of Labor of communism and attempted to block Catholic membership in its ranks by asking for a papal condemnation of the movement.[47] Even during World War II, while criticism of the Soviet Union generally had become somewhat subdued because of the temporary alliance against the Axis powers, the Church continued its unrelenting condemnations of "Godless Soviet communism."

As Catholic strongholds in Eastern Europe fell under Soviet dominance in the early postwar years, it truly became a political preoccupation for the Church – years before the Red Scare hit society in general. Especially the fates of Poland, Yugoslavia, and Hungary became major con-

---

46 Editorial, *National Review*, July 29, 1961.
47 See Donald F. Crosby, S.J., *God, Church, and Flag*, p. 5.

cerns, and the persecution of Catholic leaders, such as Archbishop Aloysius Stepinac in Yugoslavia and Joseph Cardinal Mindszenty in Hungary, gathered tens of thousands of Catholic demonstrators in New York City under the leadership of Francis Cardinal Spellman.[48] Particularly the Hungarian uprising in 1956 mobilized Catholic activists who joined other conservatives in the demand for a policy of liberation rather than "containment." The president's unwillingness to risk war by helping the rebels further strengthened the conservative dislike of his brand of "modern republicanism."

Although most of these organizing efforts originally had been made in response to the conditions of Catholics in Eastern Europe, the Church also gave attention to alleged subversion at home. Organizations such as the Catholic Information Society of New York distributed scores of anticommunist pamphlets, and some right-wing Catholics began to organize in semi-secret anti-Communist societies, "Freedom Foundations" and "Cardinal Mindszenty Foundations." In many respects these organizations were the predecessors of the John Birch Society and other radical right organizations of the 1950s and 1960s.

The Catholic Church and Senator McCarthy

When McCarthy emerged as the new champion of anticommunism in 1950, Bishop Fulton J. Sheen of New York City had already been writing anticommunist books, pamphlets and articles for twenty years. The Knights of Columbus, a Catholic lay body, which by 1954 had acquired a membership of 920,000, had since the early Cold War years set up programs to combat communism all over the country. Father John Cronin had been employed for years by the Social Action Department of the National Catholic Welfare Conference, with the purpose of compiling files on domestic communist subversion. His reports had included the later fa-

---

48 Stepinac, who had collaborated with the occupying Nazi forces and had served as councilor for the Croatian dictator Ante Pavelic, was sentenced to 16 years in prison in 1946. Joseph Cardinal Mindszenty was arrested in 1948 and charged with treason. Probably subjected to torture, the cardinal pleaded guilty on all counts, and was sentenced to death. The sentence was later changed to imprisonment. During the Hungarian uprising in November 1956, the cardinal fled to the U.S. Embassy in Budapest, which became his sanctuary for the next 15 years.

mous charges of communist subversion against Alger Hiss three years before they were made in public by Whittaker Chambers. Yet, it was first of all Senator McCarthy's Catholicism that brought public attention to the anticommunist policies of the church.

Although Joe McCarthy himself never made his religious affiliation an issue, others, supporters as well as opponents, did. For one thing, it became part of conventional wisdom that he had been talked into a crusade against communist subversion by Father Edmund Walsh of Georgetown University, despite the fact that McCarthy previously had exploited the issue as early as 1946 in his campaign for the Senate. Many political observers became preoccupied with the question of what Catholics thought of McCarthy and to what extent he "controlled" the Catholic vote.

The senator clearly had strong support in the Catholic press. Out of almost a hundred Catholic newspapers and weeklies, there were only a few, though notable and important journals such as *Commonweal* and the Jesuit weekly *America* which maintained their strong opposition to the senator. They did so amidst a heavy flack of accusations of helping the enemy. Such charges came from readers, from other parts of the Catholic press, and not least from Senator McCarthy himself.[49]

As for the American Catholic hierarchy, only one member – Bishop Bernard J. Sheil of Chicago – ever spoke out publicly against Joe McCarthy, carefully pointing out that he was speaking as a private person and not as a representative of the Church. But although some leading Catholics such as the archbishop Francis Cardinal Spellman of New York made public endorsements of McCarthy, the Church never endorsed him officially. On the other hand, given the political climate of the time, it was extremely cautious not to make any statement that could be interpreted as "anti-anticommunist."

If the opinions expressed by the Catholic press and members of the Catholic hierarchy seemed to support the popular notion of McCarthy's almost unanimous support among Catholics, how then did he fare among the lay people? The opinion polls taken at the time revealed far

---

49 Both journals repeatedly warned about the dangers, which they believed support for the Wisconsin senator posed to the Catholic Church, as well as to the country in general. *Commonweal* called McCarthy a "reckless, irresponsible bogeyman," who threatened "the basic decencies, the objectivity and the order of our national life."(June 2, 1950), p. 188; (November 5, 1954), p. 149. For Senator McCarthy's response, see Vincent P. De Santis, "American Catholics and McCarthyism," pp. 7-8.

more mixed reactions. Contrary to the public stereotype, support for McCarthy actually remained a seriously divisive issue within the Church.

As for the widespread notion that McCarthy to a large extent was able to capture and control the Catholic vote in the congressional elections of 1950 and 1952, this, too, appears to be a myth.[50] Even in his home state of Wisconsin there was no indication that this was the case. McCarthy generally had strong support in rural areas and little support in urban areas – even in urban districts that were heavily Catholic.[51] Neither did he, in the presidential election of 1952, seem to exercise any substantial influence on the Catholic vote. To the extent that Catholic voters abandoned the Democratic Party and voted Republican, it was seemingly for the same reasons as non-Catholic voters: Ike's popularity, Korea, corruption, and the like.[52]

So, regarding the question of whether support for McCarthy led any substantial number of Catholics into the conservative camp, the answer is no. To the extent that a shift to the Republican Party among Catholic voters would be considered a valid indicator of a possible turn to the right, such realignment did not occur throughout the 1950s and 1960s.[53] Not until the landslide election of 1972 did a majority of Catholics vote Republican, and even then their defection from the Democratic Party appeared to be transitory and not proportionally larger than that of Democrats in general.[54]

Not only does it appear to be a myth that McCarthy possessed the necessary influence to make a substantial number of otherwise Democratic voters shift to a Republican candidate; even the basic notion that a large majority of Catholics held a favorable opinion of him appears to be wrong. A Gallup poll taken in January 1954, while McCarthy was at the height of his career, showed that although he did have a higher following among Catholics than among Protestants, it did not come anywhere near

---

50 For an analysis of McCarthy's role in these elections, see Donald F. Crosby, S.J., *God, Church, and Flag*, pp. 70-118.
51 Crosby, *God, Church, and Flag*, pp. 88-117.
52 Crosby, *God, Church, and Flag*, pp. 88-117.
53 Like in all presidential elections since the New Deal, a minimum of three-fifths of the Catholic vote would go to the Democratic Party throughout the period. Andrew M. Greeley, *The American Catholic; A Social Portrait* (New York: Basic Books, Inc., 1977), p. 92.
54 Greeley, *The American Catholic*, p. 92.

the popular notions of overwhelming support – 58 percent as compared to 49 percent among Protestants.

One might of course argue that this is a significant difference in any case, but January 1954, December 1953 and March 1954 were actually the only months in McCarthy's four years on the national scene when his support among Catholics exceeded 50 percent.[55] Four months later, as the Army-McCarthy hearings were taking place and his popularity had begun to slip, another Gallup Poll indicated that American Catholics followed the general trend, as the number of respondents favorable towards the senator had decreased to 46 percent.[56]

To sum up, Catholics were very visible among conservative intellectuals and organizers of the 1950s. Among other things, their strong presence in the movement evidences the decline of nativism. Yet, despite the suggested affinity between Catholic church teaching and conservative ideas, the notion that Catholics in general constituted a conservative core group does not hold up. Rather than full-blown conservatives, most Catholics were simply "fellow-travelers" on a few important issues, most notably the fight against communism.

The Downfall of McCarthy

In the spring of 1954, Senator McCarthy finally self-detonated when he used a trivial case concerning an army dentist who had turned out to be a member of the American Labor Party to strike a blow at the army. When Brigadier General Ralph Zwicker refused to give the names of the officers who had been involved in the case, McCarthy publicly berated him as "not fit to wear that uniform." The army retaliated by disclosing material concerning attempts by McCarthy and his aide Roy Cohn to make the army give preferential treatment to a member of McCarthy's staff. These charges led to the Army-McCarthy hearings – the first televised public hearings ever.

Public support for the senator declined rapidly during the hearings, and within the Republican Party he was increasingly seen as a political li-

---

55 Vincent P. De Santis, "American Catholics and McCarthyism," *The Catholic Historical Review*, Vol. LI (April 1965), p. 24.
56 De Santis, "American Catholics and McCarthyism," p. 29.

ability. After the congressional election campaigns of 1950 and 1952, it had been a common perception (though not necessarily correct) that support from McCarthy had been crucial in several Republican victories, and good relations with him had been considered politically wise. In the fall election campaigns of 1954, however, even candidates in the Midwest – supposedly a bastion of McCarthyism – declined the Wisconsin senator's offer of support.

The final blow to McCarthy came on December 2, 1954, when the Senate voted to censure him for contempt of the Senate and for his abuse of General Zwicker.[57] Republican Conservatives such as Barry Goldwater, William Jenner, Everett Dirksen and John Bricker had unsuccessfully tried to work out a compromise to avoid the censure. When these attempts failed, several of them instead went all out in support for McCarthy and implied that the censure itself was a part of the Communist conspiracy. Among them was Senator Goldwater of Arizona, who talked about the "unknown engineers of censure" and "the masterminds of this fight" whose "deeds have come from the darkness." He also noted that the Communists had "skillfully shifted the leadership of the campaign into the hands of highly respectable American anti-Communists who have come to hate McCarthy for other reasons."[58] While all Democrats voted for the censure, the Republicans split on the issue. Twenty-two senators, easily identified with the right wing of the party, opposed it.

The censure almost made McCarthy a pariah in the Senate, and he soon faded into political obscurity. But the conflict of which he had become a catalyst continued long after his disappearance from the political scene.[59] To the Republican right, the Eisenhower administration's handling of the McCarthy issue became yet another source of bitterness. Especially Vice President Richard M. Nixon's job as anti-McCarthy hatchet-

---

57 Republican Senator Ralph Flanders of Vermont took the initiative to the censure. McCarthy had publicly described him as "senile," and had added that "they should get a man with a net and take him to a good quiet place." Among the other members of the Senate that McCarthy had insulted were Senator Hendrickson of New Jersey, who he described as "a living miracle in that he is without question the only man who has lived so long with neither brains nor guts."
58 1954 *Congressional Record*, Volume 100, p. 16001.
59 Outside Congress there were, however, still a great number of people on the American right who continued to demonstrate their loyalty to McCarthy. In one of the first issues of *National Review*, William F. Buckley had the senator review his pet aversion, Dean Acheson's book *A Democrat Looks at His Party*.

man created a deep-seated distrust among conservatives. The Hiss-case notwithstanding, this distrust would follow Nixon throughout the rest of his political career.

If most liberals saw the McCarthy era as a lesson in the fragility of civil liberties, most conservatives saw it as a lesson in the tremendous power of "the Liberal establishment." If McCarthy became the greatest villain in liberal demonology, he became a true martyr for the American Right. A common conservative portrait of McCarthy became that of an honest – if sometimes ill tempered – defender of American virtues, who had dared to challenge "the Liberal establishment," and had been punished accordingly. At McCarthy's death in 1957, *National Review*-editor, Willi Schlamm, wrote in the magazine's eulogy for the senator that "(He) saw the gargoyles of the Anti-Christ staring and sneering at him from everywhere, and innocently he reached out to crush them ... and it killed him."[60]

The same chord was struck more than two decades later by William A. Rusher, former publisher of *National Review* and one of the leading figures in the "draft Goldwater" movement. In his political memoirs, *The Rise of the Right*, Rusher writes that

> [McCarthy] wandered into the sights of Liberalism's mighty guns" with his speech in Wheeling, and "as a result of his charges and his reckless disinclination to retract them, was the recipient of a barrage that lasted nearly four solid years and resulted in his political destruction and (in all likelihood) his death at forty-eight in 1957."[61]

On the far right, McCarthy's censure, subsequent decline into obscurity, and actual death in 1957 formed the basis of a variety of myths and inventive conspiratorial theories. A book published by the John Birch Society, for instance, presented the theory that the senator had been poisoned with carbon tetrachloride by the Communist conspiracy just as he was on the verge of a political comeback.[62]

On balance, how did McCarthyism affect the emerging conservative movement in America? First of all, it pushed the conservative movement

---

60 William S. Schlamm, "Across McCarthy's Grave," National Review, Vol.3 (May 18, 1957), p. 470.
61 William A. Rusher, *The Rise of the Right* (New York, 1984), p. 42.
62 Medford Evans, *The Assassination of Joe McCarthy*, Western Islands (Boston, 1970).

in a more majoritarian direction. The apparent public support for the anti-Communist witch-hunt gave many conservative intellectuals a renewed faith in the political instincts of the common people, which prompted them to redefine their own political role accordingly. The role as conservative "remnant" was gradually being replaced, as the wish to enter the fray and participate directly in the political process grew stronger.[63] Likewise, the fact that it was a Catholic senator who emerged as the leading anti-Communist figure of the early 1950s made a difference. Not only did it signal that Catholicism was in the process of moving into the mainstream of American culture; it also signaled the decline of nativism as an essential feature of right wing politics.

The anticommunism of the "Old Right" had often been closely connected with anti-Catholicism and anti-Semitism. The ability to tie the fear of subversion to existing social strains had made people such as Gerald B. Winrod, Gerald L.K. Smith and William Dudley Pelley prominent figures on the far right of the 1930s.[64] McCarthy's focus on treason in the corridors of power somehow detached the idea of subversion from such strains.

Given the focus on treason and internal subversion rather than on Soviet threats to American security, the fight against Communism developed an almost abstract quality under the senator's banners. In fact, he domesticated the issue and eased the tensions between Old Right isolationists and the Cold War crusaders of the emerging New Right.[65]

For the conservative movement, the advantages of hitching on to the Senator McCarthy bandwagon were won at the expense of intellectual respectability, which many otherwise considered to be crucial to further conservative political advances. In this respect, Senator McCarthy's downfall, rather than his previous four years of power, probably had a greater

---

63 See Jonathan Rieder, "The Rise of the 'Silent Majority'" in Steve Fraser and Gary Gerstle (ed.), *The Rise and Fall of the New Deal Order, 1930-1980* (Princeton: Princeton University Press, 1989), p. 247.

64 For the best study of the far right in the 1930s, see Leo P. Ribuffo, *The Old Christian Right* (Philadelphia: Temple University Press, 1983).

65 During the 1960s, the far right's most prominent organization, the John Birch Society, was often described in the media as a nativist protestant organization, but according to the organization's own estimate, as much as 50 percent of its members were Catholics. John A. Andrew III, *The Other Side of the Sixties: Young Americans for Freedom and the Rise of Conservative Politics* (New Brunswick: Rutgers University Press, 1997), p. 105.

impact on the American Right. His witch-hunt for communists had obviously not resulted in any major political realignment. It had stirred emotions and had inspired and encouraged a great number of attacks on the State Department, on liberal intellectuals, and on specific policies of the Roosevelt and Truman administrations, but it could not automatically be translated into any significant increase in the support for conservative views as such.

McCarthy's power had almost completely been centered around his own person. His influence had been based on his senatorial prerogatives, his chairmanship of the Senate Permanent Subcommittee on Investigations, and of course on his ability to catch the attention of the media. While offering his support to conservative Republicans in congressional elections, he had never seriously attempted to channel his power and political prestige into the organization of the right outside of Congress.[66] There were no leading conservative figures waiting to take over after his fall, and there was no organizational structure to do the job in the absence of such a leader. After four years of McCarthyism, the right was hardly better organized than it had previously been. Thus, to many conservatives the most important lesson that could be drawn from the rise and fall of Senator Joe McCarthy was the need to organize from the bottom up, rather than to rely on the possible success of a leading figure.

---

66 Curiously, McCarthy's widow made an unsuccessful attempt after his death to organize a conservative research institute in honor of his memory. The purpose of such an institute would according to Mrs. McCarthy be to serve as counter to liberal organizations such as Fund for the Republic, the National Committee for an Effective Congress, and the Committee for Cultural Freedom. (Mrs. Joe McCarthy to William F. Buckley, Jr., August 20, 1957, WFB papers, Box 3).

Chapter 4

Out of Isolation

> The possibility of intervention ushered the most savage debate of my lifetime – more savage than the debate over communism in the late 1940s, more savage than the debate over McCarthyism in the early 1950s, more savage than the debate over Vietnam in the 1960s. The debate between interventionists and isolationists in 1940-41 had an inner fury that tore apart families, friends, churches, universities, and political parties.
>
> ARTHUR M. SCHLESINGER, JR.[1]

"Ideas Have Consequences"

IF THERE WAS ONE thing conservatives could agree on in the early postwar years, it was the urgent need for the creation of conservative media. There was ferment in the evolution of conservative ideas, but no forum where such ideas could be exchanged and shared with a larger audience. True enough, conservative viewpoints were expressed daily in the Hearst papers, in the New York *Daily News*, William Loeb's Manchester *Union Leader*, and in the Chicago *Tribune*, which was the most widely read newspaper in America. They were presented in the *American Legion Magazine* and in the pages of widely circulated periodicals such as *Reader's Digest* and *Life*. But such journals could not serve as standard-bearers of a political movement.

What conservatives wanted were intellectual outlets which could challenge the liberal claim that conservatives did not have any ideas – a claim that later found its most famous expression when Lionel Trilling described American conservative thinking as "irritable mental gestures which seek to resemble ideas."[2] In short, they wanted counterparts to lib-

---

[1] Arthur M. Schlesinger, Jr., "Back To the Womb? Isolationism's Renewed Threat," *Current* (November, 1995), p. 25.
[2] Lionel Trilling, *The Liberal Imagination* (New York, 1950), p. ix.

eral journals such as *The New Republic* and *The Nation*. According to John Chamberlain, conservative journalist and editor of *The Freeman*, such journals had been instrumental in creating the intellectual climate for the New Deal in the 1920s and early 1930s, and he believed that the time had come for conservative journals to have a similar impact. This view was later seconded by the editor of *National Review*, William F. Buckley, Jr., who likewise saw the New Deal revolution as the result of "the cumulative impact of *The Nation* and *The New Republic* and a few other publications on several American college generations during the twenties and thirties."³

The importance that right wing intellectuals attributed to the media partly reflected a strong conservative belief in ideas rather than in the struggle between interests as a primary force in social change. "So what do the philosophical foundations of conservatism mean to people in Kansas City and Scranton?" populist conservatives would later ask. Not much, *National Review* editor Jeffrey Hart would respond, except to the individuals "who are addicted to good prose and to theoretical perception." But the main purpose of a journal of opinion was not to reach Middle America. A magazine such as *National Review* was based on the assumption that "the intellectual class in modern society possesses unprecedented leverage."⁴ Most conservatives shared this faith in the "trickledown effect" of ideas.

According to John Chamberlain, there was no lack of talented conservative writers, but lack of a forum in which these writers could develop conservative ideas. Otherwise, they would be stifled to death by the liberal media. He was convinced that "if New York City, for example, had one good Sunday newspaper, the whole intellectual climate at the critical level would change overnight." Publishers would allegedly be more willing to publish conservative books if they knew that such books would be reviewed and reach "the bookstores of the hinterlands."⁵

Most of the prospective conservative publishers and editors realized that there was no direct correlation between a journal's circulation and its actual influence on political opinion. Both *The Nation*, with a modest circulation of about 36,000 copies a week, and *The New Republic*, with an

---

3   Trilling, *The Liberal Imagination*, p. 2.
4   Jeffrey Hart, Column, December 23, 1975. Quoted from John B. Judis, *William F. Buckley; Patron Saint of the Conservatives* (New York: Simon and Schuster, 1988), p. 379.
5   John Chamberlain, *A Life With the Printed Word* (Chicago: Regnery Gateway, 1982).

average of about 30,000, were good examples of this fact.[6] Just to reach this modest level of circulation, however, would prove to be extremely difficult for most of the conservative journals in the first postwar decade.

Regardless of political orientation, it was a financially risky business to start a journal of opinion. Even a well-established liberal journal such as *the Nation* could not exist without financial support.[7] According to an estimate made by a publishers' consultant in 1949, it would take an average of four years to establish a new journal, and the odds against the success of such a venture for a new publisher was approximately three to one.[8] Accordingly, it was only to be expected that several of the many conservative ventures into publishing would be short-lived.

Yet, funding and logistics were not the primary problems impeding the development of the conservative media. More important were the ideological and strategic disagreements that took place in the editorial offices, sometimes resulting in bitter struggles. To a large extent these struggles were reflections of the major ideological conflicts wracking the postwar American Right: traditionalists clashed with libertarians, isolationists clashed with interventionists, and elitists clashed with majoritarians. Accordingly, a closer look provides a valuable insight into the continuous struggle to define the nature and future direction of American conservatism.

In the Course of Human Events

In February 1944, while war raged on three continents, the first issue of a weekly conservative newsletter called *Human Events* was published in Washington, D.C. There was nothing spectacular about this new venture. It was a weekly four-page newsletter, usually devoted to a single essay. Yet *Human Events* was the first serious attempt to create a conservative journal for postwar America, and many conservatives, though mostly in retrospect, would see it as a messenger of things to come.

---

6   Theodore Peterson, *Magazines in the Twentieth Century* (Urbana: The University of Illinois Press, 1956), p. 364. The *New Republic* actually reached a circulation of 96,000 in 1948, when its editor Henry A. Wallace ran for the Presidency, but it soon dropped back to its usual level.
7   Peterson, *Magazines in the Twentieth Century*, p. 364.
8   Harlan Logan, "Tomorrows New Magazines," *Magazine Industry* 1 (Summer, 1949), p. 17, quoted from Peterson, *Magazines in the Twentieth Century*, p. 76.

Perhaps it is somewhat misleading to label *Human Events* in its early years as conservative. Eventually it did become an important forum for both traditionalists and libertarians, but at this stage it was first of all a dissenting voice of "Old Right" isolationist opposition to the government's foreign policy. "Isolationist" is used here as a neutral term, although by 1940 it was often used pejoratively. For that very reason most of the people it referred to preferred label themselves as "America Firsters," "noninterventionists," or "nationalists."

Human Events was founded and edited by Frank C. Hanighen and Felix Morley. Both defied the common stereotype of conservative isolationists They were not narrow-minded xenophobes, but cosmopolitans with strong personal ties to a number of European intellectuals. Contrary to the stereotypes, which emerged in the heated debate over American intervention in World War II, isolationism had traditionally covered a diverse spectrum of opinions. In general, isolationists had rarely advocated insularity. Few had advocated cultural isolation, even fewer the severing of commercial ties to the outside world. Rather, many isolationists advocated a hard-nosed economic nationalism. All in all, American isolationism had rarely been based on ideas about national self-sufficiency, just as it rarely dealt in absolutes. Its main concern had been the discussion of methods, directions, and priorities in the country's foreign policy. *Human Events* emerged out of this tradition, but the political climate had changed dramatically since the days when isolationist views belonged to the mainstream. America was now at war.[9]

Frank Hanighen, a Harvard graduate, had worked before the war as a foreign correspondent in Europe for the New York *Post* and the Philadelphia *Record*. He had authored several books on history and politics, among them the influential *Merchants of Death*, which was an early warning about what later, would be termed "the military-industrial complex."[10] The book became an important source of inspiration for the so-called Nye-Committee that was created by the Senate that same year with the

---

9 It is worth remembering that just six months before the Japanese attack on Pearl Harbor, an opinion poll indicated that 83 percent of all Americans opposed armed intervention in the war. It is important to add, though, that a majority would risk war in order to help the allied powers and defeat Germany. See Justus D. Doenecke, "American Isolationism, 1939-1941," *Journal of Libertarian Studies*, Vol. VI, No. 3-4 (Summer/Fall, 1982), pp. 209-211.

10 With H. C. Engelbrecht (New York: Dodd, Mead & Company, 1934).

purpose of investigating the role which the munitions industry had played in the American government's decision to intervene in World War I. The Nye-Committee eventually presented the thesis that the United States had been dragged into the war by foreign loans and munitions profits, and the investigations led to the passing of the so-called neutrality acts, between 1935 and 1937. After the publication of *Merchants of Death*, Hanighen was active in The America First Committee, and by the mid-1940s he remained a strong proponent of non-interventionism.[11]

Hanighen's associate, Felix Morley, came from a position as president of the Quaker institution Haverford College. He too had spent several years abroad. After graduating from Haverford, he had studied at Oxford University and at the London School of Economics, and in the late 1920s and early 1930s he had worked in Geneva as a correspondent for the *Baltimore Sun*. Upon his return to America in 1931, he became a researcher and public relations liaison for the Brookings Institution in Washington, D.C. Since then he had been a widely recognized editor of the Washington *Post*. In 1936 his work was rewarded with a Pulitzer prize. Morley was well connected. His personal friends included former president and fellow Quaker Herbert Hoover, as well as Republican Senator Robert A. Taft.

Raised in an English Quaker family, Morley shared his faith's anti-militarist and anti-imperialist outlook.[12] Yet, he could hardly be described as a typical isolationist, for he had served in Geneva as a representative of the American League of Nations Association. By the late 1930s, however, he had become increasingly hostile to the foreign policy of the Roosevelt-administration, as it involved the country still deeper in the ongoing European conflict. When in August, 1940, his opposition to American intervention in the Second World War clashed with the views of the owner of the *Post*, Eugene Meyer, he resigned.

During the first year of *Human Events*, Hanighen and Morley became associated with Henry Regnery – a young man from Chicago of German Catholic origins who was anxious to leave the family textile business and

---

11 The best account of America First is Wayne S. Cole, *America First: The Battle Against Intervention, 1940-1941* (Madison, WI: Wisconsin University Press, 1953).

12 Although Morley shared such views, he was disturbed by what he referred to as "the growing cult of Quaker socialism." Many liberals were attracted to the humanitarian side of Quakerism, while allegedly ignoring the sturdy self-reliance, which Morley saw as an essential quality of the faith. Letter, Felix Morley to Herbert Hoover, November 19, 1953. The Felix Morley Papers, Hoover Presidential Library, West Branch, Iowa.

enter the world of publishing. Regnery had graduated from M.I.T. in mechanical engineering in 1934 and had spent the following two years in Nazi Germany studying economics at the university in Bonn. His close ethnic, cultural and personal ties to Germany, which he maintained after his return to the United States, left a distinct mark on his later career as a publisher.

Regnery entered the graduate school at Harvard in 1936 as an admirer of Franklin D. Roosevelt and the New Deal, a political stance that was identical with that of most German Catholics, a pro-social reform group since at least the Progressive Era. However, lectures by the Austrian laissez-faire economist Joseph Schumpeter convinced him of the virtues of the free market.[13] Likewise, Regnery later mentioned his experiences during a summer job in the allegedly rigid bureaucracy of the Resettlement Administration among the important factors behind his "conversion" to anti-statist beliefs.[14] Concerning his non-interventionist views on foreign policy, Regnery was walking in the footsteps of his father, William H. Regnery, who had been member of the executive committee of the America First Committee, as well as its largest individual contributor.[15]

America First

The America First Committee, its brief existence notwithstanding, had been a focal point for organized opposition to the interventionist foreign policy of the Roosevelt-administration, and many of the roots of the continued right wing opposition to American interventionism in the postwar years can be found in that organization. The Committee had been formed in September of 1940. In the following fifteen months, until it was dissolved after the Japanese attack on Pearl Harbor, it had been the country's

---

13 Schumpeter had in such works as *Theory of Economic Development* (1912), and later *Business Cycles* (1939), given the entrepreneur the leading role in economic development. His later work *Socialism, Capitalism, and Democracy* (1947) was a warning against corporate capitalism, which according to Schumpeter eventually would pave the way for socialism. When the units of production became so large that their leadership became divorced from their ownership, the state would eventually take over.

14 Henry Regnery, *Memoirs of a Dissident Publisher* (New York: Regnery Publishing, Inc., 1979), p. 14 ff.

15 Justus D. Doenecke, *Not To the Swift; The Old Isolationists in the Cold War Era* (Lewisburg: Bucknell University Press, 1979), p. 98.

leading isolationist pressure group.[16] By December 1941, the America First Committee had some 850,000 members in 450 chapters all over the country (although it did not have much success in the South).[17] Its major strength was clearly to be found in the Midwest.

The organization's national headquarters were located in Chicago, and the national chairman, General Robert E. Wood of Sears, Roebuck and Company, as well as the other six members of America First's executive committee were all Midwesterners. Like William H. Regnery, most of them were businessmen.[18] Among the largest of the approximately 25,000 contributors to the committee's campaigns, advertisements and radio broadcasts (apart from Regnery), were Colonel Robert C. McCormick, the publisher of the rabidly anti-New Deal and isolationist Chicago *Tribune*, H. Smith Richardson of the Vick Chemical Company, J.M. Patterson, president of the *New York News*, and the national chairman Robert E. Wood, who himself contributed more than $10,000.[19] The most active speakers at America First rallies across the country included Senators Burton K. Wheeler of Montana and Gerald P. Nye of North Dakota, as well as the journalist John T. Flynn and Colonel Charles A. Lindbergh, who consistently expressed his belief in the necessity of a negotiated peace with Nazi-Germany. Other senatorial members included Robert M. LaFollette, Jr. (R-Wis.) and Arthur M. Vandenberg (R-Mich.).

The Midwestern tilt of the America First Committee was no coincidence. The isolationist impulse had traditionally been particularly strong among farmers and small businessmen in this part of the country. Skeptical of both big business and big government, they were convinced that military mobilization would subsidize big business and unfairly benefit industrial and urban areas elsewhere in the country at their expense. Many Midwesterners also harbored a profound distrust of the cultural

---

16 Other noninterventionist organizations included the National Council for the Prevention of War, American Legion, Women's International League for Peace and Freedom, and the Keep America Out of War Congress.

17 Wayne S. Cole, *Roosevelt and the Isolationists, 1932-45* (Lincoln: University of Nebraska Press, 1983), p. 381.

18 As an illustration of the organizational continuity on the American right, General Wood and several other America First organizers and sponsors would twenty years later be leading figures in anti-Communist organizations such as the Institute for American Strategy and the American Security Council – a national information center on domestic communist subversion.

19 Wayne S. Cole, *Roosevelt and the Isolationists*, p. 381.

values of "Eastern anglophiles," as well as a feeling that one of the primary purposes of intervention was to save Wall Street bankers and Eastern corporations from the consequences of their "foreign entanglements."[20] The America First Committee also expressed such views.

To most of these isolationists, the notion that the national security of the United States could be threatened by wars on other continents largely remained an abstraction. Particularly the conservative isolationists put their faith in airpower as a cheap and efficient way of turning the North American continent into an impregnable fortress.[21]

There were strong ties between the founders of *Human Events* and the people behind the dissolved America First Committee.[22] Apart from an initial donation of $3,000 from Joseph N. Pew, Jr., who was vice-president of the Sun Oil Company and a Republican Party leader, the journal was started on some 117 subscriptions taken from former members of Committee.[23] In addition, the editors received financial help from a number of leading America Firsters, including former chairman, General Robert E. Wood, Colonel Robert C. McCormick, Charles A. Lindbergh, and William Regnery.[24]

The editors hoped that within a short time they could increase the number of subscriptions and receive donations enough to turn the newsletter into a full-fledged national conservative magazine.[25] After a

---

20 These views were often reflected in the speeches of Midwestern political representatives such as Senator Taft, Senator Gerald P. Nye (Rep.-N.D.), Burton F. Wheeler (Dem.-Mon.), and the liberal Republican William Langer (N.D.).

21 For this idea of "Fortress America," see John A. Thompson, "Another Look at the Downfall of 'Fortress America'," *Journal of American Studies*, Vol. 26, No. 3 (December 1992), pp. 393-408.

22 Felix Morley had actually been asked to join the National Committee of America First in December of 1940, and although he agreed with 90% of the Committee's opinions, he declined. The last ten percent were crucial to him. He strongly opposed the passage of the Neutrality Act which America First advocated, since he believed that the United States should play an active part in world organization for peace by the use of any means short of military action. In contrast to this position, it was his impression that most of the members of the America First Committee were "convinced isolationists, in peace as well as in war." Letter, Felix Morley to General Robert E. Wood, January 4, 1941. The Felix Morley Papers.

23 Regnery, *Memoirs of a Dissident Publisher*, pp. 29-30.

24 Undated list of informal sponsors, Box 18, the Papers of John T. Flynn, University of Oregon Library, quoted in Doenecke, *Not To the Swift*, p. 51, n. 10. In June 1945, *Human Events* was incorporated, with Hanighen, Morley, and Regnery each owning a third of the stock.

25 Letter, Frank C. Hanighen to Henry Regnery, August 13, 1946, p. 2. *The Henry Regnery Papers*.

couple of issues they added a supplement called "Not Merely Gossip," which according to Hanighen was intended to supply the readers with news from Washington that would not otherwise get past the "iron-curtain" of the liberal media.[26] Regardless of this addition, it soon became evident that the powerfully Democratic and internationalist context of the 1940s was entirely against them, and that the interest in a conservative publication such as *Human Events* was smaller than they had anticipated. In the years that followed, the weekly circulation of the newsletter did not exceed a tiny 5000 copies.[27]

The Withering of Isolationism

One major factor inhibiting the growth of *Human Events* was an ideological reorientation that had begun on the American Right. "Old Right" isolationism began to make way for Cold War interventionism as the natural enemy abroad, for the United States changed from Nazi Germany to the Soviet Union, and thus, from a location on the far right to the far left of the political spectrum. This would create profound changes in the ideological climate.

In the national debates of 1940 and 1941, isolationists had suddenly found themselves under heavy fire, frequently accused of being an American fifth column and indiscriminately grouped with outspoken Nazi sympathizers like Father Charles E. Coughlin and the two protestant fundamentalist preachers Gerald B. Winrod and Gerald L.K. Smith.[28] Those sharing such sympathies, however, were clearly a minority among the isolationists, as were the pacifists who opposed the war on religious and moral grounds.

---

26 Vice President's Report to Human Events, Inc., September 12, 1949, p. 3. *The Henry Regnery Papers*.
27 More than half of the subscriptions to the newsletter were block subscriptions bought by corporations. Money donated in this form could either be taken as an operating expense of business or covered by a tax-exempt gift to the National Foundation for Education in American Citizenship. Of the 3,000 paid subscriptions *Human Events* had in 1945, approximately 1200 were block subscriptions. *Human Events* had a working arrangement, in which the Foundation took a small percentage for handling the overhead. Letter from Felix Morley to J.K. Lily, October 12, 1945, *The Henry Regnery Papers*.
28 An excellent study of these American extremists can be found in Leo Ribuffo, *The Old Christian Right: The Protestant Right From the Great Depression to the Cold War* (Philadelphia: Temple University Press, 1983).

Noninterventionist views were actually shared by a diverse group of people from both ends of the political spectrum. However, leftist isolationism had clearly reached its peak in the 1930s, and the majority of isolationists after the war belonged in the conservative camp.[29] Yet, many of the motivating factors behind isolationism went beyond left and right. The regional and economic factors underlying the strength of opposition to war against Germany in the Midwest and the Great Plains states have already been mentioned, but some scholars have redirected their attention towards the ethnic compound in this part of the country – particularly the strong presence of German-Americans.

In his pioneering exploration of the ethnic factor in politics, *The Future of American Politics,* journalist Samuel Lubell discarded the geographical concept of isolationism as a myth.[30] In his view, the hardcore of the movement came from ethnic groups with a pro-German or anti-British bias (e.g. German-Americans and Irish-Americans) that existed in large numbers in the Midwest. Thus, it was not indifference to the war in Europe, but rather hypersensitivity to ancient ‹ethnic and national hatreds and rivalries in European history, that made these groups embrace non-interventionism.[31] As for isolationist sentiment in the postwar years, Lubell claimed, it resembled opposition to American intervention in the two wars against Germany, which had a large German and Scandinavian component, more than it did a distinct view on present and future foreign policy. Thus, there was an element of "political revenge" against the Democrats. Many Republican politicians shrewdly used it to persistently link Cold War-frustrations to alleged failures by the Roosevelt-administration during the war against Germany.[32]

---

29 For the references to American isolationism during World War II and the early Cold War, I have relied heavily on Wayne S Cole's *Roosevelt and the Isolationists, 1932-45* (Lincoln: University of Nebraska Press, 1983), and on Justus D. Doenecke's excellent work, *Not to the Swift; The Old Isolationists in the Cold War Era* (Lewisburg: Bucknell University Press, 1979), as well as on his comprehensive bibliography, *Anti-interventionism: a bibliographical introduction to isolationism and pacifism from World War I to the early Cold War* (New York: Garland, 1987).

30 (New York: Harper & Row, 1965 [1952]), p. 133 ff. For a bibliographical guide to the discussion of ethnicity versus other explanations for isolationism, see Doenecke, *Anti-intervention,* pp. 7-20.

31 For a case study of ethnicity and isolationism, see Frederick C. Luebke, *Bonds of Loyalty: German-Americans and World War I* (DeKalb, Ill: Northern Illinois University Press, 1974).

32 Lubell, *The Future of American Politics*, p. 151.

Both during and after the war, issues related to the conditions of the German people were a clear preoccupation with the conservative isolationists. This fact gives further weight to interpretations of isolationism, which stress the role of cultural factors – most of all strong and enduring German ethnic roots and sympathies in the Midwest. This was clearly reflected on the pages of *Human Events*. Although Nazism and all its horrors were consistently denounced, the newsletter openly expressed sympathies for the German people.

During the war it denounced the air-raids on German cities, and often condemned Churchill and Roosevelt as warmongers, claiming that their call for "unconditional surrender" was just as abhorrent as many of Hitler's atrocities. After VE-day, the lack of food in defeated Germany became a major issue among isolationists. *Human Events* harshly criticized the occupational policies of the allied powers, which it claimed deliberately caused starvation as a punishment based on the principle of "collective guilt."

The journal had connections to many local and national organizers of food collections and other relief programs for Germany. Often bulk subscriptions to the journal and large quantities of newsletters and pamphlets were sold through such organizations. *Human Events* also considered initiating a relief program of its own. Henry Regnery suggested the creation of a list of "German, Austrian and possibly Italian writers, university people and others," to whom the readers of *Human Events* could send food packages. He was under the impression that "the sort of people who read *Human Events*" would be glad to have the opportunity to help "those who will be responsible for carrying on European civilization."[33]

The more general explanations of isolationism blended with a general hostility towards the New Deal and "that Man" in the White House. Likewise, American military mobilization had aroused traditional Old Guard Republican fears of "excessive" presidential power and continuous erosion of the decision-making powers of Congress, as well as of further government regulation of the economy in the name of national security. In this respect the fears of the conservative- and the leftwing isolationists went in

---

33 Letter, Regnery to Alexander Boeker in the Washington office of *Human Events*, dated October 29, 1946. *Henry Regnery Papers*, Box 31.

opposite directions. While the left feared that interventionism would mean the end of social reform at home and that it would eventually turn America into a totalitarian garrison state based on "armament economics," the right suspected that interventionism was an excuse for further social reforms, a vast increase in the size and scope of the federal government, increased taxation, more state intervention in the economy, more economic "planning," more regimentation, more government-sponsored centralization, corporatization and monopolization.

Finally, anti-Communism was also a major contributing factor to conservative isolationism. This was illustrated by the reactions to the German invasion of Russia in June 1941. Rather than increase the fear of German expansionism, it hardened isolationist opposition to intervention. Robert A. Taft was among those who found that the prospects of an American alliance with the Soviet Union was another good reason to stay out of the conflict because the "victory of communism in the world outside of America would be far more dangerous to the United States from an ideological standpoint than the victory of fascism."[34] His views on the subject were shared by the journalist and author John T. Flynn, who due to his role as co-founder of the America First Committee and his vitriolic attacks on FDR and the New Deal, had become a celebrated champion of the Old Right.[35] In his view, an alliance with Stalin would mean that Americans would have to fight in order to win a war "whose peace terms will have to satisfy Communist Russia."[36]

Some isolationists, among them Charles Lindbergh, frankly admitted that they would rather see the United States support Germany than Soviet Russia. For her part, the British-born and widely read author on pub-

---

34 Robert A. Taft, "Russia and the Four Freedoms," radio address over CBS, June 25, 1941. Quoted from Ronald Radosh, *Prophets on the Right*, p. 129.

35 Like so many other prominent figures on the postwar American Right, John T. Flynn had moved across the spectrum since the 1930s (in the election of 1936 he had supported Norman Thomas). Flynn was among the most widely read conservative authors in the 1940s and early 1950s. His book *The Road Ahead: America's Creeping Revolution* (New York: Devin-Adair, 1949) sold more than two million copies in its first year, and a condensed version reprinted in *Reader's Digest* was distributed in more than four million copies. Michael Kazin, *The Populist Persuasion: An American History* (New York: Basic Books, 1995), p. 173.

36 Talk on radio NBC Blue Network, June 26, 1941. Quoted from Radosh, *Prophets on the Right*, p. 225.

lic affairs Freda Utley found Nazi Germany "a little more likely to bear the seed of a better ordered world than Stalin's bastard socialism."[37]

Despite the significant ideological differences between radical, liberal and conservative isolationists, the prospects of intervention created a certain level of political ecumenism.[38] This was reflected on the pages of *Human Events*, where Norman Thomas, Robert M. Hutchins and former president Herbert Hoover were among the early contributors.[39]

Republic or Empire?

Whether or not it was a sincere concern, both conservative and liberal isolationists frequently justified their opposition to American intervention in World War II by referring to the fear that America would become an imperialist power. They ascribed to Albert J. Nock's charge made prior to the war that the true purpose of American intervention was to make "the world safe for U.S. investments, privileges, and markets."[40] Felix Morley argued that a new central role for both the military and the military indus-

---

37 Charles A. Lindbergh, address in San Francisco, July 2, 1941. Quoted in Doenecke, *Not To the Swift*, p. 31. Freda Utley, *The Dream We Lost; Soviet Russia Then and Now* (New York: The John Day Company, 1940), p. 298. A former communist who held a doctorate from Moscow's Academy of Science and had worked for the Comintern in the early 1930s, Utley had traveled all the way to the other end of the political spectrum and had become one of the most passionate anti-Communist agitators on the American Right. Utley's conversion had a strong aspect of personal tragedy. Her Russian husband had disappeared under Stalin's purges in the 1930s. The America First Committee endorsed her writings, and after the war she became a frequent contributor to conservative journals such as *Human Events*, *The Freeman*, and later *National Review*.
38 Liberal membership in America First included people such as the Nobel Prize-winning author Sinclair Lewis, the president of the University of Chicago Robert M. Hutchins, the architect Frank Lloyd Wright, the historian Charles A. Beard, the socialist leader Norman Thomas, the head of the CIO John L. Lewis, and the editor of *The Nation* Oswald Garrison Villard, who was forced to resign from the journal in 1940 due to his non-interventionist views. Two future presidents, John F. Kennedy and Gerald R. Ford, also contributed as students to the America First Committee.
39 Herbert Hoover's role as conservative *eminence grise* was closely connected to his quest for political rehabilitation. As FDR became more interventionist in his foreign policy, Hoover's need to distance himself from the policies of the New Deal moved him in a more isolationist direction.
40 Albert J. Nock, "The Amazing Liberal Mind," *American Mercury* (August 1938), pp. 467-472.

try in policymaking, and the acceptance of "peace through strength," would create a siege mentality and ultimately change the nature of American democracy.

In an address to Congress, Robert A. Taft, the most prominent isolationist in that body, warned that intervention would lead to a permanent global engagement which would create "an American Empire, doing what the British have done for the past 200 years."[41] He questioned whether the European democracies would welcome "an Anglo-American benevolent despotism any more eagerly than a German despotism."[42] Taft further objected that the prospects of a permanent global engagement following the war, possibly would "change the whole attitude at home" and might move the nation towards "totalitarianism."[43] Although some observers in the context of the American engagement in Vietnam would find Taft's dispassionate analysis almost prophetic, it was in fact primarily a reflection of his basic indifference to European affairs.[44] His view was in line with a longstanding tradition in which the American self-perception was first of all shaped by its sense of otherness and moral superiority to the "old world," which was seen as an incurable, inherently wicked, and decaying system.[45]

The Japanese attack on Pearl Harbor in December 1941 meant the end of isolationism as a political movement. The country's leading isolationists pledged their full support to the war effort, although most of them probably shared former President Hoover's belief that "continuous putting pins in rattlesnakes finally got this country bitten."[46] In Congress, all

---

41 Nock, "The Amazing Liberal Mind," pp. 467-472.
42 Robert A. Taft, "Shall the United States Enter the European War?" May 17, 1941 (*Congressional Record*, May 19, 1941). Quoted from Ronald Radosh, *Prophets on the Right*, p. 128.
43 Robert A. Taft, *"American Foreign Policy,"* address to the American Bar Association at Chicago, August 26, 1943. Quoted from Radosh, *Prophets on the Right*, p. 141.
44 Taft like other the World War II and Cold War isolationists has been "rediscovered" and reevaluated by revisionist historians as an early critic of American imperialism. A representative example of this interpretation can be found in Ronald Radosh, *Prophets on the Right; Profiles of Conservative Critics of American Globalism* (New York, 1975).
45 As George Washington put it in his Farewell Address, "Europe has a set of primary interests, which to us have none, or a very remote relation." Washington's "Farewell Address to the American People" was first published *in The Independent Chronicle*, September 26, 1796.
46 Letter, Hoover to Robert A. Taft, December 8, 1941, Taft Papers. Quoted from Wayne S. Cole, *Roosevelt and the Isolationists, 1932-45* (Lincoln: University of Nebraska Press, 1983), p. 503.

isolationists except one voted for war against Japan, and later against Germany and Italy.[47] However, the isolationist impulse did not die. Rather, it was channeled into more subtle forms of expression.

For one thing, isolationists continuously assailed the Roosevelt administration's conduct of the war, and called on it to state the "true objectives" of American participation. In a particularly provocative article in *Saturday Evening Post* entitled "For What Are We Fighting?," Felix Morley called for a statement of purpose. He contended that a very influential group of "Anglo-American Nazis" – a clear reference to such advocates of an "American Century" as Walter Lippmann and Henry Luce – had plans for

> a global Anglo-Saxon dictatorship ... with limited privileges for small nations which know their place and agree to keep it, with great condominiums over the rich lands inhabited by lesser breeds without the law, and with a sort of permanent earthly purgatory – enlarged ghettos strikingly like those which the Nazis design for the Jews – for the nations which have dared to strike ruthlessly at Anglo-Saxon supremacy.[48]

After the war the isolationists fought an uphill battle in their attempts to gain public support for their views on America's role in the postwar world. In August 1945, Frederick J. Libby, executive secretary of the National Council for the Prevention of War, created the Foundation for Foreign Affairs – a research bureau with the purpose of propagating noninterventionist views. William H. Regnery became the foundation's main sponsor, and both his son Henry and Frank C. Hanighen served on the Board of Trustees.

A primary concern of the organization was the fate of Germany.[49] This concern was not entirely humanitarian in nature, nor did it spring solely from the German ethnic roots. It also reflected a common perception among isolationists that a revived Germany was the key to European sta-

---

47 The dissenting vote came from Jeannette Rankin (Rep.-Mon.), who had also voted against the declaration of war against Germany in 1917.
48 Morley, "For What Are We Fighting?" p. 42.
49 The works sponsored by the organization included Freda Utley's frontal and widely read attack on the occupation policies of the Allied powers, *The High Cost of Vengeance* (Chicago: Henry Regnery Company, 1949).

bility, since by itself that nation could counter Soviet power and make a permanent American engagement in Europe unnecessary.[50] This view of the postwar situation in Europe led several isolationists to argue that the funds appropriated for all European countries under the Marshall Plan would come to better use if they were all invested in Germany. It also made them fierce opponents of the so-called "Morgenthau Plan," which in a widely quoted phrase would turn Germany into "goat pastures."[51]

The German question was the topic of several of the 46 monthly pamphlets published by Henry Regnery for *Human Events* over the next four years. These publications provided an important demonstration of the cultural complexities that characterized *Human Events* and the early conservative movement.[52] In addition to the pamphlets, *Human Events* also began to publish a number of books, beginning with collections of essays from the journal. The wish to diversify into book publishing was Henry Regnery's brainchild, and in October 1946 *Human Events* was split into two separate enterprises.[53] Human Events, Inc. run by Morley and Hanighen in Washington, D.C. would be devoted entirely to the publica-

---

50 This view was later in large part adopted by the Truman administration, as well as by the British government.
51 Worked out for the President prior to the Quebec Conference in September 1944 by his Secretary of the Treasury, Henry Morgenthau, Jr., the plan called among other things for total demilitarization of Germany and the dismantling of all its industry. It also suggested a division of the country into two separate countries (North Germany and South Germany). The plan was subsequently published in an elaborated form under the title *Germany is our Problem* (New York, 1945). In response to the plan, *Human Events* published a pamphlet with the same title, *Germany is Our Problem* in January 1946, written by Karl Brandt, a professor in agricultural economics at Stanford University Brandt's pamphlet was widely distributed, both through newsstand and mass mailings. Like the *Human Events* newsletter itself, it was strongly promoted among German-Americans through advertisements in German language newspapers. Likewise, tens of thousands of copies were sold to German-American organizations, which distributed them among their constituencies in both the United States and Germany. Letters, Alexander Boeker to Henry Regnery, January 12, 1945 and April 11, 1946. *The Henry Regnery Papers*.
52 The diverse group of authors included Felix Morley, the radical libertarian Frank Chodorov, the passionate anti-Communist Freda Utley, Robert M. Hutchins, socialist party leader Norman Thomas, and the French philosopher Raymond Aron, whom *Human Events* introduced to the American public for the first time.
53 Morley and Hanighen were clearly less enthusiastic about the venture. They found the publishing venture too risky, and would rather spend their time and funds in an attempt to turn *Human Events* into a national weekly magazine. Letter, Frank C. Hanighen to Henry Regnery, August 13, 1946. *The Henry Regnery Papers*

tion of the journal, whereas Human Events Associates (later Henry Regnery Company) in Chicago, would publish the pamphlet series as well as books.

The Henry Regnery Company went on to become one of the three most important right wing publishers in America, the other two being Caxton Printers in Caldwell, Idaho, and the Devin-Adair Company in New York. The importance of these publishing houses to the emerging conservative movement came partly from their willingness to publish books that other publishers would not touch due to their controversial nature. In this connection it is worth remembering that F.A. Hayek's *The Road to Serfdom* had been rejected by three American publishers before it was published in the country. Russell Kirk's seminal and widely respected book *The Conservative Mind*, which many self-described conservatives view as the true beginning of modern American conservatism had also been rejected by one of the major publishing houses (Alfred Knopf) before the Henry Regnery Company published it in 1953.[54]

In his first years as a publisher, Regnery mostly published books by European authors. Most of them clearly reflected his preoccupation with foreign, and especially German, issues.[55] Yet, it was also somehow a reflection of the immature state that still characterized American conservative thought in the late 1940s. As it began to acquire an identity of its own in the early 1950s, when a new generation of American conservative intellectuals began to emerge, Regnery deliberately attempted to get away from the "German" image and give more attention to American authors and domestic issues.[56]

---

54 If the Regnery company's willingness to publish books on unpopular subjects made it a noble and important venture from a right wing point of view, it was not, however, a very profitable one. Not many of its publications sold well enough to make a profit. Regnery openly admitted that the survival of the company was dependent on the transfer of funds from the family textile business. "Memorandum on the Henry Regnery Company, May, 1961, *The Regnery Papers*, Box 81. Interview with Henry Regnery, "Trade Winds," *The Saturday Review*, September 25, 1954.
55 This led to frequent but unfounded charges of anti-Semitism. Actually, the first three books published by the Henry Regnery Company in 1947 were written by Jewish authors (*In Darkest Germany*, and *Our Threatened Values* by Victor Gollancz and Max Picard's, *Hitler in Ourselves*).
56 Letter, Henry Regnery to Margaret A. Boveri, May 27, 1963. *Henry Regnery Papers*, Box 50.

From Isolationism to "Asialationism"

Most conservative isolationists faced a serious dilemma. They were caught between their growing alarm over the rising Soviet Empire on the one side, and their anti-statist sentiment on the other. Who was the greatest enemy, Communism or the state? What consequences would Cold War-interventionism have for the entire political system in America? Many saw it as a hard choice between individual liberty and collective security.

Some hardcore isolationists maintained that the threat from Communism was largely fictional – an invention made by "big business" and New Deal liberals in order to establish a corporate state in America. They adhered to John T. Flynn's prediction made during World War II, that American foreign policy after the war would be "internationalist" as a result of the fact that "militarism is the one great glamorous public-works project upon which a variety of elements in the community can be brought into agreement."[57] They also shared Flynn's fear that the United States would become "a planetary Santa Claus" in the attempt to win allies in the struggle with the Soviet Union. By the late 1940s, however, such views were held by a diminishing minority among conservatives.

For most conservatives, as for the American public in general, the period from 1947 to 1949 was a time of shocks. A near-collapse of Greece and Turkey had led to the adoption of the Truman-doctrine, and the foundations of American foreign policy had once again changed radically with the announcement in September 1949 that the Soviet Union had exploded its first atomic bomb. However, even more than events in Europe, which many, in the words of General Douglas MacArthur, saw as a "dying system" anyway, it was the defeat of Chiang Kai-Shek's Nationalist government in China in 1949 which became a catalyst for the conservative shift to interventionism.[58]

In a sense, a preoccupation with Asia had solid traditions in Republican foreign policy, going back to the Open Door-policy of the turn of the

---

57 John T. Flynn, *As We Go Marching* (New York: Doubleday-Doran, 1944), p. 207.
58 In a speech in 1950, Joseph P. Kennedy, who had remained a staunch isolationist, gave a peculiar rationale for ending American involvement in Europe. He claimed that Soviet control of the continent eventually would mean the end of Communism: "The more peoples that are under its yoke, the greater are the possibilities of revolt."("Present Policy is Politically and Morally Bankrupt," *Vital Speeches* (Jan.1, 1951), p. 171.

century.⁵⁹ Now events there had turned that part of the world into the central stage for what many saw as an apocalyptic battle between Communism and Western civilization – or, in the words of one of the chief ideologues of the new militant anti-Communism James Burnham, a "struggle for the world."⁶⁰

The situation created a strange bond between the MacArthur nationalists and the "Old Guard" isolationists. Revisionists, who had blamed FDR for his unwillingness to negotiate with the Axis powers in order to keep America out of war, now saw all attempts at diplomatic compromise as "craven appeasement."⁶¹ Rightwing advocacy of massive economic and military aid to Chiang, who Republicans saw as a powerful symbol in the struggle against Communism, as well as various proposals for direct American involvement in the conflict, clearly exposed double standards and undermined the moralistic arguments which many non-interventionists had been using in their fight to keep the United States from any commitments in Europe.

The "fall of China" also became a key element in the right wing's attempt to link the advances of Communism abroad to the political struggle against New Deal liberalism. A persistent belief that the defeat of the Chinese nationalists could largely be attributed to a group of Communists in the American government became an important element in the Red Scare. Despite the fact that many Old Isolationists previously had been strongly critical of Chiang, he was now increasingly portrayed by the right as a hero who cynically had been sold out by the State Department. Ignoring the complex nature of the conflict in China, John T. Flynn even made the farfetched claim that the president had "sold out 400 million Chinese for 400,000 American communist votes."⁶² In this fashion the problems of international communism were gradually domesticated.

This process clearly eased the transition from the isolationism of the "Old Right" to the Cold War interventionism of the "New Right." As the career of Senator Joseph McCarthy so amply demonstrated, the idea that

---

59 Since the turn of the century, Republicans had been more willing to consider intervention in Asia, partly because they saw the risk of entanglement as smaller than in Europe. America would be less likely to become seduced and "contaminated" by allies eager to improve their own position in the eternal struggle for power.
60 James Burnham, *The Struggle for the World* (New York: John Day, 1947).
61 Selig Adler, *The Isolationist Impulse* (London: Abelard-Schuman Ltd., 1957), p. 448.
62 Justus Doenecke, *Not To the Swift*, p. 178.

all advances of communism were ultimately the results of past failures, or outright treason by the New Deal liberals in power, often made it possible to have it both ways: they could support interventionist policies, while still appealing to isolationist sentiments. Accordingly, the Truman administration's 1950 decision to intervene in the Korean War did not prevent McCarthy and other self-styled avatars of the struggle against international communism from advocating an expansion of the war in the form of strategic bombings in Manchuria and China, while blaming the Truman administration for the death of "our boys."[63] The "betrayal" of the nationalist forces in China was the cardinal sin, which had now brought the war to Korea.

From "Old Right" to "New Right"

If the American Right could have it both ways for a while, the ongoing shift to interventionism was nevertheless evident. It was also reflected in growing disagreements, and eventually a split between the two editors of *Human Events*. The major causes might have been of a personal nature, but political disagreements definitely played their part too.

In Felix Morley's version of the story, an early disagreement occurred when newly elected California Congressman Richard M. Nixon called *Human Events* and suggested that the journal cooperate actively with the House Committee of Un-American Activities in the campaign against Alger Hiss and other alleged "subversives" in the Administration.[64] While Hanighen saw this as a great opportunity to promote the journal, Morley found it more important to stay above the fray and protect its intellectual credibility.[65]

This was not merely a question of ethics. It also reflected the editors' differing opinions about the type of readership that *Human Events* ought to address. Somewhat simplified, Morley insisted that the journal should

---

63 Right wingers widely supported Senator Taft's claim that President Truman had usurped authority from Congress and violated the Constitution by sending troops to Korea, and many supported the demand that Truman should resign as a consequence of this violation.
64 Felix Morley, "The Early Days of Human Events," *Human Events*, Vol. 34, April 27, 1974, pp. 26-31.
65 Felix Morley, *For the Record* (South Bend, IN: Regnery/Gateway, Inc., 197?), pp. 429-431.

be aimed at intellectuals, and he did not feel that Hanighen could provide the journal with a definite philosophical direction. Hanighen, for his part, aimed at mass circulation and allegedly saw his co-editor's semi-academic approach as an obstacle.[66]

Even more important, however, were the mounting disagreements over foreign policy. While Morley in most respects maintained his non-interventionist views, Hanighen was clearly moving towards interventionism. So was associate editor William Henry Chamberlin, who in 1953 would publish his *Beyond Containment*, which advocated "liberation" and the fall of the Soviet empire, instead of merely "containment" as the objective of the Cold War.[67] Felix Morley would later recall the conflict as "largely a result of the differences which would soon separate the "Old Right" and the "New Right" – between a generally pacific, even isolated America and an actively interventionist America."[68]

After a short struggle for the control of *Human Events*, Felix Morley resigned as president in 1950. Despite the fact that another staunch isolationist, Frank Chodorov, took over as co-editor, the editorial line of the journal gradually changed. By the mid-1950s the transformation was complete. *Human Events* had turned into a New Right advocate of Cold War interventionism.[69]

Cold War interventionist views, combined with the use of direct mail and other inventive fundraising methods, gave the journal an exposure which Morley's heresy could never have provided. *Human Events* became the nation's largest-circulation conservative journal, with a readership of 28,000 by 1956, and approximately 140,000 by 1964, but its importance to the conservative movement went far beyond that. From 1961, *Human Events* also began to arrange a series of semi-annual Political Action Conferences in Washington, D.C. Eventually, it also became an important

---

66 Felix Morley, "The Early Days of Human Events," *Human Events*, Vol. 34, April 27, 1974, p. 27
67 William Henry Chamberlin, *Beyond Containment* (Chicago: Henry Regnery Company, 1953).
68 Felix Morley, "The Early Days of Human Events," *Human Events* (April 27, 1971), p. 31.
69 In a private letter to Felix Morley, written in 1965, the radical libertarian economist Murray N. Rothbard deplored the evolution of *Human Events* after his departure: "It must be particularly distressing to you to see *Human Events*, a fine Revisionist magazine in its early days when you were one of its main founders, become an ultra-Right rag." (February 28, 1965). The Felix Morley Papers.

breeding ground for young conservative authors and journalists through internships and a scholarship program started in 1957. Perhaps most importantly, the journal and its Human Events Writing School gave several young conservative intellectuals and prospective journalists an opportunity to come to Washington, D.C. and learn their way around Capitol Hill.[70]

The Last Stand: The Fight for the Bricker Amendment

In Congress the old isolationists made their last stand in the wake of the Korean War with the fight over the Bricker Amendment, which was reintroduced into the Senate in January 1953.[71] The intention was to restrict presidential authority in foreign policy, first of all with a requirement of referendums prior to the signing of international treaties and congressional approval of executive agreements.[72] Many isolationists saw the Bricker Amendment not just as a symbolic manifestation, but as a strong weapon in the fight against the United Nations and other alleged international threats to American sovereignty.[73]

Conservatives first of all based their opposition to multilateral agreements and international commitments on the fear that New Deal liberals would use them as a Trojan horse to force social change at home. Senator John Bricker of Ohio argued that international treaties were steps in the direction of "global socialism" and seriously threatened political autonomy in America, on national as well as on state and local levels.[74] This view also made the battle for the Bricker Amendment an early step in the process of establishing a link between conservative Republicans and

---

70 Among the young conservatives who were nurtured in this way were the leaders of Young Americans for Freedom, David Franke, Doug Caddy, M. Stanton Evans, Antoni Gollan, Allan Ryskind, and Gary Russell.
71 The Amendment had previously been introduced in the Eighty-second Congress in 1951.
72 See Justus D. Doenecke, *Not to the Swift*, pp. 236-238.
73 Resistance to the UN among hardcore isolationists often resulted in the promotion of absurd notions about the possible consequences of membership. Colonel McCormick claimed that the UN was seeking to enforce polygamy in the United States, while others warned that racial conflicts or even derogatory remarks about a minority group, could mean that American citizens would stand trial in an international court. See Doenecke, *Not To the Swift*, pp. 237-238.
74 John Bricker, "U.N.Blueprint for Tyranny," *The Freeman* (January 28, 1952), pp. 265-68.

Southern segregationists within the Democratic Party. The segregationists supported the amendment out of fear that the United Nations might become involved in the black struggle for civil rights. Indeed, the NAACP had already petitioned the UN in 1947 in the hope of such an involvement.

The final defeat of the Bricker Amendment in February 1954 was a heavy and demoralizing blow for the isolationists.[75] However, the struggle itself was also a testimony to the residual strength of isolationist sentiments. Bricker's own proposal was narrowly defeated by 50 to 42 votes, with 4 not voting. A watered down version was defeated by just a single vote, and 32 Republican senators voted against the wishes of President Eisenhower.[76]

Among the last gasps of the isolationist Old Right was Colonel McCormick's organizing of a group called For America in May of 1954. Under the directorship of Brig. Gen. Bonner Fellers, For America made ambitious plans for a network of local units, youth divisions, research divisions, a speaker's bureau, field workers, film production, radio broadcasts, a book club, and several other activities. It involved the organizing efforts of well-known isolationists such as General Robert E. Wood, Dean Clarence Manion of Notre Dame, Frank Chodorov, and John T. Flynn in the attempt to create a separate constituency that could ultimately push the GOP to the Right. The idea, according to Dean Clarence Manion, was to mobilize voters, who would vote for separate electors instead of voting directly for one of the presidential candidates. These electors might then decide to vote for a candidate found among "outstanding pro-American statesmen who will have been deliberately passed over by the international socialist managers of both party conventions."[77] Regardless of such ambitions, For America was not a success, and it soon dissolved due to personal conflicts among the organizers and a general lack of public interest.[78]

---

75 For an account of the struggle over the Bricker Amendment, see Carhal J. Nolan, "The Last Hurrah of Conservative Isolationism: Eisenhower, Congress, and the Bricker Amendment," *Presidential Studies Quarterly* (spring, 1992), pp. 337–342.

76 One limited victory for the isolationists was that Eisenhower had to abstain from signing formal UN treaties on human rights. At least publicly, the U.S. would have to leave the initiative in this field to other countries.

77 "The 'International Socialist' in Both Parties," *The New Republic*, Vol.134, Number 12, p. 4.

78 See Justus D. Doenecke, *Not to the Swift*, pp. 234-35.

By the mid-fifties isolationism had lost most of its leading spokesmen. Senator Robert Taft had died in July 1953 and Colonel McCormick had died in April 1955. Most of the leading isolationists in Congress had either been defeated in the elections of 1952 and 1954 or had retired.[79] Several smaller right wing organizations such as America's Future, Inc., The Congress of Freedom, and Facts Forum were still promoting isolationist views, and a number of intellectuals were still writing for various conservative journals, but for all practical purposes, the isolationist "Old Right" had faded into oblivion.

The American Mercury *and the* Freeman

By 1950, the Red Scare had provided Republicans in Congress with a powerful weapon in the attempt to bring New Deal liberals on the defensive, but conservatives were still grappling with the problem of finding a general journal of opinion which could help give the forces on the right focus and thrust.

A potential candidate for the position was the *American Mercury*. The monthly review had gained tremendous prestige under the editorship of its founder H.L. Mencken from 1924 to his resignation in 1933, but had since had a rather unobtrusive position under shifting owners and editors. The ideological bias of the journal had also been somehow unsettled since Mencken's days, but when William Bradford Huie became editor in 1950, the *Mercury* was turned into a truculent voice of militant conservatism.

Regardless of its shifts in political allegiance, the *American Mercury* had been able to maintain a circulation between 50,000 and 90,000 copies, which was far more than any of its conservative contestants.[80] This made it an attractive outlet for many right wing intellectuals. Among the frequent contributors were the young William F. Buckley, Jr., James Burnham, Max Eastman, and Ralph De Toledano.[81]

---

79 After the election of 1954, Edwin C. Johnson (Dem.-Col.), Henry P. Dworshak (Rep.-Idaho), and William Langer (Rep.-D.D.), were the only three veteran isolationists left in the Senate, and in the House fewer than 40 remained. See Doenecke, *Not to the Swift*, p. 242.

80 Peterson, *Magazines in the Twentieth Century*, p. 380.

81 William F. Buckley, Jr. was offered editorial positions at both *the Freeman* and the *American Mercury*, but chose the latter, primarily due to the fact that its circulation was about four times that of the *Freeman*. See John B. Judis, *William F. Buckley, Jr.; Patron Saint of the Conservatives* (New York: Simon and Schuster, 1988), p. 103.

Despite the *Mercury's* potentials, its bid to become a leading conservative journal of opinion was short-lived. In August 1952 it was taken over by the speculator J. Russell Maguire. Although several of the contributors expressed their hope that the journal would become an advocate of "dynamic and sophisticated Conservatism," it soon became evident that the new owner intended to turn it into a vehicle for anti-Semitic views. Bradford and several of the other editors consequently resigned. Rather than being an active voice for the conservative camp, the *American Mercury* became an embarrassment and a political liability, and several conservative intellectuals, including former contributors such as William F. Buckley, Jr., got busy placing it outside the limits of "responsible conservative opinion."[82]

Another journal which many conservatives hoped could become a leading voice for the movement was the *Freeman*, which began publication in October 1950.[83] The name of the journal had been chosen in homage to Albert J. Nock, whose short-lived journal of the same name, published in the early 1920s, had become a model for many conservative and libertarian journalists and intellectuals. The *Freeman* was intended as a journal that could challenge liberal views, not just on current social and political issues, but on all levels of opinion. Its principles of faith printed in the first issue, showed a clear leaning towards libertarianism:

> It will be one of the foremost aims of the Freeman to clarify the concept of individual freedom and apply it to the problems of our time ... Real morality cannot exist where there is no real freedom of choice. The individual must be free to act as his own conscience directs, so long as he does not infringe upon the equal rights of others.[84]

---

82 By 1959 the *American Mercury*'s exposures of alleged Jewish conspiracies of unprecedented immensity still attracted some 61,000 readers, but the journal finally ceased publication in the early 1960's. M.K. Singleton, *H.L. Mencken and the American Mercury Adventure* (Durham, N.C.: Duke University Press, 1962), p. 241.

83 The *Freeman* was in a sense a replacement for the anti-Communist journal *Plain Talk*, which had ceased publication earlier in the same year when its main sponsor, Alfred Kohlberg, had withdrawn his support and announced his intention to sponsor a more wide-ranging conservative journal. *Plain Talk*, which had been edited by Ralph De Toledano and Isaac Don Levine, had mainly been occupied since 1946 with the exposure of "spy rings," "secret armies" and other forms of alleged communist subversion in the United States.

84 "The Faith of the Freeman," *The Freeman*, Vol.1, No.1 (October 1950), p. 5.

Apart from its political and economic concerns, the Freeman would include special departments on such topics as literature, art, and music. "Old Right" conservatives such as George Sokolsky, Raymond Moley, and John T. Flynn, whose articles had occasionally popped up in mainstream journals, could now be read on a regular basis along with libertarian economists such as F.A. Hayek, Ludwig Von Mises, and Wilhelm Roepke.

Henry Hazlitt, Suzanne La Follette, and John Chamberlain, who also served as president of the enterprise, edited the journal. Hazlitt had briefly replaced H.L. Mencken as editor of the American Mercury in 1934, but his major career since had been as an editorial writer for the New York Times, and later as a contributing editor for Newsweek. He was also the author of Economics in One Lesson, a passionate and widely distributed libertarian defense of free market capitalism.[85]

Hazlitt's co-editor, John Chamberlain, who many knew as the author of the highly acclaimed work on American Progressivism, Farewell to Reform, had just left a job as editorial writer for Life when he signed up with the Freeman.[86] As a young radical socialist, John Chamberlain had been a book reviewer for the New York Times and had gained a reputation, which later made Alfred Kazin characterize him as "the golden boy of a generation of ideologues."[87] From a position as a socialist and staunch supporter of Norman Thomas in the election of 1932, Chamberlain, like other radical intellectuals such as Max Eastman and John Dos Passos, had gradually moved across the political spectrum to end up in the conservative camp by the late 1940s. While working for Henry Luce's Time Inc., he had been part of a rightwing faction of ex-communists, which also included another contributor to the Freeman, and later co-editor of National Review, Willi Schlamm, as well as Whittaker Chambers. Inspired by economists such as Hayek and Von Mises, Chamberlain had also become a leading spokesman for libertarianism.[88]

The expectations that many conservatives had to the Freeman become evident if one looks at the 18 director-stockholders, who made up the

---

85 (New York, 1946).
86 (New York, 1932).
87 Alfred Kazin, *Starting Out in the Thirties* (Boston, 1965), p. 6.
88 The appointment of Suzanne La Follette as managing editor provided the journal with a certain element of continuity since she had worked with Nock on the old *Freeman*, and later, in the early 1930s, made a brief and unsuccessful attempt to revive his journal.

journal's board. It was a virtual "who's who" of the early conservative movement. It included people such the Austrian economist Ludwig Von Mises and former Dean of Harvard Law School Roscoe Pound, as well as some of the most active business benefactors of right-wing groups, director of Sun Oil Co., J. Howard Pew, H.W. Prentis, Jr. of the Armstrong Cork Company, and Du Pont vice-president Jasper E. Crane.[89] Pew had been one of the driving forces behind the American Liberty League in the 1930s. Both he and Crane also held prominent positions in the National Association of Manufacturers, and had been leading forces in formulating the anti-New Deal policies of that organization. Other board-members were Leonard Read, who in 1946 had founded the Foundation for Economic Education – one of the earliest organizations in the United States dedicated to spreading the gospel of libertarian economics – and the influential China lobbyist Alfred Kohlberg.[90]

Kohlberg, who was one of the *Freeman's* major sponsors, as well as its treasurer, was usually the person people talked about, when they talked about the powerful "China Lobby."[91] He had manufactured and imported textiles from China since the 1920s and counted Chiang Kai-Shek among his personal friends. Since 1946, Kohlberg had been the driving force behind the American China Policy Association, and he was also president of the American Jewish League against Communism. As far back as 1944, however, he had almost single-handedly launched an attack on the Institute of Pacific Relations, which under McCarthyism came to serve as the epitome of academic treason. It was first of all his efforts which directed the attention of politicians such as John F. Kennedy, Joseph R. McCarthy and Pat McCarran to the explosive political potential in charging the In-

---

89 Other major sponsors of the *Freeman* included Quaker Oats Co., Inland Steel Co., Wm. Volker Fund, and Chrysler Corp. (The Freeman Magazine, Inc. Notes Payable. Herbert Hoover Papers, Box 166.

90 For further details on the FEE, see Nash, *The Conservative Intellectual Movement*, pp 21-25.

91 The term was sometimes also associated with Henry Luce and his wife, Claire Boothe Luce, who was president of the America-China Policy Association. In truth, however, political support for Chiang's Chinese nationalist forces was of a more disparate nature. However, it was first of all the right-wing views of Kohlberg and his like-minded, which became associated with the "China Lobby." One of the Lobby's main political vehicles became the American China Policy Association, which was founded in 1946 with Alfred Kohlberg as chairman of the board. Among its shifting presidents were Clare Boothe Luce and the publisher of the Manchester *Union Leader*, William Loeb.

stitute and its highly acclaimed scholars with being powerful instruments of international communism.

With the help of Kohlberg, the *Freeman* did not start entirely from scratch. It was able to take over 5,200 unexpired subscriptions from the journal *Plain Talk* and add a few hundred of its own for the first issue. It received both financial help and moral support from the gray eminence of postwar conservatism, former president Herbert Hoover. As was the case with *Human Events*, and later *National Review*, Hoover was an active participant in the *Freeman's* fundraising efforts. He personally donated hundreds of gift subscriptions to friends and associates all over the country.

The financial prospects for the new journal were good. Circulation increased steadily by approximately 1,000 copies per month, and had reached almost 22,000 by the end of 1952.[92] The journal was well on its way to reaching the break-even level of 30,000 copies when a veritable battle broke out in the editorial offices. This battle went on through most of 1952 and did not cease until January 1953, when John Chamberlain, Forrest Davis, and Suzanne La Follette all handed in their resignations.

The Republican Battle of 1952

Though bad chemistry and personal disagreements played their part, the split was also related to two major issues dividing the American Right at the time. One was the movement's relationship to Senator Joe McCarthy and his witch-hunt. The other was the struggle between Robert Taft and Ike Eisenhower – a struggle that to many conservatives concerned the soul of the Republican Party.

Regarding McCarthy, Henry Hazlitt and several of the director-stockholders objected to the way in which the Wisconsin senator had become a "sacred character" on the pages of the journal.[93] The controversy was further intensified by the fact that some of those involved worked directly for McCarthy. Among these were the journal's treasurer Alfred Kohlberg, the

---

92 "Battle for the *Freeman*," *Time*, January 26, 1953.
93 "Battle for the *Freeman*".

author Freda Utley, who was a frequent contributor to the *Freeman*, and in particular the editor Forrest Davis. In one instance, Davis had been commissioned by the journal to write an article about General George Marshall's role in the shaping of U.S. foreign policy, especially in the Far East. Instead he ended up giving his manuscript to McCarthy, who delivered it as a frontal attack on General Marshall from the floor of the Senate.[94]

Support for Senator Robert A. Taft was the other major dividing issue. The struggle between him and Eisenhower for the 1952 Republican nomination was to a large extent a regional struggle between a more socially "moderate" and internationalist Eastern wing, and a more anti-statist Midwestern wing, which had maintained much of its deep-seated distrust of foreign commitments, especially in Europe. The intensity and bitterness of this conflict within the Republican Party was clearly revealed at the national convention in Chicago in 1952. Eisenhower's subsequent nomination, which led to charges of theft from many Taft-supporters, would continue to create waves on the right for a long time. To many conservatives Taft's defeat became a crucial impetus to the creation of independent organizational structures outside of the Republican Party.

In the editorial offices of the *Freeman* these events led to confrontations between Forrest Davis, John Chamberlain, Willi Schlamm and other Taft supporters on the one side, and on the other side Hazlitt and those among the editor-stockholders who favored Eisenhower and objected to the journal's open endorsement of Taft. Again, the conflict was sharpened by the fact that both Davis and Chamberlain were actively involved in the Taft campaign.[95] In order to grasp the bitterness of this conflict, it is necessary to take a closer look at what actually happened at the convention in Chicago in July 1952.

---

94 Chamberlain, *A Life With the Printed Word*, pp. 141-142. It was in this speech that McCarthy charged General Marshall of being part of "a conspiracy so immense and an infamy so black as to dwarf any previous such venture in the history of man." It was later published as *America's Retreat from Victory, the Story of George Catlett Marshall*, and McCarthy himself was credited as the author.
95 Davis was a consultant, and Chamberlain was, along with Max Eastman and John Dos Passos, founder of the Arts and Letters Committee for Robert A. Taft for President.

The 1952 Republican National Convention

The Republican right had come to Chicago with great confidence that their time had finally come. Many felt that the "me-too Republicanism" which Senator Henry Cabot Lodge, Governor Thomas Dewey (and Wendell Wilkie before him) in their opinion represented had had its chance and failed. They felt confident that Senator Taft would finally get the chance in his third bid for the nomination.

Taft had the support of GOP bosses in a majority of states, and he was already in control of some 500 of the 604 delegates needed for the nomination. Moreover, a clear majority in the Republican National Committee supposedly favored Taft, just as the list of speakers at the convention had been packed with declared supporters. Despite such clear advantages, the Ohio senator was met with an unexpected strong opposition. The Eisenhower-forces under the brilliant leadership of campaign manager Herbert Brownell had clearly done their homework.

The struggle between the two factions evolved into encounters ranging from actual fights over poster space at the hotel where both Eisenhower and Taft had their headquarters, to more serious disputes over the legitimacy of various delegations (most notably those from Texas and Georgia, and some of the Louisiana delegates). The air was loaded with mutual accusations of dirty tricks and "steamroller tactics."[96]

As for domestic policy issues, the actual differences between the two candidates could hardly account for the bitterness of the struggle, especially considering how blurred Ike's political stands still were at this point. Neither Eisenhower nor Taft was libertarian. Taft admittedly had a much clearer conservative profile than the general, but he had no intentions of dismantling the basic framework of the modern welfare state. Much to the dismay of some rightwing Republicans, he had clearly demonstrated this with his sponsorship of the Taft-Ellender-Wagner bill, which would have provided federal support for low-income housing, slum clearance and urban renewal.[97]

---

96 On the dispute over delegations, see William B. Pickett, *Eisenhower Decides to Run* (Chicago: Ivan R. Dee, 2000), pp. 201-205, and David W. Reinhard, *The Republican Right Since 1945* (Lexington: The University Press of Kentucky, 1983), pp. 80-89.

97 The bill, proposed in 1945, was finally passed in the Senate in 1948, but was killed in the House of Representatives.

In the field of foreign policy, however, disagreements between the two candidates were much more profound. As a matter of fact, fear of Taft's non-interventionist inclinations was the primary reason for Ike's candidacy, and the strong support it received from people who wanted to see the United States play a permanent stabilizing role in the postwar world – not least in western Europe, where the future role of NATO was a major point of disagreement between the two candidates. One of the people who had urged Eisenhower to run was Henry Cabot Lodge, who had personally met with the general the previous year in his effort to persuade him. After the meeting, Lodge noted in his diary that the general "will think that his duty is to prevent the Taft victory from taking place."[98]

Taft had tried to appease his critics and distance himself from the notion of isolationism. "Anybody is an idiot who calls anybody else an isolationist," he claimed.[99] Reluctantly, he had supported the intervention in Korea, just as he in principle had become reconciled with the idea of the NATO alliance. Yet it was evident to most that Taft had never fully abandoned his non-interventionist sentiment[100] His attitude towards Europe turned out to be perhaps his strongest liability. It put him clearly at odds not only with the Eastern wing of the party, but also with the assertive "new nationalism" in foreign policy represented by such people as John Foster Dulles, Richard M. Nixon, and the late Arthur Vandenberg. The senator's assurances could not allay the widespread mistrust of his willingness to defend Europe.[101] In response some of his supporters, among them the *Freeman's* editor John Chamberlain, tried to convince his critics that an "Asia-first" policy — with which Taft, with his China lobby support, was identified — by no means meant that the U.S. would abandon its commitment to Europe. On the contrary, Chamberlain argued:

---

98 Henry Cabot Lodge, "Personal Interview with General Eisenhower," July 16, 1951. Quoted from William B. Pickett, Op.Cit , p 115
99 Quoted from Forrest Davis, "Senator Taft's New Deal," *The Freeman*, Vol 1, No. 7 (December 25, 1950), p. 202.
100 Taft had originally voted against American membership of NATO, and had maintained that the Soviet Union did not pose any serious threat to Western Europe. A strong American presence in Europe would, according to the senator, provoke rather than protect. For an account of Taft's reluctant acceptance of NATO, see James T. Patterson, *Mr. Republican*, pp. 476-484.
101 Taft's mid-west campaign manager Howard Buffett, for one, sustained this mistrust by continuously denouncing the existence of U.S. military bases abroad.

> With a fixation on Europe, the West has failed to see that the way to keep Stalin from marching in Europe – or to keep him from consolidating a success if he does march in Europe – is to create a continuing chaos in his rear in Asia.[102]

In short, Taft supporters argued the senator simply represented a more narrow definition of "the national interest." This would be a foreign policy that, according to Chamberlain, would be "based upon a rational idea of the conservation of one's own energy," or as he bluntly explained it, would use Asian lives instead of American lives.[103]

The difference in strength between the Eisenhower and Taft coalitions was not big prior to the first ballot on the convention. 595 votes were secured for Eisenhower compared to 500 for Taft. Accordingly, when Eisenhower's victory became a fact after the vote switches at the end of the first ballot, it resulted in numerous charges of "theft" and "fraud." The avatar of Old Guard Republicanism in the Midwest, Colonel Robert C. McCormick, was so enraged that he advocated a complete break with the Republican Party and the founding of independent third party, the *American Party*. Although few were ready to take such drastic consequences, many questioned whether Taft could possibly have lost the nomination, if not for the schemes of the "Dewey wing" of the party. Had Taft won the disputed Southern delegates, he would, after all, have led 560 to 535 prior to the first ballot. Although the charges of theft were not really justified, they nevertheless formed the basis of a persistent myth that would galvanize conservatives and play an important part in the Goldwater-campaign twelve years later.[104]

"The Kingmakers"

"Quite candidly," the *Freeman* wrote in an open letter to Eisenhower, "the verdict at Chicago proved nothing about the popular temper of the coun-

---

102 John Chamberlain, "American Conservatism and the World Crisis; A Policy for Conservatives," *The Yale Review 40* (spring 1951), p. 409.
103 Chamberlain, "American Conservatism and the World Crisis…", p. 400.
104 Not even the contested delegates from Texas, Georgia, and Louisiana, which Taft had to give up when the so-called Langlie (or "Fair Play") resolution was passed at the convention, could have given him the victory. The total number of delegates that Taft had lost due to the resolution was only 47, and the Eisenhower got 595 votes to Taft's 500 in the first ballot.

try come Election Day. What was demonstrated at Chicago was that the Eastern, internationalist Republicans can dominate conventions."[105] However, the *Freeman* also conceded that Taft had been "in the hands of amateurs." So did most other observers. In addition to its tactical blunders, the Taft-camp had underestimated the prevalence of the "Taft-can't-win"-syndrome. It had also underestimated the level of support for Eisenhower among the Republican governors, and the impact that this group would have on the final outcome. Even more importantly, however, the Eisenhower-forces had managed to take control of the Credentials Committee. The chief architect behind the "Draft Goldwater" movement, F. Clifton White, would later recall the important lessons in the use of the Credential Committee that he had learned under Dewey's tutorship in the 1952-election. At close range he had observed "how [Dewey] chopped down 42 of Senator Taft's Southern delegates, starting the stampede that ended in the Ohioan's defeat."[106]

Taft's personality had of course also been an important factor. His other qualities aside, the senator was not exactly a charismatic figure, and he was further handicapped by his open disgust for all the baby-kissing and ballyhoo which is essential to political campaigning in the United States. After twenty years without a Republican administration, many delegates understandably had an appetite for winning that exceeded their loyalty to Taft. Most of all, the Ohio senator's electoral basis of support had simply proved to be too small in the still crucial northeastern and Pacific Coast regions.[107] To many of the delegates from these regions the political thinking of the Taft-wing still reflected, as one opponent put it, the "rural barbershop mind of 1880."[108]

Such arguments did not count for much in the prevalent right wing evaluation of the defeat. Instead it became a widespread notion that the nomination had been stolen from Taft by the Eastern wing of the party, helped by big business, New York lawyers, the media, and other alleged "kingmakers." Thus, the conflict could to a large extent be seen as a result of pro-

---

105 "Eisenhower's Opportunity," The *Freeman*, July 28, 1952, p. 719.
106 F. Clifton White, *Suite 3505; The Story of the Draft Goldwater Movement* (New Rochelle, N.Y.: Arlington House, 1967), p. 389.
107 See James T. Patterson, *Mr. Republican; a Biography of Robert A. Taft* (Boston: Houghton Mifflin Company, 1972), p. 560.
108 Bernard De Voto, "The End of the Stalwarts," *Harper's*, Vol. 204 (September 1952), p. 78.

found differences in the underlying political culture and a longstanding and deep-seated mutual suspicion between the two competing factions of the party, rather than as the result of disagreement over actual issues.

This perspective was also evident in the analysis that Taft himself made after his defeat. The senator, who prior to the convention had declined help from professional strategists from the East and had preferred to be surrounded by a staff of Midwesterners, did not focus as much on tactical errors. Rather, he pointed to "the power of New York financial interests and large numbers of businessmen subject to New York influence," as well as on the majority of influential newspapers who according to the senator had served as a mouthpiece for Eisenhower.[109]

Even if Taft shared the common right wing perception that he had lost to the "kingmakers" of the eastern establishment, he nevertheless looked more optimistically than many of his supporters on the prospects for conservative politics with Eisenhower in the White House. In a letter to his friend Felix Morley, he expressed his confidence that Eisenhower was "essentially conservative and that if we keep working with him and pushing him in the right direction, we will make real progress."[110] Taft himself, however, would not be able to work on this task for long. In July 1953, "Mr. Conservative" succumbed to cancer, and the American Right lost its leading political figure.

Conservative Principles vs. Corporate Cosmology

In the editorial offices of the *Freeman*, the battle continued throughout 1952. Although it was Henry Hazlitt who originally had brought Davis to the journal from the *Saturday Evening Post*, their political positions proved to be irreconcilable. When John Chamberlain and Suzanne La Follette gave their support to Davis, Hazlitt resigned. However, harsh criticism of the editorial line persisted from many of the director-stockholders, most

---

109 Robert Taft, "Analysis of the Results of the Chicago Convention," Robert Taft Papers, Box 488.
110 Letter, Robert A. Taft to Felix Morley, June 29, 1953. The Felix Morley Papers, Hoover Presidential Library.

notably from some of the corporate sponsors, who shared Eisenhower's pragmatic republicanism. This particularly seemed to be the case with Howard Pew, Leo Wolman, and Jasper Crane, who had denounced the editors' obvious support of the Taft camp, and claimed that the *Freeman* was being turned into a "scandal sheet."[111] The editors found this to be an untimely and intolerable interference. As Forrest Davis put it, they wanted to turn a "militant magazine appealing to strong emotion" into a "quiet, semi-academic review of economics."[112] At the annual director-stockholder meeting in January 1953, it was Chamberlain, La Follette, and Davis' turn to resign. Henry Hazlitt was subsequently brought back as editor.

To several conservative observers, the *Freeman* incident highlighted a basic tension between conservative ideology and the interests of big business. It was a struggle between the entrepreneurial ideals of conservative intellectuals, and the pragmatic style of the corporate conservatism which would come to be so closely identified with the Eisenhower-administration.[113] During the battle for the *Freeman*, several of the supporters of Davis and his co-editors warned that a victory for the "big business" faction would mean an early death for the magazine as a vibrant force in the conservative intellectual movement.[114] Such predictions turned out to be largely correct.

In 1954 Leonard Read and his libertarian Foundation for Economic Education bought what was left of the journal and made Frank Chodorov the editor. The *Freeman* continued its existence as a monthly magazine with a primary focus on libertarian economics. The position as leading voice for the new conservative movement, however, was left open for some other journal.

---

111 Memorandum, John Chamberlain to Henning W. Prentis, Jr., October 27, 1952. The Herbert Hoover Papers, Box 166.
112 "Battle for the *Freeman*," *Time* (January 26, 1953)
113 After Chamberlain's resignation, Henry Regnery wrote him a letter concerning Russell Kirk's book *The Conservative Mind*, in which he noted that Kirk, like many other conservative intellectuals, and with good reason, was "genuinely disturbed by certain aspects of American business." The Freeman episode was, according to Regnery, " a good example of the sort of thing he is concerned about" (Letter, Henry Regnery to John Chamberlain, August 26, 1953. The Regnery Papers, Box 14).
114 For an example, see Frank Hanighen to Henry Regnery, quoted in letter from Regnery to John Chamberlain, January 12, 1953, the Regnery Papers, Box 14.

Chapter 5

Finding a Voice: *the National Review*

A DECADE AFTER the first issue of *Human Events*, conservatives could find quite a few periodicals to represent their views. They could find publishers willing to print books written by American conservative intellectuals, and a few scholarly journals were also in existence.[1] Yet, the conservative movement was still left without a leading national journal of opinion. That situation changed in November of 1955, when the first issue of William F. Buckley Jr.'s *National Review* reached the newsstands.

The importance of the journal for the development of the conservative movement can hardly be overestimated. Not only was it a catalyst and a major conservative voice in the ongoing political debate, its role within the movement was even more important due to the people who were brought together and the connections that were established through the journal. As George H. Nash has noted, "To a very substantial degree, the history of reflective conservatism in America after 1955 is the history of the individuals who collaborated in — or were discovered by - the magazine William F. Buckley, Jr. founded."[2]

---

1 One early attempt to create a scholarly conservative journal was *Measure*, which Regnery published in association with the Committee on Social Thought at the University of Chicago from 1949 to 1951. Despite the work of people such as Robert Hutchins, John Nef, and Daniel J. Boorstin, the journal was discontinued after just eight issues. Conservative dreams of a successful scholarly journal did not truly materialize until 1957, when the first issue of *Modern Age* was published. The quarterly, which was edited by Russell Kirk, eventually gained international recognition and reached a circulation of about 6,000 copies. In 1959, Kirk resigned after a dispute with his associate editor, David Collier, but the magazine continued along the guidelines that he had created. For further details, see George H. Nash, *The Conservative Intellectual Movement*, p. 145.

2 George H. Nash, *The Conservative Intellectual Movement*, p. 153.

William F. Buckley, Jr.

Despite the fact that Buckley was only thirty years old when he founded the *National Review*, he had already acquired a status as the very epitome of the "New American Right." As John Chamberlain later expressed it, Buckley "more than any single figure ... made conservatism a respectable force in American life."[3] Even Ronald Hamowy, the radical libertarian editor of *New Individualist Review*, who was otherwise an outspoken critic of the role that the *National Review*-crowd had come to play on the American Right, acknowledged – albeit with a certain regret – that Buckley had become so much "identified with everything intelligent on the Right that if in the common image of modern conservatism Senator Goldwater can justly be portrayed as the sword, William Buckley is, without doubt, the pen."[4]

Buckley had graduated from Yale in 1950, and the following year he had attracted national attention for the first time with *God and Man at Yale*, the best-selling attack on his alma mater. Actually, Buckley had been admitted both to the law school and to graduate studies in political science at Yale, but he was not interested in an academic career. He wanted a more direct impact on public opinion. Several conservative journals offered him a position after his success with *God and Man at Yale*, and Buckley eventually accepted an offer from the *American Mercury*. Before he devoted himself fully to the world of publishing, however, Buckley had a brief stint as an agent for the CIA. He was recruited for the Agency by his political science professor and mentor at Yale, Willmoore Kendall, who would later join Buckley as editor of *National Review*. Kendall also introduced Buckley to another future editor of *National Review*, Professor James Burnham.

James Burnham

Burnham was not stuck in any ivory tower. Apart from being a professor of philosophy at the New York University, he worked as a consultant to

---

[3] John Chamberlain, *A Life With the Printed Word* (Chicago: Regnery Gateway, 1982), p. 147.
[4] Ronald Hamowy & William F. Buckley. Jr., "*National Review:* Criticism and Reply," *New Individualist Review*, Vol. 1, No.3 (November 1961), pp. 3-12.

the CIA's covert action wing, the Office of Policy Coordination.[5] He had also acquired fame as the author of controversial books such as *The Managerial Revolution* and *The Machiavellians*.[6] With Burnham's recommendation, Buckley joined the CIA in 1951 and went to work for Howard Hunt in Mexico City. After a year Buckley quit in order to fulfill his true ambition: to own and run a magazine, and Burnham became a key figure in this enterprise.

Like several of his future colleagues at *National Review*, Burnham had taken the journey from the far left to the far right of the political spectrum.[7] A prominent Trotskyite during the 1930s, he had actually been an early victim of "red-bashing" when the Hearst press in 1933 demanded the sacking of him and Sidney Hook from the faculty of New York University for "treasonable plotting to overthrow the American government."[8] By the late 1940s, however, Burnham's political conversion was complete. Books such as *The Struggle for the World* and *The Coming Defeat of Communism* had made him the leading American guru of an aggressive and uncompromising Cold War strategy.[9] Gone were all reservations about globalism:

> The reality is that the only alternative to the communist World Empire is an American Empire which will be, if not literally worldwide in formal boundaries, capable of exercising decisive world control. Nothing less than this can be the positive, or offensive, phase of a rational United States policy.[10]

In Burnham's apocalyptic worldview there was no middle ground between victory and surrender in the Cold War. Containment was cowardly and counterproductive "If we do not smash the communist power, we shall

---

5 John B. Judis, *William F. Buckley, Jr*, p. 80.
6 James Burnham, *The Managerial Revolution: or, What is happening in the world now* (New York: The John Day Company, 1941); *The Machiavellians, defenders of freedom* (London: Putnam and Company Limited, 1943).
7 An excellent account of Burnham's political conversion can be found in John P. Diggins, *Up From Communism; Conservative Odysseys in American Intellectual History* (New York: Harper & Row, 1975).
8 Quoted from Heale, M.J., *American Anticommunism; Combating the Enemy Within 1830-1970* (Baltimore: The Johns Hopkins University Press, 1990), p. 111.
9 Burnham, *The Struggle for the World* (London: J. Cape, 1947), *The Coming Defeat of Communism* (New York: J. Day, 1950).
10 Burnham, *The Struggle for the World*, p. 182.

cease to exist as a nation and a people," read Burnham's gloomy message.[11] By the time Burnham joined *National Review* his brand of strident anti-communism had become the glue of the conservative movement.

Gathering the National Review crowd

Buckley's first idea was to buy one of the already existing conservative journals, broaden its scope and turn it into a weekly. Circulation was naturally an important issue in this connection. Buckley was convinced that one national magazine with a circulation in the neighborhood of the major liberal journals (70,000-100,000 copies) would have a greater impact on public opinion than a number of smaller conservative journals. Several merging initiatives had previously been taken on this account. Frank Chodorov's *analysis* had merged with *Human Events*, and *the Freeman* had absorbed *Plain Talk*. In 1950, the editors of *Human Events* and the *Freeman* had discussed a possible collaboration between the two journals,[12] and in 1952 the possibilities had been explored for letting the *Freeman* take over the *American Mercury*.[13] Buckley, for his part, had negotiations with the owners of *Human Events* and the *Freeman*, but in both cases was unable to reach an agreement.

The plans for a new magazine came much closer to fruition when Buckley in 1954 found an enthusiastic partner in Willi Schlamm. An Austrian Jewish émigré and former communist, Schlamm had converted to the Right and become Henry Luce's leading foreign policy advisor at *Time* Inc. Prior to his association with Buckley, Schlamm's career had somehow been sidetracked, but he had never lost his strong desire to edit a conservative magazine. Since his departure from *Time* Inc. in 1949, he had been in search of a way to fulfill it, and Buckley's project was like an answer to his prayers.

---

11 Quoted from John P. Diggins, *Up From Communism*, p.386. War was not only inevitable, Burnham claimed, it had in fact already begun. Thus, it was a very apt reflection of the Burnhamite position that his future department in *National Review* was entitled "the Third World War."
12 Letter, Henry Regnery to John Chamberlain, December 8, 1950, Regnery Papers, Box 14.
13 Letter, Henry Regnery to John Chamberlain, July 18, 1952, the Regnery Papers, Box 14.

To both of the prospective editors, the fates of the *Freeman* and the *American Mercury* had provided valuable lessons. Willi Schlamm, who probably assumed that he would be able to influence his young partner without any formal authority, insisted that Buckley take full control of the venture in order to assure that the failures of those magazines would never occur at the *National Review*. Ironically, Schlamm himself would later become a victim of this arrangement, when in 1957 he was forced to resign from the magazine.[14]

From the outset, the masthead of *National Review* looked like a "who's who" of conservative journalism. Apart from Buckley and Schlamm, the list of editors included Burnham, Kendall, Suzanne LaFollette, and Jonathan Mitchell. Among the associates and contributors were Max Eastman, Eugene Lyons, Medford Evans, Karl Hess, Russell Kirk, Gerhart Niemeyer, E. Merrill Root, Richard Weaver, and Buckley's brother-in-law L. Brent Bozell. Later, names such as John Dos Passos, Whittaker Chambers, and the young Garry Wills would be added to the list. A goodly part of the staff was people who had formerly been associated with the *Freeman*.[15]

Standing "Athwart History, Yelling Stop"

The format of the new magazine would be like that of the *Freeman,* but a broader scope was intended. Several people advised Buckley to reach out to a larger audience by making *National Review* more wide-ranging and less doctrinaire than the *Freeman*, which according to Russell Kirk had been a publication solely aimed at an audience "wailing over the vanished terrestrial paradise of 1928."[16]

Apart from the range of topics covered, the tone in *National Review* was also to be different from that of its predecessors. Rather than scholarly

---

14 The most important instrument that Buckley used in order to maintain full editorial control, regardless of the clashes that might occur in the editorial offices, was a special financial arrangement with two separate classes of stock. Class B shares were sold to the public, but had no voting rights attached, while Class A shares, which had voting rights but no par value, all were owned by himself.

15 In addition to Willi Schlamm, and Suzanne La Follette, Forrest Davis and John Chamberlain also found a new outlet in *National Review*. So did Frank S. Meyer, Freda Utley, Frank Chodorov, and Buckley's brother Reid. See John B. Judis, *William F. Buckley*, p. 147.

16 Letter, Russell Kirk to William F. Buckley, Jr., November 29, 1955. The Buckley Papers.

and dull, it was supposed to be truculent, witty and sarcastic. As Buckley expressed it, *National Review* would not join "the mutual-admiration society of complacent American journalism."[17] Far from all conservatives were pleased with the tone in *National Review*. Russell Kirk found it "sophomoric," and F.A. Hayek at one point angrily canceled his subscription and rejected any future association with NR as a result of satirical allegations brought in the journal that UN Secretary-General Dag Hammarskjold cheated at cards.

Although this new tone was intended to give the journal a wider readership outside of academia, Buckley nevertheless held on to his unabashed elitism by stressing that the editorial line would "reject cultural concessions to the so-called 'average man.'"[18] On the contrary, the magazine would stand "athwart history, yelling Stop, at a time when no one is inclined to do so, or to have much patience with those who so urge it."[19]

The "Publisher's Statement" in the first issue of *National Review* was nothing short of a declaration of war on liberalism. The editors stated their belief that

> The nation's leading opinion-makers for the most part share the Liberal point of view, try indefatigably to inculcate it in their readers' minds, and to that end employ the techniques of propaganda ... That we may properly speak of them as a huge *propaganda Machine*, engaged in a major, sustained assault upon the sanity, and upon the prudence and the morality of the American people—its sanity, because the political reality of which they speak is a dream world that nowhere exists, its prudence and morality because their values and goals are in the sharpest conflict with the goals and values appropriate to the American tradition ...[20]

The magazine would see it as one of its most important tasks to keep track of and counter this "Liberal line." As one might expect from a right-wing magazine, labor relations made up an area in which *National Review* intended to go against the grain and "tell the violated businessman's side

---

17 Letter, F.A. Hayek to William F. Buckley, Jr., November 22, 1961. James Burnham Papers.
18 Promotional letter for *National Review*. The Buckley Papers.
19 "Publishers Statement," *National Review*, Vol. 1, No.1 (November 19, 1955), p. 5.
20 "The Editors of National Review Believe:" *National Review*, Vol.1, No.1 (November 19, 1955), p. 8.

of the story."²¹ In the area of foreign affairs this policy implied opposition to "the fashionable concepts of world government, the United Nations, internationalism, international atomic pools, etc," which according to the editors had "bewitched America's Liberal elite."²² American conservatives had converted to interventionism, but certainly not to multilateralism.

If *National Review* launched its attack on liberalism head-on, it did, however, also open a second front against the alleged conservatives who had "made their peace with the New Deal" and now preached consensus and conformity. As Buckley noted in his "Publisher's Statement:"

> Radical conservatives in this country have an interesting time of it, for when they are not being suppressed or mutilated by the Liberals, they are being ignored or humiliated by a great many of those of the well-fed Right, whose ignorance and amorality have never been exaggerated for the same reason that one cannot exaggerate infinity.²³

That Buckley was aiming at President Dwight Eisenhower's brand of "modern Republicanism" became even clearer when he warned that the complacency and the political consensus which seemingly characterized the national mood at the time were largely created by:

> An identifiable team ... bent on controlling both our major political parties – under the sanction of such fatuous and unreasoned slogans as "national unity," "middle-of-the-road," "progressivism," and "bipartisanship." Clever intriguers are reshaping both parties in the image of Babbitt, gone Social-Democrat.²⁴

Thus, while most political observers at the time tended to view Ike as the representative of a "new conservatism," Buckley and his associates strongly disagreed. Ike might have slowed the rate of growth in the public sector, but he had also accepted, and thus in fact legitimized the basic framework for the modern welfare state as bipartisan doctrine. Buckley was ready to write both him and Vice President Nixon completely out of the conserva-

---

21 *National Review*, Vol.1, No.1 (November 19, 1955), p. 8.
22 *National Review*, Vol.1, No.1 (November 19, 1955), p. 6.
23 *National Review*, Vol.1, No.1 (November 19, 1955), p. 5.
24 "The Magazine's Credenda," *National Review*, Vol.1, No.1 (November 19, 1955), p. 6.

tive movement. In fact, he and his co-editors discussed whether the first issue of *National Review* should present an open endorsement of Senator William Knowland of California as Republican candidate for the presidency in 1956, but they decided that it would be an unwise move, both tactically and financially. Instead they settled on launching the magazine with an article by Senator Knowland.[25]

"Neither good nor Conservative"

National Review's opening salvo on liberalism did not go unanswered. A characteristic attitude reflected in many comments to the first issue read something like: "yes, there is a strong need for a good conservative journal of opinion in America – not just for the sake of conservatives, but also because liberalism is plagued by fatigue without worthy opposition. Unfortunately this is not it." Writing in *Commentary*, Dwight McDonald contended that the reason why the *National Review* was not a good conservative magazine was that it was "neither good nor conservative."[26]

The fact that most reviews treated the new magazine as a curiosity and refused to take it seriously on its own merits, clearly reflected the sociopathological thesis concerning the American Right, which had come in vogue through the works of sociologists and historians such as Daniel Bell, Richard Hofstadter, and Seymour Martin Lipset. The launching of *National Review* happened to coincide with the publication of Daniel Bell (ed.), *The New American Right*—an extremely influential collection of essays which abandoned traditional explanations of political behavior and instead attempted to explain right-wing political activity as various expressions of "status anxiety."[27] According to this mode of explanation, most of the self-styled conservatives were really "pseudo-conservatives" (Hofstadter's term), driven not by ideological convictions, but by paranoid

---

25 William F. Knowland, "Peace – With Honor," *National Review*, Vol.1, No.1 (November 19, 1955), pp.9-13. Knowland had taken over the position as minority leader in the Senate after the death of Robert A. Taft, and many conservatives saw him as a potential national leading figure in the conservative movement. However, his political career ended in 1958 when he left the Senate in order to run for governor of California and lost the election.
26 *Commentary* (April 1956), p. 367 ff.
27 (New York: Criterion Books, Inc., 1955).

delusions about communism in government and by their own personal fears and frustrations. It was also this attitude that guided Dwight McDonald's review of *National Review*, which he only found worth examining as a "cultural phenomenon:"

> The McCarthy nationalists – they call themselves conservatives, but that is surely a misnomer – have never before made so heroic an effort to be intellectually articulate. Here are the ideas, here is the style of the Lumpenbourgeoisie, the half-educated, half successful provincials (and a provincial may live within a mile of the Empire State Building as well as in Kokomo or Sauk Center) who responded to Huey Long, Father Coughlin, and Senator McCarthy. Anxious, embittered, resentful, they feel that the main stream of American politics since 1932 has passed them by, as indeed it has, and they have the slightly paranoiac suspiciousness of an isolated minority group. For these are men from the underground, the intellectually underprivileged who feel themselves excluded from a world they believe is ruled by liberals (or eggheads – the terms are, significantly, interchangeable in NR) just as the economic underdog feels alienated from society.[28]

The outspoken conservative sense of suppression, which was also reflected in the pages of *National Review*, was only further reinforced by the arrogance of reviewers such as McDonald, who apparently felt that they were in a position to outline the limits of "true" conservatism and the form that a qualified and responsible opposition to their own ideas should take. But if a majority of liberal reviewers dismissed the ideological content of *National Review* as "pseudo-conservatism," how then did Buckley and his associates themselves attempt to define their position?

Ecumenical Conservatism

Looking back on the first five years of *National Review*, editor James Burnham could conclude that the journal had appealed to such diverse tendencies as:

> Libertarianism, isolationism, hard-line anti-Communism, traditionalism, McCarthyism, classic laissez-faire, DARism, States Rightsism, and various semi-crackpotisms – but managed to muddle along reasonably well

---

28 Dwight McDonald, *Commentary* (April 1956), p. 367 ff.

because all of the tendencies were negatively united in opposition to the prevailing power and ideology.[29]

As Burnham's statement indicates, "fusionism" was an important keyword to the whole *National Review* venture. Buckley's envisioned that the journal would serve as a common forum for the scattered forces of the right – that it would become a vital factor in the attempt to create a viable coalition between the various anti-liberal forces in American politics – and this vision was clearly reflected in the list of contributors. Buckley was also convinced that for all practical purposes, it would be possible in time to iron out the notable differences between the various strains of conservatism, and blend them into a coherent set of ideas.

"Fusionism" also had a practical side, based on a realistic assessment of the potential readership. By deliberately evading a more precise definition of conservatism, the editors hoped to reach an audience large enough to make the journal a profitable and thus economically independent venture. An ambiguous position in content also made it a lot easier to find sponsors for the journal. With the fates of the *Freeman* and *American Mercury* in memory, Buckley was determined not to become too dependent on just a few major contributors.

Another explanation for Buckley's unfailing belief in an ecumenical brand of American conservatism can perhaps be found in the fact that his own beliefs were a strange hybrid. He personally seemed to be able to embody most of the apparent contradictions and incoherence of American conservatism. As a result, he did not always seem to grasp the depth of the controversies that occurred from time to time among other contributors to his magazine. Despite Buckley's considerable diplomatic skills and firm intent to defuse the various ideological controversies, the relationship between the various factions at the magazine was not always one of "peaceful coexistence."

The fact that most strands of conservative thought were represented among the editors and contributors of *National Review* did not imply that they were equally important to the profile of the journal. Those who openly contested the notion of "fusionism" mostly retained only a loose affiliation with the magazine. That was the case for a number of libertarians, as well as for traditionalists such as Russell Kirk and Richard Weaver.

---

29 "Strategic Development of NATIONAL REVIEW," memorandum, James Burnham to William F. Buckley, Jr. (undated), p. 2. James Burnham Papers.

Kirk actually appeared on the original masthead, but immediately after the first issue he wrote Buckley and requested that his name be removed. He found it embarrassing, he said, if people got the idea that he had any influence upon the editorial line of the journal.[30] Besides, he did not like the idea of appearing on the same masthead as Frank Chodorov and Frank Meyer, whose reviews of his book *The Conservative Mind* had offended him deeply.[31] Kirk did, however, agree to write a bi-weekly column on the world of academia and conservative campus initiatives around the country.

Stalin's gift to the American Right

If traditionalism and libertarianism were respected components in the general outlook at *National Review*, it was clearly a militant anti-communism that served as the journal's integrating factor and mostly shaped its image. It was no coincidence that half of the editorial board was made up of militant ex-radicals, who, in the words of the historian John P. Diggins, had become "Stalin's gift to the American Right."[32] This new dominating force on the intellectual Right included Buckley's closest associates Willi Schlamm and James Burnham, as well as Frank Meyer, Max Eastman, John Dos Passos, Suzanne La Follette, and later also Whittaker Chambers. For most of these people, communism remained a central issue in their lives as they gained recognition on the right as self-styled experts.[33] Among the leftovers from former convictions that these "inverted Stalinists" now used in their efforts to extirpate the God That Failed were their crusading zeal and their passionate dislike of liberalism.[34]

---

30 Letter, Russell Kirk to William F. Buckley, Jr., November 20, 1955. The Buckley Papers.
31 A few months earlier Russell Kirk wrote William F. Buckley, Jr's father concerning Frank Meyer and Frank Chodorov's reviews of his book *The Conservative Mind:* "It is amusing while waging such battles on the frontier [against liberalism] at my own expense, to be knifed in the back by such cheerborne *condottieri* as Frank Meyer and Frank Chodorov." (Letter, July 13, 1955. The Buckley Papers).
32 John P. Diggins, *Up from Communism*; p. 3.
33 On the implications of this expert status of the ex-communists, see Hannah Arendt, "The Ex-Communists," *The Commonweal* (March 20, 1953), pp. 595-599.
34 The expression "inverted Stalinists" was coined by Isaac Deutcher in *Russia in Transition and Other Essays* (New York, 1957), p. 203.

The militant anti-communism that became the hallmark of *National Review* was among other things evidenced by perpetual calls for military expansion and was in most areas at odds with libertarian principles. One critic of the journal sarcastically remarked that:

> Through issue after issue ... we read of the "rights of the community," of five thousand years of conservative tradition, of authority and order, of the duty of the West to uplift the negro with Bible and bullwhip, of the sacred obligation all free men have to coerce Communists at home and slaughter them abroad. Where once the Right was fervently devoted to the freedoms propounded in the Bill of Rights, it now believes that civil liberties are the work of Russian Agents.[35]

Spiritual Politics

Buckley had been raised in a right-wing political climate where anti-Semitic views were a common ingredient. By the 1950s such views were still expressed by organizations such as Gerald L.K. Smith's Nationalist Christian Crusade, the Liberty Lobby, and Merwin K. Hart's National Economic Council, as well as by *the American Mercury* after its takeover by Connecticut millionaire Russell Maguire in 1952. Despite frequent attempts to associate *National Review* with such organizations, their views were not reflected on the pages of the magazine. In fact, there was a strong Jewish presence among the editors and contributors, including Willi Schlamm, Frank Meyer, Morrie Ryskind, Eugene Lyons, Ralph DeToledano, Max Eastman and Frank Chodorov. In several respects Buckley and his associates could take a good deal of the credit for successfully distancing the "respectable" right from the anti-Semitic nativism which was still prevalent among the remains of the Old Right.

Regardless of the strong Jewish representation on the editorial board, however, it was Buckley's own Roman Catholic faith that first and foremost set the religious tone of *National Review*. In contrast to the *Freeman* and most other predecessors, the spiritual dimension of anti-communism

---

35 Ronald Hamowy, "*National Review*: Criticism and Reply," p. 4.

was strongly emphasized in the pages of *National Review*, where communism was generally presented as nothing less than the ultimate challenge to Judeo-Christian civilization.

Apart from Buckley and those of his relatives who worked for the journal, the list of contributors who were also Catholic by birth included Garry Wills, Thomas Molnar, James Burnham, Erik von Kuehnelt Leddihn, and Frederick Wilhelmsen. An even more significant indicator of the Catholic dominance at the magazine, however, was the conspicuous number of editors and contributors who converted to the faith. The list included Willmoore Kendall, L. Brent Bozell, Jeffrey Hart, Gerhart Niemeyer, Russell Kirk, and Frank Meyer (who made the conversion on his deathbed in 1970).[36]

Did Buckley and his co-editors consider conservatism inseparable from religion? Did they see the existence of an objective moral order as an essential feature of all conservative thought, and was such a belief thought to prescribe a belief in something divine? Most contributors to *National Review* did subscribe to such a perception and accordingly tended to see the struggle against communism as basically a struggle between atheism and religion, just as Buckley's hero Whittaker Chambers had framed it in *Witness*. There were, however, notable exceptions. One of them was Max Eastman.

His "conversion" to conservatism notwithstanding, Eastman had maintained a view of religion as "primitive mythology," and he continued to criticize the God-intoxication of the variety of anti-communism, which he found in the views of Buckley, Jr., Brent Bozell, and Whittaker Chambers. He objected to their traditionalist notion that "freedom" could not be a goal by itself; that it only served a purpose if it fostered, ultimately, a belief in the existence of an objective moral order. To Eastman it was a contradiction in terms "to advocate freedom, and then lay down the law as to how men 'should' use it."[37] His own anti-communism, he claimed, was based on the belief that people should be allowed to live their lives as

---

36 In two 1991 numbers of *National Review*, Buckley has devoted attention to the issue of anti-Semitism on the American right, and to reflections on his own father's anti-Semitism. See "In Search of Anti-Semitism," *National Review*, Vol. XLIII, No. 24 (December 30, 1991), pp. 20-64; and "In Pursuit of Anti-Semitism," *National Review*, Vol. XLIV, No. 5 (March 16, 1992), pp. 2-32.

37 Max Eastman, "Am I A Conservative?" *National Review* (January 28, 1964), p. 57.

they wanted to, "so long as they do not encroach injuriously upon the lives of others."[38]

Despite this profound disagreement with most of the other editors, Eastman stayed on the board of NR for almost a decade. When his animus against the linkage of religion and conservatism finally made him resign in 1964, he wrote Buckley that "It was an error in the first place to think that, because of political agreements, I could collaborate formally with a publication whose basic view of life and the universe I regard as primitive and superstitious."[39]

Although the conservative worldview in *National Review* was evidently shaped by the religious beliefs of its contributors, it was nevertheless also clear that the magazine was conservative before it was Catholic. Respect for papal authority was only strong when its political implications did not conflict with basic conservative principles, and that is exactly what happened in the early 1960s after John XXIII had become pope. His *Mater et Magistra*, published in July of 1961, called for social justice and aid to underdeveloped countries, just as the succeeding Vatican Council II (1962-1965) launched a host of reforms within the Church. The papal appeals for social justice were flatly rejected by *National Review*. The journal called *Mater et Magistra* "a venture in triviality," since communism, which in its view was the prime enemy that all Catholics ought to join forces against, was hardly mentioned in the encyclical.[40]

These critical remarks led to the peculiar situation that Buckley was charged with disloyalty to his Church by liberal Catholics headed by *Commonweal* and the liberal Jesuit weekly *America*.[41] Buckley, however, felt no inclination to apologize. He remained critical of Pope John, who in contrast to the traditionally fierce anti-Communist policies of the Catholic Church in America issued more conciliatory notes in a declared attempt to ease cold war tensions between the two competing superpowers. Thus, when in 1965 the Pope called Andrei Gromyko a "man of peace," Buckley

---

38 Eastman, "Am I A Conservative?" p. 57.
39 Quoted in William F. Buckley, Jr. (ed.), *Conservative Thought in the Twentieth Century* (Indianapolis, 1970), p. xxix.
40 Editorial, *National Review*, July 29, 1961.
41 For further details on the dispute over *Mater et Magistra*, see Garry Wills, *Politics and Catholic Freedom* (Chicago: Henry Regnery Company, 1964).

noted in an editorial that with regard to political matters "the Pope is as fallible as Walter Cronkite."[42]

Further evidence of the magazine's priorities between religious loyalties and political principles may be found in the split between Buckley and his longtime friend and brother-in-law L. Brent Bozell, who in May of 1963 asked Buckley to remove him from the masthead of *National Review*.[43] Although his reasons were mostly of a private nature, mounting disagreements over the proper role of religion in the conservative movement also played a part.[44] When Bozell — who had found Buckley's remarks about *Mater et Magistra* most impious — eventually left *National Review*, he went on to establish the right-wing Catholic journal *Triumph*, of which the first issue was published in 1966.

Bozell's views were clearly becoming still more theocratic. By the late 1960s, while war was raging in Vietnam, as well as in the streets of Chicago and elsewhere in America, Bozell spelled national doom and put the blame on the Constitution. The American political order had been "bound to fail" from the very beginning, he argued, because the government was only held accountable to the people and not to God.[45] Advocacy of a state religion was a rather peculiar position to hold for somebody belonging to a religious minority which had benefited from the tradition of religious tolerance, but this paradox did not shake Bozell in his conviction that the American republic could only survive if the separation between church and state was broken down. Bozell had lost his faith in the conservative movement, which he now repudiated as an "inadequate substitute for Christian politics."[46]

---

42 Editorial, *National Review* (October 19, 1965).
43 Letter, L. Brent Bozell to WFB, May 22, 1963. The Buckley Papers.
44 For further details on the break between Buckley and Bozell, see John B. Judis, *William F. Buckley...*, pp. 317-322.
45 L. Brent Bozell, "The Death of the Constitution," *Triumph* 3 (February 1968), pp. 10-14. Quoted from George H. Nash, *The Conservative Intellectual Movement...*, P. 311.
46 *Triumph*, March 1969. Quoted from Judis, *William F. Buckley, Jr...*, Op. Cit. p.320. Bozell's views echoed those of Leo Strauss, who despite his own Jewish heritage insisted on the philosophical need for an established national religion in order to secure public orthodoxy and prevent the drift into moral relativism. See Strauss' view on theology, see Ted V. McAllister, *Revolt Against Modernity: Leo Strauss, Eric Voegelin, and the Search for a Postliberal Order* Lawrence: University of Kansas Press, 1996), and Shadia B. Drury, *Leo Strauss and the American Right* (London: MacMillan Press, 1997).

The 1960s had obviously moved Buckley and Bozell in different directions. Bozell had in many respects become a pioneer in the movement later known as the New Christian Right. In 1970, he founded an anti-abortion organization called Action for Life. Together with a group of Christian right-wing students known as the Sons of Thunder, he became involved in raids on health care clinics that allegedly counseled abortions. Buckley, on the other hand, had in several respects moved closer to the mainstream. His plea for tolerance on issues such as abortion, and his social libertarian advocacy of marijuana decriminalization, would in time put him at odds with many of the moralistic crusaders of the New Christian Right.[47]

"Hunting in the Pond where the Ducks Are"

As civil rights issues in the 1950s became pressing national political questions, many conservative Republicans saw increased opportunities for making inroads in the hitherto solid Democratic South. Conservative calls for "a choice, not an echo" implied a two-party system neatly divided along ideological lines with Republican meaning "conservative" and Democratic meaning "liberal." According to this line of thinking, the wrong political party evidently dominated the South, widely recognized as "the most conservative region in the country." Thus, in their quest for a partisan realignment, conservative Republicans should, as Barry Goldwater later expressed it, "go hunting in the pond where the ducks are."[48] This task of searching for new allies in the South was clearly reflected on the pages of *National Review*.

Despite all the talk of the "Southern tradition," which many conservatives claimed made white Southerners natural allies in a national conservative movement, this had few, if any, practical implications in terms of creating such a political realignment.[49] Judging from Southern willingness to accept federal funding, absolutely nothing indicated that the

---

47 For an account of the tense relations between Buckley and the emerging "New Right" of the 1970s, see Judis, *William F. Buckley, Jr...*, p. 367 ff.
48 Quoted from Phillip E. Converse, et.al. "Electoral Myth and Reality: The 1964 Election," *The American Political Science Review*, Vol. LIX, NO. 2 (June, 1965), p. 327.
49 Phillip E. Converse, et. al., p. 330.

South was more conservative than other regions in economic matters. The one issue that mattered was civil rights. As a part of their stand on racial relations, conservatives attempted to link the civil rights issue to the struggle against communism. The use of this strategy helped make champions of white supremacy such as Senator James O. Eastland of Mississippi, popular on the American right in general. In May of 1955, Senator Eastland responded to the Supreme Court's decision on school segregation in *Brown vs. Board of Education in Topeka* from the previous year, by claiming that the Court had been "brainwashed by left-wing groups who were part and parcel of The Communist conspiracy to destroy our country."[50] Similar views were expressed in *National Review*, albeit in a more sophisticated manner. Richard Weaver, the magazine's leading spokesman for the conservative virtues of the "Southern tradition," saw the decision in *Brown vs. Board of Education* as a case of "political fanaticism," and contended that eventually integration meant "communization."[51]

Fortunately, the catering to potential southern allies did not require the endorsement of nakedly racist views, which might hamper the magazine's quest for intellectual respectability. The defenders of white supremacy in the South had for years attempted to give their struggle a more palatable image under the banners of "States Rights" and "Constitutionalism" – both words which also had a pleasant ring to conservative ears. In the guise of "Constitutionalism" the issue was not the political and social repression of black Americans in the South, but the encroachment of the federal state.

In 1957, Buckley found just the right man to cover the civil rights struggle for *National Review* in James J. Kilpatrick, columnist and editor of the *Richmond Newsleader*. Kilpatrick was the author of *The Lasting South* and *the Sovereign States* in which he argued in favor of the states' constitutional rights to use the principle of *interposition* in defiance of federal authority.[52] A typical example of how the States Rights argument was framed in *National Review* could be seen in 1963, when he attempted to explain to the readers why all respectable conservatives ought to oppose the proposed Civil Rights Act.

---

50 Quoted from Dan Wakefield, "Respectable Racism," *The Nation* (October 22, 1955), p. 341.
51 Richard M. Weaver, "Integration is Communization," *National Review* (July 13, 1957), p. 67 ff.
52 Both books published by Henry Regnery Company in Chicago, 1957.

According to Kilpatrick, the bill would destroy the states' control of their own voting requirements, just as it would undermine property rights. Besides, he stressed, the right to vote was not an absolute right anyway, since it did not apply to children and lunatics. Kilpatrick did not deny that willful intimidation of black voters might occur, for example, in the form of phony literacy tests. However, he insisted that this was not a valid legal problem, since there was "abundant law on the books" — and had been even prior to both the Civil Rights Acts of 1957 and 1960 — to prevent and punish any such intimidation.[53] As for the proposed ban on racial segregation, the bill would impose a "requirement to serve," which according to the author was unconstitutional in any other field than public utilities such as power, water supply and telephone services. Finally, the author insisted that he did not defend racial discrimination, but merely the citizens' constitutional right to discriminate.[54]

Kilpatrick might have been sincere in his belief that federal intrusion posed a greater danger to the Republic than the institutionalized violation of civil rights in the South. So might Barry Goldwater, who took over most of Kilpatrick's arguments in his 1964 presidential campaign. But in most instances the use of such Constitutional arguments was sheer hypocrisy. Ralph de Toledano, who occasionally wrote for *National Review*, did not share the belief in Southern segregationists as natural brothers in arms for the conservative movement. In 1960, he recalled how eight years earlier he had toured most of the Southern states:

> I talked to governors, newspaper editors, businessmen, taxi drivers, elevator operators, and the minor officialdom — usually off the record. Only when I took out my notebook and pencil did I hear the Constitutional arguments and the plea for States Rights. In casual conversation with those upholding the *status Quo*, I heard the old talk about "keeping the niggers in their place."[55]

That de Toledano's observations might have been closer to the heart of the matter — also regarding the position of *National Review* — was occa-

---

53 James J. Kilpatrick, "Civil Rights and Legal Wrongs," *National Review* (September 24, 1963), p. 232.
54 Kilpatrick, "Civil Rights and Legal Wrongs," p. 234.
55 Ralph de Toledano, *Lament for a Generation* (New York: Farrar, Straus and Cudahy, 1960), p. 178.

sionally evidenced by unfortunate slips in the magazine. Thus, William F. Buckley wrote an editorial in 1957 entitled "Why the South Must Prevail" which removed the Constitutional veil from the issue. Not only did Buckley refer to the South as a legitimate cultural entity based on white supremacy, he even encouraged Southerners to openly defy the Supreme Court on the question of voting rights:

> The central question that emerges ... is whether the white community in the South is entitled to take such measures as are necessary to prevail, politically and culturally, in areas in which it does not predominate numerically. The sobering answer is *Yes* the white community is so entitled because, for the time being, it is the advanced race ... *National Review* believes that the South's premises are correct. If the majority wills what is socially atavistic, then to thwart the majority may be, though undemocratic, enlightened.[56]

When Buckley's editorial was criticized for its blunt racism by his own brother-in-law, Brent Bozell, among others, he came up with a pathetic clarification. He now argued that uneducated black and whites alike ought to be disenfranchised – a solution that Buckley argued would live up to "the spirit of the Constitution, and the letter of the Fifteenth Amendment."[57]

The "white man's burden" attitude which characterized the magazine's views on civil rights in America also framed its views on the process of decolonization in the Third World which had gained momentum by the late 1950s. Decolonization, Burnham lamented, meant the end of a "brilliantly conceived structure" and posed a mortal danger to the West, as the Third World was about to become the prime battleground in the Cold War.[58] This was also a central theme in his book *Suicide of the West*, published in 1964.[59]

Buckley was in full accord with the Burnhamite position. Africans, he contended, were generally incapable of handling their own political and economic affairs, and would continue to be so he quipped in an interview,

---

56 Editorial, *National Review*, August 24, 1957.
57 "Editorial Clarification," *National Review*, September 7, 1957.
58 *National Review*, January 29, 1961.
59 James Burnham, *Suicide of the West* (New York: The John Day Company, 1964).

until "they stop eating each other."⁶⁰ Later the same year, when Buckley was invited by conservative students to speak at the 14th National Student Congress at the University of Wisconsin, a foreign student charged him with double standards in defending colonialism in the third world, while advocating "freedom" in America. The student concluded by pointing to America's own revolutionary departure from colonialism. In response, Buckley told the student that it was "out of touch with historical reality" to compare the revolutionary activities of Founding Fathers such as Benjamin Franklin, George Washington and Thomas Jefferson with those of "semi-savages in the Congo."⁶¹

Heading for the Mainstream

By 1960, the conservative movement had reached a level of maturity which made it both natural and pertinent to evaluate and possibly revise the underlying assumptions guiding its politics. Given the fact that *National Review*, rightly or wrongly, had acquired status as the leading voice of the conservative movement in America, how then had the conservative self-perception *vis a vis* the alleged political establishment evolved in the preceding years?

In 1958, Professor Gerhart Niemeyer[62] analyzed the articles in the *National Review*, seeing in them certain basic assumptions:

1) Liberals are in power.
2) Conservatives are out of power.
3) Liberals form a solid block of people with fairly uniform and basically unchangeable views.
4) Conservatives are also a group with fairly uniform and clearly identifiable views.

---

60 Dan Wakefield, "W.F.B. Jr., Portrait of a Complainer." *Esquire* (January 1961). Quoted from Judis, *William F. Buckley, Jr....*, p. 185.
61 Quoted from Tom Huston, "NSA: The Turning Point," *The New Guard*, August, 1964, p. 10.
62 German born Gerhart Niemeyer was a traditionalist conservative, who had previously worked for the State Department and had taught political Science at both Princeton and Yale. By the time he joined *National Review* in 1955, he held a position as professor of political science at Notre Dame University.

> 5) Conservatives have no prospect of coming into power or directing the course of events, in our lifetime.[63]

According to Niemeyer, the journal used much of its energy on exposing the existence of a liberal "Establishment" and on an almost ritualistic lamentation of the neglected outsider status of conservatism. While this position might be mentally soothing to some, Niemeyer was convinced that it did not in any way promote conservative views. Indeed, if it had any political impact at all, it was that of a self-fulfilling proposition, which actually tended to make liberals react more and more as an establishment. As Niemeyer saw it, there was nothing monolithic about liberalism, and if conservatives addressed political issues "in the name of good sense," rather than in the name of a self-pitying minority demanding to be heard, they had a chance of gaining influence by "driving wedges into the ranks of liberals."[64]

Niemeyer's suggestions were later taken up by James Burnham, who by the late 1950s had somewhat softened the bombastic rhetoric and moved toward a more pragmatic brand of conservatism. Particularly the outcome of the Hungarian revolt in 1956 had made him realize that the persistent conservative advocacy of a policy of liberation in Eastern Europe was reckless and unrealistic. It was time to rethink conservatism's relationship to the political mainstream.[65]

In 1960, Burnham evaluated *National Review's* first five years of existence. In these years, he asserted, the magazine had reached most of its initial goals. It had been successful in gaining recognition as the principal conservative journal of opinion, and had become widely accepted as a common forum for all strains of American conservatism. Furthermore, it had provided the movement with a good deal of the intellectual credibility that it so desperately needed. Yet, it was also clear to Burnham that the

---

63 Quoted in memorandum from James Burnham to William F. Buckley, Jr. on strategic development of *National Review* (undated). The James Burnham Papers.
64 Memorandum from James Burnham to William F. Buckley, Jr. on strategic development of *National Review* (undated). The James Burnham Papers.
65 Burnham's new pragmatism was also evidenced by the fact that he, unlike most of the other *National Review* editors, advocated the journal's support of Richard Nixon in the 1960-election. For further details on Burnham's reconsideration, see Kevin J. Smant, *How Great the Triumph; James Burnham, Anticommunism and the Conservative Movement* (Lanham: University Press of America, 1992), pp. 69-74.

journal, with a circulation of 30-35,000 copies, had hit a ceiling for further expansion, if it chose to remain a magazine exclusively by, for, and of conservatives.

Should *National Review* rest largely content with this role, and remain a sectarian journal, or should it attempt to reach out to a wider and not exclusively conservative audience by adopting a more indirect and less doctrinaire approach to its political objectives? In that case, Burnham estimated, the magazine could reach a potential readership of 100,000, perhaps even a quarter of a million. Despite the necessary compromises involved, and the potential danger of destroying the magazine's conservative profile, Burnham adhered to Gerhard Niemeyer's suggestions. In a personal addendum to Buckley, Jr., he summed up the dilemma:

> Now I suspect that you are inwardly divided on the choice between a sectarian or side channel – or bayou – and the main stream. To be the honored, responsible, enlightened and enlightening leader of a responsive sect (I use this word in default of a better) is a sympathetic career in many ways; and a career of heroic size if the seeming side channel is in truth the main stream, and if the deviating bulk of the flood will one day – as if of its own accord – burst back into the home bed. And maybe it is so; and maybe it is enough to lecture history from the bank. But it may also be necessary to wade further out into the mud. [66]

There were clear signs in the following years that Buckley in several areas had responded favorably to the suggestions made by Niemeyer and Burnham, and that he and *National Review* increasingly recognized politics as the art of the possible. In terms of more direct forms of political action, Buckley and his associates at *National Review* would also demonstrate that they were ready to "wade further out into the mud." However the fact that the circulation of the magazine increased from 34,000 copies in 1960 to 54,000 copies in 1961 was hardly the result of a change in the editorial line.[67] Rather, it had to do with the general change in the political climate caused, or at least reinforced, by the election of John F. Kennedy as president.

---

66 Memorandum from James Burnham to William F. Buckley, Jr. on strategic development of *National Review* (undated). The James Burnham Papers.
67 The circulation figures are taken from Jeffrey Hart, *The American Dissent: A decade of modern conservatism* (Garden City, N.Y.: Doubleday, 1966), p. 31.

A sense that the political stalemate was over affected conservatives as well as liberals. Also, a good many conservative Republicans who had previously desisted from openly expressing their opposition to government policies out of party loyalty no longer had such inhibitions with a Democrat in the White House. Equally important was the fact that the conservative movement had finally found a leading national figure in Barry Goldwater after the 1960 election. This was clearly evidenced when *National Review* in 1961 sent out a fundraising letter signed by the senator and, as a result, increased the number of subscribers by 7,000.[68]

"Further Out into the Mud"

The conservative movement had clearly reached a level of maturity, where many felt ready to abandon the role as "remnant" in order to explore the possibilities of direct political action. *National Review* would in many instances serve as inspiration and clearing-house for such action. Among the activities directly sponsored by the magazine was a program of monthly "National Review Forums" on current political topics initiated in 1958 at Hunter College in New York. Also, the following year, when Nikita Khrushchev visited the United States in the name of "peaceful coexistence," *National Review* was the sponsor of a major anti-Khrushchev rally at Carnegie Hall. In time, several of the contributors to *National Review* became more directly involved in conservative politics. Among the most significant examples of such involvement were the organizing in 1960 of both the New York Conservative Party and Young Americans for Freedom.

When Wall Street lawyer William A. Rusher in 1957 had been hired as publisher of the magazine (Buckley had hitherto been both editor and publisher), his primary function had been to provide a firmer grip on the magazine's fiscal situation. Since its first year, *National Review* had lost

---

68 Goldwater, on his side, also benefited from his association with the magazine. Not only did it continuously promote his presidential candidacy strongly, but also several people from the *National Review* crowd went to work directly for the Arizona senator. Apart from publisher William A. Rusher, who was a leading force in the "Draft Goldwater movement," Buckley and L. Brent Bozell wrote several of the senator's speeches, and Bozell was also the ghostwriter of his best-seller *The Conscience of a Conservative* (Shepherdsville, Ky: Victor Publishing Company, Inc., 1960), which eventually sold some 3,500,000 copies.

approximately $100,000 every year, and it took quite an effort in terms of attracting donations and organizing occasional fundraisers among its subscribers to keep the magazine afloat.[69] However, as an important side effect the association with Rusher had also brought Buckley and *National Review* closer to the world of partisan politics. Since his graduation from Harvard Law School in 1948, Rusher had been active in the Republican Party. In 1956-57, he had been associate counsel to the Senate Internal Security Subcommittee headed by Senator Pat McCarran. However, it was first of all through his many years of activity in the Young Republican National Federation that Rusher had built up good connections to aspiring leaders within the GOP. Here he had worked closely with John Ashbrook and F. Clifton White, with whom he would in 1961 organize the "Draft Goldwater movement."

If Rusher was closer to the world of Republican politics than most of the *National Review* crowd, he was, however, also among those who most strongly expressed the need to put conservative principles over power and political expedience. He had few illusions about the GOP as a proper vehicle for the conservative cause.[70] In his view, both major political parties were nothing more than vote gathering machines and it could become necessary for the conservative movement to sever its ties to the Republican party and form a third party. In the fall of 1960, when the editors discussed whether *National Review* should bring an endorsement of Richard Nixon, Rusher opposed it on the grounds that it might work against the larger goals of the conservative movement:

> What matters for our present purposes is merely this: that it is possible for a conservative to oppose Nixon, not simply as a means of recapturing the Republican Party, but as a first step in breaking away from the Republican Party altogether—toward a third party, to be formed when the moment is ripe. A vote for Nixon, it seems to me, merely enhances the power and prestige of the present management of the Republican Party, in return for be-

---

69 See, William A. Rusher, *The Rise of the Right* (New York: William Morrow and Company, Inc., 1984), pp. 72-74.
70 In a letter to Bill Buckley, Rusher dated his disillusion with the GOP to September 1956, when the party leadership in New York unanimously nominated Jacob Javits for Senator, despite their alleged knowledge of his "undenied and unrepented associations with Communists." (October 10, 1960). The Rusher Papers.

ing given what would be accorded anyway: namely, a voice we may not even want, in a party it may prove desirable to oppose.[71]

As the Goldwater campaign became a rallying point for most of the American Right, it naturally also became a primary concern for *National Review*. Although Buckley himself for various reasons was barred from assuming the prolific role in the campaign that many had foreseen, several of the contributors to the magazine followed Rusher's example and became directly involved in it. Regardless of the final outcome, the Goldwater campaign created a tremendous boost for *National Review*, as for the right in general. The circulation of the magazine leapt in election-year of 1964 from 61,000 to 90,000 copies.[72] Just as the conservative movement itself did not share the fate of the unsuccessful Goldwater-candidacy, regardless of the numerous obituaries in its aftermath, the role of the magazine was not diminished either after the election. *National Review* would, for better or worse, continue to be the leading voice of American conservatism in the years to follow.

---

71 Letter, William A. Rusher to William F. Buckley, Jr., October 10, 1960. The Rusher Papers.
72 Jeffrey Hart, *The American Dissent*, p. 31.

Chapter 6

Third-Party Probings: The Case of the New York Conservative Party

> This country, in its majesty, is too great for any man, be he conservative or liberal, to stay home and not work just because he doesn't agree. Let's grow up, conservatives! If we want to take this party back, and I think we can some day, let's get to work!
>
> BARRY GOLDWATER,
> Speech at the Republican National Convention, 1960

Facing the Odds

BY 1960, MOST conservatives probably agreed with Goldwater's words at the Republican National Convention that the time had come for direct political action, but they did not necessarily agree on the road to dominion. Even if they felt like Goldwater that the GOP was their historic home, not everyone believed that "taking back" the GOP was possible, or even desirable in the foreseeable future. Some believed that conservatives would be in a better position by either attempting to create a bipartisan conservative coalition, or by creating an independent party. They also believed that either a bipartisan coalition or an independent party would be able to win support from a large group of voters who at the moment were beyond the reach of the Republican Party.

A bipartisan coalition would be fragile in the long run, and it would also be very difficult to get any high-ranking members of either party to risk their political life on such a venture. Regarding the third-party strategy, the American electoral system left it with very poor odds. Although third parties had been influential in several elections throughout American history, only one third party had ever won a presidential election: the Republican Party in 1860. History also suggested that it required a major crisis or an important issue, which the established parties had failed to address before any significant part of the electorate would support a third-party candidate. Conservatives hardly had such an issue in the early 1960s.

Even if one were willing to embark upon a third-party venture anyway, other questions would immediately occur. Should an independent Conservative Party be organized from the top down as a national party, or from the bottom up, as a coalition of state parties? The first possibility would require a leading figure of national standing to rally around. Candidates for such a task were indeed few, and in case one could be found in one of the major parties, would he be willing to risk his political career by running on a third-party platform? If yes, would one large-scale national campaign be enough to sow the seeds for future conservative campaigns? Would it be possible to create a national organizational network in the first attempt? If not, would failure in a national campaign then destroy the work of conservative organizations on the state and local levels? Could local conservative efforts, on the other hand, be sustained in the long run without a corresponding national effort?

Such troubling questions did far from discourage all conservatives from trying to organize independent parties. By 1960, a few efforts had already been made. Among them was an attempt in 1958-59 by Clarence Manion and others to run Hon. J. Bracken Lee as candidate for an independent Conservative Party in Utah named FOR AMERICA. Two years later, a more serious attempt was made in New York State. That effort is the main topic of this chapter.

The Founding of the New York Conservative Party

The case of the New York Conservative Party illustrates the kinds of problems conservatives got into when they openly challenged the liberal leadership of the Republican Party in New York. It also illustrates that the issue of whether conservatives should work inside or outside the GOP was not necessarily a question of either/or. Rather, the two strategies were complementary, with the immediate goal of establishing a symbiotic relationship between the independent Conservative Party and the GOP.

In 1962, a group of mostly young Republicans decided to challenge the liberal leadership of the state Republican Party. Their efforts resulted in the founding of the New York Conservative Party, which in many respects became a forerunner for the Draft Goldwater movement in that state.[1]

The organizers of the new party were headed by J. Daniel Mahoney, a New York City attorney, and his brother-in-law, Kieran O'Doherty. Neither were high profile figures in New York politics, but their project attracted the attention of several well-known and well-connected conservatives.

William F. Buckley, Jr. was actively involved in the organizing of the party from the very beginning. So were a number of his *National Review* colleagues, including William A. Rusher, William F. Rickenbacker, Suzanne LaFollette, and Frank S. Meyer, who wrote the Party's "Declaration of Principles." Other influential allies included former Governor of New Jersey Charles Edison, who served as a successful intermediary between the organizers and potential sponsors sympathetic to their cause. As for public relations and fundraising, the Conservative Party joined forces with the leading conservative expert in this field, Marvin Liebman.

As a pioneer in the use of direct mail, Liebman had become almost indispensable to the conservative movement.[2] Like so many other prominent figures on the American Right, he had taken the journey across the political spectrum from the Communist Party during the campaign for Henry Wallace in 1948 to the China Lobby and right wing politics in the 1950s. He had become executive secretary in The Committee of One Million Against the Recognition of Red China – a rightwing lobby dedicated to the prevention of the admittance of communist China to the United Nations.[3] Liebman had numerous other anti-Communist com-

---

[1] For a detailed account of the story of the New York Conservative Party by one of its principal founders, see J. Daniel Mahoney, *Actions Speak Louder* (New Rochelle: Arlington House, 1968).

[2] See Neal Blackwell Freeman, "The Marvin Liebman Story." *The New Guard*, May 1966, p.12, and Liebman's political memoirs *Coming Out Conservative; An Autobiography* (San Francisco: Chronicle Books, 1992).

[3] The organization was established in 1953 by Congressman Walter Judd (R-Minn.) and counted among its members prominent conservatives such as James Burnham, John Chamberlain, Whittaker Chambers, William Chamberlin, Ralph DeToledano, Senator Everett Dirksen, John Dos Passos, Max Eastman, William Loeb, Senator William Knowland and Barry Goldwater. They were joined by a smaller group of liberal anti-Communists including Sidney Hook and Jacob Javits. The committee founded and sponsored a couple of sub-organizations such as American Asian Educational Exchange, Inc., where Marvin Liebman served as executive vice-chairman.

mittees and right wing organizations as customers, and several of them were operated directly from his office in New York.[4]

The initial task of the New York Conservative Party was fairly straightforward: In order to run candidates in the 1962 election it would have to gather 12,000 signatures statewide, with at least 50 from each of the 62 counties in the state. Furthermore, in order to get permanently on the ballot, the Party's candidate for governor would have to get at least 50,000 votes in the election. Before the Party sent its nominating petitions into circulation, however, there were a number of tough questions that had to be answered: What exactly did the organizers hope to achieve by founding an independent party? Would a third party not simply split the conservative vote and help secure liberal victories?

Several conservative skeptics feared that this was the case and advocated a strong reform movement within the Republican Party instead. In accordance with what later became the general strategy of the "Draft Goldwater movement," the primary task for such a movement would be to erode the control of the regular organization through internal party reforms. In the particular case of New York, this effort would include direct election of district leaders, and the nomination of gubernatorial and senatorial candidates in state primaries, rather than in conventions.

A Party within a Party

In their response to critics, the organizers of the Conservative Party would first of all stress that they did not intend to create a third party in the traditional sense. They preferred to present it as an addition, rather than as an opposition to the Republican Party. When conservatives in New York chose to organize outside the GOP rather than inside in their attempts to gain influence, it was partly the result of the special electoral system in

---

4   These would include the American Jewish League Against Communism, Emergency Committee for Chinese Refugees, Committee for the Monroe Doctrine, National Committee Against the Treaty of Moscow, The Committee for Freedom for All Peoples, The Committee Against the Treaty of Moscow, American Afro-Asian Educational Exchange, Inc., American Committee for Aid to Katanga Freedom Fighters, Public Action, African-American Affairs Association, International Youth Crusade, Draft Goldwater, Miller for Vice President, Buckley for Mayor, American Conservative Union, and the New York Conservative Party.

that state. New York was one of only two states in America where Republican candidates were elected at closed conventions. Accordingly, the conservatives argued, it was very difficult, if not impossible, to shake the nomination of potential candidates out of the hands of the allegedly liberal leadership in control of the party, when such candidates could not be challenged directly in a primary.

Actually the people behind the Conservative Party were not the first ones who had come to such a conclusion. In 1957, a young Queens Republican, Eli N. Zrake, had made a serious attempt to gather influential conservatives in the state for the same purpose. Like his successors, Zrake had also been firmly convinced that Conservatives would have to organize outside the established party system if they wanted to gain influence within the state Republican Party. He had also seen the founding of a third party in New York as an important element in a national conservative effort based on subsidiaries and pressure groups in each individual state.[5] New York State with its 69 electoral votes was crucial in such an effort, given its status as the heart of liberal Republicanism. However, when Mr. Zrake suddenly died his plans were shelved.

Zrake's aspirations had later been taken a step further with the founding of the New York State Conservative Political association, which among its members counted people such as George E. Sokolsky, Edward V. Rickenbacker and William F. Buckley, Jr.[6] Among the potential party candidates considered at this early stage were Raymond Moley and Leo Wolman. However, it was not until J. Daniel Mahoney and Kieran O'Doherty came forward with their plans for a party that conservatives in New York took the plunge into electoral politics.

As mentioned, the idea behind the Conservative Party was not to create a fully independent third party, but rather a parallel organization to the state Republican Party. The Party would provide selective support of conservative or moderate candidates from any of the two major parties, though the Republicans, whether they liked it or not, were most likely to benefit from this. Only if none of the available candidates met the expectations of the Conservative Party would it run an independent candidate. Such an organization was, as Raymond Moley expressed it, intended to

---

5 Eli N. Zrake, "Program for Political Action in New York State," Speech, May 3, 1957. The William F. Buckley Papers.
6 The Buckley Papers.

"put fear of God, if they believe in God, in the people who are running the Republican Party in New York State."[7]

As for those who on principle opposed the idea of a third party, the proponents would remind them that in New York a Conservative Party would actually become a *fourth party*, due to the existence of the Liberal Party.[8] Once established, it could become to the Republican Party what the existing Liberal Party for years had been to the Democratic Party in New York State. Its purpose would be to provide a decisive "swing vote" that could move the political center of gravity to the right, just as the Liberal Party allegedly had been able to move it to the left in previous elections. As one example, the Conservative Party could have a decisive influence on the election of Republican candidates who were supposed to run against liberal Democratic incumbents in close districts. According to Eli Zrake, the cultivation of some fifty thousand supporters in a normal election year would be enough to "hold the balance of power in New York State that would offset the influence of both the ADA and liberal parties."[9]

"The Anti-Rocky Forces"

When the word came out in New York that a group of conservatives intended to challenge the state Republican Party, one local newspaper was quick to label them "the Anti-Rocky Forces," since it was assumed that their primary target was Nelson Rockefeller. Although such a statement neglected the larger political principles involved, it did rightfully stress that personalities also played a very important role in the venture. It was first of all the two leading Republican figures in the state that had incurred the wrath of the conservatives.

With one of the highest ADA approval ratings in Congress, Senator Jacob K. Javits did to most conservatives what a red rag does to a bull. Only Governor Nelson A. Rockefeller had managed to become even more

---

[7] Letter, Raymond Moley to William F. Buckley, Jr., February 19, 1957. The Buckley Papers.

[8] The President of the International Ladies' Garment Workers Union, David Dubinsky, had founded the Liberal Party in 1944.

[9] Eli N. Zrake, "Program for Political Action in New York State," Speech, May 3, 1957. The William F. Buckley Papers.

unpopular among them. To many conservatives, he alone was a perfect reason for an attempt to form an independent party. Rockefeller's political aspirations also provided a clear connection between the local efforts of right wing Republicans in New York and the national political goals of the conservative movement.

The Conservative Party had been born in the expectation of a Republican showdown prior to the presidential election of 1964, with Barry Goldwater as the most likely conservative candidate and Rockefeller as the most likely liberal contender. History had proven the position as governor in New York to be an excellent springboard for the presidency. In twenty-one national elections between the Civil War and 1948, as many as thirteen had candidates who were either governors, or former governors of New York.[10] In the early 1960s, the state was still both the most populous and the most powerful in the Union, as well as the home of most of the leading newspapers, broadcasting companies, foundations, corporations and other institutions usually associated with "the liberal establishment."

Knowing Rockefeller's political ambitions, which he so clearly had demonstrated in his attempt to win his Party's nomination in the 1960 presidential election, it was a natural assumption that he would give it another shot in '64. Rockefeller could really get his presidential bandwagon rolling if he could manage to win re-election as governor with a huge margin in 1962. The people behind the Conservative Party saw it as one of their most important objectives to prevent this from happening.

Why had Rockefeller become such a favorite hate-object of the Republican right? First of all, few within the Party were more closely identified with the notion of the Eastern liberal establishment. Conservatives saw him as the very embodiment of "me-too Republicanism" and liked to remind the voters that he had started his political career as a New Dealer, working for Harry Hopkins. Furthermore, few Republicans (outside the Party's right wing, at least) had so openly and so sharply criticized the policies of the Eisenhower administration.[11] Thus, while liberal Republicans pointed to Rockefeller as the future of the GOP – a dynamic

---

10 On the importance of New York in national elections, see Theodore White, *The Making of the President, 1960* (New York: Pocket Books, 1961), p. 181.
11 Oddly enough, it was first of all Rockefeller's alarmist calls for increased spending in national defense and his support for Senator John Kennedy's mistaken idea about the existence of a "missile gap" which infuriated conservatives.

leader who could lead America out of the complacency and stalemate of the Eisenhower years – most conservatives simply considered him a traitor to his party. Their aversion to Rockefeller culminated with the episode that has gone down in American political history as "the Compact of Fifth Avenue."[12]

"The Munich of the Republican Party"

When the Republicans gathered in Chicago for their National Convention in July of 1960, Richard Nixon already had a firm grip on the Party regulars. His nomination seemed fairly secure. Despite some conservative misgivings about the Vice President, the only potential threat to his nomination seemed to come from Governor Rockefeller, who several times had turned down Nixon's offer of a job as future Vice President.

When the 103-member platform committee had completed most of its work on the Republican convention in Chicago, Rockefeller made his move. He openly expressed his dissatisfaction with parts of the proposed platform in a form that could only be interpreted as a threat of open war on the convention floor, unless Nixon agreed to meet his demands on a number of issues. His primary concerns were in the fields of foreign policy and national defense, but he was also persistent on a number of domestic issues including social security for the aged and a more progressive and activist stand on civil rights.

The threat of havoc at the convention made Nixon agree to a private meeting in Rockefeller's Fifth Avenue apartment in New York. The terms under which it was supposed to take place appeared to be close to humiliating, but as Theodore White has pointed out, Nixon may actually have welcomed Rockefeller's arm-twisting. It did provide him with a good opportunity to distance himself from the Eisenhower era and present a new and more dynamic image, while giving Rockefeller most of the blame for his concessions to the liberals. In other words, the idea that he had been confronted with a *fait accompli* made it possible for him to move left, while still preserving his firm grip on the Party regulars.[13]

---

12 A detailed account of the event can be found in Theodore White, *The Making of the President 1960* (New York: Atheneum Publishers, 1961), pp. 180-208.
13 White, *The Making of the President 1960*, pp. 201-202.

When the meeting between the two was over, they had agreed to ignore the meticulous work of the platform committee on a number of vital issues, including civil rights, and take most of Rockefeller's proposed points to the convention in Chicago and incorporate them in the party platform.

To Republican conservatives, the whole affair was political blackmail of the worst sort. Even more than the actual changes in the platform caused by the "compact," it was the political principles involved and the arrogant procedure that infuriated them. This time the "secret kingmakers" had not even bothered being all that secretive about what they were doing. As Theodore White later put it:

> Never had the quadrennial liberal swoop on the regulars been more nakedly dramatized than by this open Compact of Fifth Avenue. Whatever honor they might have been able to carry from their services on the Platform Committee had been wiped out. A single night's meeting of two men in a millionaire's triplex apartment in Babylon-by-the-Hudson, 830 miles away, was about to overrule them; they were exposed as clowns for all the world to see. It was too much.[14]

Barry Goldwater denounced the agreement as the "Munich of the Republican Party," and changed his mind about withdrawing his name for consideration in advance. Instead he would withdraw his name on national TV. This would give him a chance to address conservatives across the nation and tell them to start organizing.

Along with the choice of Henry Cabot Lodge as nominee for Vice President, the agreement confirmed the suspicion of many conservatives regarding Richard Nixon's political integrity in general and his commitment to conservative principles in particular. The incident also provided Goldwater with an excellent opportunity to strengthen his profile as the country's leading conservative figure. Stephen Shadegg, one of the senator's speechwriters, later noted that "on that evening the drive to nominate Goldwater for the President of the United States began."[15]

After Richard Nixon's narrow defeat in November of 1960, Goldwater, like many other right-wing Republicans, held Rockefeller responsible (just

---

14 White, *The Making of the President 1960*, p. 199.
15 Stephen Shadegg, *What Happened to Goldwater?, The Inside Story of the 1964 Republican Campaign* (New York: Holt, Rinehart and Winston, 1965), p. 34.

as many conservatives would like to give him chief responsibility for Goldwater's defeat four years later). According to the Arizona senator, Nixon could have won the election by carrying some of the Southern states, had the party maintained the original platform on civil rights. In contrast to both the Democratic platform and Rockefeller's proposal, the original platform had carefully avoided any form of explicit support for sit-ins and other forms of civil disobedience, just as it had not contained any promises of federal intervention to prevent racial discrimination in employment.

Nixon could also have won, other conservatives would point out, had he carried New York State, as had the Republicans in all presidential elections since 1944. His devastating defeat in that state by 383,666 votes, was, in their opinion, mostly the result of Rockefeller's disloyal attacks on the Eisenhower administration, as well as his rather unenthusiastic campaigning for Nixon, the "Compact" notwithstanding.

In their analysis of the defeat, few bothered to mention the many conservative Republicans who had been less than lukewarm in their support of Nixon, especially after his agreement with Rockefeller. While many right-wing Republicans preferred to buy the idea that Rockefeller had twisted Nixon's arm, the agreement nevertheless also strengthened a widespread suspicion about the dubious nature of Nixon's commitment to the conservative cause. A few even welcomed a Republican defeat in the election, since it was likely to provoke an inevitable showdown between conservative and liberal forces within the Party: a struggle, which they hoped, would pave the way for a dedicated conservative candidate such as Barry Goldwater in the election of 1964.[16]

From Abstract Principles to Local Concerns

Most conservatives in New York, however, were not yet looking to 1964, but to 1962, when Rockefeller and Javits would be up for reelection. In order to prevent a predicted Rockefeller landslide, which would really get his presidential bandwagon rolling, the Conservative Party not only need-

---

16 Marvin Liebman Associates, Inc., Memorandum regarding the "organization of Americans for Conservative Action." Undated [1961]. The Marvin Liebman Papers, Hoover Institution.

ed to get on the ballot, but also to go beyond abstract political principles and present a clear-cut conservative alternative to Rockefeller's brand of Republicanism.

Unlike its Liberal counterpart, the Conservative Party could not count on a base of support from unions or other major organizations. Accordingly, the Party's campaign would mainly be aimed at the presumed conservative sentiments of the middle class, particularly in districts such as Staten Island, Queens, and homeowner neighborhoods such as Bay Ridge in Brooklyn. The Party's Political Action Manual informed its activists of the necessity to express in concrete form the Conservative Party's concern for "the hard working, self-supporting middle class which is the backbone of this country, but gets no shrift from the vote-buyers among our politicians who defer only to organized pressure groups."[17]

However, such voters were unlikely to mobilize, unless the party was able and willing to divert some of its attention to local issues. As the leader of Young Americans for Freedom David Franke pointed out, the apparent success of the conservative movement in New York, evidenced by rallies, picket lines and similar forms of political action, had first of all been created by YAF-students and other "movement" conservatives, who most often had no real stake in the local communities. Such success would not automatically result in electoral strength, unless conservatives were willing to "break out of their ideological shell and obtain a larger segment of support in their local communities."[18] Such a support would also require the recruitment of district captains from within the communities. Permanent local activities were not only necessary if the party was to maintain the interest of potential voters and not disappear in between elections, but also in order to stimulate the interest of volunteers and make local party organization prosper.

As for types of issues, the Action Manual of the Party recommended that conservatives be alert to areas which would "produce issues of a clear conservative-liberal nature," such as education, welfare, urban renewal, and juvenile delinquency.[19] The most important would include the passing of a "right to work" law for New York State, the return of political

---

17 Reprinted in Mahoney, *Actions Speak Louder*, p. 151.
18 David Franke, "Will Conservatives Ever Win in New York?" Memorandum. The William F. Buckley Papers.
19 Mahoney, *Actions Speak Louder*, p. 150.

power to local school boards (teacher pay, curriculum, required qualifications for teachers, etc.), opposition to extended rent control and an expanded ban on discrimination in private housing. Likewise, the manual advocated the adoption of a one-year minimum residence requirement for welfare payments (except for temporary emergencies). The party also addressed other social issues of the type, which some decades later would dominate the agenda of the New Right. It attacked AFDC, and argued that the state should have greater authority to remove children from welfare mothers who lived in "blatant immorality," just as it opposed the 1962 Supreme Court decision in *Engle v. Vitale*, which declared school prayer unconstitutional.[20]

Later, beginning in June of 1963, opposition to "busing" and other forms of affirmative action in the field of education also became key issues on the Party's political agenda. That month Commissioner of Education in New York State James Allen circulated a message calling for corrective action in order to remove the racial imbalance in the schools of the state. While declaring its strong opposition to affirmative action, especially if such action was to be based on a quota system, the Party carefully avoided any arguments that could be branded as racist. The Party's opposition to the proposed measures was limited to a rejection of quotas in education, as well as in housing and employment, based on the argument that such measures would only reinforce the existing patterns of discrimination.

As the 1962 election approached, the Conservative Party was ready for the first test of its electoral strength. Three months after the official opening of the party headquarters in April of 1962, there were some 112 local Conservative Party Clubs throughout the state.[21] Drawing upon the fundraising skills of Marvin Liebman, and a mailing list of some 50,000 potential conservative supporters, the Party had managed to raise $167,000 in contributions for the campaign.[22] Last but not least, all the formal requirements regarding petitions had been met at long last.

---

20 The party supported a proposal for an amendment to the federal Constitution, which would override the ban on school prayer.
21 Mahoney, *Actions Speak Louder*, p. 48.
22 Wesley McCune, "Activity of the American right wing, January 1962 to March 1963," Group Research, Inc., 1963, p. 9.

As expected, the Conservative Party did not even get close to having any of its candidates elected in the election, but its gubernatorial candidate David H. Jaquith did receive 141,877 votes – almost three times the 50,000 votes required to get an automatic place on the ballot for the next gubernatorial election. The Party's co-founder Kieran O'Doherty, who ran in the senatorial race, received 116,753 votes. Most of all, party officials delightedly pointed to the fact that outside of New York City the Party had outpolled the Liberal Party, just as they took part of the credit for the fact that a predicted Rockefeller landslide had not occurred.[23] Against an unknown Democratic contender, he had polled 55,000 fewer votes than in the election of 1958. This result, according to the conservatives, would weaken Rockefeller's status as prime contender to the position as presidential candidate of the GOP in 1964 – a status that to a large extent was based on the claim that he could deliver New York's 43 electoral votes to the party.

Regardless of how encouraging the leadership found the Party's first attempt at the polls, the election had also demonstrated how difficult it was to translate highly publicized rallies and related forms of political manifestations into actual votes. The Party's fairly limited appeal to the voters also highlighted another strategic dilemma. On the one hand, the Party had given high priority to becoming firmly rooted in the local communities across the state. Most of the local officials insisted that the Party could only grow and increase its support by engaging itself at the grassroots level in local politics and running candidates in local elections. On the other hand, there was the larger objective of getting a conservative candidate nominated for the coming presidential election.

As Frank Meyer pointed out, it could very well destroy the Party's image as a potential threat to the liberal wing of the Republican Party, if the conservative Party used a lot of energy on local elections in 1963 and nevertheless received negative results at the polls. In his view, the New York Conservative Party was more important on the state level and even the national level, as a conservative "force in being" than as a "force in action." Meyer was convinced that the Party's vote-getting potential would be

---

23 Rockefeller only won the election by 530,000 votes, which was far from an expected victory margin of approximately 800,000 votes. Rockefeller's vote was also substantially less than that given both Senator Javits and Attorney General Lefkowitz. ("Conservative Party Can Be Thorn to GOP Hopes in '66." Editorial, *Utica Press*, November 6, 1964.)

much greater in a major campaign, where it could present itself as part of a national conservative movement, than in a local election, and that the Party accordingly would be feared much more by its opponents.[24] Hence, positive action was only to be taken in 1963 when there was overwhelming evidence in favor of it.

Between a Rockefeller and a Hard Place

While the party leadership had deliberations about goals and strategies in the years to come, membership enrollment continued to grow steadily. In 1963, the NYCP had a membership of 10,329. One year later, when the Goldwater campaign was at its highest, membership had doubled to 21,590. Apparently, the interest in conservative mobilization did not decline after Goldwater's devastating defeat in the presidential election. On the contrary. By 1965, the Party had 30,936 members, and the following year, when William F. Buckley, Jr. was running as the Party's candidate for mayor of New York City, the enrollment reached 53,591.[25]

However, a growing membership would not automatically cause any profound change in the Party's chances of getting its candidates elected – nor would it necessarily bring the Party closer to its overall objective of pushing the Republican Party to the right. In order to do that, it would, for one thing, be necessary to solidify the bonds to the conservative forces within the Republican Party. The attempt to do so clearly revealed the pitfalls and problems related to the third party strategy.

In its approach to the Republicans, the Conservative Party attempted to strike a very delicate balance between appeals for cooperation in the best interest of a common cause, and thinly disguised threats of open confrontation. The appeal to conservative or moderate Republican candidates was mostly based on the argument that, as an independent party, the Conservative Party, both could deliver additional organizational support, and through its endorsement provide access to a segment of voters that was otherwise beyond the reach of the Republican Party. However, if Republican candidates or local organizations declined an endorsement, it

---

24 Letter, Frank S. Meyer to all local Party organizations, quoted from Mahoney, *Actions Speak Louder*, p. 180.
25 Mahoney, *Actions Speak Louder*, p. 135.

would automatically result in an opposing candidate. This could mean that a conservative independent candidate would run against a conservative Republican who was otherwise agreeable to the Conservative Party. Thus, as several critics of the third party effort pointed out, the strategy could eventually lead to the loss of conservative seats in Congress, due to a split in the vote.[26]

Despite such reservations, the New York Conservative Party ended up running 59 independent candidates, including former *Freeman* and *National Review* editor Suzanne LaFollette and the African-American journalist George S. Schuyler, who attempted to challenge Adam Clayton Powell in the Eighteenth Congressional District in New York City. Fifty-two of these candidates were running in districts where the Republicans had refused Conservative Party endorsement.

As one might expect, running this number of independent candidates was perceived as a hostile and provocative policy by many Republican Party officials in the state, but actually the Conservative Party also endorsed 59 Republican candidates (as well as one Democrat). Furthermore, all the independent candidates of the Conservative Party pledged their allegiance to the Republican Barry Goldwater in 1964, although that might also have been regarded as a provocation by the Republican leadership in the state.

The leaders of the NYCP were generally pleased when the results of the 1963 election became known. The Party's share of the vote in the different boroughs of New York City ranged between 5 and 14 percent, with the best result in Staten Island.[27] While the Party was still not even remotely close to a chance of having any of its candidates elected, the result was nevertheless seen as another important step into political maturity. The Party's position had been strengthened prior to the anticipated conservative-liberal showdown in 1964: the struggle to get Barry Goldwater nominated and elected.

From the very beginning of the Goldwater-campaign, the leaders of the Conservative Party were among the driving forces behind the campaign in New York. Yet, as Election Day came closer, it would prove very difficult for them to even get in on the action with an official endorsement.

---

26 See Douglas Caddy, "the Conservative Dilemma at the Polls," *The New Guard*, March 1962, p. 31.
27 The New York *Herald Tribune*, November 7, 1963. Quoted from Mahoney, *Actions Speak Louder*, p. 187.

Early in the campaign for the 1964 election, a list of the Conservative Party's candidates had been approved by the leading force behind the national Draft-Goldwater movement, F. Clifton White, in order to make sure that none of them would prevent Goldwater from accepting an endorsement from the Party.[28] However, White was not the only one the Party would have to ask. Whether or not it would be able to endorse and support Goldwater and vice-presidential candidate William E. Miller officially depended entirely on the goodwill of the Republican leadership.

The voters would have to vote for a slate of presidential electors, and the Republican State Committee would appoint these electors. The Conservative Party could not run an identical slate of electors without an agreement with this committee. An editorial in the New York *Daily News* estimated that a joint slate of Goldwater electors would attract anywhere from 140,000 to 200,000 extra votes for Goldwater, which could ultimately mean the difference between victory and defeat in the election.[29] Nevertheless, the Republican leadership in New York was hostile to the idea for several reasons.

True enough, an agreement on a joint slate had always existed between the Democratic Party and the Liberal Party – but though the Conservative Party liked to present itself as a counterpart to the Liberal Party, there were crucial differences. First of all, the Party had been founded with the explicit goal of defeating the existing leadership of the Republican Party in the state. Agreement on a joint slate could possibly be interpreted as a de facto Republican recognition of the Conservative Party and its objectives. The Republicans were also aware that the opportunity to put Goldwater and Miller on its slate was likely to create a tremendous boost for the New York Conservative Party, and rub off on its influence in state politics as well. Besides, the Republican leadership in New York was not, after all, particularly enthusiastic about the Goldwater candidacy in the first place.

Relations between the Republican leadership and the Conservative Party did not get any better when it became known in April of 1964 that about half a dozen of the Republican candidates running to represent New York State in Congress would accept conservative endorsements. As the Conservative Party had hoped, many newspapers saw this as the repu-

---

28 Mahoney, *Actions Speak Louder*, p. 238.
29 Editorial, *New York Daily News*, July 25, 1964.

diation of Rockefeller's leadership and presidential aspirations – a repudiation which had been one of the Party' key political goals. All in all, it did not come as a big surprise when the Republican leadership in New York flatly rejected the idea of a joint slate.

A letter from the Republican state chairman Fred Young to the members of the Republican state executive committee informed them that the Party would never make any political deals with what he considered "a political blackmail racket being operated by two self-serving opportunists as the spokesmen for hundreds of thousands of sincere, conservative Republicans whose political house is in the Republican Party."[30] This left the conservatives with the choice of either splitting the Goldwater vote by running an independent slate of electors for an independent candidate, or leaving the top line of its ticket blank.

The Conservative Party did make one last attempt, though, to make the Republican State committee change its mind about a joint slate. It moved closer to Fred Young's intemperate description of the Party as a "blackmail racket" by announcing that former Congresswoman Claire Boothe Luce would run as its candidate against the incumbent Senator Kenneth Keating in the upcoming election.

Not surprisingly, the challenge to Keating drew national attention to the conflict in New York. For several reasons many liberal Republicans considered the reelection of Keating of vital importance. Under the general assumption that Goldwater would lose the presidential election, the struggle for power within the Republican Party after Election Day had already set in. The fact that Keating was the only Republican candidate for the Senate who openly refused to support the Goldwater ticket gave him a special status. As one journal alleged, the New York Republican leaders probably felt that it would become easier for the Eastern wing to regain its former influence in the national Republican Party if,

> On the morning after Election Day, they can show the country a smashing Keating victory in New York – especially a victory over a member of the Kennedy clan – contrasting sharply with the defeat of Senator Goldwater, then they and other middle-of-the-road Republicans will be on the way toward regaining control of the party at the 1968 Convention.[31]

---

30 Mahoney, *Actions Speak Louder*, p. 232.
31 *U.S. News and World Report*, October 5, 1964.

In order to win, however, Senator Keating would supposedly need all the support he could get, considering that his Democratic opponent was none other than Attorney General Robert F. Kennedy. A conservative challenger such as Claire Boothe Luce was indeed likely to cause further trouble. Apart from being a prestigious figure on the Republican right, Luce was also the co-chairman of the national Citizens for Goldwater Committee. It was clear from the announcements about Luce's intention to run, though, that her candidacy would be withdrawn if the state leadership of the Republican Party changed its mind about a joint slate of electors for the presidential election. The prospect of Luce's candidacy even compelled Rockefeller to ask Goldwater to "use his influence with his followers" in the name of Republican unity.[32]

In the following week, while the possible Luce candidacy was attracting attention, several unsuccessful attempts, including a lawsuit, were made to make the state Republican leadership change its mind about a joint slate. However, when Luce announced on August 30 that she would withdraw her candidacy from the senatorial race, it was clear that the game was up. Running an opposing candidate was not a serious option, of course, for a party that was so strongly committed to the Goldwater campaign.

Republicans After All

At its state convention the Conservative Party adopted a platform which in essence was almost identical to the 1964 national Republican platform, and it also adopted a resolution endorsing the Goldwater-Miller ticket. However, as things were, the Party would have to leave the top line on its ticket blank, and hope that the voters, while voting for Goldwater on the Republican ticket, would nevertheless still vote for the Conservative Party's candidate for the Senate, and for its local candidates.

In his acceptance speech at the convention, Dr. Henry Paolucci, the replacement for Luce in the senatorial race, repeated the Party's claim that its views were in accord with the majority of Republicans in the country, while the leadership of the Republican Party in New York had been dislo-

---

32 Earl Mazo, "Goldwater Gets Rockefeller Plea," The New York *Times* (August 13, 1964), p. 1.

cated and were at odds with them. As one example, he mentioned that Jacob K. Javits and Kenneth B. Keating had been two of only five Republican senators voting for the bill expanding Social Security, while 28 Republicans had voted against it. Paolucci also reasserted the belief that the real home of Conservatism was in the Republican Party, and that the chosen third party strategy was only an intermediary solution dictated by the existing political order in New York:

> My purpose is to provide a voice for the Goldwater-Miller ticket. I am not a third party candidate, but a fourth party candidate. I stand for a return to the two-party system, but it must be a genuine two-party system.[33]

As in the rest of the country, the Republican Party in New York was hurt badly by Lyndon B. Johnson's national landslide victory on November 3. Robert F. Kennedy defeated Senator Keating, and the Party lost control of both houses of the state legislature, as well as of seven congressional seats. The state Republican leadership publicly put much of the blame for these defeats on the Goldwater movement and on the Conservative Party. In return, the latter was quick to cash in on the idea that Goldwater had been stabbed in the back by liberal forces spearheaded by the New York Republican leadership:

> Many factors influenced the outcome of the presidential contest. It is safe to say that no Republican could have won against Lyndon Johnson in 1964. But the size of the Goldwater defeat resulted largely from the deliberate sabotage done to his campaign by liberal members of his own party, ably led in their campaign of smear and harassment by New York's Nelson Rockefeller. ... Rockefeller was joined by key liberal Republicans in New York State, men like Javits, Keating, Lindsay and Halpern, in their efforts to discredit and undermine the Goldwater campaign. The performance of this cabal in 1964 proved, in spades, what most of us have known all along — that the New York Republican liberals will stop at nothing to prevent conservative leadership of the national Republican Party.[34]

---

33 Quoted in Mahoney, *Actions Speak Louder*, p. 247.
34 Fundraising letter for the New York Conservative Party (signed by William F. Rickenbacker, David H. Jaquith and Kieran O'Doherty), January 18, 1965. The Marvin Liebman Papers. Hoover Institution.

Apparently, a growing number agreed with this analysis. Contrary to what some observers predicted at the time, Goldwater's stunning defeat was not the last nail in the NYCP's coffin. As for the conservative movement in general, the Goldwater campaign had not only been a culmination, but also a new beginning. Rather than beaten and chastened, conservatives had been galvanized. The election had actually solidified the Conservative Party's position as a factor to be reckoned with in New York politics. The senatorial candidate, Dr. Henry Paolucci, had received 212,216 votes (as compared with the 141,877 votes received by David H. Jaquith in 1962), and some 31 members of the state legislature had accepted endorsement from the Conservative Party during the election. In the acknowledged citadel of liberalism, New York City, the conservative vote had more than doubled from 50,184 in 1962, to 119,971.[35]

This trend of solidification for the Conservative Party continued in the following years. It attracted a lot of publicity in 1965 when the party ran William F. Buckley, Jr. against the liberal Republican John Lindsay for mayor of New York City. Buckley received 341,226 votes, or some 15 percent of the total vote, in the election.[36] In the following years the Party's gubernatorial candidate, Dr. Paul L. Adams, placed it on "Row C," the third Place on the New York State Ballot, by outpolling his counterpart from the Liberal Party, Franklin D. Roosevelt, Jr.[37]

Finally, in the election of 1970, the Conservative Party won a seat in the U.S. Senate when William F. Buckley, Jr.'s brother James Buckley defeated GOP incumbent Charles Goodell.[38] Buckley actually validated the Conservative Party's longstanding claims that once elected, its candidates would be willing to work loyally within the Republican Party. He accepted several Republican committee assignments, and in 1974 he served as vice-chairman of the GOP Senate Reelection Committee. Six years later James Buckley was once again running for the U.S. Senate, but this time as the Republican nominee in the state of Connecticut. The fact that Buckley and a number of other former candidates of the Conservative Party would

---

35 Mahoney, *Actions Speak Louder*, p. 259.
36 Edward L. Schapsmeier & Frederick H. Schapsmeier, *Political Parties and Civic Action Groups* (Westport, Conn.: Greenwood Press, 1981), p. 121.
37 Schapsmeier, *Political Parties and Civic Action Groups*, p. 121.
38 In his campaign Buckley was endorsed by both President Nixon and Vice-president Agnew, most of all because Goodell had attacked the president's Vietnam policy.

later run as Republicans reaffirmed the original intentions behind the Party. It was not, after all, a serious attempt to create a new political home for conservatives as much as a strategically well-positioned weapon in the continuing struggle for the "soul" of the Republican Party.

Chapter 7

Preparing the Next Generation: Conservatism on Campus

The inroads that relativism has made on the American soul are not so easily evident. One must recently have lived on or close to a college campus to have a vivid intimation of what has happened. It is there that we see how a number of energetic social innovators, plugging their grand designs, succeeded over the years in capturing the liberal intellectual imagination. And since ideas rule the world, the ideologues, having won over the intellectual class, simply walked in and started to run things.

WILLIAM F. BUCKLEY, JR.[1]

Revolt on the Campus

IN THE EARLY 1960S, most conservatives still saw the nation's universities and colleges as impregnable citadels of liberalism, but the walls, many believed had started to shake. The conservative media triumphantly reported that a new generation of students was rejecting liberal dogmas, and journals and newspapers outside the movement began to write about an alleged "conservative revolt on campus." A growing interest in conservative spokesmen among American students did point in that direction. In 1962, the two most popular speakers at campuses across the country were Barry Goldwater and William F. Buckley, Jr. (followed by Martin Luther King.)[2]

---

1 William F. Buckley, Jr., "Publisher's Statement," *National Review*, Vol.1, No.1 (November 19, 1955), p. 5.
2 "College Students by Thousands Are Swept Up in Political and Social Movements," The New York *Times* (May 14, 1962), p. 32. During the decade, a number of universities became centers of conservative intellectual activity and thus particularly attractive to conservative students. Among them was University of Notre Dame, where scholars such as Stanley Parry, Gerhard Niemeyer, Stephen Kertesz (political science), Charles Rice, and Clarence Manion (law) were members of the faculty. In the South, University of Dallas became one of the new citadels of conservative thought, with scholars such as Willmoore Kendall and Frederick Wilhelmsen among the faculty.

To some extent this alleged conservative revival on the American campus reflected a general trend of students becoming more politically active. University life generally provides excellent conditions for political mobilization. However, students of the 1950s had not exactly distinguished themselves as an active force in the political life of the nation. Many progressives of the generation that vacated the campuses in the 1930s would lament that the students of the "silent generation" largely considered higher education a four-year moratorium from the real world. As the 1960-election gave promise of a generational shift in the political leadership of the country, and an end to the stalemate of the Eisenhower-era, all this was about to change.

The election of John F. Kennedy sparked a new interest in political activism among students both left and right. In time the two political wings came to share a profound distrust of American liberalism, albeit for very different reasons. Unlike Students for a Democratic Society (SDS) and other organizations on the left who presented a structural criticism of consensus liberalism, the conservative students did not dream of participatory democracy. They simply wished to replace the liberal establishment with a conservative one.

Just like older conservatives, the students expressed ambivalence about the current standing of their beliefs in society at large. In 1961, the conservative author M. Stanton Evans optimistically reported that a conservative tide was sweeping campuses all over America.[3] Yet, he also contended, though, that "the most depressing part of being a conservative student is the feeling, artfully enforced by the opposition, that one is so terribly alone."[4] Despite Evans' claim that the liberal opposition was somehow able to "enforce" such a feeling, the truth was rather that conservative students did remain a minority on campus, regardless of their newly acquired taste for direct political involvement.[5] The massive conservative student revolt that several authors prophesied, remained wishful thinking. Yet, a growing number of organizations now offered these conservative students a group identity.

---

3   M. Stanton Evans, *Revolt on the Campus* (Chicago: Henry Regnery Company, 1961).
4   Evans, *Revolt on the Campus*, p. 7.
5   To put things in perspective, the largest chapter of Young Americans for Freedom in 1962 was found at Yale University. It counted some 150-200 members in a student body of 8,000.

A Social Profile of the College Conservative

Who were the students who went against the grain and joined conservative organizations such as Young Americans for Freedom (YAF) and the Intercollegiate Society of Individualists (ISI)? How did their social background differ from that of their counterparts on the left? First of all, they generally seemed to defy the common stereotype of conservatives as children from well-to-do families. An informal survey conducted by M. Stanton Evans among 122 members of ISI indicated that more than half of the students came from families with annual incomes of $5,000 or less.[6] Another 32 percent listed their families in the $5,000-$10,000 income bracket.

These findings were generally affirmed by in a study by Richard G. Braungart, comparing the family status of YAF members with that of members of its left wing counterpart, Students for a Democratic Society (SDS).[7] Although Braungart's study did not find a strong correlation between social class and the political orientation of the students, there was nevertheless a notable difference in this respect between the two groups. While only 17 percent of the SDS members had a working class background, 39 percent of the YAF supporters had. Likewise, 55 percent from the SDS group came from upper middle class families, while only 28 percent from the YAF group did.[8]

Just as striking, however, were the class differences within YAF. Generally, the members who could be labeled as libertarians tended to come from more privileged backgrounds than did the traditionalists. They were also overwhelmingly protestants and much more likely to come from old-stock American families.[9]

Although ethnicity taken on its own did not appear to be a very important factor in the students' political orientation, Braungart's study nevertheless showed significant differences between the SDS students and the YAF students in this respect. While 63 percent from the former group came from families with "low-ethnic status" (mostly having their ethnic

---

6 Evans, *Revolt on the Campus*, p. 48.
7 Richard G. Braungart, "Family Status, Socialization, and Student Politics: A Multivariate Analysis," *American Journal of Sociology*, Volume 77, No.1, 1970, pp. 108-130.)
8 Calculated on the basis of figures from Table 3 in Braungart, "Familiy Status..." p. 119.
9 Rebecca E. Klatch, *A generation Divided, The New Left, The New Right, and the 1960s* (Berkeley: University of California Press, 1999), pp. 38-40.

background in Southern- or Eastern Europe), as much as 69 percent of the latter group came from families with "high-ethnic-status" (mostly English or northern-European background).[10] As for religion, the most notable difference between the two groups was the strong Jewish representation in SDS, 43 percent, compared to just 13 percent in the YAF group.[11] YAF seemingly had a particularly strong representation on Catholic universities such as Fordham and St. John's in New York, and Notre Dame in Indiana.[12]

The Intercollegiate Society of Individualists

One of the first attempts to create a link between the conservative intellectual community and students across the country had been the founding of the Intercollegiate Society of Individualists. As early as 1950, *Human Events* -editor Frank Chodorov had proposed the formation of an organization that could lead the way in a conservative student revolt against the liberal orthodoxy, which allegedly prevailed on American campuses. Although some found the idea of organizing individualists something of a paradox, Chodorov moved along and founded the organization in 1953.[13]

---

10 Braungart, "Familiy Status...," p. 118, table 4.
11 Braungart, "Familiy Status...," table 5.
12 The faculty at Notre Dame included leading conservative figures such as Gerhard Niemeyer, Clarence Manion, Charles Rice, and Stanley Parry.
13 A number of the organizations supporters, including William F. Buckley, Jr., later suggested that the name of the organization should be changed to Intercollegiate Society of Conservatives, in order to link the organization closer to the rest of the conservative movement. Frank Chodorov, however, opposed the change on the grounds that while individualism was a philosophical term, which was not easily corrupted, Conservatism, on the other hand, was a political creed that was always "in danger of being perverted by political considerations." According to Chodorov, local ISI clubs around the country should feel free to change their names from "individualist" to "conservative," considering that many of them became directly involved in political activities that would inevitably expose them to the ideological corruption that comes from the attempt to adopt the doctrine of limited government and the theory of the free market to the public school system, old age pensions, the use of foreign aid in the fight against communism abroad, and other areas of public policy where most conservatives were generally ready to dispense with the principle of laissez-faire. The parent society, however, ought to remain "untainted by political ideas" and keep the word "individualism" in its name. (Letter, Frank Chodorov to William H. Brady. Jr., January 14, 1961, The William F. Buckley Papers.

A man in his sixties, Chodorov was a bit old for a student leader, so William F. Buckley, Jr. became the organization's first president. After a brief time, however, Chodorov wrote him: "Am removing you as president. Making myself pres. Easier to raise money if a Jew is president. You can be V-P. Love. Frank."[14]

Although ISI's Board of Advisors included a variety of prominent conservatives, the organization was largely run by Leonard Read's Foundation for Economic Education, which had also bought *Human Events*.[15] It started out as a mailing-list operation whose primary task was to distribute FEE's pamphlets and *Essays in Brief* to students. However, several other activities were soon added, and the organization eventually left the headquarters of the Foundation for Economic Education in Irvington-on-Hudson, New York, and set up its own in Philadelphia and Indianapolis.

ISI now arranged seminars for conservative students around the country, and helped them establish their own libraries on campus.[16] It also played an important part in the founding of the Philadelphia Society, a youth version of the Mont Pelerin Society.[17] The major purpose of the organization was not to organize direct political action, but to inform, help and inspire right wing students to organize.[18] By 1961, it had some thirteen thousand members performing this task among the students on 54 campuses. In the meantime, other conservative student organizations had

---

14 Quoted from William F. Buckley, Jr., *The Jewelers Eye* (New York: G.P. Putnam's Sons, 1968), p. 347 ff.
15 It included activists and sponsors such as Dean Clarence Manion of Notre Dame, Professor E. Merrill Root, and textile magnate Roger Milliken (who would all later become associated with the John Birch Society). Another generous contributor to the funding of the American Right, John G. Pew, Jr. of Sun Oil would later become Vice President of ISI. Other prominent conservatives who became associated with ISI included Henry Regnery, F.A. Hayek, Richard Weaver, Russell Kirk, Frank Meyer, William Rusher of *National Review*, and M. Stanton Evans, who became the organization's Midwest Director.
16 The books distributed by ISI included Richard Weaver's *Ideas Have Consequences*, Russell Kirk's *The Conservative Mind*, F.A. Hayek's *The Road to Serfdom*, and William F. Buckley, Jr. and L. Brent Bozell's *McCarthy and His Enemies*.
17 The Philadelphia Society had the future director of the Hoover Institution W. Glenn Campbell as its first president, while Frank S. Meyer and Eliseo Vivas of *National Review* held the positions as vice presidents.
18 To disseminate information about conservative activities and publications in other campuses, the organization initiated two new publications in 1962; *Under Thirty*, which published selected articles from other conservative campus magazines, and *Campus Report*, which reported on conservative activities on campuses across the country.

become more directly involved in political action. The most important of these was Young Americans for Freedom (YAF), founded in 1960.[19]

The Founding of Young Americans for Freedom

The origins of YAF could be traced back to 1958, when David Franke and Douglas Caddy, both students in Washington, D.C., founded an organization called the Student Committee for the Loyalty Oath.[20] The purpose was to rally support for the strongly contested provision under the National Defense Education Act which required students who received loans and NDEA fellowships to sign an affidavit stating that they did not belong to any organization considered subversive by the United States government.[21]

Both Caddy and Franke were also involved in other conservative activities. Caddy was head of the College Young Republicans in Washington D.C., Franke was the editor of ISI's *The Individualist*, as well as the College Young Republicans' newsletter *The Campus Republican*. Both of them had also worked for *Human Events*.

In June 1960 they represented Youth for Goldwater for Vice President – a group within the Young Republican National Federation – at the Republican convention in Chicago. This brought them into contact with William F. Buckley, Jr. and his friend, the public relations expert Marvin Liebman, who were impressed by their enthusiasm and decided to take them under their wings. They were offered jobs and assistance to organize a national conservative youth organization.

Franke was given an internship at *National Review*, and Caddy went to work for Marvin Liebman. His first assignment was to organize the found-

---

19 For an elaborate history of YAF, see John Andrew III, *The Other Side of the Sixties; Young Americans for Freedom And the Rise of Conservative Politics* (New Brunswick: Rutgers University Press, 1997), and Gregory L. Schneider, *Cadres for Conservatism: Young Americans for Freedom and the Rise of the Contemporary Right* (New York: New York University Press, 1999).

20 Lee Edwards & Anne Edwards, *You Can Make the Difference* (New Rochelle, N.Y.: Arlington House, 1968), p. 287.

21 Later, support for such policies would also become a major rallying point for YAF, who in 1961 arranged a pro-HUAC demonstration with picket lines demanding continuous support of HUAC, increased surveillance of the Communist Party, and legislation denying passports to Communists (Editorial, *The New Guard*, July 1961, p. 4).

ing meeting of Young Americans for Freedom. An interim committee forwarded invitations to 120 young conservatives around the country, and 80 of them turned up in September at the Buckley family's estate in Sharon, Connecticut.

At the founding meeting in Sharon it was decided to appoint a Board of Directors numbering twenty-one members. Each director was to hold office for two years. The general Board of Directors then appointed a National Chairman, a National Director, an Organizational Director, a Treasurer and a Secretary. Robert Schuchman occupied the position as National Chairman. Douglas Caddy became the organization's first National Director. YAF was also given a National Advisory Board, which read like a "who's who" of the conservative movement. It included twenty-eight members of Congress, among them the leading conservative voices on Capitol Hill: Senators Barry Goldwater, Strom Thurmond and John G. Tower, and Representatives John M. Ashbrook, John H. Rousselot, and Donald C. Bruce.[22]

If the widely publicized "generational gap" did exist in the 1960s, it seemingly did not relate to young conservatives and their parents. They generally shared the same political views. Actually, the political identification of the parents seemed to be the single most important factor affecting the political orientation of the conservative students.[23] This was well illustrated by the number of YAFers who were children of prominent right-wingers. Among them were Suzanne and Alfred Regnery, children of publisher Henry Regnery, Lee Edwards, son of Willard Edwards of the *Chicago Tribune*, Carl McIntire, Jr., son of the notorious founder of Twentieth Century Reformation and the American Council of Christian Churches, Marilyn Manion, daughter of Dean Clarence Manion, Allan Ryskind, son of Morrie Ryskind, and John C. Meyer, son of Frank Meyer.

---

22 Other board members were William F. Buckley, L. Brent Bozell, John Chamberlain Jr, Frank Chodorov, Ralph DeToledano, John Dos Passos, Devin A. Garrity, Henry Hazlitt, Russell Kirk, Alfred Kohlberg, Marvin Liebman, M. Stanton Evans, Willmoore Kendall, William Loeb, Carl T. McIntire, J. Daniel Mahoney, Frank Meyer, Ludwig Von Mises, Thomas Molnar, Gerhart Niemeyer, Archibald B. Roosevelt, William A. Rusher, Richard M. Weaver, John Wayne, and Ronald Reagan.

23 Richard G. Braungart, "Family Status, Socialization, and Student Politics: A Multivariate Analysis," *American Journal of Sociology*, Volume 77, No.1, 1970, pp. 108-130.). Braungart's findings were also supported by M. Stanton Evans' survey of ISI students, where 81 of 121 respondents listed their parents as conservatives, and 76 of them listed both their parents as Republicans. (Evans, *Revolt on the Campus*, p. 49).

The Sharon Statement

YAF was not intended as a rival to the Intercollegiate Society of individualists (ISI). Its purpose was rather complementary. While ISI's stated goal was a conservative intellectual awakening on the campus, YAF was almost solely designated for political action by implementing and coordinating the activities of conservative youth groups. But before the students could get to work, it was essential to spell out an ideological framework for their activities. Thus, the participants at the founding meeting adopted a declaration of principles. It had largely been drafted by the young editor of the *Indianapolis News*, M. Stanton Evans, and would later be referred to simply as "the Sharon Statement." Since it has been praised as one of the most coherent expressions of modern American conservatism, it deserves some attention.

For the traditionalists reading the Sharon Statement, it stressed the necessity to affirm "eternal truths" and "transcendent values" in a time of "moral and political crisis."[24] The foremost such value was "the individual's use of his God-given free will, whence derives his right to be free from the restrictions of arbitrary force." God was explicitly mentioned after careful deliberation, in an unsuccessful attempt to discourage Randian "objectivists" and other radical libertarians from becoming too interested in the organization.

As Rebecca E. Klatch has pointed out, there were some striking similarities between the Sharon Statement and the Port Huron Statement issued two years later by YAF's ideological counterpart, Students for a Democratic Society. Both opposed the existing order of "corporate liberalism" and expressed a populist faith in participatory democracy and libertarian ideas about decentralization and local control.[25] However, unlike the Port Huron Statement, the Sharon Statement was also implicitly aiming at the Constitutional debate on "states rights," which had been triggered by the civil rights movement. The statement confirmed the primacy of "the several states, or to the people, in those spheres not specifically delegated to the Federal Government."[26]

---

24 The Sharon Statement is reprinted in most of the publications issued by YAF. It is quoted here from Suzanne Scholte (ed.), "High School Organization Manual," Young Americans For Freedom, Inc, Sterling, Virginia, (no date).
25 Rebecca E. Klatch, *A generation Divided*, pp. 30-36.
26 Scholte, "High School Organization Manual."

Regarding economic policy, the statement repeated the libertarian notion that there was no halfway house between laissez-faire capitalism and "collectivism:"

> When government interferes with the work of the market economy, it tends to reduce the moral and physical strength of the nation; that when it takes from one man to bestow on another, it diminishes the incentive of the first, the integrity of the second, and the moral autonomy of both.[27]

As for anti communism, the third leg of postwar conservatism, the Sharon Statement singled out international Communism as the greatest single threat to the rights of American citizens and the national sovereignty of their country. The United States, it contended, should "stress victory over, rather than co-existence with, this menace."[28] Thus, like most of the conservative movement, YAF apparently did not see any contradiction between the wish for a minimal state and the requirements of victory in the Cold War. But below the glossy surface of the Sharon statement, the unresolved tensions between such irreconcilable priorities would continue to cause trouble.[29]

After the meeting in Sharon, William F. Buckley, Jr. told the readers of *National Review* how impressed he had been by the energy and enthusiasm of the participants:

> What is so striking in the students who met at Sharon is their appetite for power. Ten years ago, the struggle seemed so long, so endless, even, that we did not dream of victory. ... the difference in psychological attitude is tremendous.[30]

Most of the practical work involved in running YAF was initially left to Marvin Liebman. Buckley's own role in the organization would remain

---

27 Scholte, "High School Organization Manual."
28 Scholte, "High School Organization Manual."
29 As an indication of the primary importance of anti communism to the YAF venture, it is worth noting that the word "conservative" was deliberately left out of the name of the organization. According to Lee Edwards, who took part in the founding meeting in Sharon and served on the first board of directors, the word was omitted out of fear that it would scare liberal anti-Communists and libertarians away from the organization. Despite the attempted "fusionism," anti-communism remained the crucial component in the credo of the American Right.
30 *National Review*, September 24, 1960.

largely inspirational, but several of the other *National Review*-editors and the journal's publisher William A. Rusher became more directly involved, and they were determined to maintain a certain level of authority in the hands of "grown-up conservatives." They did realize, though, how important it was that YAF appeared as a genuine youth organization run and controlled by young people (or at least relatively young, the maximum age of members was 39). When one of the organization's major sponsors Howard Pew – a man who liked to be in control of the ventures he supported – wanted to extend his influence over YAF through a suggested senior advisory council, Buckley warned that it would make YAF look "like the front operation of the senile class."[31]

Finding a Place in the Movement

From the outset YAF had strong ties not only to the *National Review*-crowd, but also to other parts of the movement. It cooperated with several foundations in the effort to educate a new breed of leaders, and in association with *Human Events*, it sponsored political action conferences twice yearly in Washington, D.C. Here, hundreds of young conservatives would meet to discuss organizational strategies. Likewise, YAF arranged a series of summer schools in cooperation with the Tuller Foundation for the Advancement of Economic Understanding, and in 1962 Leonard Read's Foundation for Economic Education at Irvington-on-Hudson, N.Y. formalized a summer program for students known as "The FEE School of Political Economy." YAFers also flocked to Washington to attend the annual School of Anti-Communism, sponsored by Fred C. Schwarz's Christian Anti-Communism Crusade.[32]

In addition to the conferences and summer camps, YAF also set up a national speakers bureau, a film service, a special hotline service advising local chapters on demonstrations, pickets, etc., a book service, and a campaign materials service, providing bumper stickers, badges and the like. It also offered a Washington employment service, which it hoped would in time expand into a national young conservative job service – an idea that

---

31 Letter, William F. Buckley, Jr. to Barry Goldwater, July 12, 1962. The Buckley Papers.
32 "YAF Roundup: Anti-Communist School," *The New Guard*, July 1964, p. 18.

in the 1980s would be adopted by the Heritage Foundation and other conservative think-tanks.³³

In March of 1961, the first issue of YAF's own monthly journal *The New Guard* was published. The editorial contended that "Ten years ago this magazine would not have been possible. Twenty years ago it would not have been dreamed of. Thirty five years ago it would not have been necessary."³⁴ Apart from articles on both domestic and foreign policy issues, *The New Guard* also served the purpose of reporting on YAF- and other right-wing activities from around the country. Later YAF complemented its journal with two other monthly publications: the *Washington Report*, which provided conservative views on Congressional matters, and (from 1964) the newsletter *Report on the Left*. Other newsletters published by YAF-chapters around the country had names such as *Freedom Writers* (Maine), *The Challenger* (Georgia), *The New Nationalist*, Buffalo, N.Y., *The Patriot* (Boston University), and *The Liberty Bell* (Richmond County).³⁵

One of the first events, which attracted the attention of the national media to YAF, was its first rally in March 1961. Some 3,000 young conservatives gathered in the Manhattan Center in New York. At least as many had turned up, but could not get in. The featured speaker of the evening was Barry Goldwater, and awards were given to institutions or persons who in the view of the organization had made "contributions to American conservatism and the youth of the nation."³⁶ Among the recipients were William F. Buckley, Jr., Russell Kirk, George Sokolsky, and HUAC. The turnout for the rally made the New York *Times* write the following day that "something is afoot which could drastically alter our course as a nation."³⁷

The media were even more amazed the following March, when this relatively obscure conservative youth organization gathered some 18,000

---

33 See Niels Bjerre-Poulsen, "The Heritage Foundation: A Second-Generation Think Tank," *Journal of Policy History*, Vol. 3 (No. 2, 1991), p. 163 ff.
34 *The New Guard*, Vol. I, No. I, March, 1961, p. 3
35 The YAF-publications added themselves to a growing list of conservative campus journals from around the country. This list also included journals such as *Insight and Outlook* published at University of Wisconsin, *The New individualist Review*, published by ISI at the University of Chicago, *Analysis* (University of Pennsylvania), *The Liberator* (University of Tulane), *The Campus Conservative* (Jackson, Mississippi and University of Miami, *Foundation* (Columbia University), *The Southern Conservative*, and *Man and State* (California Universities), and *The Conservative Review* (New York City College).
36 M. Stanton Evans, *Revolt on the Campus*, p. 121.
37 *New York Times*, March 4, 1961, p. 1.

people in Madison Square Garden. However, the high turnout was not, as some claimed, a sign that a genuine conservative tide was about to sweep the country. Although YAF did have about twice as many active members as SDS, the rallies in New York gave a bloated image of the organization's actual strength.[38] They were skillfully manufactured political events intended to create the appearance of a rising conservative tide. Marvin Liebman, from whom the organizers learned the strategy, would later recall how he himself had learned about the importance of perception while organizing the Committee of One Million:

> I had learned a political rule of thumb: perception is more important than reality. The perception that we were a powerful lobbying group speaking for one million Americans was far more important than the reality. What it came down to was one individual – me – with a circle of influential allies who could get all these VIPs to sign the public statements we wrote on behalf of the "millions," thus creating the illusion of an enormous people's movement. It was a technique I first learned from Marxist propagandists. And it worked.[39]

William Rusher, for one, did indeed believe that there was a real growth in the support for the Right, and a growing urge among many conservatives to become actively involved in the political fray. However, privately he too conceded that part of the success was made by mirrors, and that the real strength remained far from the picture painted from the media: "I know the YAF story from the inside," he wrote L. Brent Bozell, "and it is considerably less impressive than the public facade Marvin has so ably created."[40]

Apart from speeches by Barry Goldwater, John Tower, and other leading conservatives, a central element in the spectacular New York events was an award ceremony, where the organization paid tribute to its heroes

---

[38] Marvin Liebman would later claim that also the membership of YAF was highly inflated. The actual number, according to him, was probably closer to 5,000 members than to the stated 25,000 (interview with Marvin Liebman in Gregory L. Schneider, *Cadres for Conservatism*)

[39] Marvin Liebman, *Coming out Conservative* (San Francisco: Chronicle Books, 1992), p. 111.

[40] Letter, William Rusher to L. Brent Bozell, September 28, 1961. William A. Rusher Papers.

and mentors of the older generation. In 1962, awards were to be given to former President Herbert Hoover, Richard Weaver, Senator Strom Thurmond of South Carolina, John Dos Passos, Ludwig Von Mises, M. Stanton Evans, John Wayne, and Roger Milliken – one of the right wing's most generous sponsors. However, YAF had also decided to give a medal to a more notorious right wing celebrity, General Edwin A. Walker.

For a movement craving for respectability, the general was definitely made of the wrong stuff. Walker had become a martyr to many on the far Right, when the U.S. Army in 1961 removed him from his post as commander of the twenty-fourth Infantry Division in Germany for spreading right wing propaganda to his troops. (see chapter 8). Now he was associated with organizations such as the John Birch Society and Christian Crusade, and toured the country with warnings that the United Nations and the United States Department of Defense were working for the communist conspiracy.

General Walker's presence made both Thomas J. Dodd and Herbert Hoover decline the invitation to attend the rally. Hoover, for his part, had been advised by his political consultants to avoid any connection with the general.[41] The situation became even worse when Barry Goldwater and John Tower also refused to appear if General Walker was present. In response, YAF issued an official statement claiming that the general was too busy to attend the rally. But Walker insisted that it was no trouble at all, and YAF finally had to go through the embarrassment of withdrawing both the award and the invitation. The fact that he had been nominated in the first place demonstrated that the far right and particularly the John Birch Society at that time had considerable influence within the organization.

YAF and the Civil Rights Struggle

The organizers of the rally in New York were presumably happy about their decision to withdraw their award to General Walker, when later that same year he led a violent white mob in Oxford, Mississippi. Here it waged war against 400 marshals and 300 soldiers in order to prevent the enroll-

---

41 Letter Charles B. Coates to Miss Bernice Miller (Hoover's secretary), January 5, 1962. The Herbert Hoover Papers, Box 396.

ment of the black student James Meredith at the University of Mississippi. Like most of the conservative movement, YAF attempted to walk a fine line in its opposition to civil rights. It would avoid overt racism and instead clothe its position in constitutional and anti-statist arguments. But how could the defense of institutionalized racial discrimination under the banners of "states rights" be reconciled with declared emphasis on the primacy of individual freedom – in this case the individual freedom of African-Americans? The answer is that it couldn't.

The events that followed James Meredith's attempted enrollment at the University of Mississippi in 1962 provided an illuminating example of YAF's unsuccessful attempts to square the circle. In *The New Guard* editor Lee Edwards wrote about Meredith:

> As conservatives we understand and support the theory of states' rights but as conservatives concerned about freedom and respectful order, we cannot endorse lawlessness, insurrection or racism. If Meredith is a "tool" of the NAACP he is a charlatan of the worst stripe. But if he is a young man with a family interested in the best education, we wish him well as he pursues his course of studies.[42]

The argument was indeed strange. Apparently it was Meredith's personal motives and not the legal and moral principles involved which would dictate whether Edwards was for or against his enrollment at University of Mississippi – whether he was for or against racial segregation.

YAF took a more official stand on civil rights at its second national Convention in 1963. One of the adopted resolutions stated that the organization opposed civil rights legislation which would "interfere with an individual's liberties in order to favor any race, class or group of individuals."[43] The ambivalence of the statement was emblematic of the attempt by the "respectable" right to have it both ways. After all, ending the interference with an individual's liberties on the basis of race was what the civil rights movement was all about.

---

42 Lee Edwards, "Meredith at Mississippi," *The New Guard* (November 1962), p. 4.
43 "YAF's 2nd National Convention; Bob Bauman Re-elected National Chairman," *The New Guard* (November-December, 1963), p. 16.

Battling the NSA

In the following years, YAF engaged itself in many of the issues that also concerned the rest of the conservative movement: opposition to the Test Ban Treaty, the wish for restraints on labor unions through right-to-work laws, cuts in federal spending, and welfare reform. The organization adopted Marvin Liebman's tactics of setting up "front groups" working on single issues. Among them were the Student Committee for a Free Cuba and the National Student Committee for Effective Social Welfare, whose goal it was to counter the ideas of a domestic Peace Corps, the National Service Corps. However, the primary concern of the organization was quite naturally student politics. It lamented the alleged exclusion of conservative ideas on campus, just as it eagerly defended the principle of *in loco parentis*. Like the Marxists, YAF believed that the university had a responsibility for the moral education of its students – an education that would reflect the values of the cultural mainstream which they, regardless of their outsider status on campus, claimed to represent.

A primary target of YAF activities on the campus was the allegedly liberal National Student Association. The goal was to make students all over the country vote against affiliation with NSA. In September 1960, Howard Phillips, then President of the Student Council at Harvard University, claimed that NSA had "abused the rights of individual students, diminished the strength of our country, and weakened our position in the eyes of students from other nations."[44] In consequence he announced the formation of the Committee for A Responsible National Student Organization (CRNSO). At the first national YAF convention in held in New York City in September 1962, the delegates passed a resolution urging conservative students to work within as well as against the National Student Association in order to strengthen the conservative position within the student community.[45] Two years later YAF adopted a ten-point program for 1965, which among its declared goals had a decrease in the representation of NSA from 15 percent of the nation's colleges to only 10 percent.[46]

---

44 Quoted from Tom Huston, "The Rise and Fall of NSA" in *the New Guard* (April 1964), p. 8.
45 Gary Russell, "YAF Charts Far-Ranging Program for Victory," *The New Guard*, November 1962, pp. 8-9.
46 *The New Guard*, January 1965, p. 25.

YAF often found a particularly responsive audience for such views in the system of fraternities and sororities across the country. Accordingly, many YAF-chapters made the preservation of this system amid attacks from the NSA and other liberal organizations a major concern in student politics. When YAF organized a national "STOP NSA" committee, it advised its members to expose the "anti-Greek nature of the Association" in order to enlist local Greek chapters in the fight against NSA.[47]

Endless Struggles

YAF was ambitious, well connected and well financed, but its performance was nevertheless far from optimal. Almost from the beginning, the organization was weakened by factional strife, attempted hostile takeovers, and purges. There were several reasons for this. The fusionist credo expressed in the Sharon Statement did not provide useful ideological guidelines, and the organizational structure was very vulnerable. From the outset, it was very difficult for the national board to exert influence on the membership and activities of the local chapters.

Another part of the explanation might have been the very fact that YAF was an organization run by young people in pursuit of a career in politics. Some of them were no doubt easily tempted by the opportunities offered by the various forces struggling for the control of the organization.

One cause for controversy was the issue of how closely YAF should be connected to the Republican Party and the Young Republican National Federation. Even more controversial, however, was the issue of how closely it should be connected to the *National Review*-crowd. This issue resulted in the organization's first major crisis in the summer of 1961. By that time three major factions had evolved in YAF: the *National Review*-crowd, the John Birch Society-crowd, and the Rockefeller-crowd.[48] In their efforts to

---

47 Tom Huston, "You, Too, can STOP NSA!" *The New Guard* (September 1964), p. 12.
48 In his attempts to move in a favorable position for the 1964 nomination as the Republican Party's presidential candidate, Rockefeller had courted a number of leading YAF-members, including Douglas Caddy, and convinced them that he was a genuine conservative. Rockefeller also had another axe to grind. Buckley and several other people from the *National Review* crowd had been involved in the organizing of the New York Conservative Party, which was also strongly supported by YAF. One result of Rockefeller's foothold within the organization was that Douglas Caddy went against the National Policy Committee of YAF and openly attacked the New York Conservative Party (Letter to the editor, the *Wall Street Journal*, March 9, 1962).

sever YAF's strong ties to Buckley and his associates, the latter two formed a strange alliance.

The first signs of an attempted takeover appeared when Douglas Caddy, Scott Stanley (the leading bircher in YAF), and a number of other board-members wanted to end the association with Marvin Liebman, who had so far handled fundraising, public relations, administration, and other practical matters involved in the organizing of YAF.[49] Soon charges were flying back and forth between the board members. Caddy and Stanley went as far as to suggest conservative sponsors to withhold financial support to YAF until Liebman had been removed.

The conflict was not old before William Rusher intervened. He was convinced that the attack on Liebman was the first step in an attempt to wrestle control of the organization away from the *National Review*-crowd, and he was not willing to let that happen.[50] YAF was intended as a youth organization in the sense that it would be run by and for young people, but Rusher wanted *National Review* to remain in charge of the larger ideological outlines. A memo sent from William A. Rusher to Buckley, Liebman and Meyer in September of 1961, provides a revealing insight into their perception of the YAF venture:

> We took this lusty infant into Marvin's office and proceeded to treat it as another Committee of One Million, only this time with teenagers on its letterhead. We even spoiled the teen-agers outrageously, giving them offices, secretaries, credit cards and expense accounts that would have been entirely appropriate to (say) the activities of the McGraw-Edison Committee on Public Affairs, but which were wildly beyond the experience of the young people in YAF.[51]

The crisis had demonstrated just how difficult it was to recruit young leaders who were both ambitious and controllable. Yet Rusher reminded Buckley that it was imperative for *National Review* to "find or found" or-

---

49 For further details on the entire episode, see John A. Andrew III, *The Other Side of the Sixties*, pp. 116-120.
50 Memo, William A. Rusher to William F. Buckley, Jr., March 12, 1962. William A. Rusher Papers.
51 Memo from William Rusher to William F. Buckley, Jr., Marvin Liebman and Frank Meyer, September 5, 1961. William Rusher Papers.

ganizations such as YAF in order to avoid the risk of seeing them "develop <u>without</u> our guidance or blessing."[52]

Rusher, Buckley and their associates won the first round of the battle, among other things, by flying in members from all over the country to a board meeting, and by expanding the number of board members from 21 to 27 in order to strengthen their majority. Rusher did not succeed, though, in his attempt to persuade two-thirds of the board to expel the leading rebels, and he was aware that more trouble was likely to follow.[53] He expressed his concern in a memo to Buckley:

> I am now inclined to think that there are going to be conservative mass organizations whether Kennedy (or Buckley!) wants them or not. But there is plenty to be gloomy about, if we cannot develop a better relationship to the action organizations of the Right than we are managing to maintain in the case of YAF.[54]

As a result of this first crisis in YAF, the organizational structure was streamlined, and in order to avoid the takeover of local chapters by birchers and other undesired elements, the national director was given the authority to revoke the membership of both individuals and local chapters. Upon Marvin Liebman's suggestion, YAF hired a full-time executive in August 1961 to take care of fundraising and other practical matters.[55] His name was Richard Viguerie, he had worked for John Tower in the election of 1960, and he could be expected to remain loyal to the *National Review*-crowd. In order to recruit new members for YAF, Viguerie and Liebman used *National Review*'s list of subscribers, as well as a couple of other mailing lists, to make a successful venture into direct mail.[56] It was in these years, while working for Liebman and YAF, that Richard Viguerie acquired many of the fundraising skills that in the late 1970s would make

---

52 Memo from William Rusher to William F. Buckley, Jr., Marvin Liebman and Frank Meyer, September 5, 1961. William Rusher Papers.
53 Rusher wanted to expel Scott Stanley and William Cotter, and hoped that Douglas Caddy would see " the writing on the wall." Letter, William Rusher to William F. Buckley, Jr., March 7, 1962. William A. Rusher Papers.
54 Memo, William A. Rusher to William F. Buckley, Jr., March 12, 1962. William A. Rusher Papers.
55 Memorandum, YAF, August 12, 1961. William F. Buckley Papers, Box 17.
56 F. Clifton White & William J. Gill, *Why Reagan Won* (Chicago: Regnery Gateway, 1981), p. 74.

him one of the central figures of the New Right. Liebman also taught him the critical importance of creating the illusion of mass. Only 2,000 members actually paid dues to YAF, but Viguerie was told that "it's important that membership be perceived at 25,000."[57]

Despite the organizational changes, rivaling factions, charges of improper use of funds, attempted takeovers, and purges would continue to mark the history of YAF.[58] The birchers were purged in 1965, the Wallacites in 1967, and in 1969 the libertarians followed after a strong bid for control of the organization.[59] The tensions between traditionalists and libertarians had been evident all along, but conflicting views on the war in Vietnam, and particularly the issue of the draft, ended in irreconcilable conflict.

YAF in Electoral Politics

In 1960, the campaign to nominate Barry Goldwater as candidate for the vice-presidency had been a catalyst for the formation of YAF. Four years later his nomination, this time as presidential candidate, once again became a focal point for the organization's activities. YAF now counted more than 25,000 members, spread over approximately 700 campuses across the country. In the preceding years many YAF chapters had taken part in electoral politics at the state and local level. In the 1962 local elections in New York City, the organization had been involved in 17 races (albeit mostly with poor results). Seven of the candidates had themselves been YAF members. YAF had also been actively involved in the campaigns for politicians such as Donald Bruce of Indiana, Jack Cox (gubernatorial candidate) in Texas, Bill Cramer in Florida, and Joel Broyhill in Virginia. Now the turn had come to a national campaign.

Goldwater was in many ways an unusual idol for a student organization. The senator was worlds apart from William Buckley, Jr., Russell Kirk, and other conservative idols. Many of the students were well aware that

---

57 Quoted from Rick Perlstein, *Before the Storm* (New York: Hill and Wang, 2001), p. 162.
58 One of the most well publicized scandals occurred in 1985, when YAF chairman Robert Dolan was forced to resign after charges that he had diverted a substantial amount of the organization's money to cover private expenses.
59 By 1969, an estimated 20 to 40 percent of YAF's membership were libertarians. Klatch, Op.Cit., p. 225.

Goldwater was not himself a college graduate, and that his books *The Conscience of a Conservative* and *Why Not Victory?*, which were widely distributed by conservative youth organizations and frequently hailed as nothing less than milestones in American Conservative thought, did not contain many lines written by the senator himself. But although some considered Senator John Tower of Texas, who was a former college-professor, a more congenial candidate, Goldwater was for better or worse the leading political figure in the conservative movement, and YAF hailed him as the embodiment of conservative virtues.

From the outset of the campaign to nominate the senator from Arizona, YAFers supplied much of the energy required for canvassing. They organized Students-for-Goldwater groups, held campus rallies, arranged mock conventions on campuses across the country, and took polls. Many YAF chapters cooperated with the local Goldwater clubs, walked stairs and rang doorbells in order to acquire information about the strength of Goldwater in the polls.

YAF was also the driving force behind the organizing of "Youth for Goldwater." Although this organization was not directly controlled by it, the leadership was nevertheless completely dominated by YAF members. The national steering committee of Youth for Goldwater included five members of YAF's board of directors, among them its National Chairman.[60] In September 1964 YAF also joined forces with Young Republican National Federation, College Youth for Goldwater, and the Young Democrats and Independents for Goldwater-Miller, and formed a special campaign organization called the Young Americans for Goldwater-Miller.

Apart from the work done through these organizations, several national board members and other leading YAF organizers went to work directly in the Goldwater presidential campaign. The press division of the Republican National Committee hired *New Guard*-editor Carol Bauman and former editor and co-founder of YAF Lee Edwards, along with board members George McDonnell and Mary Ann Ford. YAF's national treasurer Lammot Copeland, Jr. and national board member Fulton Lewis III both became special aides to Vice Presidential candidate William E. Miller.[61]

---

60 "YAF Roundup: YAF for Goldwater," *The New Guard*, July 1964, p. 18.
61 *The New Guard*, September 1964, p. 23.

In his account of how Goldwater won the Republican nomination, F. Clifton White, the man behind the "draft Goldwater movement," would later praise YAF for its contribution. During the actual campaign, however, the relationship between White and the organization was rather strained, which was well illustrated, when White sarcastically remarked after the New Hampshire primary that the YAF vote apparently had not come in yet. [62] Thus, White, who had unwisely been sidetracked prior to Goldwater's failure in that primary, insinuated that the YAFers were too confident of their own political abilities.

The enthusiastic YAFers, however, were not given much of a chance to prove him wrong, particularly not after the primaries. There were members who came to work directly for Goldwater's campaign-staff, but the organization itself was, like most of the conservative movement, relegated to a marginal position.

Yet, the Goldwater-campaign became a very important field of practice for many future conservative leaders. In the following years many of them would be given a chance to use the skills they had acquired in student politics. Tom Huston went to work for President Nixon in the White House. As a deputy to YAFer Pat Buchanan, Huston gave name to the notorious "Huston Plan," President Nixon's elaborate program of domestic spying and harassment of political enemies by abuse of the IRS and other government agencies. Other leading YAFers working for the Nixon-administration included Carol Bauman and Randall Teague. Former YAF chairman Robert Bauman was elected to Congress in 1973 and represented Maryland until a sex scandal stopped his political career in 1980.

By that time, many former YAFers were playing important roles in the rising conservative "counter-establishment" that helped bring Ronald Reagan to power. Among them were Phillip Crane, Pat Buchanan, Howard Phillips, Donald Divine, Bruce Eberle, and Richard Viguerie, whose fundraising skills were instrumental.[63] Other prominent figures of the New Right who had started their political engagement in YAF included the editor of the *American Spectator* R. Emmett Tyrrell, and the late John T.

---

62 Quoted in William K. Wyant, Jr., "Stakes High As Factions Fight For Control of Republican Party," in *Ultraconservatism in the 1964 Presidential Campaign*, special issue of the St. Louis *Post-Dispatch* (undated), p. 6.

63 Pat Buchanan became Reagan's Director of Communications, Howard Phillips headed Conservative Caucus, and Donald Divine became President Reagan's Director of the Office of Personnel Management.

Dolan, chairman of the National Conservative Political Action Committee (NCPAC). ISI as well contributed with a number of former disciples, including Edwin Feulner, Jr., head the conservative think tank the Heritage Foundation, and Richard V. Allen, who would serve as President Reagan's National Security Advisor.

In retrospect, how does one assess the political impact of the conservative student organizations compared with that of their left-wing counterparts? When both organizations were at their peak, YAF had twice as many members as SDS, and while the latter collapsed in the turmoil of the late 1960s, YAF outlived it by several decades.[64] Today the organization is still alive, though now a shadow of its former self. Yet, it is mostly SDS and the New Left that come to mind when people talk of the student movement. Neither numbers nor longevity can change this assessment. For a couple of years, the widespread resistance to the war in Vietnam gave SDS a political leverage that YAF never had.

Ironically, however, the excesses of SDS and its even more radical offspring also triggered a backlash, and thus probably did more to promote the conservative cause than YAF did. In the end, the major contribution of the conservative student organizations was not the creation of a mass movement, but the recruitment and training of future leaders. YAF and ISI could not take much of the credit for the many young Americans who turned right with Reagan in the early 1980s. For one thing, YAF was almost completely absorbed by an endless stream of purges and lawsuits, which at one point threatened to destroy the organization completely. Still, many of the people who now advised the President could think back on their political baptism in one of these two organizations. Student politics had provided a crucial field of practice for many of the political activists who now headed the conservative counter-establishment.

---

64 Braungart, Margaret M. & Richard G. Braungart, "The Effects of the 1960s Political Generation on Former Left- and Right-Wing Youth Activist Leaders," *Social Problems*, Vol. 38, No. 3, August 1991, p. 301.

Chapter 8

The Respectable- and the Not-so-respectable Right

"Danger on the Right"

IN 1961, THE national media discovered "the radical right." Suddenly, there was a steady flow of cover stories and special reports on the threat of right wing extremism. Several of them warned their readers that the greatest threat to American democracy no longer came from the left, but from the right.[1] Soon numerous books contributed to the state of alert, and in Congress the growing concern triggered calls for federal investigations and HUAC investigations.[2]

The White House was also paying attention. President Kennedy and his advisors began to explore possible ways of disrupting the activities of right wing groups.[3] Attorney General Robert F. Kennedy encouraged President of UAW Walter P. Reuther to prepare a memorandum on "The Radical

---

1   For examples, see Stanley Mosk & Howard Jewel, "The Birch Phenomenon Analyzed," The New York *Times Magazine*, August 20, 1961, p. 12 ff. "Subversion of the Right," *The Christian Century* 78 (April 12, 1961), pp. 379-380, Alan Barth, "Report on the Rampageous Right," The New York *Times Magazine* (November 26, 1961), "Thunder on the Right: The Conservatives, the Radicals, the Fanatic Fringe" (cover story), *Newsweek* (December 4, 1961), "The Ultras," *Time* (December 8, 1961).
2   The list of books includes Gene Grove, *Inside the John Birch Society* (Greenwich, 1961), Murray Clark Havens, *The Challenge to Democracy: Consensus and Extremism in American Politics* (Austin: University of Texas Press, 1965), Mark Sherwin, *The Extremists* (New York: St. Martin's Press, 1963), and Irwin Suall, *The American Ultras: The Extreme Right and the Military Industrial Complex* (New York: New America, 1962).
3   As historian John A. Andrew III reveals in his book *Another Side of the Sixties: Young Americans for Freedom and the Rise of Conservative Politics* (New Brunswick: Rutgers University Press, 1997), the Kennedy-administration even went as far as to use the IRS and other government agencies in a covert effort to curb the activities of the John Birch Society and other right wing organizations. Some of these efforts took place under a secret program entitled The Ideological Organizations Project (pp. 151-168).

Right in America Today."[4] The result was a report, which in all its shrillness had a striking resemblance to the far Right's warnings of an impending communist takeover.[5]

What Reuther described was a genuine threat to American democracy; a threat that required a proactive administration policy of "containment." A policy of "appeasement" would in Reuther's view only make matters worse.[6] He suggested that a number of radical right organizations should be added to the Attorney General's list of subversive organizations, since they were totalitarian, predicated upon secrecy, and posed "a far greater danger to the success of this country in its battle against international Communism than [did] the domestic Communist movement."[7] Other measures would include a prompt revocation of the federal tax exemption that a number of groups enjoyed under the National Education Program.[8]

Extremists in Arms: The Case of General Walker

According to Reuther, the most serious threat came from the radical right's infiltration of the Armed Services. Here was "an immediate and special problem requiring immediate and special measures."[9] The report further stimulated an existing concern in the White House over the political opinions of some of the military chiefs. A couple of generals and an admiral had already been eased out. Others were difficult to touch. In the case of Air Force chief of staff Curtis ("Bombs Away") LeMay, who uninhibitedly expressed his rightist views in public, the Kennedy administration had come to the conclusion that any attempt to muzzle him was

---

4 Letter, Victor G. Reuther to Robert F. Kennedy, December 19, 1961. Robert F. Kennedy Attorney General Papers, John Fitzgerald Kennedy Library, Boston Mass. See also memo "Re Reuther memorandum on the 'Radical Right'", Andrew F. Oehmann to Robert F. Kennedy, November 7, 1963. Robert F. Kennedy Attorney General Papers, John Fitzgerald Kennedy Library.
5 Andrew F. Oehmann to Robert F. Kennedy, November 7, 1963. Robert F. Kennedy Attorney General Papers.
6 Reuther, "The Radical Right in America Today," p. 12. Robert F. Kennedy Attorney General Papers.
7 Reuther, "The Radical Right in America Today," p. 15.
8 Reuther, "The Radical Right in America Today," p. 18.
9 Walther P. Reuther, "The Radical in America Today", p. 9. Robert F. Kennedy Attorney General Papers.

most likely to backfire.[10] The same did not apply to General Edwin A. Walker, whose dismissal nevertheless fueled a public controversy.

A 1958 National Security Council directive had commissioned commanding officers to provide their troops with a basic knowledge about the nature of the Cold War. The officers were also offered literature that would serve the purpose. Walker was an army general in charge of the 24th Division stationed in Germany, and in that capacity, he had chosen materials produced by The John Birch Society and other far right organizations in his efforts to instill patriotism and "Americanism" in his soldiers and their relatives. He had also encouraged them to consult the ACA-index – a rating of all members of Congress made by the far right-organization Americans for Conservative Action – before they cast their votes.

Secretary of Defense Robert McNamara found this to be a case of political propaganda by a federal employee and thus a violation of the Hatch Act of 1939. When reports of Walker's "political seminars" surfaced in the media, the White House put pressure on the Pentagon to relieve the general of his command until the affair had been investigated.[11]

According to a press release dated June 12, 1961, Walker was admonished following a speech to 200 soldiers and their dependents, in which the general had "made derogatory remarks of a serious nature about certain prominent Americans, the American Press, and TV industry and certain commentators, which linked the persons and institutions with Communism and Communist influence."[12] The official report of the incident found that Walker's actions had "exceeded the limits of propriety for an officer of the Army," but apart from the admonition, no further action was taken.[13] However, Walker subsequently offered to resign, and his offer was accepted.

Now the far right had a new martyr. The *New York Mirror* contended that "No matter how it is sliced, General Walker seems to have committed the crime of being excessively patriotic, of preferring his own country to

---

10 Oral history interview with Deputy Secretary of Defense Roswell L. Gilpatrick, 1970, p. 111. John Fitzgerald Kennedy Library.
11 Oral History interview with Deputy Secretary of Defense Roswell L. Gilpatrick, John Fitzgerald Kennedy Library, Boston, Mass.
12 Press release, Department of Defense Directorate for News Services, June 12, 1961. John Fotzgerald Kennedy Library.
13 Press release, Department of Defense Directorate for News Services, June 12, 1961. John Fotzgerald Kennedy Library.

Soviet Russia."[14] Soon he was warning audiences across the country that the United Nations and the United States Department of Defense were working for the communist conspiracy. To many on the left, Walker came to embody the potential threat of a right wing coup within the Armed services. He served as the model for the demagogic villain in Fletcher Knebel's book *Seven Days in May* (1962), just as General Jack D. Ripper – the madman who initiates an unprovoked nuclear attack on the Soviet Union in Stanley Kubrick's 1964-movie *Dr. Stangelove* – had more than a passing resemblance to him.

In February 1962, Walker made an unsuccessful attempt to become the Democratic Party's candidate for governor of Texas. Later that year, liberal fears of Walker's subversive inclination were confirmed. On September 30, 1962, he traveled to Oxford, Mississippi and led the charge against the federal marshals, who were there to secure the enrollment of James Meredith at the University of Mississippi.[15] Ironically, five years earlier, as commander of the Arkansas Military District, Walker had been in charge of the integration of Little Rock High School.

Upon the request of Attorney General Robert Kennedy, he was now charged with conspiracy, insurrection, and rebellion, and amid protests from Strom Thurmond and other right wing politicians, he was briefly confined to a mental hospital in Missouri for psychiatric evaluation.[16] The general himself claimed to be a "political prisoner" of the Kennedy administration.[17] Mentally stable or not, General Walker had become an icon of right wing radicalism in America.

---

14 Quoted from Rick Perlstein, *Before the Storm* (New York: Hill and Wang, 2001), p. 148.
15 It was not the last time that Walker's name would catch national attention. After the assassination of President Kennedy, it became clear that the general had actually been Lee Harvey Oswald's first target. On April 30, 1963, Oswald allegedly took a shot through a window in Walker's Dallas-home and missed the general by a few inches.
16 A rambling open letter from Walker to President Kennedy just four days earlier concerning the Cuban threat to national security might very well have helped convince the Kennedy-administration that Walker was mentally unstable. The letter implicitly threatened the president with widespread public rebellion unless he came down hard on Cuba: "Without a modicum of respect, such a mood could rebel in revulsive repudiation of its traditional bounds against the untraditional escalation of intrusive and compulsive accommodation." Open letter, Edwin A Walker to President John F. Kennedy, 26 September 1962. The Presidential Papers of John F. Kennedy, White House Central Files. John Fitzgerald Kennedy Library, Boston, Mass.
17 Chris Cravens, Edwin A. Walker in *The Handbook of Texas Online*, www.tsha.utexas.edu/handbook/online/articles.

Locating the "Radical Right"

Just who or what was this "radical right" that General Walker supposedly represented? The term covered a very diverse group of organizations. Some of them were national in scope; others were regional or local. Some had substantial memberships; others were fund raising enterprises or mere letterhead groups whose publications and activities were largely sponsored by a single or a few eccentric donors. In their coverage of the right, some journals and newspapers conscientiously made distinctions between violent "hate-groups," paramilitary organizations, "radical reactionaries," and respectable conservative groups. Just as often, however, anything from the Ku Klux Klan to Young Americans For Freedom was simply lumped together as "the radical right," "the far right," or "the extreme right."

According to an analysis made in August 1963 for the Kennedy-administration, the "radical right" spent some $15 -$25 million annually and could be heard on the airwaves of at least a thousand of the country's radio stations.[18] These broadcasts included those made by the Life-Line Foundation. Created in 1958 by one of America's richest men, Texas tycoon H.L. Hunt, the foundation sponsored a daily program, "Life Lines," which by 1962 was broadcast seven days a week on close to 300 radio stations in 42 states.[19] Hunt also sponsored a pamphlet by the same name, which was distributed to some 40,000 people three times a week.

Other prominent right wing broadcasters included the former dean at the University of Notre Dame, Clarence Manion, who had aired his own Manion Forum since 1954. Each week the program supplied radio and television audiences with something Manion poetically described as a "beacon of hope" in a country where all three branches of government were "writhing in the tentacles of the International Socialist octopus."[20]

---

18 Mike Feldman, "Memorandum for the President on Right-Wing Groups," August 15, 1963. The Presidential Papers of John F. Kennedy, White House Central Files. John Fitzgerald Kennedy Library.
19 Feldman, "Memorandum for the President on Right-Wing Groups," p. 4.
20 "Manion Forum Fourth Anniversary October 1954-1958" (pamphlet). The Manion Papers, Box 5. In these programs, which according to Manion would serve as "an antidote to the venom of foreign ideologies and so-called "liberalism," he and a host of other prominent right-wing figures would denounce everything from the Marxist income tax" to "senseless and harmful 'foreign aid.'" Speakers included "Old Guard" conservative members of Congress such as J. Bracken Lee, William Jenner, William F. Knowland, Joe McCarthy, Karl Mundt, Barry Goldwater and Burton K. Wheeler, as well as conservative celebrities such as William F. Buckley, Jr., ex-New Dealer Donald R. Richberg, and General Douglas A. MacArthur.

A number of Protestant organizations were also prominent within the "radical right." Among these were Howard Kershner's Christian Freedom Foundation, which from 1950 published the journal *Christian Economics*; the Christian Crusade, headed by the Rev. Billy James Hargis of Oklahoma – a pioneer of "televangelism" and direct mail – and the Church League of America, headed by Major Edgar C. Bundy. The Reverend Carl McIntire was the director of Christian Beacon, Inc. and in charge of the "Twentieth Century Reformation Hour" – a program carried nationwide on more than 400 radio stations.

McIntire was also the man behind the country's leading protestant fundamentalist organizations, the American Council of Christian Churches (ACCC), and the International Council of Christian Churches (ICCC). By principle, the fundamentalist organizations scorned the earthly realm and did not want to be a part of any political movement. Yet, their strong anticommunism, combined with the prospects of vastly increased funding and membership, often compelled them to overcome their traditional reluctance towards working with secular organizations.[21]

Organizations such as Christian Crusade, the Life Line Foundation, and the Manion Forum had existed for years, some for decades, but only occasionally had they attracted the attention of the national media.[22] It was first of all the activities of the John Birch Society that now created a hype and made the term "radical right" a household word.

The John Birch Society

The John Birch Society had been founded in December of 1958 by former candy manufacturer Robert Welch and a group of invited co-founders,

---

21 To mention one example, James Hargis of Christian Crusade began in 1961 to organize "Anti-Communist Leadership Schools" across the country. The list of speakers at these events included some of the most prominent figures of the secular right

22 Other groups included American Coalition of Patriotic Societies, Christian Crusade, Congress of Freedom, the Conservative Society of America, and We, the People! The Conservative Society of America, based in New Orleans, published the newspaper *The Independent American*. Among the ideas promoted by Congress of Freedom, founded in 1951, was the demand that the entire Warren Supreme Court be impeached. We, The People! founded in 1955 and headed by former Secretary of Agriculture Ezra Taft Benson, had repeal of the income tax as one of its primary political objectives. The organization also published the journal *Free Enterprise*.

most of them well-known figures from other enterprises on the far right. Welch had served on the board of the National Association of Manufacturers for seven years, but had now retired in order to devote himself to the exposure of a worldwide communist conspiracy. This conspiracy, he claimed, had infiltrated the American government at all levels. The mission of his new organization was to expose the conspiracy and save the nation.

Welch named his venture after an American Baptist missionary who during the revolution in China had done work for the American Secret Service. John Birch had been killed by communist soldiers in a rather obscure episode, and Welch had since attempted to make him a martyr for the anti-Communist cause.[23]

The co-founders and early members of the society included "Mr. China-lobby" Alfred Kohlberg, former Assistant Secretary of State Spruille Braden, and Merwin K. Hart, president of the National Economic Council. Likewise, several of the conservative movement's leading sponsors were active members, including Roger Milliken, Pennsylvania oilman J. Howard Pew, former New Jersey Governor Charles Edison, Brig. Gen. Bonner Fellers, Vice-Chairman of Americans for Constitutional Action, General A.C. Wedemeyer, and General Edwin A. Walker.

If conservatives in general expressed a strong belief in the power of ideas, then most "radical right" put their faith in the power of exposure. The result was an endless stream of books and pamphlets aimed at alerting the American public to the web of subversive forces which – most often in the disguise of liberalism – had taken over the country. The John Birch Society also put a great deal of faith in the printed word. The organization would expose the workings of the communist conspiracy through the publication of periodicals, pamphlets and books, just as it would mobilize letter-writers and open reading rooms throughout the country.[24]

But Welch also wanted to go beyond exposure. He wanted to emulate communist tactics and engage in "counter-infiltration." The society would work in cadres, small local chapters of 10-30 members, who would

---

23 In 1954, Welch had published *The Life of John Birch* (Chicago: Henry Regnery Company), where the unknown missionary was lauded as a symbol of "the ordeal of his age."
24 Apart from pamphlets and bulletins, the organization published the journal *American Opinion*, as well as a steady stream of books from its publishing house, Western Islands, in Belmont, Massachusetts.

meet in private homes. These local chapters would organize "front groups," disrupt meetings, and attempt to infiltrate school boards, community organizations, trade groups or local chambers of commerce. They would also attempt to gain influence within the Republican Party by organizing at the precinct level.

Welch was convinced that it was imperative to organize *outside* the GOP, regardless of the prospects of some day winning the presidential nomination for a conservative favorite such as Barry Goldwater, to whose campaigns in Arizona he had donated money. The importance of a right wing counter-establishment would be even greater with a slick opportunist such as Richard M. Nixon as Republican candidate: "what good could such a man be to us, even as president, unless outside forces and accomplishments made it opportunistic and expedient for him to ride an anti-Communist wave which those outside forces had created?"[25]

In his *Blue Book of the John Birch Society*, Robert Welch expressed his goals for the size and scope of the organization: "I think that a million members is all we would want, at least in the United States. For we need disciplined pullers at the oars, and not passengers in the boat."[26] He had no need to worry about too many passengers. Though bigger than most other conservative groups, the membership of the society never came anywhere close to this upper limit. By 1963, it had an estimated 60,000 members. The main office in Belmont, Massachusetts, employed some 44 full-time workers, and approximately 30 paid and 100 volunteer "coordinators."[27]

According to the organization's own figures, the annual budget, which had been a mere $130,000 in 1959, skyrocketed to $2 million in 1964 – the year of the Goldwater-campaign. Membership dues raised some 30 percent of this amount. The Society had its strongest support in suburban areas in the Sunbelt. In Southern California it even captured control of key positions in the California Young Republican Federation and had two of its members (John Rousselot and Edgar Hiestand) representing their state in Congress. Apart from local chapters, the John Birch Society established

---

25 Robert Welch, *The Blue Book*, p. 111.
26 Robert Welch, *the Blue Book*, p.153.
27 J. Allen Broyles, "The John Birch Society: A Movement of Social Protest of the Radical Right," *The Journal of Social Issues*, Vol. XIX, No. 2, April 1963, p. 51.

a speakers bureau, some 40 bookstores, and approximately 100 right-wing libraries, including 7 or 8 travelling "bookmobiles."[28]

A Conspiracy So Immense...

The views of the John Birch Society were practically identical with the views of its founder, Robert Welch. The organization's manifest *The Blue Book of the John Birch Society*, was largely a reprint of Welch's marathon speech at the founding meeting. Here one could read a political program which supported "states rights," demanded impeachment of Earl Warren and the rest of the Supreme Court, proposed a repeal of the income tax, withdrawal from NATO, and an end to foreign aid. It was another of Welch's books, however, which attracted the largest media attention: *The Politician*.

The manuscript for *The Politician* was privately circulated to select recipients in 1958, and in 1962 Welch published a slightly sanitized version of it.[29] The book reflected the retired candy manufacturer's firm belief in a vast communist conspiracy that took the most deceptive forms. Thus, Welch could reveal in his book that the President of the United States, Dwight D. Eisenhower, was actually an agent for this communist conspiracy.[30]

Welch described three stages of Communist influence in the White House: 1. FDR, who thought he could use the Communists to promote his personal ambitions, but ended up being used by them instead, 2. Truman, who was well aware that he was being used by the Communists, but accepted that this was the price he had to pay in order to become President. 3. Eisenhower, who was himself a Communist traitor.[31]

Ike was apparently surrounded by allies. Among the other leading agents of the Soviet conspiracy were General Marshall and the president's brother Milton, who was his superior and boss within the Communist

---

28 Mike Feldman, "Memorandum for the President on Right-Wing Groups," p. 3.
29 (Belmont, Mass.: Western Islands, 1962).
30 Confronted with this claim, Russell Kirk responded: "Eisenhower is not a Communist, he's a golfer!"
31 The relevant part of the manuscript is quoted in Green, Barbara, Katryn Turner, Dante Geronimo, "Responsible and Irresponsible Right-Wing Groups; A Problem in Analysis," *The Journal of Social Issues*, Vol. XIX, No. 2 (April, 1963), p. 17.

Party. They received all the help they could need from the United Nations under the leadership of the "homosexual, pro-Communist Secretary-General Dag Hammerskjold."[32]

Most surprising to Welch and probably to most of his readers as well, was the conclusion, reached "after careful consideration," that Secretary of State John Foster Dulles, despite his hard-line anticommunist rhetoric, was also a communist agent. His clearly defined role was "always to say the right things and always to do the wrong ones."[33] Dulles' brother, Head of the CIA Allen W. Dulles, was also a communist agent. That explained the downfall of Senator Joseph McCarthy, who had been "done for the moment he began casting glances at the CIA ... he was never allowed to expose its true nature as the most Communist-infested of all the agencies of our Government."[34]

The key to understanding Welch's surprising choice of targets was his use of a principle of reversal: the cunning Communists said they were in favor of things they were really against in order to trick ordinary Americans to be against them. Thus, when Khrushchev criticized UN Secretary General Dag Hammerskjold, who according to Welch was an agent of the Kremlin, it was simply part of a clever scheme to keep him at his post. Based on such logic, Welch's estimate that America was "60-80% Communist" seemed less surprising. If this principle of reversal might seem confusing to many, they could seek comfort in the fact that Welch had simple solutions to most political issues. The apparent complexity of many issues, he contended, was merely a smokescreen cleverly orchestrated by the communist conspiracy.

With a communist infiltration of 60-80%, one might naturally expect to find subversive elements in all walks of life. In a speech in California, Welch told his audience that 7,000 of the nation's protestant ministers could "fairly be called Communists or Communist sympathizers."[35] Considering that Welch frequently denounced supporters of such measures as

---

32 Green et. al., "Responsible and Irresponsible Right-Wing Groups; A Problem in Analysis," p. 136.
33 Quoted from Gene Grove, *Inside the John Birch Society* (Greenwich, Conn.: Fawcett Publications, Inc., 1961), p. 24.
34 Grove, *Inside the John Birch Society*, p. 30.
35 Quoted from a report by the Office of the Attorney General in the state of California to the Honorable Edmund G. Brown, Governor of California, July 7, 1961, p. 3. The Manion Papers, Box 71.

fluoridation, mental health programs and federal aid to education as agents of the communist conspiracy, 7,000 must have been a conservative estimate on his part.

In several of the many alarmist reports on the John Birch Society published in the early 1960s, Welch was portrayed as a dangerous warmonger. In fact he was an ardent isolationist, who believed that the communist threat was primarily domestic and that increases in the defense budget were part of a collectivist scheme for further centralization of power in the United States:

> Although our danger remains almost entirely internal, from Communist influences right in our midst and treason right in our government, the American people are being persuaded that our danger is from the outside, is from Russian military superiority. And under the excuse of preparing to match that military might, or defending ourselves from this threat of outside force; in other words, under the guise of fighting Communism, we are being stampeded into the biggest jump ever towards, and perhaps the final jump right into socialism and then the Communist camp.[36]

In a letter to Barry Goldwater written in 1965, Welch elaborated on his view that the military threat of the Soviet Union was largely fictional:

> The Communists have not made any of this progress through military victories. Their pretended military might has been used only for prestige, bluff, and negotiations. The Communist advance has been entirely dependent on the cunning, cruelty, and ruthlessness of their conspiratorial activities. They have now taken over some forty countries, always by subversion and guerilla activities from within, never by armed attack from without.[37]

Proponents of the *National Review* -line of anti-communism found Welch's neo-isolationist ideas and narrow focus on domestic communism extremely harmful. William Rusher viewed the organization as "a Mecca for

---

36 Robert Welch, *The Blue Book of The John Birch Society* (Boston: Western Islands, 1961 [1959]), p. 22.
37 Letter, Robert Welch to Barry Goldwater, November 4, 1965. Denison Kitchel Papers, Hoover Institution.

every crackpot in America" and Marvin Liebman found it imperative to create a national organization which would "lessen and/or supercede the influence of the John Birch Society" and promote a "responsible" conservative foreign policy based on a strict definition of the national interest.[38] Such a foreign policy would strengthen NATO, SEATO and other military alliances, cut all financial and political support of the UN to the minimum required in order to maintain membership, and link all types of foreign aid to the overall goal of fighting Communism. There were other attempts to undercut the appeal of Robert Welch and his endless charges of betrayal and conspiracy, but it would take another three years before Buckley and his associates were ready to attack the John Birch Society and its founder head-on.

In the meantime, the national media continued to warn their audiences of the birchers' attempts to infiltrate and take over other organizations, including the Republican Party, a process which might eventually endanger American democracy itself if the necessary precautions were not taken.

Such warnings vastly overrated both the authoritarian inclinations and the political potential of the John Birch Society. Despite all the talk of "counterinfiltration," Welch and his followers did not challenge the basic tenets of democracy, just as it was a far cry from their advocacy of nutty conspiracy theories to the Klan, the Minutemen, and their violent attempts to subvert the law of the land. The birchers showed no disregard for the rule of law and they generally adhered to the rules of democratic debate. Even a slogan like "Impeach Earl Warren" was in its own silly way a tribute to the cornerstone of American democracy: the system of checks and balances. This was also the answer that the California Governor Pat Brown got when he asked his Attorney General for a report on the organization: it was "a nuisance, not a peril."[39]

---

38 Letter, William Rusher to L. Brent Bozell, September 28, 1961. The William A. Rusher papers. Marvin Liebman, "Memorandum regarding Committee for an American Foreign Policy," January 2, 1962, p. 1. The Buckley Papers.

39 The expression was borrowed from an article by Senator J.W. Fulbright in *Congressional Record*, April 18, 1961).

The Consensus-school and Right Wing "Extremism"

If the birchers did not violate any laws, or intend to do so, in what sense, then, could they be characterized as extremists? Birchers and their likeminded were extremists, sociologists Seymour Martin Lipset and Earl Raab would argue in 1970, because they rejected the belief in an open "marketplace of ideas."[40] They were political moralists, who were unwilling to accept ambiguity. Their belief that most problems were basically simple opened the door for conspiracy theories, and made political disagreement synonymous with treason. In other words, Lipset and Raab saw anti-pluralism – or "monism" as they called it – as the key component of extremism.

The implicit assumption behind this approach was of course that all statements presented by the radical right should be taken at face value, without any room for rhetorical style.[41] Otherwise, many anticommunist statements by President Kennedy and other mainstream politicians would also qualify them to the label of political "extremism." But to Lipset and Raab the basic motivation of the radical right was altogether different from that of the political mainstream, and thus had to be analyzed within a separate conceptual framework.

This approach, first of all inspired by Theodore Adorno's study of *The Authoritarian Personality*, had dominated the field since the early 1950s. It turned the attention of scholars towards the socio-psychological sources of support for the American Right. The historians and sociologists who ascribed to this approach might disagree about the proper balance between personal disposition and the role of social and economic strains on certain groups in society, but they generally agreed that right wing beliefs were abnormal and should be treated as a pathology.[42]

---

40 Seymour Martin Lipset & Earl Raab, *The Politics of Unreason; Right-Wing Extremism in America, 1790-1977*, 2nd ed. (Chicago: The University of Chicago Press, 1978), p. 6.

41 For an attempt to make a distinction between "responsible" right wing groups and "extremists," see Barbara Green, Kathryn Turner & Dante Geronimo, "Responsible and Irresponsible Right-Wing Groups; A Problem in Analysis," *The Journal of Social Issues*, Vol. XIX, No. 2 (April, 1963), p. 3. See also Michi Ebata, "Right-Wing Extremism: In Search of a Definition," in Braun, Aurel & Stephen Scheinberg (eds.), *The Extreme Right; Freedom and Security at Risk* (Boulder: Westview Press, 1997), pp. 12-35.

42 T.W. Adorno, et. al., *The Authoritarian Personality* (New York, 1950).

A particularly illuminating example of this approach was an article by Professor Herbert McClosky entitled "Conservatism and Personality."[43] Based on a sample of some 1200 people in Minnesota, McClosky suggested a strong correlation between conservative beliefs and factors such as intelligence, knowledge and education. "By every measure available to us," he wrote, "conservative beliefs are found most frequently among the uninformed, the poorly educated, and so far as we can determine, the less intelligent."[44] McClosky did not attempt to define just what he meant by the terms "conservative" and "liberal," although he postulated (with unintended irony) a strong correlation between "liberal tendencies" and "greater precision in speech and thought." He also found if safe to conclude that there was a clear correlation between conservatism and feelings such as alienation, anomie, bewilderment, and submissiveness:

> Conservatism, in our society at least, appears to be far more characteristic of social isolates, of people who think poorly of themselves, who suffer personal disgruntlement and frustration, who are submissive, timid, and wanting in confidence, who lack a clear sense of direction and purpose, who are uncertain about their values, and who are generally bewildered by the alarming task of having to thread their way through a society which seems to them too complex to fathom.[45]

According to the author this correlation was only natural, since conservatives were most likely to come from "the classes that are socially and psychologically depressed."[!][46] Thus McClosky was attempting to combine the view of conservatism as a personal disorder with a view which first of all saw it as the result of social strains.

This perspective had found its quintessential expression in 1955 in *The New American Right*, an anthology edited by Daniel Bell.[47] The rise of McCarthyism had undoubtedly encouraged several of the influential contributors to view the masses not as victims of greedy businessmen and

---

43 *American Political Science Review* 52 (March 1958), pp. 27-45.
44 McClosky, "Conservatism and Personality," p. 35.
45 McClosky, "Conservatism and Personality," p. 37.
46 McClosky was, however, gracious enough to concede that "doubtless, many of us know individual conservatives whose personalities differ in key ways from the prototypic pattern described here." (p. 43).
47 (New York, 1955), later revised and published as *The Radical Right* (New York, 1963).

special interests, but first and foremost as victims of their own anxieties. The followers of right wing movements were first of all motivated by fear of cultural, social and economic displacement, it was argued. It was less important whether such displacement was real or imagined, since it was the sense of powerlessness and alienation in their everyday lives that made these people search for answers outside the political mainstream, thus making them the likely victims of the right wing's manichean worldview and simplistic propaganda.

Historian Richard Hofstadter stressed that such an approach to the study of the American Right did not intend to neglect the structural and historical context, nor to replace concepts such as class, power, racial divisions, and ethnicity with status anxiety and other problems of personal adjustment. He and the other authors of *The New American Right* were "not trying to deny the obvious, but to go beyond it."[48] Yet, it is difficult to escape the sense that Daniel Bell, Richard Hofstadter, and their co-authors used a separate conceptual framework of socio-psychological concepts exclusively for the study of "pseudo-conservatives" and other alleged "extremists." A framework which they would never have applied in the attempt to explain the political behavior of liberal Democrats or moderate Republicans. Such activities were still described in the realm of interest politics.[49]

Hofstadter and his colleagues were in fact applying a narrow definition of a rational political mind in which the major defining characteristic was "tolerance." This concept was, as Terence Ball has pointed out, "predicated on a particular political theory – interest group liberalism – whose practices (and prejudices) the studies of (in) tolerance then serve [d] to legitimize if not insulate from criticism."[50] At the same time, the concept

---

48 Richard Hofstadter, "Pseudo-Conservatism Revisited – 1965" in *The Paranoid Style in American Politics and Other Essays* (Chicago: The University of Chicago Press, 1979 [1965]), p. 83.

49 The most profound critique of the socio-psychological approach to the study of the American Right has been raised by Leo P. Ribuffo in his brilliant book *The Old Christian Right* (Philadelphia: Temple University Press, 1983). See also Michael Paul Rogin, *Ronald Reagan, the Movie* (Berkeley: University of California Press, 1987), Christopher Lasch, *The True and Only Heaven: Progress and Its Critics* (New York: Norton, 1991), and Terence Ball, "The Politics of Social Science in Postwar America," in Lary May (ed.), *Recasting America; Culture and Politics In the Age of Cold War* (Chicago: The University of Chicago Press, 1990), pp. 76-92.

50 Terence Ball, "The Politics of Social Science in Postwar America."

made it irrelevant to deal with the political ideas and concerns of the "pseudo-conservatives" at face value. As Leo Ribuffo has noted: "If extremists differed tactically, psychologically, and perhaps 'anthropologically' from 'rational men,' then without apparent contradiction, liberals could bar them from the 'open marketplace of ideas.'"[51] Even if one does not question the motives or the ideological baggage that led liberal scholars to label a good deal of America's avowed conservatives as "pseudo-conservatives," the socio-psychological approach still had severe weaknesses.

If support for right-wing organizations was to be interpreted as a reaction to economic strains and structural transformations in American society, then why did the presence of such organizations seem to be a permanent feature of American political culture, regardless of fluctuations in the economy? One should expect less support for the far right in times of prosperity such as the early 1960s.

Empirical studies have not substantiated the assumption that people who feel powerless or alienated, or suffer from conflicting indicators of social status are most likely to be "seduced" by right-wing propaganda. In his fine study of Fred C. Schwarz' Christian Anti-Communist Crusade, Clyde Wilcox concludes that:

> The picture which emerges from the multivariate analysis is one of rationality. Support for the crusade did not come from personality disorders, status anxiety, or alienation. It came instead from conservative Republicans who attended fundamentalist churches where politics was discussed, who believed in the inerrancy of the Scriptures, and strongly disliked Communists.[52]

In the same vein, the Attorney General of California concluded in 1961 that the membership of the John Birch Society mostly consisted of "wealthy businessmen, retired military officers and little old ladies in tennis shoes." In other words, not exactly the kind of people than one would usually characterize as social and political outsiders.

The proponents of the status theory responded to this objection by focusing on more subtle forms of displacement. The magic of the status-

---

51 Ribuffo, *The Old Christian Right*, p. 241.
52 Clyde Wilcox, "Popular Backing For the Old Christian Right: Explaining Support For the Christian Anti-Communism Crusade," *Journal of Social History* (Fall, 1987), p. 129.

theory was that it seemingly worked just as well for conservatives who clearly belonged to society's elite. Given the widespread anti-elitism in American culture, Seymour Martin Lipset and Earl Raab noted, "many of the American elite are status-anxious, feel threatened and insecure, and react politically to this sense of being under attack."[53] However, if such obscure sources of anxiety could have the same radicalizing effect, then most people were likely victims, and if so, then how come only a minority of them actually joined or supported "radical right" organizations?

Charges that the "radical right" constituted a genuine threat to American democracy became still more frequent as it became clear that the conservative Senator Barry Goldwater of Arizona actually had a real chance of winning the Republican nomination in 1964. Several liberal observers saw his candidacy as evidence that birchers and their like-minded had infiltrated scores of local party organizations and were about to take over the entire Party. What was the reality behind such charges?

"The Radical Right" and the Goldwater-campaign

The John Birch Society did not officially promote Goldwater's candidacy, but maintained to be an educational organization raised above the fray of politics. It was, however, true that many birchers were involved in the campaign, and that the organization used it effectively to boost its membership and to improve its foothold in the Republican Party at the precinct level. In a few states birchers were also found at higher levels in the Goldwater-campaign.[54]

This was most evident in California, which accounted for more than a quarter of the organization's entire membership. Goldwater's advisory committee here included Walther Knott (of Knott's Berry Farm), who was associated with the Society, as well as with Christian Crusade and a number of other "radical right" enterprises. Other leading members in the

---

53 Lipset & Raab, *The Politics of Unreason*, p. 29.
54 At point during the Goldwater-campaign, it was also revealed that Denison Kitchel was or had been a member of the John Birch Society. However, Kitchel and his wife, who had both been early members of the organization, had terminated their membership in June of 1960, as soon as a copy of Robert Welch's manuscript "The Politician" had come into their possession. Letter, Denison Kitchel to Robert Welch, Jr., June 8, 1960. The Denison Kitchel Papers.

Golden State included Republican Representatives John Rousselot and Edgar Hiestand.

In 1964, Rousselot became The John Birch Society's national director of public relations and publisher of the its journal, *American Opinion*. He was also one of Goldwater's field coordinators, and after the Republican National Convention he contended that more than one hundred of the delegates and alternates had been birchers.[55] Even if this figure was somewhat exaggerated, it nevertheless supports the claims that quite a number of birchers were actively involved at the grassroots-level.

Rousselot's claim also indicates that Goldwater's campaign-staff was walking a fine line. One the one hand they welcomed active individual involvement of birchers and like-minded "radicals" in the campaign. On the other hand they attempted to keep their organizations at arms length in order to avoid stigmatizing charges of "extremism." Goldwater's refusal to openly repudiate the John Birch Society made him unnecessarily vulnerable to such charges.

At the party convention in San Francisco, two of Goldwater's rivals, Nelson Rockefeller and William Scranton, both introduced amendments to the party platform which denounced extremism and explicitly mentioned the John Birch Society. Both were of course aware that Goldwater in the previous years had been asked several times to do this, and that each time he had refused on principal grounds. As long as the organization did not violate any laws, he argued, there was no need to single it out.

In the past, Goldwater had on several occasions expressed admiration for the birchers. In April of 1961, when the Senate Internal Security Subcommittee had considered investigating the activities of the John Birch Society, Goldwater had publicly cautioned his fellow senators, arguing that many would become embarrassed when they discovered that they were dealing with some prominent people from their constituencies:

> I don't know why this society is called ultra-conservative, when its sole purpose is to fight communism. I know liberal Democrats as well as conservative Republicans who belong. Its purpose is to study communism and disseminate news about communism. Of course in every organization you'll find some who slip. But I have been very impressed with the high quality of these people.[56]

---

55 *San Francisco Examiner*, July 16, 1964.
56 "Goldwater Cautions Congress On Probe Of Birch Society," *Nashville Banner* (April 5, 1961).

Goldwater had in fact publicly expressed his personal opinion that Robert Welch was a liability as head of the society and ought to resign, but he found the media's treatment of the organization hysterical, and the notion that it constituted a potential threat to American democracy completely phony.[57] Conservatives, he argued, had always had to deal with the extreme right, just as liberals had always had to deal with the extreme left. The Right had organizations like the John Birch Society and the Left had organizations like ADA, Goldwater argued, and as long as they abided by the Constitution he had no quarrel with that.[58]

While Goldwater himself on principle refused to denounce The John Birch Society, other conservatives found it imperative to publicly distance themselves from the "radical right" in order to avoid being kept on the defensive. The *National Review crowd* gave up the idea that prudence was bound to creep in sooner or later and turn the John Birch Society and like-minded organizations into "responsible" vehicles of conservatism. They were ready to write them out of the conservative movement like they had previously done with other groups on the American Right.

The Gatekeepers

In the late 1950s, William F. Buckley, Jr. had led the way in severing the ties to nativist and anti-Semitic elements and organizations.[59] Likewise, the radical libertarians – particularly the followers of Ayn Rand's "objectivism" – had been written out of the movement. Although conservatives generally shared the objectivist faith in the virtues of the free market, they had little else in common with Rand, who, like Karl Marx, saw religion as

---

57 See Barry Goldwater interviewed by Gore Vidal in *Life*, June 9, 1961. Reprinted in Gore Vidal, *United States; Essays 1952-1992* (New York: Random House, 1993), pp. 827-840.
58 Gore Vidal, *United States; Essays 1952-1992*, pp. 827-840.
59 One step was to inform all contributors to *National Review* that if any of them appeared on the masthead of the (by now strongly anti-Semitic) *American Mercury*, they would not be able to write for his journal in the future. ("Confidential memorandum to writers for *National Review*," April 1, 1959. The Buckley Papers box 6). One notorious spokesman of the old nativist right, Gerald L. K. Smith actually himself wrote William F. Buckley and advised him to remove his name from *National Review's* mailing-list, since it could become a potential embarrassment for Buckley and the journal. (Letter, Gerald L.K. Smith to William F. Buckley, Jr., May 18, 1961. The Buckley Paper, box 16).

opium for the unenlightened masses, and preached the evils of altruism and the "virtue of selfishness."[60] As Garry Wills noted:

> It is treason, betrayal from within, for conservatives to endorse any fanatic who agrees with certain methods which conservatives must use to implement their view of man. I like money and dislike socialism; so, for his own reasons, does the devil; so, for her own reasons, does Ayn Rand. This does not make the three of us allies.[61]

Exclusion from the movement was probably not a traumatic condition for Rand, who for her part had denounced modern conservatism as an "embarrassing conglomeration of impotence, futility, inconsistency and superficiality."[62] It was a far more difficult task to convince birchers, who generally saw themselves as godfearing patriotic anti-Communists that their organization was beyond the pale and did not belong in the movement.

The *National Review*-crowd had on several occasions attempted to outline the difference between the "radical right" and "responsible" anti-Communists in general terms. According to Eugene Lyons, the defining characteristic of the radical right was the propensity to link all kinds of domestic grievances to the communist issue, thus blurring the real challenge of international Communism:

> Every American has the right to dislike the income tax, social security, desegregation, the TVA, fluoridation, the national diet, the United Nations, NATO, foreign aid, etc., etc. He has the further right to believe that these things can help the communists or threaten the American way of life. But he does not have the right, in common sense, to insist that some or all of these things are dimensions of communism and must be opposed as an intrinsic part of the struggle against communism. Let him fight against them under other, more appropriate banners. The central communist challenge to mankind is too important to be obscured and diluted by injecting an array of extraneous issues.[63]

---

60 Ayn Rand, *The Virtue of Selfishness; A New Concept of Egoism* (New York: New American Library, 1964).
61 Garry Wills, "But is Ayn Rand Conservative?" *National Review* (February 27, 1960), p. 139. See also Whittaker Chambers' classic review of Rand's novel *Atlas Shrugged*: "Big Sister is Watching You" *National Review* (December 28, 1957), p. 596.
62 Quoted from Eliza Simmons, "Who's an Objectivist?" *The New Guard* (May 1962), p. 21.
63 Eugene Lyons, "Anti-Communism and the 'Radical Right'" *The New Guard* (January 1962), p. 8.

Setting guidelines for responsible conservative opinion was one thing. Attempting to write a specific organization such as the John Birch Society out of the movement, however, was quite another. Buckley and his associates had several reasons to be cautious. Some of them were strategic. After all, the society had more members than most of the "responsible" organizations. Could the conservative movement afford to leave them out? If so, how would an open split be used by liberal critics?

Buckley and Rusher also had considerations about the direct impact on *National Review*. How many subscriptions would be cancelled? What damage would open repudiation of the society inflict upon the finances of the *National Review*? How would it affect personal relations with sponsors and associates who were birchers, or at least sympathetic to the organization? Robert Welch, Jr. had actually been among the initial sponsors of *National Review*, and privately he and Buckley had remained on friendly terms so far.[64] Furthermore, both Buckley's former partner Willi Schlamm and *National Review*-contributor Morrie Ryskind were birchers. So was the journal's leading sponsor Roger Milliken.

One *National Review*-contributor, Richmond *Newsleader*-editor James Kilpatrick, had previously experienced the wrath of Welch and his supporters when he described the society's campaign to impeach Earl Warren as preposterous. The result had been more than 400 letters from angry birchers. "This has been the most incredibly disciplined pressure group ever to come my way," he warned Buckley, "and we are frankly a little stunned by it."[65]

Nevertheless, in early 1962 Buckley met with Barry Goldwater, Russell Kirk, William J. Baroody, Jr., and a couple of other conservative organizers in Palm Beach. The purpose of the meeting was to find the best way to distance their brand of responsible conservatism from Welch's endless stream of conspiratorial accusations. In this context, the best way meant the way that caused least disruption of the movement, financially and

---

64 In order to get his support for the venture, Willi Schlamm had even told the wealthy candy manufacturer that the prospective journal "would have to count on the literary contribution of Robert H. W. Welch, Jr., author of two of the finest pamphlets this country has read in a decade." Letter, Willi Schlamm to Robert Welch, Jr., July 4, 1955. William F. Buckley Papers, box 4. Schlamm later became associate editor of the John Birch Society's journal *American Opinion*.
65 James Kilpatrick to William F. Buckley, Jr., March 27, 1961, William F. Buckley Papers, box 15.

otherwise. They decided to limit the casualties by focusing on Welch personally, and avoiding any direct criticism of the regular birchers.[66] Thus, Buckley who had once tried to save McCarthyism from McCarthy now took it upon himself to save the John Birch Society from Robert Welch.[67] His article triggered debate among conservatives and led to the cancellation of a couple of hundred subscriptions of *National Review*, but it did not impede the liberal tactics of guilt by association.[68] After all, not many, even among conservatives, believed in the assumption that the majority of birchers probably disagreed with most of Robert Welch's farfetched ideas and truly belonged in the conservative mainstream.

Writing the Birchers Out of the Movement

In 1965, after having learned a hard lesson from what the extremist-issue had done to the Goldwater-campaign, Buckley finally decided to attack the John Birch Society head-on. This time the purpose was not to prompt Welch to resign, but to write the entire organization out of the conservative movement once and for all.[69] Rather than focusing on Welch's notorious charges that Eisenhower was an agent of the communist conspiracy, Buckley turned his attention to recent utterances in the organization's magazine *American Opinion* and found plenty that was just as outrageous.

Medicare was described as a deliberate effort to "destroy the independence and integrity of American physicians" and create a shortage that would give room for physicians and nurses from "communist provinces." The civil rights movement and civil rights legislation were described as "part of the pattern for the communist takeover of America."[70] "Is there in fact substantial disagreement between the membership at large, and the

---

66 William F. Buckley, Jr., "The question of Robert Welch", *National Review*, February 13, 1962, pp. 83-88
67 Before publishing his repudiation, Buckley privately informed Welch of his intentions and motives. Letter, William F. Buckley, Jr. to Robert Welch, January 29, 1962. William F. Buckley Papers, box 20.
68 Letters William A. Rusher, to William F. Buckley, Jr., March 7 and March 12, 1962. William A. Rusher Papers.
69 *National Review*, October 19, 1965, pp. 914-920, 925-929.
70 Quoted from William F. Buckley, Jr, "On the Right," syndicated column released August 17, 1965. William F. Buckley Papers.

leadership of the JBS?" Buckley asked, leaving the salvageable birchers with a last avenue of retreat.[71]

Judging from the response, the answer was no. Out of the first 200 responses to his column, only two agreed with his objections to the silly statements in *American Opinion*.[72] Quite a number of respondents wondered whether he too had betrayed the anticommunist cause and had become part of the grand conspiracy.

Now that the cat was out of the bag, Buckley and the *National Review* crowd used their influence in various organizations to put distance between "responsible" conservatives and the radical right. Thus, the leadership of the American Conservative Union cancelled its participation in a conference arranged by "We, The People!" with the following explanation:

> The board believes that the conservative movement cannot survive an association with groups dominant at your meeting which have compromised basic American principles and cast those principles in terms which are irresponsible and fall far short of an accurate analysis of the crisis confronting this country. Conservatism cannot triumph if it allies itself with ideologies which bear no relationship to responsible conservative thought and action.[73]

Conservatives were clearly attempting to let go of their siege mentality. It was no longer considered an unaffordable luxury to contend that the enemy's enemy was not necessarily a friend, regardless of his anti-Communist credentials.

Severing formal ties to various organizations was of course far easier than keeping individual radicals out of the movement. In many conservative enterprises the local chapters had a high degree of autonomy, as was the case in YAF where birchers and others associated with the "radical right" continuously were in charge of some local chapters around the country. Nevertheless, the fact that a line had been drawn in the sand evidenced the growing maturity of the conservative movement. Faced with the wild charges and the nutty theories of the birchers and their like-

---

71 Buckley, Jr., "On the Right," August 17, 1965.
72 William F. Buckley, Jr, "On the Right," syndicated column released August 21, 1965. William F. Buckley Papers.
73 Telegram from Robert E. Bauman, reprinted in "Bruce Deserts Conservatives," *Free Enterprise* (October 1965). William A. Rusher Papers.

minded, conservatives had been forced to outline the limits of "responsible" conservatism. It was no longer possible to simply condemn the evils of Communism without also acknowledging the limits of its influence.

Chapter 9

The Reluctant Crusader

> In election after election for nearly thirty years, the American people have been denied the opportunity to vote for – nay even to listen to – a conservative candidate for the presidency
>
> WILLMOORE KENDALL, 1964[1]

"A Choice, Not an Echo"

THURSDAY EVENING, July 16, 1964, Senator Barry Goldwater stepped to the podium at the Republican national convention in Cow Palace, San Francisco and accepted the nomination as his party's candidate for the upcoming presidential election.[2] Finally, here was the day that conservatives had been looking forward to for decades. They had "taken back" the party, and in the process they had repudiated the common assumption that a presidential candidate could not win the Republican nomination without the support of the eastern establishment. They had stunned their liberal opponents with a well-organized *coup d'etat*. Now the time had come to abandon the pragmatic nature of the party system and instead create a division along ideological lines. The conservatives were ready to offer "a choice, not an echo."

The story of Barry Goldwater's candidacy in the presidential election of 1964 falls in three parts. The first part is the story of one of the most successful ventures in American political history, the "draft Goldwater movement" which ultimately won him the nomination. The second part

---

1   Willmoore Kendall, "What Goldwaterism is all about," *The New Guard* (October, 1964), p. 9.
2   Goldwater had won the nomination with 883 delegates, as opposed to 214 for Scranton, 114 for Rockefeller, 41 for Romney, and 27 for Margaret Chase Smith.

is the story of why and how Goldwater got buried in a landslide election that paved the way for Lyndon B. Johnson's "Great Society." The third part of the story was added after the presidential election of Ronald Reagan in 1980. It tells of how conservatives amidst predictions of demise maintained their control of the GOP and continued the development of a political infrastructure which 16 years later would help Ronald Reagan to the White House.[3] This idea of continuity from the Goldwater-campaign to the triumph of the New Right will be explored in the last chapter of this book. First, however, we must take a closer look at the conservative champion of the 1960s, Senator Barry Goldwater of Arizona, and the changes within the American polity that made his nomination possible.

"Mr. Conservative"

How could a second-term senator from a small state with only five electoral votes acquire the status of being the country's leading conservative politician? One part of the explanation is that Goldwater had stepped into a void in the late 1950s. Since the death of Senator Robert Taft in 1953, the Republican right had been in search of a leading figure.

Goldwater had not begun his career in Congress as a dedicated Taft-supporter. He had been elected in 1952 by hanging on to Eisenhower's coat tails. By 1957, however, he had become a persistent critic of the president's pragmatic politics, and on April 8, 1957 he took a crucial step towards his future status as "Mr. Conservative," when he openly attacked the fiscal policy of the Eisenhower-administration, claiming that it did not offer the American public an alternative to liberal policy, but merely a "dime-store New Deal."[4]

Goldwater was not a particularly prominent member of the Senate. He had not sponsored any major legislation. Yet, in many ways the fact that he had not become an "insider" in Washington only made him more attractive to "movement" conservatives. Prior to the 1960 Republican national convention, several people approached Goldwater and asked him to

---

3   For one example, see White, F. Clifton & W.J. Gill, *Why Reagan Won; A Narrative History of the Conservative Movement* (Chicago: Regnery Gateway, 1981).

4   Quoted from Richard Hofstadter, *The Paranoid Style in American Politics* (Chicago, 1979 [1964]), p. 97.

enter the race for the presidential nomination. One of them was Clarence Manion, who tried to organize a "Committee of One Hundred" with the purpose of securing the nomination for the Arizona senator. Goldwater declined the offer, but was forthcoming and did not rule out that he would be willing to run at a later stage. One of the senator's key advisors, Frank Brophy, even indicated that Goldwater would perhaps prepare the soil for a future candidacy by asking delegates from Arizona, Alaska, and Alabama to place his name on the ballot.[5]

Clarence Manion had also nurtured other plans for the promotion of Goldwater: The senator should publish a book in order to strengthen his position as the GOP's leading conservative spokesman. This project eventually resulted in *The Conscience of a Conservative*, which was ghostwritten by L. Brent Bozell.[6] The book became a national bestseller and eventually sold more than four million copies, but although it did have a profound impact the senator's status, Clarence Manion's expectations nevertheless reflected an outspoken naivete concerning the requirements of a national political campaign. He was convinced that the very success of the book would first win Goldwater for the campaign and then the campaign for Goldwater.

Goldwater did briefly enter the campaign at the 1960 Republican national convention when the delegations from South Carolina and Arizona tried to nominate him in defiance of Richard Nixon, but his candidacy was largely a symbolic protest against Nixon's "compact of Fifth Avenue" – his pact with Nelson Rockefeller. However, Goldwater's withdrawal speech provided him with an excellent opportunity to address all conservatives in the country. He called upon them to remain loyal to the party, but also stressed that the time had come for conservatives to get to work if they wanted to take back the party. Nixon's alleged sellout had made it easier for Goldwater to have it both ways: To come across as both a conservative rebel and a Republican loyalist.

In the following years, Goldwater continued to strengthen his position within the Party. As chairman of the Senatorial Campaign Committee, he visited all parts of the country and became well acquainted with dozens of state and county chairmen. In 1961 alone, he had 225 speaking engage-

---

5   Lee Edwards, *Goldwater* (Washington, D.C.: Regnery Publishing Inc., 1995), pp. 105-109.
6   (New York: Manor Books Inc., 1960).

ments around the country. The senator also explored new means of spreading the conservative gospel. Beginning in 1960, he published a newspaper column three times a week, entitled "How Do You Stand, Sir?" Originally written for the Los Angeles *Times*, it was published in some 148 papers by 1962.[7]

By 1963, Goldwater was probably the country's most popular politician, next to President Kennedy, although his popularity probably had more to do with his personality than with his political views. His image defied common stereotypes of a conservative politician. A former successful businessman with rank as major general in the Air Force Reserve, he was perfectly suited for the role as all-American hero. He was good looking, he had verve, and furthermore, a reputation for talking straight and being honest, even when it wasn't politically expedient.

Despite the fact that his political rhetoric was loaded with frontier mythology and tales from the glorious days of free enterprise when his grandfather settled in the Southwest, Goldwater was a modern man. Not much of a traditionalist in the first place, he had an outspoken faith in hi-tech. Whereas Russell Kirk, the traditionalist, dreaded cars and denounced them as "mechanical Jacobins, Goldwater the libertarian loved to hit the Arizona highways in his Stingray. He was, in the words of Roger Kahn "every bit as much the simple cowpoke as Franklin Roosevelt was the simple New York apple farmer."[8]

The Rise of the Sunbelt

Goldwater's charm notwithstanding, his political ascendancy was most of all a reflection of the major demographic and economic changes which the country was experiencing in the 1960s. The senator was an icon of the rising "Sunbelt." The increasing importance of the these parts of the country, both economically and politically, was among other things evidenced by the newly won status of cities such as Los Angeles, Dallas and Houston as centers of financial power.

By the end of World War II, a quarter of all the country's banking resources had been concentrated in New York. By 1964, the Big Apple's

---

[7] The column was actually ghostwritten by one of Goldwater's speechwriters, Stephen Shadegg.
[8] "Goldwater's Desperate Battle," *The Saturday Evening Post* (October 24, 1964), p. 20.

share had decreased to just 12 percent. Particularly the South had experienced a remarkable industrial growth. In 1940, the population of that region had been 65 percent rural. By 1960, it was 58 percent urban.[9] Lower wages, low corporate taxes, right-to-work-laws, and free plant sites in new industrial parks were some of the measures used to lure outside companies to the South and the Southwest. Likewise, federal programs and a lion's share of defense contracts and military installations were important factors in the remarkable economic growth of the region.

The process was also changing the balance of power within the GOP. By the early 1960s, the Midwestern bastions of conservative republicanism which had been so closely associated with the presidential campaigns of Robert Taft, had been joined by a growing force of party organizations from the South and the Southwest. Goldwater's candidacy was a perfect expression of this economic and political ascension.

Time and again, Goldwater stressed the gap between the values of the liberal elite and the "frontier" values of his own local community. He largely ignored the role that defense contracts, federal highway construction, hydraulic projects and other government programs had played for the development of his home region. His was a tale of how his own family had settled in the far West without any help from the federal government – a tale of private initiative that made the desert bloom, not with federal aid, but in spite of federal intrusion. This notion of conservatism as a defense of localism was also at the core of Goldwater's ardent support of "states rights." What particularly made many Southern segregationists pay attention was his insistence that despite his own personal dislike of racial segregation, he would not as president have the right to impose such views "on the people of Mississippi."[10]

"Operation Dixie"

Here was of course a major part of the reason why this Republican senator from Arizona was so attractive to the once "Solid South." Goldwater's cam-

---

9   Dewey W. Grantham, *The South In Modern America; A Region at Odds* (New York: HarperCollins Publishers, 1994), p. 261.
10 Barry Goldwater, *The Conscience of a Conservative* (New York: Manor Books Inc., 1974[1960]), p. 38.

paign would reflect the rapid growth of a real two-party system in that region, triggered first of all by the split within the Democratic Party over civil rights. For many Southern Republicans, the campaign's primary purpose was to energize the GOP in their region. Senator John Tower of Texas later reflected on the impact of the Goldwater-campaign in his homestate:

> Barry was like a genie that popped out of Aladdin's magic lamp. He gave us three wishes: We asked for financial contributions – and the money rolled in; we asked for energetic campaign workers – and volunteers came in the droves; and, as our final wish, we asked for a young, attractive, articulate, energetic candidate for the U.S. Senate to run against the liberal Democratic incumbent, Ralph Yarborough. By 1963, we had funds, manpower, and George Bush.[11]

Race was of course not the only factor contributing to the growth of the GOP in the South. The region's increasing integration into the national economy and the growing number of Northerners that had settled in Dixie during the previous decade were also important. However, it was first of all the politics of race and the growing tensions between the policies of the national Democratic Party and the views held by many Southern democrats which had encouraged them to drop their reservations about the party of Lincoln.

The development in the direction of a two-party system in the South had been evident at least since the defection of the so-called "Dixiecrats" in the election of 1948, where Senator Strom Thurmond of South Carolina challenged President Truman. Symbolically, Thurmond had since switched to the Republican Party and would join Goldwater at several of his rallies in the South.

In the election of 1952, Eisenhower had successfully carried Tennessee, Florida, Texas, and Virginia, and four years later he had managed to add Louisiana to the list. In 1957, his popularity in the region faded after his use of federal troops in the battle over school integration in Little Rock, Arkansas, but that same year, GOP National Chairman H. Meade Alcorn launched "Operation Dixie" as a sustained effort to make inroads in Southern politics. The midterm elections of 1958 had given Republican

---

11 John G. Tower, *Consequences; A Personal and Political Memoir* (Boston: Little, Brown and Company, 1991), p. 166.

congressional candidates a modest total of 606,105 votes in the eleven Confederate states. Four years later, however, the number of Republican votes in these states had increased more than three times, to 2,083,971.[12] The party had also won an important victory, when John Tower of Texas became the first Republican U.S. Senator from the Old Confederacy. The Lone Star State could become an important gateway to the South for a Southwestern candidate such as Goldwater.

Given the relative weakness of the Republican Party-organizations in the South, "Operation Dixie" had provided a new breed of ambitious young conservative politicians with excellent opportunities for fast ascent to leadership. In 1964, the average age of GOP state chairmen in the South was just over thirty-six.[13] Among the "new breed" conservatives were John Grenier and Peter O'Donnell, Republican state chairmen in Alabama and Texas, respectively. Both would become leading figures in the "draft Goldwater" movement.

Undoubtedly, Goldwater benefited from years of Republican mobilization in the South, but in return his personality and his political profile did much to remove longstanding reservations about the GOP in that region. Conservative commentators such as James J. Kilpatrick worked hard to convince Southern voters that Goldwater symbolized everything they revered. Apart from being critical of the UN, skeptical of foreign aid, and eager to further limit the powers of organized labor, the man from Arizona stood for "States Rights, strict construction, limited government, private enterprise, and America First, last and always."[14]

Many seemingly agreed with Kilpatrick. The senator's supporters in the region were often more dedicated to him than to the Republican Party as such. Partisan loyalty would grow stronger in the years to come, but Goldwater was probably the only Republican candidate in the election of 1964 that could win in the South. That was a key element in the strategic considerations of the people behind "the Draft Goldwater Committee." Before they could test their assumption, however, they would have to pass two hurdles: first they would have to get Goldwater to run, and then they would have to help him win the nomination.

---

12 Figures quoted from "Can Goldwater Win?" (unsigned), manuscript. William A. Rusher Papers.
13 John H. Kessel, *The Goldwater Coalition.; Republican Strategies in 1964* (Indianapolis: The Bobbs-Merrill Company, Inc., 1968), p. 40.
14 James Jackson Kilpatrick, "Goldwater Country," *National Review* (April 9, 1963), pp. 281-82.

The Draft Goldwater Committee

Shortly after Nixon's defeat in the presidential election, Goldwater's speechwriter and former campaign manager Stephen Shadegg arranged a meeting between the senator and a group of influential businessmen headed by Roger Milliken and Charles Barr, at the Jefferson Hotel in Chicago. Although it was not openly discussed, the real concern of Milliken and his associates was to get a sense of whether Goldwater had any possible interest in the 1964 nomination.[15] The meeting hardly made them any wiser.

Eleven months after the meeting arranged by Shadegg, on October 8, 1961, twenty-two conservative Republicans met, once again at the Jefferson Hotel in Chicago, to discuss strategies that might secure Barry Goldwater the party's nomination for president in 1964. Roger Miliken and Charles Barr were also among the participants this time, but the driving force came from a group of ex-Young Republicans, headed by F. Clifton White, Congressman John Ashbrook of Ohio and William A. Rusher.[16] From their days in YR they had maintained an informal network of people who were now active in senior Republican politics. Just by gathering these people, Rusher estimated, they could become a strong influence in the GOP.[17]

But the organizers had more than an informal gathering in mind. These people would become the hard core of a nationwide political organization, which in the following three years would work for the nomination of Barry Goldwater as the next republican presidential nominee. The organization would later become publicly known as the "Draft Goldwater Committee," but at this stage it was still just an informal committee, operating quietly – some would say secretly – to secure the necessary support for Senator Goldwater, if he agreed to run in 1964.[18]

---

15 Shadegg, Stephen, *What Happened to Goldwater?* (New York: Holt, Rinehart and Winston, 1965), p. 38.
16 Among the participants were also Ned Cushing of Kansas, Ione Harrington and Congressman Donald Bruce of Indiana, Robert F. Chapman of South Carolina and former Republican National Committeeman Frank A. Whetstone of Montana. Among those who later joined the ranks of the organizers were Wirt Yerger, state Republican chairman in Mississippi, Peter O'Donnell and Tad Smith of Texas, and Governor Don Nutter of Montana.
17 Letter, W. A. Rusher to L. Brent Bozell, September 20, 1961. William A. Rusher Papers.
18 F. Clifton White's own account of the organizing of the movement can be found in *Suite 3505; The Story of the Draft Goldwater Movement* (New Rochelle, N.Y.: Arlington →

During Goldwater's presidential campaign three years later it became common to describe the widespread support for the Arizona senator in the basic party structure as the revenge of the Taft-Republicans. The Arizona senator was, wrote the *New Republic*, "the chosen instrument of that passion for vengeance which endures in the Taftites a decade after his death."[19] There was some truth to that, but the key people behind the "draft," F. Clifton White and William Rusher, had actually both been closely associated with Thomas Dewey in New York. White had served as chairman of "Youth for Dewey" in 1948, and had later continued his loyalty to Dewey as national chairman of the Young Republicans.

White would later say that his reservations about Taft had mostly been of a pragmatic nature. It was first of all lack of faith in Taft's chances of winning an election that had prompted him to work for Eisenhower in 1952, hoping that along the way the general could somehow be steered in a more conservative direction. By 1957, however, he and Rusher had lost faith in Ike's moderate conservatism and had approached the Old Right elements of the party instead.

White had more than devotion to offer them. Despite an academic background as college professor, he had gained a reputation as one of the shrewdest and most efficient campaign-organizers in the Republican fold. In 1958, White served as campaign manager in the conservative New York State Senator Walther J. Mahoney's attempt to wrestle the gubernatorial nomination from Nelson Rockefeller. Two years later he had worked for Nixon's presidential campaign. Soon after Nixon's defeat, however, he began to make elaborate plans for a Conservative alternative to the "me-too Republicanism" of the eastern establishment.

White and his associates established a headquarters for the operation in an obscure office in New York City (in its correspondence, the so far nameless committee simply used the address, "Suite 3505" for identification.) From this office White and his assistant Rita Bree coordinated the work of the embryonic movement. They meticulously gathered informa-

---

← House, 1967). William A. Rusher has told his version of the story in *The Rise of the Right* (New York: William Morrow and Co., 1984). See also Stephen Shadegg, *What Happened to Goldwater?* (New York: Holt, Rinehart and Winston, 1965), Karl Hess, *In a Cause That Will Triumph* (New York: Doubleday & Company, Inc., 1967), and Barry Goldwater's own political memoirs Goldwater, *With No Apologies* (New York: William Morrow and Company, Inc., 1979), and *Goldwater* (New York: Doubleday, 1988).

19 "Who's for Barry?" *The New Republic* (July 20, 1963), p. 3.

tion about all the state and local branches of the Republican Party, their leadership, major contributors, and likely delegates. White began travelling around the country, attempting to recruit conservative delegates for his Goldwater campaign. Often, he would open his speeches by saying: "we're going to take over the Republican Party and make it the conservative instrument of American politics."[20] There was just one minor problem, though: persuading Senator Goldwater to play his intended part.

The Man Who Did Not Want to Be President

Although Goldwater had accepted the position as the country's leading conservative figure, it was nevertheless evident that he did not lust for the presidency. The fact that he had eventually accepted the support from South Carolina and his home state Arizona at the 1960 Republican national convention was not an indication of presidential ambition, he would later argue, but merely part of an attempt to push Nixon in a more conservative direction.

His apparent reluctance to run could of course be interpreted as a gimmick. To many supporters, it was an essential part of his appeal that he seemed more concerned with the spreading of the conservative gospel than with personal political ambitions. Yet, judging from his persistent reluctance, which along the way created serious difficulties for the organizers of the draft, there is no reason to doubt that his reservations were genuine. Was 1964 the right year for a conservative candidate? Goldwater feared that his candidacy might deflate a politically immature conservative movement. At some occasions he also aired the opinion that 1968 would be a much better year, since Kennedy by then would be prohibited by law from re-election.

However, most of Goldwater's reservations were of a more personal nature. In 1964 his Senate seat would be up for reelection. After 1960 he had lambasted Lyndon B. Johnson for running for both the vice presidency and the Senate at the same time, so he could hardly himself run for two offices now. Was he willing to give up his place in Congress for a symbolic crusade?

Furthermore, Goldwater openly expressed doubts about his own qualifications for the Oval Office. "I'm not even sure that I've got the brains to

---

20 White, *Suite 3505; The Story of the Draft Goldwater Movement*, p. 163.

be President of the U.S.," he told one reporter.[21] Likewise, he had doubts that his political style and instincts were compatible with common expectations to a president. In a letter to Frank S. Meyer he wrote: "I have never been much of a leader, but more of a pusher, and I think I can do more in that role that I can by stepping out in front."[22]

Like Taft before him, Goldwater did not show much interest in the ballyhoo, which is an essential part of presidential politics. He was, as his speechwriter Karl Hess expressed it, "not very hot on the handshake circuit."[23] Also, he consistently defied the common political wisdom of attempting to be all things to all men, by sticking to unpopular positions on a variety of issues. As one of his supporters, Senator Norris Cotton of New Hampshire noted, Goldwater seemingly made "a fetish of frankness."[24] So, even though Goldwater's honesty, integrity, candor, and brashness were among the major causes for his personal popularity, they would also turn out to be his greatest liabilities in the presidential campaign.

Goldwater's refusal to sugarcoat the conservative pill and his tendency to shoot from the hip scared many voters away and detracted attention in the news from his well-prepared speeches. It also forced him and his staff to spend a good deal of their energies on explaining and modifying previous statements. Goldwater was so eager to demonstrate his integrity that he would attack tobacco subsidies in North Carolina, Medicare among the senior citizens of Florida, anti-poverty programs in poverty-stricken West Virginia, and farm subsidies in Iowa and the Dakotas. Likewise, the straightforward sometimes casual – manner in which he talked about Cold War issues, often gave his audience the impression that a nuclear war with him in the White House would be just another day at the office.

The Rivals

If Goldwater's brashness furthered the adoration of many dedicated conservatives, it also made many fellow Republicans dread the thought that

---

21 Quoted from "Peddler's Grandson," *Time*, July 24, 1964, p. 22.
22 Barry Goldwater to Frank S. Meyer (undated), William F. Buckley Papers, box 25.
23 Karl Hess, *In A Cause That Will Triumph* (Garden City, N.Y.: Doubleday & Company, Inc., 1967), p. 2.
24 Charles Mohr, "Close Look at a Puzzled Candidate," *New York Times Magazine* (May 17, 1964), p. 11.

he might win the presidential nomination. Their fears triggered a frantic search for alternatives. Nelson Rockefeller had of course been a major contender for a long time, but his candidacy had been weakened by his scandalous divorce of his wife of thirty-one years, and his subsequent remarriage to a much younger woman. Other potential nominees were Governor George Romney of Michigan, Henry Cabot Lodge, who served as Lyndon B. Johnson's ambassador to Vietnam, and Pennsylvania Governor William Scranton.

Richard Nixon was also waiting on the sideline. Although he told the press after his humiliating defeat in the 1962 gubernatorial election in California that they would not "have Nixon to kick around any more," he was a political animal who could not be counted out. However, Nixon was clearly not in a position to take charge. His only real chance would be a deadlock at the Republican National Convention in which case he would be ready to offer his candidacy.

Organizing the Goldwater coalition

Goldwater had once noted that it would be difficult to find a candidate who could satisfy all factions of the Republican Party: "Rockefeller would be hard to sell in the Middle West. I would be hard to sell to the Eastern Seaboard, and Nixon would be hard to sell to anybody."[25] From the outset it was one of F. Clifton central ideas that Goldwater did not have to be sold to the Eastern Seaboard in order to win the nomination. In order to win, he would remind potential supporters, Goldwater did not need a majority of the popular vote, but merely a majority in the Electoral College. Accordingly, the strategy would be selective to target majorities in the right constellation of states. White was ready to largely give up the North and the East in advance. In his estimate, the Arizona senator would at best be able to pick up some 11 out of 132 electoral votes A winning coalition, White would argue, could be created from a coalition of small states, joining Southerners and Westerners with the old Taft Republicans of the Midwest. The big states would have to be left to the democrats.

---

25 Quoted from Mark Sherwin, *The Extremists* (New York: St Martin's Press, 1963), p. 39.

His strategy ran counter to the liberal Republican's argument that the GOP had to take big industrial states such as New York, New Jersey, Pennsylvania, and Michigan in order to win, and that since these states had powerful unions and influential ethnic minorities, it would take a moderate Republican to woo them away from the Democrats. This was of course a major argument for the nomination of a candidate such as Nelson Rockefeller.

The conservative response was that Rockefeller might do better than Goldwater in his homestate New York, but that it didn't really matter as long as Kennedy would win in that state anyway. White and his associates did expect to win in states such as Ohio, Indiana, Iowa, Wisconsin, and perhaps Illinois, as well as in the Mountain States. California, with its 40 electoral votes, was labeled as "undecided" and naturally targeted as a major battleground in the election.

The most important part of the equation, however, was the Southern vote. This vote, it was argued, would not be available to just any Republican candidate, and certainly not to Rockefeller, but in a contest with Kennedy, Goldwater could get as much as 100 of the 270 electoral votes at stake in the once "Solid South."[26] All in all, according to the people behind the Goldwater-movement, their candidate would be able to win the presidential election with a total of 280 electoral votes, as compared with 196 for Kennedy. The next step was to go out and convince Republicans across the country that this estimate was more than wishful thinking.

During 1962, Clifton White personally visited some 28 states in order to establish contacts, and by the beginning of 1963, the organization had contacts within the GOP in 42 of the 50 states.[27] Liaisons within the student organizations YAF and ISI were also in place, and White's assistant Rita Bree was well connected in the National Women's Federation.[28] Furthermore, it was part of White's plan to have a contact in every county and congressional district in the country by the middle of 1963, as well as to have established the leadership for a citizens' organization in each state well before Goldwater hopefully declared his candidacy. In time it would also be a crucial task for the committee to develop liaisons to influential

---

26 The estimate of electoral votes was reprinted in "'Draft Goldwater' Move Starts—Its Meaning," *U.S. News & World Report* (April 29, 1963), pp. 42-45.
27 Letter, F. Clifton White to Roger Milliken, January 9, 1963. William A. Rusher Papers.
28 Letter, F. Clifton White to Roger Milliken, January 9, 1963. William A. Rusher Papers.

and conservatively inclined organizations such as the American Medical Association, the Farm Bureau, the National Chamber of Commerce, and the National Association of Manufacturers.

The basic organizational principle of the still secret Goldwater-movement was to work from the bottom up. Two thirds of the delegates would not be elected in primaries, but at party conventions. Hence the plan was to organize volunteers at the precinct-level and fill vacant committee posts with dedicated conservatives. In 1962 almost all of the states would have precinct caucuses, which would name precinct, community and county committeemen. These people would still serve two years later when delegates for the state conventions were to be picked. Thus, a primary task of the organization was to make sure that dedicated conservatives were selected for these precinct positions.

Next, attention would move on to the county- and congressional district levels. An elaborate system was set up to keep track of the delegates. Most states would have a designated Goldwater leader, who would be a member of the delegation. This person was supposed to pass on information to the other Goldwater delegates in his state. In addition to this, an outside man would observe and forward information regarding the delegates.[29]

A so-called "buddy system" was also set up. Goldwater delegates were assigned to socialize with less dedicated delegates in order to insulate them from pressure from the "stop-Goldwater" forces.[30] The idea behind this elaborate organizational system was that by fighting scores of small, unpublicized battles, the battle could be halfway over before it had even been noticed on the state and national levels. This was the blueprint for a conservative *coup d'etat*.

Gathering delegates for Goldwater was of course the primary task for the movement, but keeping delegates away from Rockefeller was also important, particularly as long as Goldwater had not yet entered the race. One way of securing this was through the support of favorite son candidacies, which, if necessary could lock up various state delegations for the time being. Rockefeller should not be allowed to run unopposed in any of the primary elections. With a little luck, he could even be persuaded not to run against favorite sons in a number of primaries.

---

29 Stephen Shadegg, *What Happened to Goldwater?*, p. 138.
30 Shadegg, *What Happened to Goldwater?* p. 139.

While some Goldwater delegates were secured by organizing from the bottom up, others were secured by organizing from the top down. This was possible in states such as Indiana, Missouri, and Illinois where the party leadership supported Goldwater. In other states such as Iowa, White and his allies fought their way to control. In many states the liberal and moderate Republicans never knew what hit them. As William Rusher would later recall:

> While the media continued to yawp about the inevitability of Nelson Rockefeller, the Goldwater forces watched the senator's strength, in terms of delegates pledged and probable, plus those likely to be elected in early 1964 in the primary states, edge upward toward the point of unstoppability.[31]

The Young Republicans

The College Young Republicans were already controlled by White and his associates. The next step was to win control of the National Young Republicans who played a key role in their plans. With its approximately 400,000 dues-paying members, YR was one of the largest political groups in the country and the Arizona senator was clearly a very popular candidate here.[32] Under the leadership of F. Clifton White and William Rusher in the mid-1950s, YR had experienced a decisive shift to the right. However, in 1961, White and Rusher's faction, often referred to as the "syndicate," had lost control of the leadership in the organization, and the faction now in control evidently had strong connections to the Rockefeller forces.

For the "syndicate," seizing control of YR at the 1963 national convention was a crucial step in the effort to win the nomination for Goldwater the following year. In return, other forces within the Party sensed the danger and were determined to maintain the existing leadership. The result was a bitter struggle over the national chairmanship. It provided White

---

31 William A. Rusher, *The Rise of the Right*, p. 156.
32 William K. Wyant, Jr., "Stakes High As Factions Fight For Control of Republican Party," in *Ultraconservatism in the 1964 Presidential Campaign*, special issue of the St. Louis *Post-Dispatch* (undated), p. 5.

with an excellent opportunity to demonstrate all his political skills, not least his ability to win control over the credentialing process.[33] Eventually the "syndicate's" candidate, Donald "Buz" Lukens – a dedicated Goldwater-supporter and an active participant in the "Draft Goldwater"-movement, won by two votes. A straw poll taken among the delegates at the convention indicated an overwhelming support for his position: Goldwater had an eight-to-one margin of support over Nelson Rockefeller as presidential candidate.[34]

Exposed!

Throughout most of 1962, the "draft Goldwater Committee" had to work on a low level of intensity. The senator was occasionally briefed about the progress made by White, but he still did not give much encouragement in return. Actually, he appeared to be very annoyed by the efforts at his behalf. Since it was obviously difficult to raise money on behalf of an unwilling candidate, the financial situation got so bad that F. Clifton White had to invest his personal savings in the project.

Despite all the hardship, the committee could hold its first full-scale meeting in the first days of December. More than fifty people showed up in Chicago to attend it. The group now included Republican chairmen from three Southern states; John E. Grenier of Alabama, Wirt Yerger of Mississippi, and Peter O'Donnell of Texas, as well as Congressman William Brock of Tennessee. It soon turned out, however, that not all of those attending the meeting were equally dedicated to the cause. News of the meeting was leaked to the public by a reporter from the liberal Republican journal *Advance,* who had somehow managed to attend.[35] His presence at the meeting caused uproar when it was disclosed, but neither the organizers nor any of the other participants seriously challenged the sub-

---

33 The struggle is described in details in Rick Perlstein, *Before the Storm*, pp. 217-222.
34 "NSA, Young GOP, Young Dems," *The New Guard*, September, 1963, p. 9. Another poll taken by YAF in early 1964 confirmed the picture: as many as 82.7 percent of the participants in the Young Republican Leadership Training school in Washington, D.C. backed Goldwater, while Governor Scranton, with only 5.2 percent, was the nearest contestant (*The New Guard*, February, 1964, p. 16).
35 *Advance* (Spring, 1963), pp. 18-21.

stance of his report. The committee had been exposed; it could no longer work in secrecy.

According to the *Advance*-reporter, Clif White had explained the advantages of a "draft:" It gave Goldwater a maximum of freedom for personal political maneuvering, it made him less of a political target, and intra-party attacks could be better and more freely handled by that organizers of the draft than by the senator himself. White had also assured the participants that Senator Goldwater himself had been "very helpful" in the organizing of the movement.

When confronted with the issue, Goldwater flatly denied any knowledge of the committee's work: "I don't know a thing about it. I don't know who the group was, where they met or what it's all about," he told the press.[36] The senator also stressed that he did not want anyone to paint him into a corner. It was his neck, as he put it. Goldwater did, however, leave a tiny opening for the committee: "I still plan to run for the Senate two years from now" he said, but added that he might not "since things change and its too early to be absolutely certain."[37] Now that their venture had become publicly known, White and his associates would repeatedly stress that the main thing was the Conservative cause, not one particular candidate. Yet, it was difficult to see any alternatives to Goldwater on the horizon.

White and his associates were still doing everything within their power to obtain even the slightest sign of encouragement from the senator. In January of 1963, William A. Rusher wrote the senator that their organization was "very probably the last one that will ever seek, in a serious and systematic way, to turn the GOP into more conservative channels."[38] The following month, when spirits in the committee had reached a new low, *National Review's* Frank Meyer wrote another appeal to Goldwater. He explained that he had taken the liberty to write because he felt that "the future of the United States" was at stake."[39]

---

36 Cabell Phillips, "G.O.P. Group Opens Goldwater Drive," The New York *Times*, December 4, 1962.
37 Phillips, "G.O.P. Group Opens Goldwater Drive."
38 Letter, William A. Rusher to Barry Goldwater, January 18, 1963. F. Clifton White Paper, Olin Library, Cornell University.
39 Letter, Frank Meyer to Barry Goldwater, February 11, 1963, Denison Kitchel Papers, Hoover Institution.

Meyer was convinced, he wrote, that a major partisan realignment was taking place "equivalent to the change F.D.R. made thirty years ago when he broke the long Republican ascendancy."[40] It was Goldwater's "duty" to provide leadership to "a responsible and sober conservative alternative to the ruinous Liberal leadership."[41] Even a defeat would leave a powerful conservative opposition. Of course Goldwater had compelling reasons not to announce his candidacy prematurely. Meyer's wish was merely that the senator would not do anything, publicly or privately, that would discourage "those who look to you; to take whatever steps are necessary to make yourself an available candidate."[42]

Barry Goldwater's answer to Frank Meyer somehow encouraged White and his associates to press on. Although Goldwater claimed that he still hoped he wouldn't have to step in front, his response was nevertheless close to a commitment to run: "I doubt that I am the only man who can give leadership at this moment, but if that be true, it will be proven, and I don't think I have ever ducked anything in my life..."[43]

In March of 1963, Goldwater told reporters that he had done everything he could "to convince these people that I am not their man."[44] He also stressed that he had no ongoing contact with the committee. The otherwise precise *Advance*-report talked about a liasion between the Committee and the Goldwater staff. Both sides categorically denied this. The senator asked reporters if they wouldn't assume that if he decided to become a candidate – which he wouldn't – that he would also create his own organization?[45] Still, such statements did not compel the committee to give up its project. Someone even suggested that the word "draft" could be taken literally and that the senator could be forced to run, if necessary.

In April 1963, White's committee was formalized as the National Draft Goldwater Committee. Since the organizers considered it wise that someone with a regular position within the GOP headed the drive, the seat as national chairman was given to Texas State Republican Chairman Peter

---

40 Letter, Meyer to Goldwater, February 11, 1963, Denison Kitchel Papers.
41 Letter, Meyer to Goldwater, February 11, 1963, Denison Kitchel Papers.
42 Letter, Meyer to Goldwater, February 11, 1963, Denison Kitchel Papers.
43 Letter, Meyer to Goldwater, February 11, 1963, Denison Kitchel Papers.
44 Jack Bell, "Goldwater Not Interested in Draft Move," *Boston Sunday Herald*, March 3, 1963.
45 Bell, "Goldwater Not Interested..."

O'Donnell.⁴⁶ White became the national director. Senator Goldwater responded to the news of a formal national organization working for his nomination by declaring "I am not taking any position on this draft movement. It's their time and their money. But they are going to have to get along without any help from me."⁴⁷

The organizers were more than satisfied with this reaction. They saw Goldwater's neutral stance as a signal to press on. Later the same month Goldwater told the press that he had given up trying to stop the drive to nominate him. It was, as he saw it, a natural result of a widespread frustration among a majority of Republicans with the "me too" politics of the party leadership.⁴⁸ Eighty percent of the delegates to the Republican National Convention in 1960, the senator claimed, had been conservatives, and they had felt let down by the platform. Yet, they had believed that Nixon was far more conservative than liberal and had become disenchanted during the campaign, as they discovered that he was just another 'me too' candidate.⁴⁹ Thus, Goldwater would conclude that the GOP had really lost the 1960 election because it was "not Republican enough."⁵⁰

When did Goldwater finally decide to go along with White and his "draft," and seek the Republican nomination? Since 1962 White had discreetly corresponded with Goldwater about the progress made by the committee. "I do not indicate to anyone, including Peter [O'Donnell], that I am sending you these informal reports," White wrote the senator in June 1963, "as I am sure that if more than two people know something in politics, it soon becomes general knowledge."⁵¹

---

46 The Texan was well suited to serve as a liaison between the Republican right and the grass roots of the conservative movement. A wealthy oilman, O'Donnell was a major financial supporter of *Human Events* and other conservative ventures through his O'Donnell Foundation. He was also a trustee of both ISI and the American Enterprise Institute, just as he served on the National Advisory Board of YAF.

47 "Republicans Start Second Goldwater Draft for '64," The New York *Times*, April 9, 1963, p. 23.

48 Edward T. Folliard, "Goldwater Shrugs Off '64 Boom 'Can't Stop it,'" The Washington *Post*, April 27, 1963, p. A1.

49 In the years following the Goldwater-campaign, Nixon shrewdly managed to repair his image with conservatives, and in 1968 he attracted a large conservative following. It lasted until July of 1971, when the president announced his intentions to visit China. Nixon's last bit of conservative support was lost over wage-price controls, his visit to Moscow, and the SALT treaty.

50 Folliard, "Goldwater Shrugs Off '64 Boom 'Can't Stop it,'" p. A1.

51 Letter, F. Clifton White to Barry Goldwater, June 7, 1963. The Denison Kitchel Papers.

The informal correspondence between the two indicates that at least in early summer 1963, Goldwater had made up his mind about running. By then he clearly expressed his appreciation for the work White was doing on his behalf: "Congratulations on the smooth operation which produces its evidence not daily but hourly."[52] Rather than help White and his associates in their undertaking, however, the senator asked his long-time friend Denison Kitchel to quietly set up a campaign office in Washington, D.C. Another friend and advisor, GM executive Jay Hall, began to quietly investigate Goldwater's prospects around the country. However, it would take more than six months before the senator from Arizona finally went public and announced that he was a candidate for the 1964 presidential election. Strategic considerations or genuine hesitation, it was a major blunder to wait that long. As Goldwater would later concede, "the late entrance was a handicap from which we never recovered."[53]

Popular Support for Goldwater

When F. Clifton White in 1967 wrote his own account of the "draft Goldwater" movement, he dismissed the idea that Goldwater's nomination had been a *coup d'etat:* "Actually I prefer to think that all we did was give direction and focus to a great grassroots movement."[54] However, judging from the opinion polls concerning the senator's support, White's assessment requires some important qualifications. First of all, it is important to distinguish between support in the general public, support among regular Republican voters and support among party activists.

The latter group was clearly much more enthusiastic about Goldwater than Republicans in general. These activists were the grassroots that White was referring to. When the Associated Press took a poll among Republican state and county leaders in the fall of 1963, it revealed that more than 85 percent of them considered Goldwater the party's strongest card against Kennedy.[55] Many of them adhered to the idea that a "hidden" con-

---

52 Letter, Barry Goldwater to F. Clifton White, June 12, 1963. The Denison Kitchel Papers.
53 Barry Goldwater, *With No Apologies*, p. 170.
54 F. Clifton White, *Suite 3505*, p. 37.
55 "Goldwater Wins Wide Lead in Poll," The New York *Times* (November 3, 1963), p. 1.

servative vote would be activated if the Republican Party managed to provide a clear alternative to the politics of the Kennedy administration.

Goldwater's support was also quite impressive in a national poll of Republican leaders taken by *U.S. News & World Report in* October 1963.[56] At this time, months before he officially declared his candidacy, the senator already had the support of a majority of Republican leaders; not just on the state and county level, but also among members of Congress (56%). The Republican governors were the only group where Goldwater did not have a majority (33%). Five months later – right after the New Hampshire primary, which had been a major disappointment for the Goldwater forces – another Gallup poll indicated that out of the 1840 county chairmen who had responded to the survey, 878, or more than 60 percent preferred Goldwater. The closest rival was Nixon, who was preferred by 383 respondents. Only 117 supported Rockefeller.[57]

What the polls reveal about the nature of Senator Goldwater's support is a striking difference between the views of party activists and non-activists. According to political scientist John Kessel, 32.4 percent of those actively involved in party affairs preferred Goldwater as nominee, while only 16.3 percent of the Republicans who took no active part in the campaign had the Arizona senator as their preferred candidate.[58] The activist/non-activist distinctions were not as pronounced among the Republicans who preferred someone else, but found Goldwater almost as good (31.0% and 28.4% respectively), but it was clear in the group who were "unhappy about Goldwater:" 36.0 percent of the activists, but more than half – 55.3 percent – of the non-activists shared this view.[59]

Even as Senator Goldwater passed the point of unstoppability by winning the California primary on June 2, 1964, very few voters jumped on the bandwagon. A Gallup poll released the same month not only gave President Johnson a 77 percent to 18 percent margin over Goldwater, it also indicated that a majority of Republican voters (55%) preferred

---

56 "Will It Be Goldwater, Rockefeller, or —?" *U.S. News & World Report* (October 7, 1963), pp. 46-48.
57 George Gallup, "With the 'Pros' It's Goldwater," March 29, 1964, Quoted from New York Goldwater for President Confidential Report No. 4, April 1, 1964, The Denison Kitchel Papers.
58 John H. Kessel, *The Goldwater Coalition*, pp. 128-130.
59 Kessel, *The Goldwater Coalition*, pp. 128-130.

William Scranton as their party's presidential candidate.[60] What made matters even worse for Goldwater was that a majority of those who preferred other candidates (60%) were particularly unhappy about the possible nomination of him.[61] However, the polls also indicated that Scranton and other Republican alternatives were as likely as Goldwater to be buried in a Johnson landslide was. In other words, Goldwater-supporters did not have any compelling reasons not to vote according to their convictions. If the Party was going down to defeat anyway, then why not stick to the candidate they really wanted?

Goldwater himself was well aware that he did not stand a chance against Lyndon B. Johnson, but the year before when he had decided to run, his opponent had been John F. Kennedy, and the entire political situation had been different. Although the senator could not match Kennedy's charisma, he had in many other respects been a perfect opponent for the late president. If Kennedy, his Irish Catholic background notwithstanding, represented the near-aristocracy of the Northeast, then Goldwater embodied the rugged individualism of the emerging "Sunbelt." Personally he felt that as a clear-cut alternative he might have a chance, albeit slim, of defeating Kennedy.[62] In Goldwater's view, even a narrow defeat—within 5 percent—would be a victory for the conservative cause. It would be something that the movement could build on in the future.

When John F. Kennedy was assassinated on November 22, 1963, the rules of the game changed completely. In a sense, Goldwater was now running against both the memory of the dead president and against his successor, Lyndon B. Johnson, who in addition to his popularity and his impressive political skills was given plenty of goodwill by the American public to carry out "Kennedy's legacy." Furthermore, it is a fair assumption that a good deal of Goldwater's previous support in the polls had been an expression of opposition to the Kennedy-administration. Obviously, it had been a crucial part of the Goldwater-strategy in the South

---

60 Only 34 per cent preferred Goldwater. Quoted from John H. Kessel, *The Goldwater Coalition; Republican Strategies in 1964* (New York: The Bobbs-Merrill Company, Inc., 1968), p. 102.
61 Philip E. Converse, Aage R. Clausen, and Warren E. Miller, "Myth and Reality: The 1964 Election," in Cosman, Bernard & Robert J. Huckshorn (eds.), *Republican Politics: The 1964 Campaign and Its Aftermath For the Party* (New York: Frederick A. Praeger, 1968), p. 56
62 For Goldwater's own account of his deliberations, see Barry Goldwater (with Jack Casserly), *Goldwater* (New York: Doubleday, 1988), pp. 138-139.

that the senator could pick up the "anti-Kennedy vote." Now he was suddenly challenging the first Southern president since the Civil War.

The assassination also raised problems of a more personal nature for Goldwater. Just as the death of President Kennedy affected the national mood tremendously, it was also evident to many that it made him even less enthusiastic than before about his own campaign. He often appeared as if he was merely going through the motions, and the tone of his speeches and statements was frequently downright defeatist. But although he and his staff knew that he did not stand a chance in the election, there was no way he could back down at this point without inflicting severe damage on the movement. What was at stake, in Goldwater's view, was the future direction of American conservatism.

Chapter 10

Conquering the GOP

> Here was a new breed of delegate, most of whom had never been to a national convention before. They were going not as a reward for faithful service, not to see the sights of San Francisco, and certainly not to ride the bandwagon of a winner. They were going there for one purpose: to vote for Barry Goldwater. To woo them away to another candidate would be as difficult as proselytizing a religious zealot.
>
> ROBERT NOVAK[1]

The "Arizona Mafia" Takes Over

FOR THE ORGANIZERS of the "Draft Goldwater Committee," January 3, 1964, was a milestone. Senator Goldwater finally announced his candidacy. It was also, however, a day of great disappointment. Not a single one of the organizers, who for almost three years had worked to secure Goldwater the nomination, was now invited to join the inner-circle of his campaign team.

The members of Draft Goldwater Committee still had the organization that the candidate needed, and had at least hoped that they could become a citizens' committee, but the senator was quick to announce that the entire operation was being taken over by the Goldwater for President Committee. There was an understandable resentment about the way in which the entire organizational network which White and his Committee had established was simply taken over by what would become known as the senator's "Arizona Mafia." The whole operation would be headed by the senator's personal friend Denison Kitchel.

---

1 Robert D. Novak, *The Agony of the G.O.P. 1964* (New York: The MacMillan Company, 1965), pp. 345-46.

Denison Kitchel was without doubt the person who was closest to Goldwater. After having completed his education at Yale and Harvard, Kitchel had settled in Arizona, where he practiced law. He was knowledgeable in corporate affairs, particularly in labor-management relations, and had previously worked with Senator Goldwater on legislative matters. But he had never managed a campaign; nor had he any experience in national politics. It would soon become clear that his political instincts were virtually nonexistent.

Dean Burch, who became Kitchel's administrative assistant, did not have any national political experience either. His primary seasoning came from four years as Goldwater's administrative assistant in the 1950s. A third member of the "Arizona Mafia," Richard Kleindienst, had been state chairman of the Republican Party in Arizona and was probably the only member with any real political experience. Goldwater made him Director of Field Operations, a job that White was the obvious choice for.[2]

From the outset it was evident that Goldwater's campaign staff lacked political professionals. The senator was certain to get plenty of loyalty, but would he also get the constructive criticism he needed? Richard Kleindienst warned Goldwater about picking too many teammates without national experience.[3] So did Peter O'Donnell, who felt that the campaign would get unfortunate "loner" connotations if the senator's staff were completely dominated by people from his home state. "This is a national drive for the nomination," O'Donnell stressed, "your top leadership must reflect this."[4]

His arguments did not make much of an expression on Goldwater, who found it crucial to be surrounded by people he knew and trusted – people who, unlike the organizational loyalists, the "movement" conservatives, the proponents of states' rights, and the foreign policy hawks, were most concerned with his personal interests. In his memoirs he would later add another, albeit no very convincing, explanation for why he ignored the advice about the composition of his campaign staff: he was so

---

2   During the campaign Kleindienst left the Goldwater team to run his own campaign for Governor in Arizona. He won the Republican nomination, but like his former boss he was defeated in the election by a liberal Democrat.

3   Richard Kleindienst, *Justice: the memoirs of Attorney General Richard Kleindienst* (Ottawa, Ill.: Jameson Books, 1985), p. 30.

4   Letter, Peter O'Donnell to Barry Goldwater, January 12, 1964. William A. Rusher Papers.

dead sure that his campaign was doomed from the very beginning that he would "only ask friends to walk down a dead-end road with me."⁵ Actually, many of the people he had passed by were very realistic about the senator's odds in a presidential election, but had nevertheless kept walking down that road for several years prior to his final decision to run.

As for F. Clifton White, it had now become obvious to everyone that Goldwater did not like or trust him regardless of his skills and devotion. Perhaps part of the explanation was the very fact that he was actually a shrewd technician, whose primary concern was not political principles but winning elections. The man who had been the driving force in mobilizing Goldwater supporters all over the country, the man who had the most detailed knowledge of Republican affairs in all parts of the country, the man who in contrast to the rest of Goldwater's staff had prior experience in presidential campaigning, was eventually offered a job as Kleindienst's assistant. It was almost an insult, and White was so disappointed, Goldwater later recalled, that he was "on the verge of tears."⁶ Although White first declined the offer, he was persuaded to stay on. However, his relationship to Kleindienst remained tense, and in the middle of February he withdrew from the campaign.

Goofing up in New Hampshire

The first major test for Goldwater and his campaign team was the primary in New Hampshire in March. Just two weeks before the election, Goldwater had secured 48 delegates in Oklahoma and North Carolina without much national attention, but the primary in New Hampshire, where only 14 delegates were at stake, was followed much closer by the national media. Goldwater campaigned extensively in the state; he had the support of strong Republican machinery, the state's senior senator, Norris Cotton, and the largest newspaper, William Loeb's Manchester *Union Leader*. Nevertheless, he was beaten by a write-in campaign for Henry Cabot Lodge.

Goldwater's weak performance made his campaign strategists realize that most of the primaries would largely be a waste of time and energy.

---

5   Barry Goldwater, *Goldwater*, p. 157.
6   Goldwater, *Goldwater*, p. 164.

They would not bring their candidate closer to the nomination. After all, 715 of the 1308 national delegates would not be elected. Traditionally, primary victories are necessary in order to convince county and state leaders that they are backing a likely winner, but the essence of White's strategy had been to take over the county and state organizations and make sure that they were controlled by dedicated Goldwater-supporters. Thus, in most states Goldwater's participation would mostly be a matter of principle. In contrast, Rockefeller, whose support was to be found among rank-and-file Republicans, relied on state primaries as the road to the nomination.

Apart from raising serious doubts about Goldwater's ability to reach beyond the converts, the New Hampshire primary also created another problem, which the senator would have to struggle with throughout the entire presidential campaign. His speeches gave him a reputation of being a verbal gunslinger. The problem was not a lack of well-prepared speeches, as much as the fact that the senator usually followed up by "shooting from the hip" to the audience. These improvised sessions usually made far better headlines than his written essays on conservative principles. Since the senator rarely provided enough information to place his remarks in the proper context, they were frequently distorted. Particularly two statements made in New Hampshire would haunt Goldwater throughout the campaign: 1) that tactical nuclear weapons could be used in case of an enemy attack, if the commander of NATO considered it necessary (According to some of the reporters present, Goldwater said "commanders"), and 2) that Social Security ought to be made voluntary.

As for the NATO commander's permission to use tactical nuclear weapons, it had actually been the policy of the United States under both Eisenhower and Kennedy, but it reinforced Goldwater's image as "trigger-happy." The senator's view that Social Security should be made voluntary was repeatedly presented by the Rockefeller camp and much of the media as an intention to destroy the entire program.[7] The Rockefeller forces exploited the issue by reproducing a distorted version of Goldwater's position from a local newspaper, and mailing it to every Social Security recipient in New Hampshire. And there were many who felt strongly

---

7   See Stephen Shadegg, *What Happened to Goldwater?* (New York: Holt, Rinehart and Winston, 1965), pp. 95-96.

about Social Security in New Hampshire. In 1964 only Nebraska, Iowa and Missouri had a higher percentage of senior citizens than the Granite State.[8] In the months following, the senator remained on the defensive, spending a good deal of his time on the campaign-trail clarifying previous statements.

After his failure in New Hampshire, Goldwater frankly admitted that he had "goofed up somewhere." Baroody and Kitchel's glaring incompetence had not exactly made things easier for him. As a result of the failure, F. Clifton White was brought back into the campaign team and promoted to co-director of field-operations. He would be in charge of the states using the convention system to pick their delegates, just as he would become the chief strategist at the National Convention. Goldwater also picked Karl Hess as his new speechwriter (and passed over Brent Bozell, who had written his two books *The Conscience of a Conservative* and *Why Not Victory?*).

Barry in the Golden State

Although the general strategy was that Goldwater could secure the necessary number of delegates mainly from state conventions, most observers found it crucial that he demonstrated his ability to attract popular support by winning at least one major primary: California. In a "winner takes all" primary as much as 86 delegates were at stake. Not only were these delegates important, but a victory in California would also help him to win over party leaders in the Midwest who were inclined to support a conservative candidate like Goldwater, but concerned about his electability.

Polls taken in April and May had clearly indicated that Lodge was the candidate whom the largest number of Republicans in California would prefer to see as president: (33%), followed by Goldwater (26%), Nixon (18%), Rockefeller (10%), Romney (3%), Scranton (2%), and Smith (1%) (7% remained undecided). Thus, there was some merit to the claim that a majority of Republicans in the state preferred a "moderate" candidate. But Lodge was not an option – Rockefeller was, and if the choice was restricted to Goldwater and him, the polls indicated that Goldwater held a 46 per-

---

8 Theodore H. White, *The Making Of the President 1964* (New York: Atheneum Publishers, 1965).

cent to 27 percent lead.⁹ Yet, the primary would turn out to be a close contest between the predominantly liberal counties in the northern part of the state and the conservatives ones in the southern part.

Southern Californian counties had experienced a significant shift to the right in the previous decade. The brand of Western progressivism, which in the past had been represented by legendary figures such as Earl Warren and Hiram Johnson, was truly in decline here. A clear indication of this process had been given in 1962, when Richard Nixon had to fight hard to win the Republican gubernatorial nomination over hardcore conservative Joseph Shell.¹⁰

One issue that became particularly important in Goldwater's California campaign was defense policy. The senator was a strong proponent of air power, just as Robert Taft had been before him. Not surprisingly, this preference found many supporters in Southern California, where jobs and wealth to a large extent had been created by the rise of the aerospace industry. In Los Angeles, San Diego, Orange, and Santa Clara counties, which contained more than half of the state's population, an estimated 83 percent of all manufacturing jobs created between 1950 and 1962 could be traced to aerospace expenditures. Likewise such expenditures accounted for 62 percent of the net influx of new residents.¹¹ As one might expect, it helped create a political climate that was congenial to a candidate like Barry Goldwater.

Another major asset working for the Arizona senator was the extensive network of conservative grassroots. Organizations such as the Young Republicans of California, YAF, and the John Birch Society provided impressive footwork. In Los Angeles County alone, some 8,000 volunteers worked for the Goldwater campaign, compared with just 2,000 working for Rockefeller.¹² Much of the credit for Goldwater's army of volunteers belonged to Robert Gaston of YR, who himself estimated that he controlled some 80

---

9 Quoted from Kessel, *The Goldwater Coalition*, p. 82.
10 Robert D. Novak, *The Agony of the GOP: 1964* (New York: MacMillan, 1965), p.86. The GOP in California still had a liberal wing which strongly opposed Goldwater. It included groups such as the Committee of Responsible Republicans, and Senator Thomas Kuchel was among the leading figures.
11 Quoted from Michael Miles, *The Odyssey of the American Right* (New York: Oxford University Press, 1980), p. 265.
12 John H. Kessel, *The Goldwater Coalition*.

percent of the operation.¹³ It would take 13,000 signatures to qualify as a candidate for the statewide ballot. The candidates had a period of thirty days to do this, but it was important to do it as quickly as possible, since the first to collect the required number of valid signatures would be first on the ballot. By two o-clock on the very first day, the Goldwater volunteers had already collected more than 18,000 signatures, and within two days they had collected some 85,000.¹⁴ The fundraising effort also demonstrated the efficiency of the Goldwater volunteers. Of the $ 5.5 million raised on the senator's behalf in the Republican primaries, as much as $2 million were raised and spent separately for the California primary. ¹⁵

Two of the leading figures in Goldwater's successful organization were William Knowland and Pete Pitchess, sheriff of Los Angeles County. Knowland, who in 1953 succeeded Robert Taft as majority leader, had been a potential national leader of the conservative movement in the mid-1950s. In 1958, he ran for Governor of California, with anti-union legislation, including a "right-to-work law" as a key issue in his campaign. Although Knowland lost the election, he had managed to create well-organized conservative machinery in the state, and most of his 1958 campaign staff was now working for Goldwater.¹⁶ Knowlands handling of the campaign, however, did not impress Goldwater, who eventually fired him and flew in replacements from Washington, D.C.

In northern California, where Rockefeller was strongest, the Goldwater forces employed a number of unorthodox methods. One of them was massive distribution of Phyllis Schlafly's book *A Choice Not an Echo*.¹⁷ Rus Walton of the United Republicans of California, who subsequently analyzed the effect of this method, claimed that support for Goldwater was 20 percent stronger in the precincts where the book had been distributed than in other precincts with voters of comparable economic, educational, and occupational backgrounds.¹⁸

---

13 White, *The Making Of the President 1964*, p. 125.
14 White, *The Making Of the President 1964*, p. 125.
15 A remarkable $1 million of this amount was raised by Henry Salvatori, who would later become a member of Ronald Reagan's famous "kitchen cabinet."
16 See Kurt Schuparra, "Freedom vs. Tyranny: The 1958 California Election and the Origins of the State's Conservative Movement, *Pacific Historical Review*, Vol. 63 (November 4, 1994), pp. 537-560.
17 (Alton, Ill.: Pere Marquette Press, 1964).
18 Stephen Shadegg, *What Happened*, p. 124.

Goldwater's biggest problem in the California primary was probably the Rockefeller force's recurrent charges that he was outside the Republican mainstream, and that his campaign was in the hands of "radical right" organizations aiming to take over the GOP. It was correct that the birchers were quite visible in the campaign. California was, after all, a stronghold for the organization. Bob Gaston, the powerful leader of the Young Republicans in California was a bircher. So was the leader of the California YAF and Walther Knott, who served on Goldwater's advisory committee.

Yet, the notion that the GOP was in danger of being taken over by the "radical right" could not be substantiated. According to Republican State Chairman Caspar W. Weinberger, it was "mathematically impossible, and realistically improbable" that the Republican State Central Committee could be captured. California was, after all, an open primary state.[19]

Despite Goldwater's superior organizational network, the race with Nelson Rockefeller remained a close one to the end, but in the last days before the election, the Goldwater forces were helped by an event in the governor's private life. Rockefeller's private life had for a long time been a serious political liability, but he had managed to force the issue somewhat in the background. However, just three days before Election Day, it flared up again when his new wife gave birth to a son. Here was a taste of something would later become a dominant theme in American elections: Rockefeller became an early victim of the "family values" controversy.

When the polls closed on June 3 and the votes were counted, Rockefeller had carried 54 out of 58 counties in California. Goldwater narrowly won the primary anyway, due to his pluralities in Los Angeles, Orange and San Diego counties (Los Angeles county alone had 36 percent of all the state's voters). After the victory, Richard Kleindienst had no doubt about who Goldwater could thank for his victory: "all those little ladies in tennis shoes that you called the right-wing nuts and kooks, they're the best volunteer political organization that's ever been put together."[20]

Regardless of whether it was his superior campaign machinery or the untimely addition to the Rockefeller-dynasty that eventually gave Goldwater the victory in California, he had now passed the biggest hurdle on the rocky road to the Republican nomination. Conservatives already re-

---

19 Wallace Turner, "Ultras a Minority of California G.O.P." The New York *Times,* May 17, 1964, p. 44.
20 Quoted by David Broder in the *Washington Star,* July 16, 1964.

joiced over the fact that the voters this time would be offered "a choice not an echo."

Next Stop San Francisco

Although Goldwater's victory in the California primary had almost made his nomination at the Republican national convention in July a foregone conclusion, his opponents within the party nevertheless mobilized a last dramatic effort to stop him. They picked up the theme that Rockefeller had been playing for the past year: Goldwater was a loner, controlled by radical elements outside the party, and the struggle for the nomination was not a choice between liberals and conservatives, but a choice between "moderates" and "extremists."

A couple of days after Goldwater's victory in California, the "moderates" made one last major effort to stop him before the national convention. The attempt took place at the Governor's Conference in Cleveland. The Republican governors were probably the group within the party that was least enthusiastic about the prospect of a Goldwater candidacy. Traditionally, very few governors share the anti-statist sentiments that were at the core of the senator's political program. In 1964, there were sixteen Republican governors, and only three of them supported his candidacy.[21] Thus, the conference provided a proper forum for this last desperate attempt to rally behind an alternative candidate. This candidate could enter the stage in case the "moderates" managed to bring the national convention to a deadlock. While semi-secret meetings were being held, and a major effort was made in order to persuade Governor George Romney to run, Goldwater was bombarded with accusations of being a radical loner, completely out of touch with the Republican mainstream. Even Richard Nixon, who had otherwise been determined to remain neutral for the time being, felt compelled to declare that for "the future of the party, it would be a tragedy if Senator Goldwater's views as previously stated were not challenged – and repudiated."[22]

---

21 The governor's of Montana, Oklahoma, and Goldwater's homestate Arizona.
22 Quoted from F. Clifton White, *Suite 3505...* p. 368. For the events at the Conference of the Governors in Cleveland, see also Theodore H. White, *The Making of the President 1964*, pp. 150-163.

Romney eventually decided that he was not going to run after all, but the attempts to shake delegates in order to derail the Goldwater-train at the upcoming convention continued. Governor Scranton, who had found yet another compelling reason to oppose Goldwater when the senator voted against the Civil Rights Act in July, now offered himself as the moderate's standard-bearer. He told the viewers on national television that Goldwater "had given every evidence of being a man who is seeking not to lead the Republican Party, but to start a new political party of his own."[23] His campaign became intense, but short-lived. Henry Cabot Lodge resigned as ambassador to Vietnam and joined his effort. If they were to stop Goldwater at the convention, they would need each and every uncommitted delegate, plus some two hundred of the delegates already committed to the Arizonan. Indeed, this was not a very likely scenario; particularly not since – as someone in the Scranton campaign put it – the Goldwater people seemingly "had rewired the switchboard of the Party."[24]

As the trenches within the GOP got still deeper, both wings were anxiously awaiting any sign of encouragement from the party's father figure, Dwight Eisenhower. The moderates hoped that an open endorsement from Ike could derail the Goldwater-train in the last minute. The Goldwater team hoped that he would at least remain neutral.

Eisenhower posed a dilemma for the conservatives. They acknowledged his popularity, and many probably shared the widespread personal affection for him. Yet, most of the conservative rhetoric basically ignored his presidency and pretended that there had not been a Republican in the White House since before the dreaded New Deal.

For his part, Ike undoubtedly felt uneasy about Goldwater and preferred to see a candidate such as Scranton win the nomination. One of Goldwater's staff-members later described how Ike on one occasion appeared as if he was "afraid that Barry would drop a nuclear bomb or repeal Social Security right in front of him."[25] Perhaps recalling the deep wounds that his own nomination had created within the party, Eisenhower was nevertheless determined to stay above the fray and attempt to bridge the gap between the two wings. On a more pragmatic note, he also

---

23 Quoted from Kessel, *The Goldwater Coalition*, p. 102.
24 Theodore H. White, *The Making of the President 1964*, p. 166.
25 Quoted in Denison Kitchel, "Explaining Things to Ike," *National Review* (April 30, 1976), p. 447.

realized that neither Scranton not Romney had a chance of stealing the nomination from Goldwater. Neither had Rockefeller, who Eisenhower furthermore had a strong personal dislike for.

What did Scranton, Rockefeller, Nixon, Romney and other Republicans who attacked Goldwater at this late stage really hope to accomplish? Did they sincerely believe that he could be intimidated to leave the race, or that a sufficient number of committed Goldwater-delegates would have second thoughts if they spoke out? Or were they already looking beyond the presidential election in November, hoping that they would be in a position to pick up the pieces afterwards? In any case their strong charges rubbed salt into wounds that had never healed and helped set the stage for a bitter fight at the Republican National Convention in San Francisco.

"So Where do You Stand, Sir?"

From the outset, Goldwater had announced that his presidential campaign would not pursue a clash of personalities, but "an engagement of principles."[26] He intended to challenge the political philosophy of the welfare state with a program based on traditional values, individual responsibility, self-reliance and "law and order." Who were the people assigned to flesh out such a program?

Apart from Denison Kitchel, the most influential person on the senator's campaign team was probably William Baroody. A close friend of Goldwater, Baroody was the leader of a then small conservative think tank called the American Enterprise Institute (AEI). He brought a couple of his colleagues from AEI with him to the campaign team, among them Charles Lichenstein, Gerhard Niemeyer, and Karl Hess. Niemeyer became one of Goldwater's leading advisors in the field of foreign policy, Hess the candidate's favorite speechwriter. The team also included W. Glenn Campbell, a former Director of Research at AEI who had since become the director of another conservative think tank, the Hoover Institution on War, Revolution and Peace at Stanford University.

Considering the fact that Goldwater was a practical politician who often felt uneasy in the company of intellectuals, he could count an impres-

---

26 Kessel, *The Goldwater Coalition*, p. 49.

sive group of university professors among his advisors. Among them were Stefan Possony, Karl Brandt, Stanley Parry, Paul W. McCracken (University of Michigan), Raymond J. Saulnier (Columbia University), Warren Nutter (University of Virginia), and Milton Friedman (University of Chicago).[27]

As chief economic advisor, Friedman left a clear stamp on the candidate's political program. Government should not concern itself with price stability or an active policy of economic stabilization, Goldwater now argued, clearly reflecting Friedman's view that government-attempts to counter the business cycle would only rock the boat further, create inflation, and prolong recessions.[28]

Despite the help of Friedman and other economists, it remained inherently difficult to dress up Goldwater's fiscal conservatism as good news for all voters. This candidate had no sense of "voodoo economics" and no "Laffer-curve" to sugarcoat the pill. Besides, 1963-64 was not a good time to preach fiscal conservatism. It was difficult to sell anti-keynesian views while deficit spending was doing wonders for the American economy.

Combating "Big Government" and "Big Labor"

The senator's economic views as presented during the campaign might not have done much to win over potential voters, but many of his views on social policy actively scared them away. In his bestseller *The Conscience of a Conservative*, Goldwater had argued that while Marxism no longer posed a real threat to American society, "welfarism" did. It was even more dangerous because it was more compatible with the political processes of a democratic society, and, hence, more difficult to combat.[29]

---

27 "Goldwater's Brain Trust," *U.S. News and World Report*, July 27, 1964.
28 There were some other areas, though, where Goldwater did not adopt the views of his economic advisor. Among those were some of Friedman's central ideas on monetary policy, as well as the belief that the dollar should be cut loose from gold. Goldwater also maintained certain protectionist ideas, which did not go well in hand with Friedman's belief in undiluted laissez-faire capitalism. In 1962, he had voted against the law that gave the president the authority to engage in the so-called Kennedy round of GATT negotiations.
29 Goldwater, *The Conscience of a Conservative*, p. 70 ff.

Most of Goldwater's statements on poverty and welfare seemed to reflect a blatant "blame it on the poor" attitude. He clearly rejected the idea of structural poverty as a liberal illusion. In response to the argument that many were poor because they lacked adequate skills or did not have an education, Goldwater told the Economic Club of New York: "The fact is that most people who have no skill, have had no education for the same reason —low intelligence or low ambition."[30] In accordance with the views of his economic advisor Milton Friedman, Goldwater also saw the existence of minimum wages as part of the problem rather than as a safeguard against poverty. If these were removed, there would be little or no unemployment.

Though many liberals and "moderates" were appalled by Goldwater's unrestrained assault on welfare, his views in this field nevertheless struck a chord with anti-statist sentiments that were shared by many Americans. His attacks on Social Security, on the other hand, were political poison. The system was based on an entirely different principle, insurance, and it enjoyed widespread support in the American public. Though the candidate argued that he merely wanted to privatize the system in order to save it from a likely bankruptcy, the issue inflicted severe damage on his campaign.

Goldwater was also hurt by his wish to abandon farm price supports and his suggestion that the federal government should sell the Tennessee Valley Authority. Although he later denied having made such a proposal, it was easily verified.[31] He had even repeated his suggestion several times upon request. Only in the face of strong public reactions did he modify his proposal so that not all TVA-services, but only steam generating plants and fertilizer-production should be sold off.

Labor relations were probably the field in which Goldwater had had the highest profile during his time in Congress. Actually, his involvement in politics had begun during a campaign for "right to work" laws in Arizona, and in 1958 he had made the fight against "labor bosses" the central theme in his campaign for re-election to the Senate. Goldwater had served on the Senate Labor and Public Welfare Committee, and from 1957-60 on the Select Committee on Improper Activities in the Labor or Management Field (the McClellan Committee).

---

30 "Excerpts From Address Here by Senator Goldwater," The New York *Times*, January 16, 1964.
31 For one example, see Stewart Alsop, "Can Goldwater Win in 1964?" *Saturday Evening Post* August 24, 1963, p. 21.

So what, if anything, did Goldwater the ardent advocate of "right to work" laws have to offer union members? Freedom from government interference, he would answer. "I'm probably the voice most loudly heard in defense of labor's right to strike," he told one interviewer.[32] Critics could of course respond that striking did not make much sense if the unions had been stripped of all the powers that could have made such a move effective.

Keeping the "Movement Conservatives" at Arm's Length

"Movement conservatives" remained conspicuously absent from the inner circles of the campaign. Goldwater apparently preferred to stick to a small group of people whom he knew and trusted, rather than to engage himself with them.[33] Stephen Shadegg would later recall how he and most of the other activists who had secured Goldwater the nomination had been dismissed afterwards:

> The finance men, who had raised more than three and a half million dollars to help Goldwater win the nomination, were each given a handsome presentation wristwatch and dismissed. The regional directors, with the exception of John Grenier, did not even rate this much attention. Clif White, Wayne Hood, Dick Hermann, Loyd Waring, Ed Failor, and I were allowed to depart without being told our services had been appreciated or asked by Kitchel, Burch, or the Senator himself to participate in the general campaign. ... All [the] whose brave and almost quixotic early efforts had been ratified by the action of the Republican convention on Wednesday night were now excluded from the inner circle of the candidate they had created.[34]

---

32 Interview by Robert Joseph Allen, July 3, 1963. Denison Kitchel Papers.
33 The people he trusted also included Congressman John J. Rhodes of Arizona, Senator Carl Curtis of Nebraska, Senator Norris Cotton of New Hampshire, former Senator William Knowland of California, the candidate's press secretary Tony Smith, and his research director Edward A. McCabe – a Washington lawyer and former counselor to President Eisenhower.
34 Shadegg, *What Happened to Goldwater?* p. 168. In Shadegg's book, his strong personal disappointment over the marginal role he was assigned in the campaign can be felt on every page. He had handled Goldwater's two senatorial campaigns, but in 1962 he attempted to fulfill his own political ambitions and sought the Republican nomination in order to run against Goldwater's eighty-five-year-old Democratic colleague in the Senate, Carl Hayden. Shadegg (unsuccessfully) ran against Goldwater's wishes and advice, and the senator did not easily forgive him for this alleged breach of faith. During the Republican primaries in 1964, however, he was recruited once again to handle Goldwater's campaign in Oregon.

Conquering the GOP

In his story of the "Draft Goldwater" movement, White conveys the same image of Goldwater. Here is a man who does not express any gratitude to the people who have made it possible for him to win the nomination, and who willingly accepts that his advisors are isolating him from the conservative movement:

> Many an intelligent and effective conservative was forced out by the palace guard and the Senator never, to my knowledge, raised a hand to save them, if indeed he was even aware of the massive throat-slitting that was carried out in his name. Peter O'Donnell, Bill Buckley, Brent Bozell, Mr. X – these were only a few in the long and ever-growing list of casualties mowed down by the Arizona Mafia.[35]

In fact, White himself was kicked out in the cold for the second time by Goldwater's palace guard. It was well known in the Goldwater camp that he had hoped his successful efforts would be rewarded with the GOP National Chairmanship, but already on his night of triumph in San Francisco, the press could tell him that Dean Burch would be Goldwater's choice for the job. Burch was only thirty-six and had no experience in national politics, but unlike White, he was from Arizona. The driving force behind the "Draft-Goldwater" movement was offered a job as director of Citizens for Goldwater-Miller – an organization he by use of his old national network actually managed to turn into an effective vehicle for the campaign. It took more than two weeks after his nomination before the candidate himself took the time to talk to White in person.

According to Goldwater, most members of the "braintrust" opposed the appointment of White to this position, which would be crucial to the campaign. His abilities untold, it was argued that White was not a team player.[36] The opposition to White was particularly strong from William Baroody, who saw him as a stand-in for the *National Review*-crowd – people he for a variety of reasons wanted to keep away from Goldwater.

White was no stand-in, but he did have the support of most movement-conservatives, not just because he deserved the job and was the best qualified candidate, but also because many of them already looked beyond the election to the continuing struggle within the Republican party. In the likely event that Goldwater lost in November, White would be in a

---

35 F. Clifton White, *Suite 3505...*, p. 278.
36 Goldwater, *Goldwater*, p. 188.

much better position than Burch -who did not have any power base of his own – to maintain conservative dominance in the party leadership.

From the early stages of the campaign, Baroody and the "Arizona-mafia" had done their best to minimize the influence of the *National Review crowd* on the campaign. Already in September 1963, William F. Buckley and L. Brent Bozell had approached a longtime friend and key advisor to Goldwater, Dr. Jay Gordon Hall of General Motors, who had arranged a dinner for them with the senator. Their major purpose was to suggest the creation of committee of college professors who would endorse his candidacy. When they arrived for the dinner, it turned out that Kitchel and Baroody had been included in the arrangement as well. A suspicion that the true purpose of their presence at the dinner was to keep Buckley and Bozell away from Goldwater was strengthened a couple of days later when the *New York Times* printed a mysterious little story:

> The Goldwater for President ship has just repelled a boarding party from the forces who supposedly occupy the narrow territory to the right of the Arizona Senator. William F. Buckley, Jr., editor of the right-wing *National Review*, and L. Brent Bozell, who also writes for the magazine, cornered some Goldwater aides the other day. They wanted to join the campaign organization, they said, on the policy-planning level. Feeling that what their candidate needs least is more support from the far right, Goldwater advisers used an old political dodge. They played dumb. They just could not seem to understand what the *National Review* men were getting at. Mr. Buckley and Mr. Bozell reportedly emerged from the conference with no share of the Goldwater command and wondering if they wanted any.[37]

Although the participating Goldwater-advisors denied it when asked directly, Buckley and Bozell naturally suspected that someone present at the dinner had leaked the story to the *Times*. Baroody's suggestion that the room could have been bugged did not seem all that persuasive.[38]

When Goldwater many years later published his political memoirs, he felt compelled to address the incident, which, he claimed, had major repercussions on his campaign. "I'm convinced today that Baroody leaked

---

37 "Random Notes From All Over: Goldwater Aides Counter Right," The New York *Times* (September 16, 1963), p. 30.
38 Stephen Shadegg, *What Happened to Goldwater?* p. 70.

the report," he wrote, "So are Kitchel and others."³⁹ The motive, according to Goldwater, was fear of competition. Unfortunately, Baroody himself had passed away and could no longer confess. Although Goldwater claimed he was "simply too busy to keep track of who was saying what to whom" and did not know about Baroody's efforts to keep the *National Review* crowd at arms length from the campaign, his reflections on the whole incident nevertheless seemed apologetic:

> Buckley, Bozell, and Bill Rusher were virtually shut out from any significant campaign assistance. It was an undeserved, unconscionable act on our part. All are men of the highest integrity and solid conservative views. They should have been on board, talking with me and others and offering feedback on issues, strategy, the media, our opposition, everything. Later, realizing what had happened, I was heartsick about the matter. But what could I say? What could I do? It was too late.⁴⁰

It remains difficult to believe that three of the most central figures in the conservative movement were being kept away from the campaign without the knowledge of the candidate himself. Goldwater must somehow have sanctioned Baroody and Kitchel's position that working with Buckley and his associates might hamper the attempt to reach beyond the converts.

The wish to keep Buckley at arm's length was also illustrated by another incident in May of 1964. The conservative leader had been invited to speak at a youth rally in Madison Square Garden, but Dean Burch vetoed the decision and replaced him with Ronald Reagan. Goldwater subsequently wrote Buckley and apologized. The official explanation was that all the speakers at the rally were supposed to be active Republican political figures.⁴¹ However, Buckley himself was convinced that he had been sacrificed in an attempt by the Goldwater camp to court Dwight Eisenhower, who, as Buckley later explained to Ronald Reagan, "went nuts" at the mention of his name.⁴² Perhaps Ike's dislike of Buckley had been fur-

---

39 Goldwater, *Goldwater*, p. 147.
40 Goldwater, *Goldwater*, p. 148.
41 Letter, Barry Goldwater to William F. Buckley, Jr., May 21, 1964. William F. Buckley Papers.
42 Letter, William F. Buckley, Jr. to Ronald Reagan, August 5, 1964. William F. Buckley Papers.

ther reinforced by the fact that *National Review*-editor seriously worked on the idea of drafting him as Goldwater's vice-presidential running mate.[43]

The canceling of Buckley's speech was not an isolated incident. There would continue to be friction between the "movement" conservatives, including the people who had organized the "draft," and the group of personal advisors who were now running the campaign. Conservatives would remain loyal to Goldwater throughout the campaign, but many of them would since express more ambivalent feelings about his contribution to the cause.

It would be impossible to imagine the Goldwater campaign without the years of ideological mobilization and organizational preparation made by the conservative movement. On the other hand, the movement desperately needed a national political leader in order to make the plunge into politics. The man from Arizona was simply the only option.

On Thursday evening, July 16, 1964, Senator Barry Goldwater took the stage at the Republican national convention in Cow Palace, San Francisco and accepted the nomination as his Party's candidate for the upcoming presidential election.[44] Finally, here was the day that conservatives had been looking forward to for decades: they had "taken back" the party.

The Arizonan's liberal opponents were stunned by the well-organized *coup d'etat* they had just experienced. The Goldwater-forces had repudiated the common assumption that a presidential candidate could not win the nomination without the support of the Eastern establishment. Goldwater's victory, however, did by no means end the strife within the party. Bitterness ran deep. The senator's opponents, for their part, maintained that Goldwater was outside the political mainstream. Thus, they helped the democrats make "extremism" a central theme in the election.

"The tactics of totalitarianism"

It was Rockefeller who had first introduced the "extremist" theme one year earlier during the Young Republicans National Convention. When

---

43 Plans discussed in memo, William A. Rusher to William F. Buckley, Jr. and James Burnham, June 17, 1964. William A. Rusher Papers. Rusher personally feared that open support for the idea in *National Review*, would make the crowd around the magazine look "somewhere between faintly amusing and downright ludicrous."

44 Goldwater had won the nomination with 883 delegates, as opposed to 214 for Scranton, 114 for Rockefeller, 41 for Romney, and 27 for Margaret Chase Smith.

the media made alarming reports about the strong support among the delegates for radical measures such as a constitutional amendment to prohibit a Federal income tax (the "Liberty Amendment"), the New York governor used the opportunity to warn the public that the Republican Party was "in real danger of subversion by a radical, well-financed and highly disciplined minority, ... operating through ... the tactics of totalitarianism."[45] In his so-called "Bastille Day Declaration", July 14, 1963, he had elaborated on the theme:

> Every objective observer at San Francisco has reported that the proceedings there were dominated by extremist groups, carefully organized, well-financed, and operated through the tactics of ruthless, roughshod intimidation. These are the tactics of totalitarianism. Unfortunately, this cannot be brushed off as irresponsibility. For youth is responsible. The leaders of the Birchers and others of the radical right lunatic fringe — every bit as dangerous to American principles and American institutions as the radical left — who successfully engineered this disgraceful subversion of a great and responsible auxiliary of the Republican Party are the same people who are now moving to subvert the Republican Party itself.[46]

Rockefeller, who consistently had appealed to party unity as long as he himself was considered the frontrunner for the Republican nomination, had taken the issue one step further in August 1963, when he explicitly said for the first time that he could not support Goldwater if the Arizona senator turned out to be a "captive of the radical right."[47] Since then, the "extremist" theme had become still more dominant in the effort to stop Goldwater. As it became clear after the California primary that neither Rockefeller nor any of the other possible candidates would be able to secure the necessary number of delegates beforehand, the only option left seemed to be to create or provoke a situation at the convention which might derail the Goldwater-train

---

45 Quoted from William A. Rusher, "The Draft-Goldwater Drive: A Progress Report," *National Review* (September 10, 1963), p. 186.
46 Quoted from Michael Kramer & Sam Roberts, *"I Never Wanted To Be Vice-President of Anything!" An Investigative Biography of Nelson Rockefeller* (New York: Basic Books, 1976), pp. 274-75.
47 Quoted from Barry Goldwater, *Goldwater*, p. 144.

The stop-Goldwater-forces had probably hoped that they could more or less repeat the events at the convention in 1952, where the Taft-coalition soon began to dwindle, but here was one important difference between Taft's situation and Goldwater's: the loyalty of the delegates.

The Scranton-letter

One of the benefits of the well-prepared conservative grassroots mobilization was delegates who would stick like wallpaper. According to F. Clifton White, the Goldwater delegates were of a brand-new breed. "Nothing could shake them," White recalled, "I cannot conceive of any large-scale desertions we could have suffered."[48]

Nevertheless, Scranton's staff had made a last desperate attempt to stop Goldwater by sending him a letter signed by their candidate. The letter, which arrived in Goldwater's headquarters on Monday, July 12, accused the senator of being a minority candidate, who had "bought, beaten and compromised" enough delegates to win the nomination. "With open contempt," the letter claimed, Goldwater's managers had regarded the delegates as "little more than a flock of chickens whose necks will be wrung at will." It was indeed a strange argument. True, Goldwater had not done as well in primaries as in state conventions, but he had nevertheless received almost twice as many votes as his closest competitor, Nelson Rockefeller.

The insults went on throughout the letter, which attempted to convince Goldwater that regardless of all the clever arithmetic, he had no chance of winning:

> You have too often casually prescribed nuclear war as a solution to a troubled world ... You have too often allowed the radical extremists to use you ... You have too often stood for irresponsibility in the serious question of racial holocaust ... You have too often read Taft and Eisenhower and Lincoln out of the Republican Party.

---

48 F. Clifton White, *Suite 3505*, p. 350.

The letter ended its barrage of charges by concluding that:

> Goldwaterism has come to stand for nuclear irresponsibility. Goldwaterism has come to stand for keeping the name of Eisenhower out of the platform. Goldwaterism has come to stand for being afraid to forthrightly condemn right-wing extremists. Goldwaterism has come to stand for refusing to stand for law and order and maintaining racial peace. In short, Goldwaterism has come to stand for a whole crazy quilt collection of absurd and dangerous positions that would be soundly repudiated by the American people in November.[49]

Goldwater was stunned by the vicious attack. He and Scranton had been good friends, and the governor had been his favorite vice-presidential running mate. The senator later claimed that he would also have endorsed Scranton if he himself had lost the California primary. Although he was hurt, Goldwater did not take up the glove. The letter was returned unanswered, but only after 4,000 copies of it had been distributed to all delegates and alternates in town.

Just what Scranton's staff had in mind when they sent the letter, which the governor had authorized but neither seen nor signed, remains a mystery. The impact, however, was evident: It enraged the Goldwater delegates and strengthened their commitment, just as it effectively destroyed any hope of reconciliation at the convention. Goldwater would later go as far as to argue that Scranton's letter had not only affected his campaign, but indeed the future course of the conservative movement.[50] For the Arizonan and his supporters, the letter would evidence that he had mostly lost the election in November because he had been backstabbed by Republican liberals who supplied all the ammunition for the Johnson campaign. "Some day I might write a book about the campaign," Goldwater later wrote to his former speechwriter Stephen Shadegg, "and if I do, I will call attention to the basic fact, that my defeat was insured on July the 15th by the stiletto job Rockefeller and Scranton and others had done on me."[51]

---

49 Quoted from Stephen Shadegg, *What Happened to Goldwater?* (New York: Holt, Rinehart and Winston, 1965), p. 152 ff.
50 Goldwater, *Goldwater*, p. 181.
51 Letter, Barry Goldwater to Stephen Shadegg, June 23, 1965. Denison Kitchel Papers, Hoover Institution.

Steamroller tactics

Several other incidents worsened the conflict within the GOP. One was the work of the Platform Committee. Goldwater's opponents claimed that the senator's supporters broke with all traditions concerning how the committee should work, and rolled over all opposition to his policies. [52] Although such committees are usually made up of one member from each state, which often means disproportionate influence to conservatives from small states, amendments are often introduced at the floor where the larger industrial (and often more liberal) states have greater strength. Goldwater's opponents could argue with some right that despite Platform Chairman Melvin Laird's efforts, this part of the process was being ignored. Apparently, Goldwater had little interest in the traditions concerning this symbolic display of unity.

Although the Scranton forces did have some influence on the platform writing, they were denied concessions in three crucial areas: civil rights, the control of nuclear weapons, and "extremism." The Goldwater camp managed to defeat proposed moderate amendments concerning civil rights and nuclear weapons, just as it defeated two proposals denouncing "extremism within the party." The final civil rights plank consisted of only 66 words. It promised "full and faithful execution," but the Goldwater-forces rejected a proposed pledge to "enforcement." They also included a provision promising equal opposition to the rapidly evolving threats of inverse discrimination."

As for the platform-amendments on "extremism," Scranton proposed the first one, asking for explicit mention and condemnation of the John Birch Society along with the Ku Klux Klan and the Communists.[53] It was a thinly

---

[52] A key player in the attempt to secure a strong conservative stamp on the party-platform was Senator John Tower of Texas, who previously had served as an important link between the draft organization and Goldwater. There was also another important connection between the platform committee and the Goldwater camp: William Baroody's son, William Baroody, Jr. served as Chairman Melvin Laird's administrative assistant.

[53] Scranton presented the issue as a choice between welcoming or rejecting "radical extremist groups" in the GOP: You have two points of view from which to choose. One says that "A lot of people in my home town have been attracted to it — that is, the John Birch Society — and I am impressed by the type of people in it. They are the kind we need in politics. They are generally impressive, intelligent people." The other point of view, with which I agree, says that the radical extremist groups are alien to our shores. I can find in them no saving grace whatsoever. Our platform should say so. Frankly, I cannot for one second conceive why you would hesitate to specifically name the John Birch Society as a prime example of this weird presence in America. Quoted from John H. Kessel, *The Goldwater Coalition* (New York: The Bobbs-Merrill Company, Inc., 1968), p. 109.

disguised Goldwater trap, and the senator did not fall into it. The Goldwater forces probably could have accepted the content and wording of an alternative amendment forwarded by George Romney, since it simply denounced extremism without explicitly mentioning the John Birch Society. However, many Goldwater advisors felt it would be interpreted as a sign of weakness and an invitation to further trouble if they went along with the proposal.

The platform Committee's rejection of the proposed amendments, and particularly the resolute way in which it was done, further angered Goldwater's opponents, who claimed to be the victims of steamroller tactics. But their proposals had been rejected fair and square, in strict accordance with party rule, and Goldwater had no intentions of handing out olive branches now to opponents who had called him "every dirty name in politics."[54] Instead he wanted to stress that a historical transition of political leadership was taking place: conservatives were taking over the party.

Accordingly, the Goldwater forces occupied most of the key spots in the national organization. Symbolically, New York was left unrepresented for the first time in party history. Though virtually unknown outside of Arizona, Dean Burch was appointed Chairman of the Republican National Committee. Several people around Goldwater, including Richard Kleindienst, who was a personal friend of Burch, had recommended Ohio State Chairman Ray Bliss, who was respected by all factions within the Party. However, Goldwater had felt let down by Bliss in his struggle for the nomination and preferred the loyal Burch, thus once again demonstrating his preference for personal loyalty to tactical skills and political expediency.

Picking a running mate

Goldwater's unwillingness to make compromises with his opponents was also reflected in his choice of running mate. Gerald Ford had been under consideration. So had Bill Scranton, who Goldwater later claimed had been his first choice. The Pennsylvania governor would have balanced Goldwater's candidacy both politically and geographically, but his letter to the Arizonan the night before the nomination had once and for all eliminated him from the list of possible candidates.

---

54 Goldwater, *Goldwater*, p. 185.

Governor George C. Wallace of Alabama, who had proven in his short presidential campaign that the "white backlash" was not confined to the South, had personally courted Goldwater in order to become his vice-presidential running mate. He had not ruled out the possibility of a third-party candidacy – a move that would seriously harm the Arizonan's chances in Dixie – but Goldwater was not tempted by the idea of teaming up with a man who was both an outspoken racist and a registered member of the Democratic Party.[55] Instead his choice fell upon William E. Miller of New York.

In some respects Miller balanced the Goldwater ticket: he was a Northeastern Catholic with a Polish-American wife. But while Miller was from the East, he was no "Eastern Republican." He was a conservative brother-in-arms who had opposed the policies of the Eisenhower administration even more vigorously than Goldwater himself had. He was not likely going to give the Goldwater-ticket any significant shares of the Eastern vote, but since that was largely written off anyway, it did not affect Goldwater's choice. The clear message that the Arizona senator did no longer intend to reach out to the other wing of the party was not only stressed by the fact that he did not pick a moderate running mate, but also by the fact that he did not bother to consult any of the party leaders before he made his choice.

Among the things that Goldwater liked about Miller was his sharp tongue and his ability to "drive Lyndon Johnson nuts." The senator hoped that it could somehow provoke the president to enter the fray. The fact that Miller was a Roman Catholic also suited Goldwater fine. He hoped that it would compel Lyndon Johnson to pick another Roman Catholic, Robert F. Kennedy as his running mate. Finally, Miller was also a popular choice among most movement-conservatives. In his home state he enjoyed the support of the New York Conservative Party, and he was also strongly recommended by F. Clifton White and his associates. White, who apparently saw Miller's vice-presidential candidacy as a way of gaining back some influence in the Goldwater campaign, had actually hired Marvin Liebman to run a campaign for Miller's candidacy at the convention.[56]

---

55 Wallace's courtship is described in Dan T. Carter, *The Politics of Rage* (New York: Simon & Schuster, 1995), pp. 219-225.
56 Marvin Liebman, *Coming Out Conservative*, p. 168.

"Extremism in the Defense of Liberty is No Vice!"

Along with the Scranton-letter, the controversy over the proposed amendments to the party platform, and the choices for National Chairman and vice president, two other incidents also rubbed salt into the wounds of the GOP during the national convention. One was the mayhem that broke out when Nelson Rockefeller took the stage in order to defend the minority resolution on "extremism." The other incident was triggered by Goldwater acceptance speech.

When Nelson Rockefeller took the podium, the booing and chanting began the moment he opened his mouth. It was soon accompanied by hoots, howling, the tooting of trumpets, and the beating of drums. Rockefeller, however, was defiant. He clearly knew which buttons to push in order to underscore his message that "extremists" were subverting the party. While the TV cameras were running he talked about "infiltration and take-over of established political organizations by Communist and Nazi methods." The Goldwater-camp had not orchestrated the disturbance, but it clearly suffered the consequences of the images that came across to the viewers at home. "How many votes Barry Goldwater lost on that night alone could never be calculated," White later wrote in his memoirs of the campaign, "but I would wager they ran into the hundreds of thousands, perhaps millions, when his opponents were done branding him and his supporters by unmistakable implication as extremists, anti-civil rights fanatics and nuclear warmongers."[57]

Goldwater's acceptance speech after his nomination became even more controversial. It truly represented a break with the tradition of closing ranks within the party after the factional struggle for the nomination. Emblematic of the entire campaign, it served to arouse those who were already predisposed in his favor, while it did almost nothing to reach out for new supporters. Goldwater told his opponents that "anyone who joins us in sincerity we welcome. Those who do not care for our cause, we do not expect to enter our ranks in any case..."[58] The senator later stated that the speech was a deliberate attempt to illustrate that it was his intention to take the Party in a new direction: "The address had to make clear that this

---

57 F. Clifton White, *Suite 3505*, p. 398-399.
58 Transcript in the New York *Times*, July 17, 1964, L, p. 10.

was a historic break."⁵⁹ It certainly served its purpose, but unfortunately the concluding remarks of Goldwater's speech not only took his campaign in a new direction, but also an unintended one.

Rarely in American political history has a concluding remark been as ill timed as when Goldwater paraphrased Marcus Tullius Cicero. After months where the senator had constantly fended off charges that he and/or the majority of his supporters were "extremists," he now ended his speech by reminding his audience that "extremism in the defense of liberty is no vice!" just as "moderation in the pursuit of justice is no virtue." Many listeners were simply flabbergasted.

Richard Nixon, who with an eye to the election of 1968 had assumed the role as the champion of party unity, later recalled that he felt "almost physically sick" while Goldwater "opened new wounds and then rubbed salt in them."⁶⁰ In Nixon's view, the senator could have unified the party first and then moved it to the right. His confrontational tactic was "an unforgivable folly."⁶¹

As one might expect, several leading Republicans were quick to express their grave concern over Goldwater's speech, and demanded a clarification of his concluding remarks. Rockefeller reacted with "amazement and shock" to Goldwater's statement, which in his view raised "the gravest of questions in the minds and hearts and souls of Republicans in every corner of our party."⁶² Former President Eisenhower, whose active support many considered vital to the Goldwater campaign, was also deeply disturbed and asked Goldwater to clarify his "extremism" statement. Ike was particularly annoyed by the fact that Goldwater's statement was being interpreted widely as an endorsement of the John Birch Society – all in all an understandable reaction considering that the organization's founder, Robert Welch, had called the former president "a conscious agent of the Communist conspiracy." However, it was not only opponents of Goldwater who found the speech disturbing. F. Clifton White, who had not seen

---

59 Goldwater, *Goldwater*, p. 186.
60 Richard M. Nixon, *The Memoirs of Richard Nixon* (New York: Grosset & Dunlap, 1978), p. 260.
61 Nixon, *The Memoirs of Richard Nixon*, p. 260.
62 Quoted from the New York *Times*, July 18, 1964, p. 1.

the speech beforehand, later admitted that he was "as stunned as anyone that night by the abrasive quality of his words."[63]

It is quite difficult to comprehend how it could elude Goldwater and his staff that the statement was likely to trigger such reactions. In a letter to Richard M. Nixon, Goldwater later explained that it had been his intention to express that "whole-hearted devotion to liberty is unassailable and that half-hearted devotion to justice is indefensible."[64] In a sense that was close to President Kennedy's statement that America would "pay any price, bear any burden," but Goldwater's speech did not provide any context which could explain how the statement was to be understood.[65] Rather than the high-minded engagement of principles that he had originally announced, Goldwater would spend a major part of his remaining campaign on the defensive, trying to convince potential voters that he was not a dangerous extremist after all.

---

63 F. Clifton White, *Suite 3505*, p. 407.
64 Letter (draft), Barry Goldwater to Richard M. Nixon, August 1964. Denison Kitchel Papers, Hoover Institution.
65 Harry Jaffa had provided the quote from Cicero which formed the basis of Goldwater's controversial statement, but he had never intended it to be part of the acceptance speech. According to the senator's former speechwriter Stephen Shadegg, the manner in which the acceptance speech had been composed provided the pattern for other statements by the candidate during the remainder of the campaign: "Ideas and phrases gathered together under Baroody's supervision [were] edited by McCabe, Kitchel, and Hess, until all unity of thought and style was completely destroyed." Shadegg, *What Happened to Goldwater?* pp. 165-66.

Chapter 11

The Anatomy of a Landslide

> The Goldwater election was the most important thing in the '60s. The people that you see in this town [Washington] today ... the conservatives from the Heritage Foundation all the way over, are all people who were activated by the Goldwater election. It was the Goldwater election that allowed the conservatives to take over the Republican Party, allowed all their groups to get going and brought them all together in a community. So that was the central, most important event in the whole period
>
> DAVID KEENE[1]

Unforgiving

BARRY GOLDWATER entered his campaign for the highest office as the candidate of a party that was in a state of civil war. To an ardent supporter such as Representative Bob Dole of Kansas, Goldwater's victory had anchored the party after years adrift. He rejoiced in the fact that it was now possible to "go out and make speeches for spending cuts and sound conservative principles, certain that we won't be undercut by the leaders of our party."[2] On the other hand, many liberal Republicans maintained that the conservatives, who according to Henry Cabot Lodge simply did not understand the modern world, had hijacked the party. In consequence, several of these liberals found open defection acceptable, if not even imperative under the circumstances. Among them were Governor George Romney of Michigan, Senator Case of New Jersey, Senators Keating and Javits, Representative John Lindsay of New York, and former presidential candidates Harold Stassen and Thomas Dewey, who all openly endorsed

---

1 Quoted from Rebecca E. Klatch, *A generation Divided, The New Left, The New Right, and the 1960s* (Berkeley: University of California Press, 1999), p. 85.
2 "Republicans; the New Thrust," *Time*, July 24, 1964, p. 19.

Lyndon B. Johnson. Other Republican senators simply avoided active support for Goldwater and did their best to detach their own reelection-campaigns from his bid for the presidency. Any association with his candidacy, they feared, could be a political kiss of death. The *Herald Tribune* endorsed a democratic presidential candidate for the first time ever and more than eighty officials from the Eisenhower-administrations signed an open attack on Goldwater.[3]

It would have been politically expedient for Goldwater to swallow his pride and taken initiatives which could bring some of these "moderates" back into the fold for the final stages of the campaign, but at this point he was simply too hurt. In 1952, Ike had extended his hand to the defeated Taft just hours after their bitter struggle for the nomination had ended. Goldwater, for his part, found it much harder to overcome his personal bitterness towards Scranton and others that had called him names and portrayed him as a dangerous extremist.

For weeks Goldwater delayed a meeting which was intended to contain the damage done by the acceptance speech and bring the Party together for the final months of the campaign, but on August 12, he finally met with Eisenhower and a number of leading moderates, including Nixon, Rockefeller, Romney, and Scranton. The meeting, which was set in Hershey, Pennsylvania, was followed by a press conference, intended as a chance for Goldwater to make a new departure. However, the senator was defiant and refused to make any real concessions. According to Nixon, an infuriated Eisenhower said afterwards "You know, before we had this meeting I thought that Goldwater was just stubborn. Now I am convinced that he is just plain dumb."[4]

In order to keep up appearances, the Goldwater campaign persuaded Eisenhower to participate in the recording of a TV program entitled "Conversation at Gettysburg." Here Goldwater supposedly clarified his views to Ike. The program hardly convinced many skeptics. Eisenhower was about as helpful to the Arizonan as he had been to Nixon in 1960, which is to say: not very. He called the charge that Goldwater was a warmonger "actual tommyrot," but he never explicitly endorsed him.

---

3   For other defections, see Rick Perlstein, *Before the Storm*, pp. 455-459.
4   Richard Nixon, *The Memoirs of Richard Nixon*, p. 262.

The Politics of Race

If Goldwater's views scared many moderate republicans away, they also attracted new constituencies to the party. As predicted, the senator was able to cash in on the growing tensions which the civil rights revolution had triggered within the New Deal coalition. Whether the GOP should actively exploit the Democratic split through a "Southern strategy" had for years been a controversial issue within the party.[5] Goldwater's nomination in San Francisco provided an affirmative answer. The defeat of the Party's Eastern establishment meant a rejection of the attempt to stress the legacy of Lincoln and compete with the liberal Democrats in the civil rights field. The GOP would no longer cater to black constituencies who voted Democratic in overwhelming numbers anyway.

Of course such a shift had a price. Part of it was the loss of most of what was left to the Republicans of the black vote. But based on a cynical assessment of the potential gains from white voters in the South that was not a bad bargain. Furthermore, the surprising strength of Governor George C. Wallace in several primaries outside the South suggested that the political gains of Goldwater's stand on civil rights would not necessarily be confined to Dixie.[6] Lyndon B. Johnson was genuinely concerned. "Alabama is coming into Maryland, Alabama is going into Indiana," he told Hubert Humphrey.[7]

In a letter to Goldwater just prior to the national convention, Dean Clarence Manion of the "Manion Forum" also assured the senator that the backlash against the Civil Rights demonstrators was already in motion in the metropolitan areas of the North, and that the democratic votes given to Wallace in Indiana could become his. "With these Democratic votes, you cannot lose Indiana next fall," Manion contended.[8] He was further convinced that "what Wallace did in Indiana, Wisconsin and Maryland, he could have done as well or better in Ohio and Illinois."

---

5 The vote in the Senate on the Civil Rights Act of 1960 illustrated the changing Republican attitude: No Republican voted against the Act, but thirty one Republican senators simply stayed away from the session.
6 George Wallace received about 34 percent of the vote in the Wisconsin primary, 30 percent in Indiana and 43 percent in Maryland.
7 Telephone Conversation between LBJ and Hubert Humphrey, May 13, 1964, Recordings of Conversations, no. 3450, White House Series, Recordings and Transcripts of Conversations and Meetings, Lyndon B. Johnson Presidential Library.
8 Letter, Clarence Manion to Barry Goldwater, June 12, 1964. Clarence Manion Papers.

Despite the fact that many supporters, particularly in the South, would have liked to see Senator Goldwater exploit the civil rights revolution even further, he attempted to walk a fine line on the issue. On the one hand he consistently expressed his personal dislike of racism, and frequently mentioned that he had been an active supporter of the NAACP in Arizona and fought legal segregation in public schools and elsewhere. He even told students at Phillips Academy that "If I were a Negro, I don't think I would be very patient."[9] On the other hand he defended "states rights" as an essential constitutional principle concerning the proper role of the Federal government. The Supreme Court's decision in *Brown vs. Board of Education* could not make him change his mind:

> The Constitution is what its authors intended it to be and said it was – not what the Supreme Court says it is ... I therefore support all efforts by the States, excluding violence of course, to preserve their rightful powers over education.[10]

While Goldwater disagreed with the principles of the *Brown* decision, he nevertheless contended that he agreed with its objectives:

> It so happens that I am in agreement with the objectives of the Supreme Court, as stated in the Brown decision. I believe it is both wise and just for Negro children to attend the same school as whites that to deny them this opportunity carries with it strong implications of inferiority. I am not prepared, however, to impose that judgment of mine on the people of Mississippi or South Carolina or tell them what methods should be adopted and what pace should be kept in striving toward that goal. That is their business, not mine.[11]

Goldwater's intellectual ammunition on civil rights issues was provided by Yale professor Robert Bork and William H. Rehnquist. The latter was then working for Denison Kitchel's law firm in Phoenix, where he had made his mark as a staunch opponent of local antidiscrimination laws. With the help of these two advisors, Goldwater presented the standard

---

9 Quoted from Lee Edwards, *Goldwater* (Washington, D.C.: Regnery Publishing Inc., 1995), p. 231.
10 Barry M. Goldwater, *The Conscience of a Conservative* (New York: Manor Books Inc., 1974[1960]), p. 37.
11 Goldwater, *The Conscience of a Conservative*, p. 38.

conservative argument against Federal intervention on behalf of the African-American citizens, whose civil rights were blatantly violated in the South: Social justice and compassion had to make way for larger principles involved, and further legislation – or even worse: demands for strict enforcement of such legislation – were not acceptable ways of ameliorating existing inequities. In any case such violations remained "essentially local problems [that were] best dealt with by the people most directly concerned."[12]

Barry Goldwater's political support in the South increased further on June 19, 1964, when he was one of the six Republican senators who voted against the Civil Rights Bill (he was not the only one, as he would later claim in his memoirs[13]). He strongly denied that his opposition to the bill was motivated by any "Southern strategy," and maintained that his vote was based entirely on the belief that some of its provisions were unconstitutional. "If my vote is misconstrued, let it be, and let me suffer the consequences," Goldwater said on the Senate floor.[14]

Given his view of the Civil Rights Act, would Goldwater attempt to repeal it if elected? No, he assured the press, he would faithfully execute the law. The senator acknowledged that his was a minority view and that the legislative branch in this case had spoken for the majority of the American people.

Many Southern supporters had hoped that Goldwater would make at least one speech in the South, which might be interpreted as a defense of segregation, but he didn't. As a matter of fact, Goldwater hardly touched upon the issue of civil rights while campaigning in Dixie. He was honoring an agreement made with President Johnson on July 24, that neither would attempt to exploit the sensitive issue in their speeches.[15]

Racial tensions remained the one issue that Johnson feared could seriously hurt him. Accordingly, he had happily agreed when Goldwater surprisingly had offered to keep race relations out of the campaign. However,

---

12 Goldwater, *The Conscience of a Conservative*, p. 30.
13 Barry Goldwater & Jack Casserly, *Goldwater* (New York: Doubleday, 1988), p. 171.
14 Quoted from Goldwater & Casserly, *Goldwater*, p. 172. For further details on Goldwater's views on civil rights legislation, see Niels Bjerre-Poulsen, "'Hunting in the Pond Where the Ducks Are:' Conservative Opposition to Civil Rights Legislation in the 1964 Election and Beyond." In Helle Porsdam (ed.), *Folkways and Law Ways: Law in American Studies* (Odense: Odense University Press, 2001), pp. 73-89.
15 Barry Goldwater, *With No Apologies*, p. 193.

the president and his staff did not trust Goldwater's intentions. A memorandum dated July 28, 1964, simply concluded: "Goldwater's meeting with Johnson was a cover. It was not designed to keep Johnson from attacking him on his civil rights record — he wishes to be attacked for this."[16] The president even suggested that the FBI should investigate whether the Goldwater-camp was behind the ongoing riots that summer.[17] Johnson would discover, however, that Goldwater was shooting straight.

Although the agreement probably gave Johnson an advantage over Goldwater, the latter did not have to address the race issue openly. Given the widespread American custom of negative voting, he did not even need to oppose the principles of civil rights and racial equality in order to win the segregationist vote, as long as it remained clear that, unlike the current administration, he would not use the power of the Federal government to enforce it. It must be noted, however, that although Goldwater questioned the right of the federal government to enforce integration in the South, he did not question its right to secure the voting rights of African-Americans, "even if it means with troops."[18]

If Goldwater personally downplayed the issues of segregation and civil rights while campaigning in the South, his local supporters often remained blunt in their use of them. A pamphlet distributed by Florida Volunteers for Goldwater featured a large picture from the signing of the 1964 Civil Rights Act, under the headline "LBJ shakes hands with King." The text below read: "If you want to restore states' rights and constitutional government, then get busy *and throw the liberals out.*"[19]

The 1964 presidential election would clearly demonstrate that commitment to the New Deal coalition was disintegrating in many Southern

---

16 Anonymous, Memorandum, "Re: Current political situation," July 28, 1964. The Office Files of Bill Moyers, Lyndon B. Johnson Presidential Library.

17 Telephone Conversation between LBJ and John Connally, July 23, 1964, Recordings of Telephone Conversations, No. 4320, White House Series, Lyndon B. Johnson Presidential Library. Quoted from Jeremy D. Mayer, "LBJ Fights the White Backlash; The Racial Politics of the 1964 Presidential Campaign" *Prologue: Quarterly of the National Archives and Records Administration* (Spring 2001), vol. 33, no. 1 (www.nara.gov/publications/prologue/lbj1964a.html#f55).

18 *New York Post*, May 11, 1961. Quoted from Robert A. Goldberg, *Goldwater* (New Haven: Yale University Press, 1995), p. 154.

19 "A Call for Volunteers," *Facts About the Campaign for President*, Florida Volunteers for Goldwater (undated).

constituencies as racial politics were given higher priority than economic issues. In Mississippi, Goldwater would eventually receive 87 percent of the vote, and in the region taken as a whole, 71 percent of the white voters supported him.[20] "Volunteers for Goldwater" groups naturally stimulated the process by attempting to convince voters that Republican conservatism could provide a respectable ideological framework for resistance to further racial integration, and that the time had come to "forget meaningless party labels."[21]

"Why Not Victory?"

Another major area where Goldwater offered the voters "a choice, not an echo" was foreign policy. He rejected the notions of appeasement and "peaceful coexistence." Victory over Communism was the one goal that all foreign policy initiatives should be subordinated to, be it foreign aid or support for the United Nations. If one compares Goldwater's views in his best-selling book *Why Not Victory?* with those expressed by Robert Taft in his 1952 campaign book *A Foreign Policy for Americans,* it becomes evident how profoundly the year in between had changed the outlook of the Republican Right.[22] Unlike "Mr. Republican," Goldwater wholeheartedly supported America's global interventionism, and he recognized the need for the elaborate system of pacts and alliances that had been developed during the 1950s (which is by no means to say that he and the American Right had converted to multilateralism). America had to stand up and challenge the "schoolyard bully" and alliances such as NATO were effective instruments to that end. *Why Not Victory*, rejected the principle of "containment" and echoed Republican "rollback" rhetoric of the early 1950s:

---

20 Dewey W. Grantham, *The South in Modern America; A Region at Odds* (New York: Harper Collins Publishers, 1994), p. 247. For evidence that race was the central issue in the Deep South, see James L. Sundquist, *Dynamics of the Party System* (Washington, D.C.: The Brookings Institution, 1983), pp. 352-363.
21 *Facts,* Pamphlet, distributed by Florida Volunteers for Goldwater (undated).
22 Barry Goldwater, *Why Not Victory?* (New York: MacFadden Books, 1964 [1962]). Taft, Robert, *A Foreign Policy For Americans* (New York: Doubleday & Company, Inc., 1951).

> Peace for Russia means defeat for the United States, and no amount of appeasement or soft talk will dissuade the Russians from their determined effort to rule the world or destroy it.[23]

In Goldwater's manichean worldview, Communism remained monolithic. He lambasted the Kennedy-Johnson Administration for trying to distinguish between "good" and "bad" communists. The increasing Sino-Soviet split and other cracks in the communist bloc were largely dismissed as bogus. The struggle with Communism, Goldwater told the German magazine *Der Spiegel*, was:

> A struggle between Godless people and the people of God, and if you want to put it in its basic form, it's between slavery and freedom. It's now worldwide. I claim that we cannot live with these two philosophies in the world forever. Sometime there'll be only one.[24]

In accordance with this worldview, Goldwater also opposed the idea of disarmament. "The only real disarmament will come when the cause for arms is removed. In our case that cause is Communism," the senator argued in *Why Not Victory?*[25] In the summer of 1963, Goldwater further bolstered his status as a hard-line anti-Communist, when he opposed the Test Ban Treaty.[26]

A former pilot in the airforce, Goldwater fully shared the Republican right's reverence for airpower. In 1959, during the planning of *The Conscience of a Conservative*, L. Brent Bozell privately summarized Goldwater's view on foreign policy in a letter to Dean Clarence Manion:

> He is OK on foreign policy. E.g.: he wants to say in the book that when there is trouble in the world, we should fly B-52s over the trouble — and if it doesn't dissipate, drop something.[27]

---

23 Barry M. Goldwater, *Why Not Victory?*, p. 47.
24 Quoted from James Reston, "Goldwater's Dilemma, "the New York *Times*, July 11, 1964, p. L9.
25 Goldwater, *Why Not Victory?*, p.84.
26 In all fairness it must be added, though, that the senator did not oppose the idea of a treaty, but merely the fact that the one in question, in his view, was based on trust in the Soviet leaders, rather than on adequate inspection.
27 Letter, L. Brent Bozell to Clarence Manion, April 17, 1959. Clarence Manion Papers, Box 68, folder 4.

Although the image as tough and uncompromising gunslinger undoubtedly was an important part of Goldwater's attraction to many of his devoted supporters, his campaign team nevertheless realized during the presidential campaign that it was necessary to soften some of his confrontational views in order to reach beyond the devotees. As one example, Goldwater no longer advocated the breaking of diplomatic relations with the Soviet Union as a matter of principle, although he did maintain that such a step could be a "strong diplomatic sword" if used "at the proper time."[28]

Still, Goldwater's hawkish attitudes undoubtedly scared many potential voters away. The one factor that really made him vulnerable to charges of being a trigger-happy warmonger, however, was the seemingly casual way in which he discussed the possible use of nuclear weapons. Nothing, with the exception of his views on Social Security, would haunt him as much throughout his presidential campaign as the charges of nuclear irresponsibility. The senator's opponents frequently portrayed him as a dangerous madman, ready to start the battle at Armageddon.

Although Goldwater's hawkish statements on foreign policy, as well as the candid way, in which he put them forward, undoubtedly were unsettling to many, their content did not represent any radical departure from the views of the Republican mainstream. One might argue that it was merely a return to the policy of "brinkmanship" introduced by the Eisenhower-administration. It is worth remembering that Ike, who the liberal media now frequently contrasted to Goldwater as an example of prudence and conservative moderation, used nuclear threats no less than five times during his presidency, e.g. in the conflict with China over the islands of Quemoy and Matsu.

Goldwater's largely monolithic view of Communism was also well in the tradition of the Eisenhower administration, as was the dismissal of uncommitted "neutrals" in the third world as Communist dupes. Yet, the Arizona senator constantly faced charges of "extremism" and attempts to associate him with the "radical right." His views on foreign policy were frequently presented as expressions of "the world according to [John Birch Society leader] Robert Welch." Such charges missed the point. Goldwater's worldview was Manichean, but so was the one presented in "NSC-68." In

---

28 "Issues and Answers," interview with Howard K. Smith, ABC News, Sunday, May 24, 1964, transcript, Goldwater Papers.

several respects the senator's perception of the ongoing conflict with Communism was substantially different from the pessimistic and alarmist views presented by organizations such as the John Birch Society.

In most of the radical right's propaganda, Communism took the shape of an amoral omnipotent superman, constantly expanding, uninhibited by the maelstrom of history, and standing of the verge of final victory and world conquest. The view presented by Goldwater, on the other hand, was much more optimistic. Under the influence of advisors such as Warren Nutter and Gerhart Niemeyer, the senator described a Soviet system that was economically weak and bound to eventually fall apart. "It's in the cards. The whole Communist empire is moving. It's cracking."[29] The Soviet system had "so many intrinsic faults," Goldwater told members of the American Legion in Dallas, that it would "collapse if it wasn't braced from the outside as we've been bracing it."[30] What the United States had to do in order to speed up the process was to stop wheat sale and other forms of trade with the Soviet Union that could delay its final breakdown.

Vietnam: the Great Non-Issue of the 1964 Election

By the spring of 1964, the American government was sinking still deeper into the quagmire in Vietnam. Like his predecessor, President Johnson was reluctant of a full-scale American engagement in a war that could ultimately destroy his elaborate plans for a "Great Society." Yet, he had decided to ride the tiger's back rather than become the president "who saw Southeast Asia go the way China went."

While the president assured the American public that he did not intend "to send American boys nine or ten thousand miles from home to do what Asian boys ought to be doing for themselves," he and his advisors had already worked out elaborate plans for an escalation of the American engagement. Johnson had asked the Pentagon to prepare plans for air strikes against North Vietnam as early as February, and by May the White House had drafted a congressional resolution which would authorize an escalation of American military action.

---

29 Barry Goldwater, *Why Not Victory?* p. 126.
30 "Transcript of Senator Goldwater's Address to American Legion in Dallas," the New York *Times* (September 24, 1964), p. 30.

Naturally, President Johnson and Senator Goldwater had different opinions about how the engagement in Vietnam should be handled. Goldwater opposed a ground war in Vietnam and expressed the traditional Republican reliance on American airpower. He also argued that the US should either win quickly or pull out, and years later he still maintained that he could have ended the war in a week or two, if necessary by making "a swamp out of the North."[31] But despite disagreements over tactics, both candidates adhered to the same conceptual framework and generally agreed about what was at stake in Vietnam. So did most of the media and a clear majority of Americans at this point, and the war never really became an issue during the 1964 campaign.

Even the official statements in August 1964 concerning the alleged North Vietnamese aggression in the Gulf of Tonkin were largely taken at face value by Congress and the American public. They did not trigger much investigative reporting by the media either. The military engagement in Vietnam clearly enjoyed bipartisan support, although an outspoken opposition to it did exist. The alleged incident in the Gulf of Tonkin, and the swift action taken by the Johnson-administration further triggered a traditional "rally 'round the flag" response which made it even more difficult for Goldwater to use the Vietnam issue in the ongoing presidential campaign.

Another important reason why Vietnam did not become a central theme in the election was simply that both candidates agreed that it shouldn't be. Actually, Goldwater had addressed the issue of the war in his acceptance speech:

> Yesterday it was Korea; tonight it is Vietnam. Make no bones of this. Don't try to sweep this under the rug. We are at war in Vietnam. And yet the president, who is commander-in-chief of our forces, refuses to say, refuses to say, mind you, whether or not the objective over there is victory. And his secretary of defense continues to mislead and misinform the American people.[32]

Nevertheless, the senator soon proposed to leave the war out of the presidential campaign. President Johnson, who clearly had most to gain by de-

---

31 Burton Bernstein, "AuH$_2$O," *The New Yorker* (April 25, 1988), p. 64.
32 Quoted from Lee Edwards, *Goldwater*, p. 272.

tracting attention from the issue, was somewhat surprised by the offer, but happily accepted it. Thus, the candidates met privately and struck a deal: they would discuss different opinions about military tactics, but not the larger issue of why American forces were in Vietnam in the first place.[33] The dramatic escalation of the engagement was allowed to continue with only a minimum of public attention.

Despite Goldwater's agreement with the president, there was one issue concerning the war in Vietnam that would nevertheless do severe damage to his campaign. In a discussion of strategic options in the attempt to expose enemy supply-lines in Vietnam, the senator mentioned that the use of low-yield atomic weapons to defoliate the forest was technically possible. Soon the story was out that Goldwater advocated the use of nuclear weapons against the enemy in Vietnam.

This was clearly a distortion of his remarks. He had mentioned the use of atomic devices for defoliation as one of several suggestions that had already been made, and he had added: "I don't think we would use any of them."[34] The last part of the quote was simply deleted in most accounts. Like Goldwater's alleged intent to end Social Security, it turned out to be a story that just wouldn't die. It kept the senator on the defensive, just as it diverted attention from Johnson's escalation of the war. The president could easily play the role of the moderate peace candidate, as long as Goldwater was casted for the role as irresponsible warmonger.

Many Principles, Few Solutions

Goldwater had expressed his hopes that the presidential campaign could become an engagement of principles, but most of the voters wanted more than that. They wanted to hear conservative solutions to their everyday problems. The senator did have specific proposals in some areas, but he never really managed to present anything resembling a genuine program. There were of course several explanations for this.

To some extent it was a reflection of the political immaturity of the conservative movement at this stage, but one may also argue that it is the

---

33 Barry Goldwater, *Goldwater*, p. 193.
34 Quoted from David Lawrence, "What Goldwater Said on A-bomb," the New York *Herald Tribune*, May 28, 1964.

nature of conservative politics to be based on reaction, rather than on positive steps towards political change. As Goldwater had stated in his bestseller *The Conscience of a Conservative,* his aim was "not to pass laws but to repeal them." Thus, his inability to flesh out conservative principles was partly a reflection of his belief that "less was more" when government action was concerned.

General observations about the nature of conservatism, however, did not make life on the campaign trail easier for Goldwater. It was difficult to generate enthusiasm and mobilize voters without the ability to present alternatives to the solutions offered by the Johnson administration.[35] To make matters worse, a 1963 memorandum by Raymond Moley had inspired the Goldwater team to separate the logistical functions from the policy functions in order to insulate the candidate from getting distracted by local issues or particular attacks by the opposition.[36] The general idea was that the candidate should stick to principles, rather than attempt to be all things to all men, but the policy often caused bitter frustration and discontent among the regional directors when their requests for the inclusion of specific issues of local concern in the senator's speeches were ignored.

Sticking to principles also meant a high degree of redundancy in Goldwater's speeches. They became repetitious, and often downright boring. Only towards the end of the campaign did his team realize the need to change strategy and beef them up with specifics, but the change came too late to have any significant impact on the outcome of the election.

Another glaring example of Kitchel and Baroody's inept handling of the campaign was the attempt to block a televised speech by Ronald Reagan, then co-chairman of California Citizens for Goldwater-Miller. In the last desperate weeks of the campaign, Reagan offered a well-tried speech, as well as money for airtime, raised specifically for that purpose by a

---

35 Goldwater's attempt to address the Hispanic voters illustrates the point: "I know you have not received the recognition to which you are justly entitled," the senator stated in a proposed letter in Spanish. He conceded that Latinos had "special problems," yet never attempted to spell out what some of these problems were. Likewise, he did not promise anything specific, apart from his "strongest and sincerest energies to the solution of these problems." ("Translation of Suggested Letter to be Signed by Barry M. Goldwater, And to be Addressed in Spanish to Latin-Americans" (undated). F. Clifton White Papers).
36 Kessel, John H., *The Goldwater Coalition* (New York: The Bobbs-Merrill Company, Inc., 1968), p. 132.

group of California businessmen.[37] Kitchel and Baroody, who were afraid that the speech would once again highlight controversial issues such as Social Security, attempted to take over the airtime and use it to rebroadcast the senator's awkward conversation with Eisenhower in Gettysburg. Only when Goldwater himself took the time to listen to a tape of Reagan's speech did Reagan get the permission to hold it.[38]

The speech, "A Time for Choosing," which was televised nationwide on October 27, 1964, turned out to be the most effective TV-program in the entire campaign. It became an instant classic and subsequently made Reagan a rising star of the conservative movement.[39]

Running against Fear

Although Goldwater was the challenger, he never took the offensive. Most of the time he was simply too busy clarifying previous statements and rebuking misquotations. The extremist issue still haunted him as well. Richard Rovere warned that Goldwater's anti-Federalism would Balkanize the United States, and many others portrayed him as the likely creator of a totalitarian police state. Baseball star Jackie Robinson charged the senator with being "a political bedfellow with some of the slimiest elements in the nation, such as the Ku Klux Klan and the John Birch Society." Walther Reuther called the Republican Party platform plus Goldwater "a prescrip-

---

37 This was largely the group of people, who would later become known as Reagan's "kitchen cabinet."

38 In his memoirs and in interviews, Goldwater would later erroneously recall that the speech had originally been written for him: "I read it and said this speech was not for me. To tell you the truth, I don't believe I had the ability to read this speech and get across all the innuendoes that it has, so I suggested that they give it to Ronald Reagan, and that's the speech that got him started." (John Kolbe "The Warrior Comes Home" *The Phoenix Gazette*, December 3, 1986). However, the speech was actually Reagan's from beginning to end – a speech he in his own words had given "hundreds of times before." (Ronald Reagan, *An American Life* (New York: Simon and Schuster, 1990), p. 139).

39 Apparently it is difficult to determine just how successful the speech was in financial terms. In *Packaging the Presidency; A History and Criticism of Presidential Campaign Advertising* (New York: Oxford University Press, 1984) Kathleen Hall Jamieson writes that the address was "a financial success, raising over half a million dollars." (p.175) Reagan, however, has given a much bolder estimate of the financial impact of the speech: "it ultimately raised eight million dollars for Goldwater and the party." Ronald Reagan, *An American Life*, p. 143.

tion for World War III," and C. L. Sulzberger simply concluded that if Goldwater entered the White House "there might not be a day after tomorrow."[40]

Goldwater, the son of a Polish Jew, also had to swallow the fact that several opponents found compelling comparisons between his candidacy and Hitler's rise to power. Roy Wilkins of the NAACP compared the senator to "a man [who] came out of the beer halls of Munich, and rallied the forces of Rightism in Germany.[41] When Goldwater went on a trip to Germany, he included a visit to the American Seventh Army's recreational area in Berchtesgaden. In Daniel Schorr's report for the CBS News, this was presented as a visit to "Hitler's onetime stamping ground." Without any shred of evidence, Schorr also told his audience that "there are signs that the American and German right wings are joining up, and the election campaign is taking on a new dimension."[42]

Goldwater's Jewish background notwithstanding, Dr. Joachim Prinz, president of the American Jewish Congress, also forwarded charges of anti-Semitism. "A Jewish vote for Goldwater," he declared, "is a vote for Jewish suicide." The Republican candidate was, according to Dr. Prinz, surrounded by "every hate group in the United States, every anti-Semite in America."[43] Meanwhile the American Nazis headed by Lincoln Rockwell were claiming that Goldwater's candidacy represented a Jewish take-over of the Republican Party.

Though Goldwater was mostly a libertarian, he increasingly addressed the type of social and moral issues that by the late 1970s would become essential features in the appeal of "the New Right." The senator spoke out against pornography and the breakdown of traditional family values, just as he introduced the "law and order" theme which just four years later had a major impact on the presidential election. His campaign was also able to tap into the anger and frustration that many Christian conservatives felt after the Supreme Court's 1962 decision *in Engle v. Vitale* which banned prayer in public schools. The decision had undoubtedly added new converts to the conservative movement.

---

40 *New York Herald Tribune*, August 7, 1964, p. 4. Quoted from Lionel Lokos, *Hysteria 1964; The Fear Campaign against Barry Goldwater* (New Rochelle, N.Y.: Arlington House, 1965), p. 135. Reuther quoted from the New York *Times*, July 16, p. 19, Sulzberger quoted from Lokos, p. 204.
41 The New York *Times*, July 14, p. 30
42 Quoted from Barry Goldwater, *Goldwater*, p.176.
43 The New York *Times*, September 27, p. 57.

A major theme in Goldwater's outbursts of social conservatism was the link between the spirit of New Deal liberalism and the decay of the nation's moral fiber. The liberals fostered permissiveness, while banning "Almighty God from our schoolrooms."[44] According to Goldwater, America's moral problems were inseparable from the country's economic system. The central issue in the election, he told an audience in Prescott, "is a choice of what sort of people we want to be."[45] If the country wanted to stop its drift and decay, it would have to "take the bureaucratic shackles off," and once again put its "main reliance on individuals, on hard work, on creativity, investment, and incentive."[46] Thus, Goldwater implied that the problem of crime in the streets would be solved by the virtues of the market, and by moral leadership.

Despite these attempts in the last month of the campaign to increasingly address social and moral issues, they never really caught on. Part of the explanation for this was probably that the candidate himself did not really feel comfortable with them. In the Reagan years, Goldwater's true inclinations became evident when he clashed with the New Religious Right, and in the early 1990s he further alienated many social conservatives with his ardent defense of gays in the military. More importantly, perhaps, the attempt to stress themes of social conservatism in a national election was simply premature. With the exception of the civil rights revolution, which was already reshaping the political landscape, it was not until the social upheaval of the late 1960s that such issues truly began to create anti-liberal sentiment and move votes to the right.

Mud Wrestling

How did Johnson and his spin-doctors perceive the Goldwater campaign, and how did they attempt to neutralize their opponent? First of all, the president never felt that Goldwater seriously threatened his re-election, but his ambition was to bury the Arizonan in a landslide that could pave the way for a major reform program. Among the people who would help

---

44 Quoted from Richard Hofstadter, "Goldwater and Pseudo-Conservative Politics," in *The Paranoid Style in American Politics and Other Essays* (Chicago: The University of Chicago Press, 1979 [1965]), p. 117.
45 Hofstadter, "Goldwater and Pseudo-Conservative Politics," p. 119.
46 Hofstadter, "Goldwater and Pseudo-Conservative Politics," p. 118.

the president do that were Abe Fortas, Clark Clifford, historian Eric F. Goldman, John Kenneth Galbraith, George Reedy, and Bill Moyers, who was in charge of the campaign. Later in life Moyers, now in charge of the Public Broadcasting System, would lament how political debates in the United States had degenerated into "the verbal equivalent of mud wrestling."[47] In 1964, however, he was a champion wrestler.

Johnson's team could rejoice in the fact that most of the ammunition for the campaign had already been provided by the struggle within the GOP. In order to convey the idea that a Goldwater presidency would spell disaster for the country, the Johnson camp could simply quote Scranton, Rockefeller, Javits and other of their opponent's fellow Republicans.

Eric F. Goldman had suggested this central message to the president in September of 1964. In his view, the president should question the very notion that Goldwater was "conservative" and instead describe the senator's philosophy as "a ridiculous hodge-podge, leading — if it leads any place — to radical change."[48] John Kenneth Galbraith, for his part, found it imperative that Johnson completely avoided the concepts of liberalism and conservatism. In his view, the president should stick to "moderation," "responsibility," and their opposites.[49] Galbraith also cautioned the president not to debate Goldwater under any circumstance, arguing that the senator's "simplifications lend themselves well to television debate."[50]

The most remarkable event in President Johnson's campaign against Goldwater was a particularly distasteful TV-commercial, which exploited the senator's trigger-happy image. In this so-called "daisy commercial," which aired September 7, 1964, a little girl is counting as she plucks petals from a daisy. Suddenly an ominous male voice begins a countdown to a nuclear blast. As a mushroom cloud envelops, there is a voice-over by President Johnson and then the final message: "Vote for President Johnson on November 3 ... the stakes are too high for you to stay home."[51]

---

47 Bill Moyers, "Old News and the New Civil War" (editorial), The New York Times, March 22, 1992
48 Eric F. Goldman, "Memorandum for the President," September 24, 1964. Office Files of Bill Moyers, Lyndon B. Johnson Presidential Library.
49 John Kenneth Galbraith, "Points on Campaign Strategy, 1964," memorandum, August 3, 1964, p. 1. The Office Files of Bill Moyers, Lyndon B. Johnson Presidential Library.
50 Galbraith, "Points on Campaign Strategy, 1964."
51 For further details on the "daisy commercial and its impact, see Kathleen Hall Jamieson, *Packaging the Presidency; A History and Criticism of Presidential Campaign Advertising* (New York: Oxford University Press, 1984).

Although Goldwater was never mentioned in the ad, the implication was clear and the impact tremendous. As Tony Schwartz, the man who conceived the ad, later explained: "It was comparable to a person going to a psychiatrist and seeing dirty pictures in a Rorschach pattern."[52] The "daisy commercial" was only aired once, but except for George Bush's Willie Horton commercial in 1988, no other political ad has ever created such uproar. It has been said that it was removed from the campaign in response to the numerous complaints, but actually the ad had been designed to run only once. Bill Moyers and the other people behind it were well aware of how controversial it would be.[53] There was no need to pay for more commercial time, when the ad itself became an issue. All three major networks subsequently aired it in its entirety.

Financing the Goldwater campaign

Amidst the gloomy perspectives for November 3, conservatives could find only a few encouraging signs in the ongoing campaign, and one of them was the way in which it was being financed. Here they saw the declining influence of eastern corporate money, and a growing number of alternative financial channels. Conservative Republican "grassroots" played a more important role than in previous elections, and accordingly, the campaign was less dependent on the financial support of the "establishment."

For the first time direct mail was used as a major source of funding. Whereas the Nixon-Lodge campaign in 1960 had received contributions from some 40,000 people, the Goldwater-campaign received donations from almost two million people.[54] Only 28 percent of the Republican campaign funds in 1964 were reported to come from donations of $500 or more, compared to 88 percent in the 1952 election.[55] Indeed, it was not a lack of funds that defeated Goldwater. All in all, some $13 million were contributed to the campaign, and although it was a fairly expensive campaign by the standards of 1964, the Republican National Committee

---

52 Quoted in Jamieson, *Packaging the Presidency*, p. 200.
53 Bill Moyers, Memorandum to the President, September 13, 1964. Office Files of Bill Moyers, Lyndon B. Johnson Presidential Library.
54 The *New Guard*, December 1964, p. 7.
55 Hess, Stephen & David Broder, *The Republican Establishment* (New York: Harper & Row, 1967), p. 51.

nevertheless had a $500,000 surplus by the time it was over.[56] Although some conservatives would later take pride in this outcome, it was mostly the result of the RNC's rather ill-advised principles of not running a deficit on the advertising budget. By the time the committee had raised the money for a last-minute blitz of Goldwater-commercials, the networks had run out of timeslots to sell. Hence the surplus.

As Nicol C. Rae has noted, direct-mail and other new methods of fundraising, combined with the large degree of independence that the "Draft-Goldwater movement" operated with in relation to the national party machinery, were important factors in the candidate's ability to take the unconciliatory ideological stances which had so infuriated the party moderates at the national convention in San Francisco. The innovations introduced in the Goldwater-campaign demonstrated the shape of things to come. In time they would make fund-raising experts such as Richard Viguerie key players in the conservative counterestablishment.

The Myth of the Hidden Conservative Vote

Confronted with the prospects of a landslide victory for Johnson on November 3, the Goldwater-camp usually responded by affirming their belief in a dormant conservative majority which would wake up in time for the election because it was finally offered "A Choice Not An Echo."

Goldwater had already referred to this hidden conservative vote, when he withdrew his candidacy at the Republican convention in 1960: "We must remember that Republicans have not been losing elections because of more Democratic voters. Now, get this. We have been losing elections because conservatives too often fail to vote." [57] Four years later Goldwater's campaign manager Denison Kitchel would tell television viewers that "A majority of voters in the United States favor conservative principles and philosophy but they have never had the opportunity – I shouldn't say never – in a long time to have [a] choice."[58]

---

56 Carol Bauman, "Can Conservatives Keep Control of the Republican Party?" *The New Guard* (December 1964), p. 7.
57 Quoted from John H. Kessel, *The Goldwater Coalition* (New York: The Bobbs-Merrill Company, Inc., 1968), p. 48.
58 Interview with Denison Kitchel, NBC-Television, July 17, 1964. Quoted from Philip E. Converse, et. al., "Myth and Reality: The 1964 Election," p. 6.

Very few of the opinion polls taken during the campaign supported the notion of a hidden conservative vote. One exception was a survey made for the Republican National Committee by Public Opinion Research of Princeton. It indicated that there were more people who considered themselves Conservative than Republican (41% and 26%, respectively). This, conservative organizers argued, meant that there was indeed a large "hidden vote" which the right type of candidate could tap into. Also, when given the choice between labeling themselves as either "conservative" or "liberal," 65 percent of the Republicans chose the former and only 14 percent the term "liberal." Of the Democrats, 30 percent claimed to be conservative, while 42 percent used the term liberal. Last but not least, as much as 41 percent of the independent voters claimed to be conservative, while only 29 percent claimed to be liberal.[59]

However, "liberal" and "conservative" are slippery terms, indeed, and if the survey itself was not misleading, then at least the inferences that some Goldwater-supporters made from them turned out on to be dead wrong. On election day, Barry Goldwater was buried in a historic landslide. He lost by nearly 16 million votes, the greatest margin ever. With 61 percent of the popular vote, Lyndon B. Johnson's victory was even bigger than Franklin D. Roosevelt's in 1936 was. The landslide hit traditional Republican strongholds such as the suburbs of the East and the Midwest, and the Republican Party lost as much as 530 seats in various legislatures around the country.

A comparison with Herbert Hoover's defeat in 1932 is suggestive. Like Hoover, Goldwater only carried six states, but whereas all the states where Hoover won had been located in the Northeast (Vermont, Maine, New Hampshire, Connecticut, Delaware, and Pennsylvania), all the states that Goldwater now won were located in the South and the Southwest (Alabama, Georgia, Mississippi, Louisiana, South Carolina, and Arizona). Vermont, a true Republican bastion, voted for a Democratic president for the first time in history. The political map of the United States was clearly being redrawn.

As one might expect, the GOP was also badly hurt in the congressional elections. It had a net loss of 38 House seats and 2 Senate seats.[60] The

---

59 Reprinted in Stephen Shadegg, *What Happened to Goldwater?*, pp. 221-228.
60 Although the two elections are not directly comparable, it is worth noting that six years earlier in the 1958 election following the Sputnik-crisis, the Republicans had actually lost 48 seats in the House, and 13 in the Senate.

losses were concentrated among conservative Republicans. Forty of the Representatives who lost had ADA scores of 20 or less. In the short term, the actual loss for the conservative coalition in Congress was even greater than the numbers indicated, since a number of Southern Democrats broke ranks and began to take more moderate positions on a number of issues. In 1963, the conservative coalition had prevailed in 63 percent of the House roll-call votes. In 1965, it only had its way in 25 percent of the votes.[61]

The notion of a hidden conservative vote had clearly turned out to be a myth. Goldwater would have needed to find millions of new dedicated conservative voters in order to compensate for the abandonment of voters in the "mushy middle." Obviously, that did not happen. In fact, evidence suggests that conservative Republicans already turned out at much higher rates than moderate Republicans, regardless of whether the candidate was conservative or not.[62]

Goldwater had not faced a great hidden pool of conservative voters, but, at best, a pool of undecided voters, who could have tilted either way. To them he did not have much to offer. Perhaps he and his staff had erroneously seen the letters-to-the editor in journals and newspapers as adequate expressions of public opinion. As Converse, Clausen, and Miller put it in their analysis of the campaign:

> It is to the world of "letter opinion," or one like it, that the Goldwater campaign, in its original design, was addressed. At least until its late stages, the campaign assumed an electorate with near-total ideological comprehension and sensitivity.[63]

Some conservative commentators responded to Goldwater's defeat by pretending that it had never happened. They chose to celebrate the event that almost 27 million "dedicated conservatives," despite the hysteria and confusion, had emerged and voted for Goldwater. The nature of the campaign, and the considerable success the liberals had in portraying Goldwater as "irresponsible," they contended, made it very unlikely that the senator had

---

61 Mary Beth Norton et. al., *A People and A Nation* 2nd edition (Boston: Houghton Mifflin Company, 1986), p. 946.
62 See Philip E. Converse, et. al., "Myth and Reality: The 1964 Election," p. 50.
63 Converse, et. al., "Myth and Reality: The 1964 Election," p. 73.

merely been the beneficiary of a routine Republican vote.[64] This notion that 27 million devoted conservatives had voted for Goldwater was ridiculed by the libertarian economist Murray Rothbard, who in a letter to his fellow-libertarian Felix Morley wrote:

> If those permanently self-deluded people think that the "27 million" form the hard-core of ultra-conservatism, then, indeed, let them all form a nationwide third party, run Bill Buckley on it, and see how many votes they get! They'll find that the hard core had dwindled out of sight.[65]

A Harris poll supported Rothbard's View. It indicated that only 6 million of the voters could be characterized as dedicated Goldwater-supporters, who wanted a take-over of the GOP, while the other 21 million were simply faithful Republicans, who stuck with their party regardless of the candidate.[66]

What Went Wrong?

Some of the major factors contributing to Goldwater's defeat were fairly easy to point out. A booming economy made conservative alternatives to the reigning keynesianism seem largely irrelevant to many voters. Equally important was the fact that Goldwater was running against an incumbent president, who had served for less than two years and was able to skillfully use the national sense of loss over his predecessor in the campaign. Furthermore, the GOP was, after all, the minority party. The Democrats did not only control the executive branch, but also a majority of state legislatures and about two thirds of the country's governorships.

Yet, many conservatives still questioned the notion that their candidate had been given a fair chance to demonstrate the true strength of American conservatism in the election. Had liberal members of his own party not fatally stabbed him in the back? Had the media not deliberately distorted his views? Could a better strategy and better management of the campaign not at least have cut the Republican losses substantially?

---

64 For an example of this view, see M. Stanton Evans, "The Prospects for Conservatism," *ACU Special Report*, 1966 (not paginated).
65 Letter, Murray N. Rothbard to Felix Morley, February 28, 1965. Felix Morley Papers.
66 Quoted from John A. Andrew III, *The Other Side of the Sixties;* Op. Cit., p. 208.

In order to protect their claim to majority status, they would point out those responsible for Barry's burial in the election: 1) the "liberal establishment," including a good many fellow Republicans, who had served the unholy alliance of Big Business, Big Government and Big Labor against Goldwater's "marching mobs of the frustrated,"[67] 2) the biased national media, which had grossly misrepresented Goldwater's views and deliberately presented him to the American public as a dangerous warmonger,[68] and 3) the "Arizona Mafia," which, in the words of Senator John Tower, had not only conducted a "monumentally inept" campaign, with a "penchant for putting the candidate in the wrong place to say the wrong thing at the wrong time," but had also isolated him from the conservative grassroots.[69]

Goldwater's own propensity to shoot from the hip had made matters worse. There is no doubt that a majority of the national media was strongly biased in their presentation of his ideas, but on the other hand, consistency and unambiguous wording were not exactly his primary virtues. Even reporters who were determined to give him fair press coverage often faced a serious dilemma: should they report what he said or what he intended to say?

Some would later interpret Goldwater's losing battle in 1964 as a populist revolt, a quixotic struggle against the moneyed interests of the East and their henchmen within the GOP. They would among other things point to the fact that large parts of the business community, which traditionally had been affiliated with the Republican Party, had supported Johnson this time. The changing allegiance of Big Business was indeed quite remarkable. The Johnson camp had found the best possible catalyst for a move to the Democratic camp when Henry Ford II in July of 1964

---

67 John Dos Passos' expression, in "The battle for San Francisco," *National Review*, Vol. XVI (July 28, 1964), p. 640.
68 Nothing indicates that the national media on its own had any major impact on the final outcome of the election, but a number of leading voices from liberal newspapers would later admit that Goldwater had been given shabby treatment. Among them were Tom Wicker of the New York *Times*, who found that "the image never did do credit to the man, and there are not many politicians of whom that can be said" (NYT, July 28, 1966). As for the media's role in Goldwater's defeat in the West and the Midwest, see Erik August Devereux, *The Partisan Press Revisited: Newspapers and Politics in the United States, 1964-1968* unpublished Ph.D. dissertation (The University of Texas at Austin, 1993).
69 John G. Tower, *Consequences*, p. 166.

was persuaded to publicly endorse the president. Representatives from many of the country's largest corporations soon followed him.

For the majority of these corporations, which in time had come to accept the basic tenets of the welfare state, and in many areas had developed a symbiotic relationship with the federal government, Goldwater first of all represented unpredictability. The senator's frontier-rhetoric of rugged individualism, and his talk of restoring entrepreneurial virtues, appealed more to the representatives of small business than it did to corporate America, which had grown accustomed to federal subsidies, tax incentives, research grants, and loan guarantees.

The campaign cash reports of the Business Council are suggestive: four years before, in the 1960 presidential election, CEOs had contributed $250,000 to Richard Nixon's campaign and only $35,000 to John F. Kennedy's. In 1964, they gave the Democratic candidate the lion's share of the money for the first time in modern presidential history. Lyndon B. Johnson received $140,000, while Goldwater only received $90,000.[70] Thus, there were some grounds for interpreting the election as an expression of the dualism between small business and the hard-working middle-class on the one side, and the unholy alliance of Big Government, Big Business, and Big Labor on the other. Goldwater himself had also played this populist theme, when he told a journalist from the German magazine *Der Spiegel* about the nature of the resistance to his candidacy from within the Republican Party:

> I know the widely held theory, and I have never heard it disputed in my life, that the Eastern money interests – the large banks, the financial houses – have most always been able to control the selection of the Republican candidate. They want to be able to control not the foreign policy as you and I think of foreign policy based on peace and war, but the foreign policy of this country relative to interest rates, gold balances, values, etc., and in my case they don't have this control and they are getting quite frantic in their efforts to have somebody get me out.[71]

The "Arizona Mafia's" handling of the campaign had caused frustrations in conservative ranks, but it had also made it easier to swallow the final

---

70 Kim McQuaid, *Uneasy Partners; Big Business in American Politics 1945-1990* (Baltimore: The Johns Hopkins University Press, 1994), p. 129.
71 Interview in *Der Spiegel*, July 8, 1964. English transcript printed in *U.S. News & World Report*, July 20, 1964, p. 70 ff.

defeat, since conservatives could maintain that they had won the nomination for Goldwater, while it was the "Arizona Mafia" who had lost the election for him. The "Mafia's" days as spokesmen for American conservatism were numbered in any case. As William Rusher had already assured an associate just after Goldwater's nomination:

> Now that Goldwater has actually won the nomination, there is a temporary surfeit of Arizonans around the place; but I counsel you to keep your eye on the ball. Either Goldwater will win in November, in which case the whole Kremlinology of the Goldwater movement will become vastly more important ... , or — as we must soberly assume is likelier — he will lose, in which case the conservative ball will snap rapidly back into the hands of Suite 3505.[72]

Establishing a Beach-head

Many conservative leaders were ready to admit after the election that all notions of a hidden well of like-minded voters had proved to be an illusion. Yet, despite the outcome, the national campaign for Goldwater had far from been in vain. It had established a political beachhead and created an organizational momentum. To mention just a few examples, YAF had experienced a significant growth in membership during the campaign, and would continue to do so in the aftermath. *National Review* had increased its circulation from 61,000 to 94,000 copies.[73] The task ahead now was to prepare for the long haul and continue with the development of a conservative "counter-establishment."

As early as September, William F. Buckley, Jr. had openly talked about Goldwater's "impending defeat." In his characteristic pompous prose, he had warned an audience of Young Americans not to uphold any illusions of a "Silent Majority" that would flock to the polls at Election Day and win the election for Goldwater:

---

72 Letter, William A. Rusher to Donald G. M. Coxe, Esq., August 7, 1964. William A. Rusher Papers.
73 In the second half of 1964, YAF increased its membership by 5,400. John A. Andrew III, *The Other Side of the Sixties; Young Americans for Freedom and the Rise of Conservative Politics* (New Brunswick: Rutgers University Press, 1997), p. 211.

> Any election of Barry Goldwater would presuppose a sea-change in American public opinion; presuppose that the fiery little body of dissenters, of which you are a shining meteor, suddenly spun off nothing less than a majority of all the American people, who suddenly overcame a generation's entrenched lassitude, suddenly penetrated to the true meaning of freedom in a society where the truth is occluded by the verbose mystifications of thousands of scholars, tens of thousands of books, a million miles of newsprint; who suddenly, prisoners all those years, succeeded in passing blithely through the walls of Alcatraz and tripping lightly over the shark-infested waters and treacherous currents, to safety on the shore.[74]

American conservatism, Buckley contended, was not yet ready to move beyond its "remnant" status. The likely event of a stunning Goldwater defeat would not be a nail in the conservative coffin, but merely another step on the road to future elections. The success of the campaign did not depend on how Goldwater would fare in the national election, but on how much momentum his candidacy would create for the organizing efforts of the conservative movement:

> If it were not for the presence of Goldwater as candidate for the Republican Party our opportunity to proselyte on a truly national scale would not exist. Now is precisely the moment to labor incessantly to educate our fellow citizens, now that so many of them feel required to listen, because the choice must be made at the polling booth. The point of the present occasion is to win recruits whose attention we might never have attracted but for Barry Goldwater.[75]

A Struggle for the Soul of the Republican Party

The dust had not settled after the Johnson landslide before the struggle over who should point out the future direction for the GOP began. "Goldwater is out. The Moderate Republicans are back in control," wrote Roscoe Drummond in the New York *Herald Tribune*. "Thus ends the par-

---

74 William F. Buckley, Jr., speech at the annual meeting of Young Americans for Freedom in New York City in September 1964. Reprinted in *the New Guard* (December 1964), pp. 10-14.
75 Buckley, Jr., "Speech at the annual meeting of YAF...," pp. 10-14.

ty's experiment with extreme conservatism."[76] Many of the Republicans who had been reluctant to support Goldwater interpreted the outcome of the election likewise. Nelson Rockefeller found that "a natural consequence of events would be that moderates would control the national party organization."[77] On December 4, 1964, he met in Denver, Colorado, with the other members of the Republican Governor's Association in order to discuss the party's future. Their deliberations resulted in the so-called "Denver Declaration," drafted by an appointed committee consisting of Scranton, Romney, Rockefeller, and Babcock. One paragraph in the declaration read:

> We need to appeal to all Americans. We need to become inclusive rather than exclusive. We need to win elections and serve America as a great broadbased political party, far greater and far more effective than any narrow, exclusive political clique can ever hope to become.[78]

The intention was clear; they hoped to rid the party leadership of Goldwater's allies. Some conservatives, including John Grenier, left more or less voluntarily. National Chairman Dean Burch was forced to resign in January of 1965, and was replaced by Ray Bliss. In the end, however, the conservative wing of the party experienced little more than a temporary setback. Almost two decades later F. Clifton White would argue that it had in fact never lost its control of the party after the Goldwater defeat, "but it took them fifteen years to find out what the hell to do with it."

Rebuilding the Infrastructure

Goldwater's candidacy might have been buried in a landslide, but the aspirations of the conservative movement were not buried with it. Intent to cut the losses and continue the momentum, a group of leading conservatives met just five days after the election to discuss the future of the movement. Among them were William F. Buckley, Jr. and Frank Meyer of *Na-*

---

76 The *New York Herald Tribune* (January 15, 1965), p. 33.
77 Quoted in New York *Times* (November 5, 1964), p. 1.
78 Quoted from John H. Kessel, *The Goldwater Coalition* (New York: The Bobbs-Merrill Company, Inc., 1968), p. 313.

tional Review, Robert Bauman, Chairman of YAF, and GOP Congressmen Donald Bruce and John M. Ashbrook. Their purpose was to create a new umbrella organization in order to "provide leadership and material for existing conservative-oriented organizations."[79] They would point to the one organization which more than anything had been crucial in creating the pervasive liberal climate which Goldwater had been up against: the Americans for Democratic Action (ADA).

ADA members occupied key positions in the federal government on all levels up to the newly appointed Vice President Hubert Humphrey, who had been one of the organization's founders in 1947. The goal of a new conservative counterpart to ADA would be to learn from its success and emulate its operations.

The founders named their new organization the American Conservative Union (ACU). They envisioned it as the central organization in a new conservative "counter-establishment." It would have interlocking directorates with a number of other conservative organizations, it would employ lobbyists, run a speakers bureau, publish reports and pamphlets, etc. Perhaps the organization could best be described as a YAF for grown-ups.[80]

Ex-Congressman Donald C. Bruce of Indiana – a staunch Goldwater-supporter, who had just been defeated in the Johnson landslide – became the new organization's first chairman. Other prominent conservatives such as L. Brent Bozell, Peter O'Donnell, Jr., John Chamberlain, John Dos Passos, Stefan Possony, and William A. Rusher joined the leadership. As often before with such conservative ventures, Marvin Liebman went to Charles Edison of McGraw-Hill in order to get the initial funding.[81] Liebman also left another imprint on the organization, as it adopted his poli-

---

79 "Confidential Preliminary Report on the American Conservative Union" (undated), William A. Rusher Papers.
80 From the outset, ACU was indeed tightly connected with YAF. Robert and Carol Bauman were put in charge of ACU staff personnel, and a seat on the ACU board was reserved for the chairman of YAF.
81 ACU started out with a first-year budget of $400,000, but only managed to raise some 218,000. After just one year the organization was in serious financial trouble, and most of the staff quit. However, Liebman was called in once again, and found the money to keep ACU afloat. "GOP's Bruce Recruiting 'Conservative Eggheads', Minneapolis *Star* (March 20, 1965); Russell Freeburg, "Top Officials Quit Conservative Group," Chicago *Tribune* (April 11, 1966), Paul Hope, "Right-Wing Tree Defoliated," Washington *Star* (Feb. 11, 1966).

cy of "appearance" by setting up front groups. Among these groups was the Conservative Victory Fund, the American Legislative Exchange Council, and the National Journalism Center headed by M. Stanton Evans.

One crucial decision that the board had to make was how closely ACU would be affiliated with the Republican Party. Some would stress the need to maintain a strong conservative influence in the regular Republican Party. Was it likely that the ACU could win acceptance as the party's "strong right arm?" Or would any attempt to gain such a status be met by opposition from alleged moderates within the party? In any case, an official endorsement from the conservative champion Barry Goldwater was seen as a very important step on the road to recognition.

The Arizonan, however, had other plans. His friend and close advisor Denison Kitchel wanted to organize a new leading conservative organization based on mass membership. Denison Kitchel announced an expected membership of 500,000 by mid-1966, and on several occasions he spoke of a future membership in the millions Goldwater's former aides Karl Hess and Tony Smith would run the Free Society Association (FSA), as it was to be called, and it would have the senator as its nominal head. Once again the *National Review*-crowd and the people behind the "Draft-Goldwater" movement had been let down by their champion. Their bitterness was understandable. It appeared to them that Goldwater was rewarding the ineptitude of the people, who in the eyes of many had completely mismanaged his presidential campaign.

FSA never came anywhere close to the membership and influence that Kitchel dreamed of. By 1966 it had some 40,000 members, and the financial situation was not too good. Two years later it was all over. The association closed due to a lack of funding.

Long before the end of FSA, however, Goldwater had officially endorsed the ACU and taken the initiative to form a loose confederation which united the two organizations along with YAF and Americans for Constitutional Action (ACA).[82] The goal was to coordinate the activities of the four organizations and make them work together toward the election of 1968. Goldwater himself was no longer the champion of this coalition, but conservatives already had their eyes on a man whose political career had been launched in the darkest hour of his campaign: Ronald Reagan.

---

82 The project was launched in August 1966.

Epilogue

"We're the new liberals of the Republican Party. Can you imagine that?"
BARRY GOLDWATER
to Bob Dole, 1996[1]

Phoenix

IN THE AFTERMATH of the 1964 presidential election, historian Richard Hofstadter noted the irony in the fact that it was Goldwater's nomination which had paved the way for the Great Society:

> No other Republican could have made such a startling contribution to the first really significant and general extension of the New Deal since the 1930's. It was his campaign that broke the back of our postwar practical conservatism."[2]

If Hofstadter could have reflected on the Goldwater-campaign and the fate of American conservatism ten years later, he would probably have noted other ironical twists of fate. Despite all the obituaries, the conservative wing of the Republican Party had prevailed, while the liberal wing had virtually been destroyed. American political parties have been compared to worms: if they are chopped in two, one of the parts will wriggle away and regenerate itself. Seen in retrospect, it was the conservative part of the GOP that kept wriggling. How can we explain this development? What happened between Goldwater's devastating defeat in 1964 and the conservative ascendance in the late 1970s? To what extent did the Gold-

---

1 Quoted from Michael Murphy, "Conservative Pioneer Became an Outcast," *The Arizona Republic* (May 31, 1998).
2 Richard Hofstadter, "Goldwater and Pseudo-Conservative Politics," p. 115.

water-campaign itself serve as a catalyst for the process, and what role did the emerging conservative counter-establishment play?

Southern Strategies

If there was one Republican who sensed better than anyone where his party was going after 1964, it was Richard Nixon. He understood that the right would continue as a major force and managed to place himself in an ideal position to bridge the gap between the two camps in the party.[3] He also understood that the major source of continuing conservative strength was the tremendous changes in the political landscape of the South.

Although Nixon would later claim that the Goldwater campaign had been a detour on the road to a two-party South, and that Goldwater had won the wrong Southern states and scared away the moderates in the border states, the Republican gains in the region were nevertheless impressive.[4] In addition to Goldwater's electoral victories, seven Republican Congressmen had been elected there. The Arizonan had been the first Republican ever to win in the state of Georgia, just as that state elected its first Republican Congressman since Reconstruction. In four other Southern states (Virginia, Tennessee, North Carolina and Arkansas) Goldwater would also have won, had it not been for the increased voter participation of African-Americans and their solid support of Lyndon B. Johnson.

How exactly had the Goldwater campaign changed Southern politics? Republicans had already made gains in the South in the Eisenhower years, but Goldwater's gains were not simply a continuation of this process. Whereas most of the gains during Ike's presidency had been made in the

---

3   Nixon would skillfully cater to the conservatives by enrolling a number of leading figures from the Goldwater movement in his efforts to win the presidential election in 1968. Several of them also went to work for him once he had entered the White House. Among them were Peter O'Donnell and Richard Kleindienst, who became Nixon's Attorney General. From YAF came, among others, Tom Huston and Pat Buchanan, who became a major speechwriter for the president. In 1972 they were joined by Howard Phillips, who became the president's Director of the Office of Economic Opportunity.
4   Nixon quoted in Dan T. Carter, *The Politics of Rage*, p. 326. The fact that Goldwater had the strongest support in the Deep South and won 87 percent of the vote in Mississippi indicates that the race issue was crucial to his victory here.

upper South, 233 of the 507 southern counties that Goldwater carried in the election had never voted Republican before.[5]

As pointed out by Thomas B. Edsall and Mary D. Edsall, the 1964 campaign clearly changed the public perception of were the two major parties stood in racial politics. As late as 1962, the respondents in a poll conducted by the National Election Studies had not seen any significant differences between the parties on such issues as fair treatment in jobs and housing. By late 1964, however, 60 percent of the respondents in a similar poll found that the Democratic Party was more likely to support fair treatment in jobs for blacks, while only 7 percent said the Republican Party. The rest – 33 percent of the respondents – did not think there would be any difference between the parties.[6] When asked about the parties' views on school integration, the response was almost identical (56%, 7%, and 37%, respectively).[7]

According to political scientist Barrie E. M. Blunt, the changing public perception of the partisan views on racial politics was well justified. The Goldwater campaign did create a partisan polarization in the U.S. House of Representatives, based on the issue of racial liberalism.[8]

Prior to the 1964 election, Republican members of the House had generally held far more liberal views on racial issues than had the democratic members. Goldwater's presidential campaign caused "an abrupt and lasting change ... whereby Democrats and Republicans completely switched their views in this area," Blunt argues.[9]

However, Professor David S. Castle has argued that although a clear change in alignment did take place after 1964, the effect of Goldwater's candidacy on this development was minor.[10] Instead Castle points out that changes in the substantive content of civil rights legislation by the introduction of measures such as open housing requirements and "busing," might have increased resistance to further civil rights legislation among a

---

5 Robert A. Goldberg, *Goldwater*, p. 235.
6 Thomas Byrne Edsall with Mary D. Edsall, *Chain Reaction; The Impact of Race, Rights, and Taxes on American Politics* (New York: W.W. Norton & Company, 1992), p. 35 ff.
7 Edsall & Edsall, *Chain Reaction*, p. 35 ff.
8 Barrie Edwin Millen Blunt, "The Goldwater Candidacy: Its Effects on Racial Liberalism in the House of Representatives," *Presidential Studies Quarterly*, Vol. 15, No.1 (Winter 1985), pp. 119-127.
9 Blunt, "The Goldwater Candidacy...", p. 126.
10 David S. Castle, "Goldwater's Presidential Candidacy and Political Realignment," *Presidential Studies Quarterly*, Vol.20, no.1 (Winter 1990), pp. 103-110.

number of Republican representatives. It is also likely that a number of Southern Democrats in return adopted a more positive attitude to such legislation under the effective presidential leadership of Lyndon B. Johnson.[11]

Thus, David Castle doesn't find that Goldwater candidacy in itself was a crucial factor in the partisan polarization in racial politics, but he does find it crucial in another respect. On the organizational level, it caused "nothing less than a Republican revolution in southern politics." By strengthening the young Republican organizations and giving them the required experience in precinct work, it effectively paved the way for a two-party system in the region and made it possible for the GOP to translate its new profile in racial politics into electoral votes. While the GOP was changing Southern politics, however, the party in return was being "southernized," and this process strengthened the conservative forces within the party even further.[12]

Between 1965 and 1967 the number of Republicans in Southern state legislatures nearly doubled (from 113 to 223).[13] At the presidential level, Republican gains in the South also continued in the following decades. The candidacy of George Wallace delayed the process in 1968, but after his departure in the 1972 campaign, Nixon managed to win all of the South's electoral votes. Although the race issue, which had triggered much of the change, faded in the 1970s – or took on more subtle forms – many Southerners maintained their support for the GOP. Feeling that they had been betrayed by the liberal national leadership of the Democratic Party, and having lost their traditional reservations about Lincoln's party, they felt free to follow the conservative inclinations of their region and continue to support it.

The importance of this change in political orientation was further increased by the continuing shift of political and economic power to the Sunbelt. In the 1970s, this was evidenced by a massive migration to the region. While economic stagnation in the first seven years of the decade dealt severe blows to the manufacturing centers of the North, contributing to the loss of almost one million jobs in that part of the country, the

---

11 Castle, "Goldwater's Presidential Candidacy and Political Realignment," p. 105.
12 Castle, "Goldwater's Presidential Candidacy and Political Realignment," p. 105.
13 James L. Sundquist, *Dynamics of the Party System* (Washington, D.C.: The Brookings Institution, 1983), p. 291.

Sunbelt provided more than 200,000 new manufacturing jobs. As a side effect, this migration to a region, which most often provided a hostile environment for organized labor, further weakened the unions, a traditional bastion of liberalism.

Helped along by Ronald Reagan's popularity in the South, the GOP made further inroads on all political levels in the election of 1980. The party won more than 45 percent of the senatorial and gubernatorial contests in the former Confederate states.

The Decline of Liberalism

By the late 1960s, a host of other factors were also rewiring the political switchboard. The Democratic Party was under attack from both left and right after the disastrous party convention in Chicago in 1968. Four years later things got even worse with the nomination of George McGovern as the party's presidential candidate. American liberalism was in a profound crisis of identity and political scientists saw a major partisan realignment in the making. The extent to which that actually happened is still a matter of debate.

In the early 1980s, an opinion poll showed that the number of Americans who described themselves as "conservative" now by far outnumbered those who ascribed to the liberal label.[14] It was evident that a major change had taken place since the triumphant years of American liberalism in the first half of the 1960s. Perhaps conservatives had moved towards the center of American politics in the preceding years, but evidently the center had also moved to the right. As one former YAF leader now working for the Reagan-administration put it:

> My political views are no different than they have been, but there has been a change toward the mainstream – not that I went to the mainstream, but the mainstream came to where we were, led by Reagan. Before, I was on the outside; now I'm in the middle of the mainstream.[15]

---

14 David Frum, *Dead Right* (New York: BasicBooks, 1994), p. 6.
15 Quoted from Braungart, Margaret M. & Richard G. Braungart, "The Effects of the 1960s Political Generation on Former Left- and Right-Wing Youth Activist Leaders," *Social Problems*, Vol. 38, No. 3, August 1991, pp. 297-315.

To what extent could the conservative movement take credit for this shift? What was the relationship between the intellectual elite that shaped the conservative movement and the opinion of those at the receiving end? We can measure the growing membership in many conservative organizations, the increasing circulation of conservative publications at certain points in time, the changes in funding made available for conservative campaigns, and the growing support for conservative policies and candidates, but how do we measure the general impact of the conservative movement? It played an important role in displaying liberal weaknesses, but it was not the primary factor behind the decline of liberalism.

Rather, a complex web of factors has contributed to the right-turn since the late 1960s. Cultural polarization, the unfulfilled expectations of the Great Society, the division over the war in Vietnam, "stagflation", political struggles over abortion women's rights, affirmative action, tax rates and welfare expenditures were among the key factors. OPEC, the Ayatollahs in Iran, and skyrocketing crime rates also did their part to further deepen the crisis of American liberalism. Once the preconditions for a political shift to the right had fallen into place, however, the conservative counter-establishment was there to make the best of it.

As mentioned, racial politics had moved to the forefront of political debate, albeit often in disguise. The polarizing effect which was already evident in the election of 1964, was further increased in the following years by issues such as "open housing," "busing," and various affirmative action-measures. By the time Ronald Reagan moved into the White House, conservatives were no longer defending the constitutional right to discriminate, but instead calling for "equal opportunity" for white Americans allegedly subjected to "reverse discrimination."

Reagan, once a fierce opponent of the 1964 Civil Rights Act, could present himself as a true defender of equality by opposing the liberal conception of group rights and group remedies – a conception which had been expressed in the Burger Court's decisions in *Griggs v. Duke Power Co.* (1971), and *Fullilove v. Klutznick* (1980). What Reagan suggested was a formal racial neutrality based on the assumption that racial discrimination was a thing of the past, and that all past injustices which might justify the notion of "group rights" had long since been remedied. The law should be "color-blind" and solely concerned with the rights of individuals. Rather than oppose the notion of civil rights, conservatives had now redefined its primary purpose as the protection of citizens from coercive social engineering by the courts and by the federal government.[16]

Several of Goldwater's views, which in 1964 had been widely viewed as extreme, had within just a few years become part of Republican orthodoxy. This was clearly the case with his "law and order" theme, which four years later, after antiwar protests, inner-city riots and soaring crime rates, revealed its true potential. While the population grew by 10 percent in the years from 1960 to 1966, the crime rate went up by 60 percent. In the following five-year period the increase was as much as 83 percent.[17]

The shift to the right on the issue of "law and order" was further stimulated by a series of widely unpopular Supreme Court decisions concerning the rights of criminal defendants (*Mapp v Ohio, Miranda v Arizona, Gideon v. Wainwright,* and *Escobedo v. Illinois*). Many conservatives linked these decisions with other controversial decisions by the Warren-court (most notably *Engle v Vitale,* the 1962-decision on school prayer), and successfully presented them as part of general assault on traditional American values. "Legal usurpation" became a major theme on the American Right. Supreme Court justices were accused of imposing their own liberal values on the American public in the name of constitutional interpretation. Such charges became an even more efficient means of bringing new converts into the conservative fold after the Court's 1973 decision in *Roe v Wade* legalized abortion.

"Neos" and "Populists"

A major shift in the economy also changed the context in the cut and thrust of national public policy. After decades of almost uninterrupted growth, the economy slowed down in the late 1960s, and unemployment and inflation rose sharply. One result was a growing political mobilization within the business community. In his 1979 book *A Time for Truth,* former Secretary of the Treasury William Simon told the business community that unless they reached for their pocketbooks and helped finance

---

16 As Thomas Byrne Edsall & Mary D. Edsall have noted, Reagan had an outspoken ability to use race-neutral language, which nevertheless "implicitly evoked submerged racial and cultural conflict." *Chain Reaction,* p. 184.

17 Figures quoted from Edsall & Edsall, *Chain Reaction,* p. 52.

a conservative "counterintelligentsia," then the GOP was "destined to remain the Stupid Party and to die."[18]

As Simon was writing, such a change in attitude was already noticeable. In the search for theoretical and intellectual justification for alternatives to the Keynesian welfare state, many corporations were channeling funds to conservative interest groups, PACs, legal foundations, and "think tanks." William Baroody's American Enterprise Institute saw a tenfold increase in its budgets between 1970 and 1980, from less than $ 1 million to $ 10.4 million, and new conservative think tanks such as the Heritage Foundation emerged.[19]

A new important source of candidates for key positions in this counterintelligentsia were the group of disenchanted liberals, who became known as the "neoconservatives."[20] This relatively small group of people – centered around journals such as *Commentary* and the *Public Interest*, and

---

18 William Simon, *A Time for Truth* (New York:: Berkley Books, 1979), p. 255. Simon himself was a gray eminence in the creation of his proposed "counterintelligentsia." Not only was he affiliated with several conservative enterprises, including the leading conservative think tanks: As President of the John M. Olin Foundation, he was also a major sponsor of these enterprises. His affiliations included the Heritage Foundation, the Hoover Institution, the Manhattan Institute, and the Institute for Educational Affairs. For more on the changing attitudes within the business community, see David Vogel, *Fluctuating Fortunes; the Political Power of Business in America* (New York, 1989), p. 101 ff.

19 Robert K. Landers, "Think Tanks: The New Partisans?" *Editorial Research Reports* 1:23 (June 20, 1986), pp. 462-63. Conservative policy research institutes also received increased amounts of money from wealthy foundations. The most generous donor was probably the Scaife Foundation, which by 1980 gave as much as $13 million of its $18 million in annual grants to conservative organizations. See Robert G. Kaiser & Ira Chinoy, "How Scaife's Money Powered a Movement" Washington *Post* (May 2, 1999), p. A01. On the organizing of the New Right network in the late 1970s and early 1980s, see Sidney Blumenthal. The Rise of the Counter-Establishment; From Conservative Ideology to Political Power (New York: Times Books, 1986).

20 Among the most prominent neoconservatives were Norman Podhoretz, Nathan Glazer, Daniel Patrick Moynihan, Ben Wattenberg, Michael Novak, Seymour Martin Lipset, Irving Kristol., and Jeane Kirkpatrick. Not all of them were equally happy about the label. Norman Podhoretz once suggested that "neo-liberal" perhaps would have been a more fitting label than "neo-conservative" for the people in question. Norman Podhoretz, "The Adversary Culture and the New Class," in B. Bruce-Briggs (ed.), *The New Class?* (New Brunswick, N.J.: Transaction Books, 1979), pp. 30-31. For more on neo-conservatism, see John Ehrman, *The Rise of Neoconservatism: Intellectuals and Foreign Affairs 1945-1994* (New Haven: Yale University Press, 1995), Sidney Blumenthal, *The Rise of the Counter-Establishment* (New York: Times Books, 1986), pp. 122-165, Godfrey Hodgson, *The World Turned Right Side Up* (Boston: Houghton Mifflin Company, 1996), pp. 128-157.

think tanks such as the American Enterprise Institute, the Hoover Institution at Stanford, and the Center for Strategic and International Studies at Georgetown University – soon managed to take over much of the intellectual leadership on the Right. Many of them held positions at some of the country's most prestigious universities. Unlike much of the conservative intelligentsia, they were not cultural outsiders; and thus generally better at attracting the media's attention. These intellectuals could effectively assume the role as Trojan horse for the conservative movement.

The neoconservatives did not just differ from the "Old Right" (as it was now called) in political background, but also in ethnocultural placement. Whereas Catholics dominated the *National Review*-crowd, there was a clear Jewish dominance among the neoconservatives. Professionally, many of them had a background in the social sciences and in liberal policy-making. Perhaps that was one of the major reasons the neoconservatives generally had fewer reservations about social "tinkering" than did the "Old Right" intellectuals.[21] As such, the neocons were perfectly suited to become part of a new conservative "managerial elite." Unlike many traditionalists, they were also unambiguous in their celebration of corporate capitalism. The "neos" harbored no nostalgia for the antebellum South.

While the neoconservatives were making their contribution to the intellectual credibility of American conservatism, others were working to move it in a more majoritarian direction. With a new emphasis on social and cultural issues, the idea was to tap into the resentment of white working-class ethnics.[22] As Paul M. Weyrich, one of the leading spokesmen for this new brand of "populist conservatism" put it, the New Right would appeal to blue collar, rather than to blue blood.[23]

---

21 For an account of the clash between traditionalist beliefs and the social-scientific approach of the neo-conservatives, see Brigitte Berger & Peter L. Berger, "Our Conservatism and Theirs," *Commentary* (October, 1986), pp. 62-67.
22 Among the best accounts of this rise of populist conservatism are Thomas Byrne Edsall & Mary D. Edsall, *Chain Reaction; The Impact of Race, Rights, and Taxes on American Politics* (New York: W.W. Norton & Company, 1992), Jerome L. Himmelstein, *To The Right; The Transformation of American Conservatism* (Berkeley: University of California Press, 1989), and Jonathan Rieder, "The Rise of the Silent Majority," in Steve Fraser & Gary Gerstle, *The Rise and Fall of the New Deal Order, 1930-1980* (Princeton, N.J.: Princeton University Press, 1989) pp. 243-269.
23 Paul M. Weyrich, "Blue Collar or Blue Blood? The New Right Compared with the Old Right," in Robert W. Whitaker, *The New Right Papers* (New York: St. Martin's Press, 1982), pp. 48-62.

Actually, the notion of populist conservatism was not an invention of the 1970s, but rather an idea whose time had come. In an effort to broaden his appeal, Goldwater had several times during his presidential campaign struck the theme of speaking on behalf of an alleged constituency of "silent Americans." Although these hard-working and law-abiding citizens were the backbone of American society, the argument went, they were being ignored by a political establishment which was busy catering to noisy and well-organized interest groups. In 1964, the notion of a hidden conservative vote, which would suddenly rush to the polls if provided with a real choice, evidently turned out to be a mirage. But four years later, when Richard M. Nixon picked up Goldwater's theme of the "silent majority" in a country tormented and polarized by war and racial strife, the impact was clear.

Another major source of inspiration to the new populist appeal was undoubtedly Alabama governor George C. Wallace. In his presidential campaigns in 1968 and 1972, a truculent anti-elitism was among the factors that made him the most successful third-party contender since the beginning of the century. Conservative activists were swift to adopt many of the key elements in his message. In 1975, Paul M. Weyrich and Kevin Phillips – the noted author of *The Emerging Southern Majority* and the brain behind Nixon's "Southern strategy –were both part of an attempt to combine the social agenda of the populist conservatives with the traditional goals of the Republican right. The idea was to create a political alliance between George Wallace and Ronald Reagan, and the organizational vehicle for this attempt was the Committee for the New Majority, founded by William A. Rusher, Howard Phillips of the Conservative Caucus, and Senator Jesse Helms.

Many traditionalist conservatives had severe reservations about such initiatives. Indeed, some argued that the very notion of "populist conservatism" was an oxymoron, since populism and conservatism expressed widely different perceptions of democracy. How could the majoritarian principles of the populists go hand in hand with the core traditionalist idea that indirection is the best way to secure organic change? traditionalists would ask. But fewer listened to them now. The leading voices of the New Right – often political strategists or fundraising experts rather than intellectuals – no longer felt much of a need to legitimize their political ideas in an existing conservative tradition.

The resistance which the populist conservatives encountered from Frank Meyer, William F. Buckley, Jr., and other spokesmen of "the Old Right," fully exposed the tensions between elitist and populist strains of the right. The populists dismissed the brand of conservatism represented by Buckley and the *National Review* crowd as "a surviving High-Church religion" struggling to remain "uncontaminated by mass culture and politics."[24] Kevin Phillips was even ready to write Buckley and his friends out of the new conservative movement as largely obsolete:

> Hell, Wallace isn't going to hook up with Squire Willy and his Companions of the Oxford Unabridged Dictionary. Nor can we expect Alabama truck drivers or Ohio steelworkers to sign on with a politics captivated by Ivy League five-syllable word polishers ... Most of the "New Conservatives" I know believe that any politics or coalition has to surge up from Middle America ... not dribble down from Bill Buckley's wine rack and favorite philosophers shelf ... There was of course a time when Bill Buckley was anti-establishment – back in the long ago days when he was an Irish nouveau-riche cheer leader for Joe McCarthy. But since then, he's primed his magazine with cast-off Hapsburg royalty, Englishmen who part their names in the middle, and others calculated to put real lace on Buckley's Celtic curtains."[25]

In its efforts to create a political mass base, the New Right attempted to tap into the country's large pool of socially conservative Protestant fundamentalists. In order to overcome a widespread reluctance in that group towards involvement in earthly matters, it was necessary to redefine a conservative political agenda in moral terms. Anything from soaring crime rates, drug addition, and the growing number of single parents, to gay rights and the denial of school prayer now had to be placed in the context of secularization and the breakdown of the traditional American family.

The effort was helped along by the Supreme Court's judicial nationalization of the Bill of Rights during the 1970s and the expansion of federal authority in areas such as education and employment. The introduction of national standards and the threat of the IRS to revoke the tax-exempt

---

24 Kevin Phillips, Column (July 17, 1975). Quoted from John B. Judis, *William F. Buckley.*, p. 378.
25 Quoted from Judis, *William F. Buckley, Jr...*, p. 379.

status of Christian schools practicing de facto racial discrimination were some of the major factors that led to the organizing of the Christian schools movement.

In the following years the Christian Right would fight *against* abortion, homosexual rights, the teaching of evolution in public schools, and pornography. They would fight *for* school prayer, home schooling, a family tax, and the general attempt to promote the role of religion in public life.

Regardless of the extent to which the Christian Right became the nuts and bolts within the party machinery, its core remained unappealing to the majority of American voters. To the leadership of the GOP and to Christian Right-activists alike, the dilemma was evident. By tightening their grip on state and local party organizations, and by disproportionate electoral participation, the Christian Right could get their candidates nominated; but as long as they scared away non-committed voters from the party, they would be doomed in general elections.

Conservatism without tears

The "populists" had learned one important lesson from the brief history of postwar conservatism. In order to broaden their appeal to lower-middle-class voters, they would have to express their beliefs in positive terms and they would have to spell out actual policy proposals.[26] In short, conservatives had to convey a sense of vision. One could argue that the very notion of a conservative vision is an oxymoron, and that conservatives suffer from an inherent inability to translate their political sentiments into formulae and specific aims, since by nature they tend to be based on instinct and experience rather than on theorizing and rational analysis. With Ronald Reagan as the champion of the movement, however, it seemed possible to square the circle.

Although many Americans probably voted against Jimmy Carter, rather than for Ronald Reagan, it was nevertheless clear that with the for-

---

26 In the election of 1972, it was once again confirmed that the majority of voters had a hard time swallowing the Goldwater brand of conservatism in its undiluted form. One of the young lions of the movement, John Ashbrook of Ohio, in response to widespread conservative dissatisfaction with the policies of the Nixon administration challenged the president in the Republican primaries. Ashbrook received less than 10 percent of the vote in all the primaries he participated in.

mer actor as the leading figure, conservatives of the 1980s were able to offer something that the Goldwater movement had not been able to deliver. While Goldwater had mostly talked about repealing laws and Gerald Ford's conservatism had mostly manifested itself in the veto of 64 bills, Reagan had adopted many liberal premises in order to present what George F. Will once called "conservatism without tears." Alternative welfare measures gave the impression that conservatism mostly differed from liberalism in its choice of methods, that it merely applied different means to the same end. Edwin J. Feulner, president of the Heritage Foundation, whose blueprint for the Reagan administration, *Mandate for Leadership*, gave it a reputation as "Reagan's think tank," talked about the attempt to create a whole new mindset among conservatives: "In the past so many of our activities have been against things. Now how do you start thinking more positively in terms of conservative initiatives?"[27]

Due to Reagan's activist politics, conservatism no longer appeared as a reactive force, but as an innovative one, and the president himself was the perfect embodiment of this new style. As his biographer Lou Cannon would later put it: "When Reagan spoke, ordinary Americans did not have to make the mental translation usually required for conservative Republican speakers. He undermined the New Deal in its own vernacular."[28]

With Ronald Reagan in the White House, conservatives benefited from a nostalgia for a simpler past and a longing for moral restoration. It was morning again for those who felt trapped in post-modern multicultural America. Notions such as "supply-side economics" were intended to convince low-income voters that they too would benefit from conservative economic policy.[29] Conservatism was no longer a thankless persuasion.

---

27 *New York Times*, December 5, 1980. Quoted from James Allen Smith, *The Idea Brokers; Think Tanks and the Rise of the New Policy Elite* (New York: The Free Press, 1991), p. 195.

28 Quoted from William E. Leuchtenburg, *In the Shadow of FDR: From Harry Truman to Ronald Reagan* (Ithaca, N.Y.: Cornell University Press, 1985), p. 225.

29 President Reagan's Director of the Office of Management and Budget, David Stockman, caught hell when he carelessly told a reporter from *The Washington Post* that the "supply-side" tax cuts were "a Trojan horse [designed] to bring down the top rate." It was merely "trickle down" economics which had been relabeled because it was "hard to sell 'trickle down' to the public." Quoted from Phillip H. Burch, *Reagan, Bush, and Right-Wing Politics: Elites, Think Tanks, Power, and Policy; The American Right Wing Takes Command: Key Executive Appointments* (Greewich, Conn.: JAI Press, 1997), pp. 45-46.

Persistent Tensions within the Conservative Movement

The organizational- and ideological continuity from the Goldwater campaign of 1964 to Reagan's victory in 1980 has often been pointed out. Historian John Morton Blum notes that Goldwater had spoken in what would become "the authentic voice of American conservatism."[30] "As late as 1988," he argues, "support for Goldwater in 1964 remained a litmus test of the Republican right."

The symbolism is appealing to chroniclers of American conservatism: In the ashes of the Goldwater-campaign, the movement found its new star, Ronald Reagan. Or as George Will has put it, "Goldwater's message was given wings by Reagan's mellifluous voice."[31] But perhaps the line of progression is not quite as clear as these quotes suggest, and the affinity between the conservative champion of 1964 and his successor not as strong as most conservatives like to think.[32]

Unlike Reagan, Goldwater openly expressed his dislike of many key issues on the New Right's social agenda. A ban on abortion was one of them. The senator was pro-choice and supported Planned Parenthood. His wife Peggy had once been the president of the organization in Arizona, and he publicly expressed the view that "If a woman wants to have an abortion, by God, that's her body."[33] According to Charles Lichenstein, research director in the Goldwater campaign, this had actually been Gold-

---

30 John Morton Blum, *Years of Discord; American Politics and Society, 1961-1974* (New York: W.W. Norton & Company, 1991), p. 159.
31 Quoted from John B. Judis, "Barry's Way" The New Republic, Vol. 218, No. 27 (June 22, 1998), pp. 15-16.
32 In fact, Goldwater himself did not wholeheartedly support Reagan's political ascendancy, just as Reagan actually asked Goldwater to stay out of California during the gubernatorial election in 1966. Ten years later, the Arizonan supported Gerald Ford rather than Reagan, the conservative favorite. The decision reflected a pragmatism that from time to time brought him at odds with "movement" conservatives. Goldwater was convinced that a split in the party would ensure a Democratic victory. His private advice to President Ford during the campaign indicated that his concern for the success of the Republican Party was greater than his dedication to the conservative movement. "You are not going to get the Reagan vote," he privately told Ford. "These are the same people who got me the nomination and they will never swerve, but ninety per cent of them will vote for you for President, so get after Middle America." Letter, Barry Goldwater to Gerald Ford, 5/7/1976, James Connor Files, Box 30, Gerald R. Ford Library.
33 Roger Rosenblatt, "Our National Buzzard," interview with Barry Goldwater, *Men's Journal*, August 1994, p. 49.

water's view all along: "I know for a fact that his views against outlawing abortion were exactly the same in '64 as in the '70s and '80s," Lichenstein told *U.S. News & World Report* in 1998. "But it wasn't an issue then."[34]

To the surprise of many, Goldwater would also become a champion of gay rights. "As long as a man doesn't do harm by what he does, or with whom he associates, he can be as gay as he wants to be," Goldwater told an interviewer, "I have a grandson who's gay."[35] Such views, and the brashness, with which he expressed them, made him the unlikely hero of many liberals. Two decades earlier he had been compared with Robert Taft and labeled a "pseudo-conservative." Now Goldwater was seen as the real thing, a token of genuine conservatism, while Jerry Falwell, Pat Robertson, Richard Viguerie and their like-minded had assumed the roles as "pseudos."[36]

Goldwater's clash with the Religious Right highlighted some of the fissures within the conservative movement. In some respects, the maturing of the movement had made conservatives less inclined to keep political disagreements behind closed doors. They split over issues ranging from trade, nationalism, foreign policy and immigration, to abortion and the legalization of drugs. Old tensions persisted and new ones emerged. In the 1990s, some of them would crystallize in the split between "neoconservatives" and "paleoconservatives," when the latter group assumed the role as the leading proponents of a culture rooted in localism, a strong (white) ethnic consciousness, and a neo-isolationist foreign policy.[37]

Fundamental to such views was a profound distrust of transnational corporations and the managerial class that runs them. Leading paleoconservatives would argue that the neoconservatives had not just served as a Trojan horse for conservatism within the establishment, but also as a Trojan horse for managerialism *within* the conservative movement.[38] The new conservative elite, they argued, was no longer able or willing to stem the

---

34 Quoted in Michael J. Gerson, "Mr. Right," *U. S. News & World Report* (June 8, 1998).
35 Rosenblatt, "Our National Buzzard," p. 49.
36 For one expression of this view, see Crawford, Alan, *Thunder on the Right: The "New Right" and the Politics of Resentment* (New York: Pantheon Books, 1980).
37 My understanding of paleoconservatism has been greatly helped by Professor Edward Ashbee's, "Politics of Paleoconservatism," *Society*, Vol. 37, No. 3 (March/April, 2000), pp. 74-84.
38 For one example, see Justin Raimondo, *Reclaiming the American Right* (Burlingame, CA: Center for Libertarian Studies, 1993).

tide of centralization and globalization in order to "resist the absorption of the American nation into a multicultural and multiracial globalist regime."[39] Thus, the seeds were sown for yet another revolt on the Right.

The Irony of Conservative Success

Is the story of postwar American conservatism ultimately a story of success or failure? Conservatives themselves seem to oscillate between overconfidence and profound disillusion. The first half of the 1980s and the year(s) following the midterm-elections in 1994 were periods of triumph for the movement, and many political scientists argued that a major realignment had finally taken place. A Republican Party controlled by its right wing had seemingly become the new majority party. Many conservatives were themselves ready to use the word "revolution." After a while, however, disappointment set in, and conservatives had to realize that their achievements had fallen short of any revolutionary change.

For years they had been able to dominate the Republican Party. The party had occupied the presidency for twelve consecutive years and controlled one or both houses in Congress for several years as well. Yet, the basic structures of the welfare state were still in place. In 1987, New Right-activist Paul Weyrich argued that while conservatives had gained influence, they did not have any real power because they did not hold any "territory."[40] The movement had leaders, activists, and supporters, but in order to win national elections it still had to win over new constituencies.

This task had previously been facilitated by the conceptual framework provided by the Cold War. It was difficult to find a new social glue which could replace anticommunism. As Weyrich later noted, secularization could not easily take the place of world communism, since "In the secular humanist empire there is no single bad organization or evil leader which can be used to symbolize a system which is a threat to America and which needs to be defeated."[41]

---

39 Samuel Francis, *Revolution from the Middle* (Raleigh: Middle American Press, 1997), p. 211.
40 Paul M. Weyrich, "The Reagan Revolution That Wasn't" *Policy Review* (Summer, 1987), pp. 50-53.
41 Paul M. Weyrich, "Will the Conservative Movement Survive?" *Free Daily* (February 15, 2000) http://www.freedaily.com. Weyrich's own suggestion for a new issue which could unite conservatives was privacy – perhaps a surprising choice from a man whose main political target hitherto had been abortion rights.

Ironically, conservative dreams of a "revolution" had among other things been thwarted by the anti-radical nature of the American political system itself, and by the fact that most Americans were too conservative in Oakeshott's temperamental sense to support any sweeping ideological changes. The neoconservative writer Midge Decter has argued that:

> there can be no reliably, steadfastly conservative White House in the United States of America, just as there can be no sudden conservative congressional revolution. The country does not work that way. And in truth, we should all be on our knees in gratitude that it does not. For, let us never forget, whatever is sauce for the goose can on some propitious day become sauce for the gander. Thirty years ago, after all, there were leftists in our midst who also proclaimed a "revolution" — indeed a variety of interlocking revolutions — and the country was saved from them not so much by the countervailing force of conservatism as by the stolidity and, yes, basic contentment of the general populace."[42]

Thus, no conservative "revolution" swept the country, but the movement continued to conquer new territory and in some areas managed to change the entire political discourse. It had become institutionalized and professionalized. Think tank fellows, fundraisers, and political consultants had replaced the intellectuals turned amateur political activists who characterized the movement in the 1940s and 1950s.

Conservatives had clearly done best with ordinary American voters when they had been able to present a positive political program, as was the case with the "Reagan-revolution" in the early 1980s; but even under such favorable circumstances they had been unable to dismantle the basic structures of the welfare state. Yet, one might argue that the conservative movement helped trigger processes that were eating at the welfare state from below. Some of these processes would later work under the control of President Clinton and other neo-liberals, eager to demonstrate their fiscal responsibility. Thus, it was Clinton who in 1996 signed into law an old conservative proposal for the decentralization of Federal welfare.

Clinton's remarkable resurgence after 1994 was to a large degree a result of his ability to hoist his conservative opponents with their own

---

[42] Midge Decter, "On the Future of Conservatism; A Symposium", *Commentary*, Vol. 103, No. 2 (February 1997). www.commentarymagazine.com.

petard. In January 1996, Clinton declared that "the era of big government is over." He adopted and modified conservative approaches to welfare and to crime, as well as the goal of balancing the budget. Such policies evidenced the extent to which the "vital center" in American politics had shifted to the right over the past decades. As such it should have given conservatives plenty of reason to rejoice. However, it had also deprived them of the ability to paint the familiar picture of liberal excesses. With an allegedly liberal president already cutting deep in welfare programs, the so-called "Reagan Democrats" — often people with limited economic means – had little incentive to vote for a fiscal conservative, who, on principle, would cut even deeper.

In 1960, Barry Goldwater had expressed the hope that conservatives would someday take back their "historic home," the Republican Party, and so they had. In this respect, the organizing of the conservative movement had been a major success. The effort to replace the New Deal order had been less successful. Often, conservatives had been able to appeal to anti-statist sentiments, to patriotism, to a longing for order, to dreams of a less complex society, or simply to the pocketbooks of well-to-do voters, but so far they had not been able to spell out a coherent political program that could decidedly win over a majority of American voters for a sustained period of time.

The growing strength of the Christian Right within the Republican Party had not made things easier. It had tapped into new resources for the movement, but its social agenda had also polarized the general voting public even further and scared away potential allies. Although conservatives were still "standing athwart history, yelling stop," the relentless forces of modernism had not been halted. The conservative movement was still at sea searching for the America it set out to reclaim almost half a century before.

Bibliography

Manuscript collections

William F. Buckley, Jr. Papers, Manuscripts and Archives Department, Yale University, New Haven, Connecticut.

James Burnham Papers. Hoover Institution Archives, Stanford University, California.

John Chamberlain Papers. Hoover Institution Archives

Ralph De Toledano Papers. Hoover Institution Archives

Barry M. Goldwater Papers (presidential campaign), Olin Library, Cornell University, New York

Barry M. Goldwater Papers, Arizona Historical Foundation, Arizona State University, Arizona

Jeffrey Hart Papers, Hoover Institution Archives

The Herbert Hoover Papers, Herbert Hoover Presidential Library, West Branch, Iowa

The Papers of Lyndon B. Johnson, White House Central File, Lyndon B. Johnson Library, Austin, Texas

Denison Kitchel Papers, Hoover Institution Archives

Marvin Liebman Papers, Hoover Institution Archives

Clarence Manion Papers, Chicago Historical Society, Chicago, Illinois

Felix Morley Papers, Herbert Hoover Presidential Library

Office Files of Bill Moyers, Lyndon B. Johnson Presidential Library, Austin, Texas

Office Files of George Reedy, Lyndon B. Johnson Presidential Library, Austin Texas

Henry Regnery Papers, Hoover Institution Archives

The Papers of the Republican National Committee, 1964-1965, Olin Library, Cornell University, Ithaca, New York

William A. Rusher Papers, Library of Congress, Washington, D.C.

The Right Wing Collection, Iowa University, Iowa City

Arthur M. Schlesinger Papers, John Fitzgerald Kennedy Library, Boston, Mass.

Theodore Sorensen Papers, John Fitzgerald Kennedy Library, Boston, Mass

Roswell L. Gilpatrick Papers, John Fitzgerald Kennedy Library, Boston, Mass

The Presidential Papers of John F. Kennedy, White House Central Files. John Fitzgerald Kennedy Library, Boston, Mass.

Robert F. Kennedy Attorney General Papers, John Fitzgerald Kennedy Library, Boston Mass.

Stephen Shadegg Papers, Center for American History, University of Texas, Austin, Texas

Robert A. Taft Papers, Manuscripts Division, Library of Congress, Washington, D.C.

F. Clifton White Papers. Olin Library, Cornell University, Ithaca, New York

Dissertations

Allitt, Patrick, *Catholic Lay Intellectuals in the American Conservative Movement* (UMI Dissertation Information Service, UC, Berkeley, 1986)

Devereux, Erik August, *The Partisan Press Revisited; Newspapers and Politics in the United States, 1964-1968* (Ph.D dissertation, The University of Texas at Austin, 1993)

Toy, Eckard Vance, *Ideology and Conflict in American Ultraconservatism, 1945-1960* (Ph.D. Dissertation, Dept. of History, University of Oregon, 1965)

Schneider, Gregory Lee, *Young Americans for Freedom* (Ph.D. Dissertation, Dept. Of History, University of Illinois at Chicago, 1996)

Books

Adler, Selig, *The Isolationist Impulse* (London: Abelard-Schuman Ltd., 1957)

Adorno, T.W., et. al., *The Authoritarian Personality* (New York: Harper, 1950)

Alert Americans Association, *First National Directory of "Rightist" Groups* (Sausalito: The Noontide Press, 1962)

Alexander, Charles C., *Holding the Line: The Eisenhower Era, 1952-1961* (Bloomington: Indiana University Press, 1975)

Allitt, Patrick, *Catholic Intellectuals and Conservative Politics in America, 1950-1985* (Itchaca: Cornell University Press, 1995)

Andrew III, John A., *The Other Side of the Sixties; Young Americans for Freedom and the Rise of Conservative Politics* (New Brunswick: Rutgers University Press, 1997)

Apter, David E. (ed.), *Ideology and Discontent* (London: Free Press of Glencoe, 1964)

Auerbach, M. Morton, *The Conservative Illusion* (New York: Columbia University Press, 1959)

Bachrack, Stanley D., *The Committee of One Million: "China Lobby" Politics, 1953-1971I* (New York: Columbia University Press, 1976)

Barber, James David, *The Pulse of Politics; Electing Presidents in the Media Age* (New York: W.W. Norton & Company, 1980)

BIBLIOGRAPHY

Barry, Norman (et. al.), *Hayek's "Serfdom" Revisited* (London: The Institute of Economic Affairs, 1984)

Barry, Norman P., *The New Right* (London: Croom Helm, 1987)

Bass, Jack & Walter DeVries, *The Transformation of Southern Politics* (New York: New American Library, 1977)

Bell, Daniel (ed.), *The Radical Right* (New York, Doubleday & Company, 1963)

Bell, Jack, *Mr. Conservative: Barry Goldwater* (Garden City, N.Y.: Doubleday & Company, Inc., 1962)

Bennett, David H., *The Party of Fear* (Chapel Hill: The University of North Carolina Press, 1988)

Blumenthal, Sidney, *The Rise of the Counter-establishment; From conservative ideology to political power* (New York: Times Books, 1986)

Blumenthal, Sidney & Thomas Byrne Edsall (eds.), *The Reagan Legacy* (New York: Pantheon Books, 1988)

Boaz, David (ed.), *Left, Right & Babyboom; America's New Politics* (Washington, D.C.: Cato Institute, 1986)

Boskin, Joseph, *Opposition Politics: The Anti-New Deal Tradition* (Beverly Hills: The Glencoe Press, 1968)

Boston, Thomas D., *Race, Class and Conservatism* (Boston: Unwin Hyman, 1988)

Braeman, John (ed.), *The New Deal; the National Level* (Columbus: Ohio State University Press, 1975)

Braun, Aurel & Stephen Scheinberg (eds.), *The Extreme Right; Freedom and Security at Risk* (Boulder: Westview Press, 1997)

Brennan, Mary C., *Turning Right in the Sixties; The Conservative Capture of the GOP* (Chapel Hill: The University of North Carolina Press, 1995)

Broyles, J. Allen, *The John Birch Society: Anatomy of a protest* (Boston: Beacon Press, 1964)

Buchanan, Patrick J., *Conservative Votes, Liberal Victories* (New York: Quadrangle/the New York Times Book Co., 1975)

Buchanan, Patrick J., *Right From the Beginning* (Boston: Little, Brown and Company, 1988)

Buchanan, Patrick J., *The Great Betrayal* (Boston: Little, Brown and Company, 1998)

Buckley, Jr., William F., *God and Man at Yale* (Chicago: Henry Regnery Company, 1951)

Buckley, Jr., William F., *Up From Liberalism* (New York: McDowell, Obolensky, 1959)

Buckley, Jr., William F., *Quotations From Chairman Bill* (New Rochelle, N.Y.: Arlington House, 1970)

Buckley, Jr., William F., *Keeping the Tablets; Modern American Conservative Thought* (New York: Harper & Row, 1988)

Buckley, William F., *The Jeweler's Eye* (New York: G.P. Putnam's Sons, 1968)

Buckley, William F. & L. Brent Bozell, *McCarthy and His Enemies* (Chicago: Henry Regnery Company, 1954)

Burch, Phillip H., *Reagan, Bush, and Right-Wing Politics: Elites, Think Tanks, Power, and Policy; The American Right Wing Takes Command: Key Executive Appointments* (Greewich, Conn.: JAI Press, 1997)

Burner, David & Thomas R. West, *Column Right* (New York: New York University Press, 1988)

Burnham, James, *The Struggle for the World* (New York: John Day and Company, 1947)

Burnham, James, *Containment or Liberation?* (New York: John Day and Company, 1953)

Burnham, James, *Suicide of the West* (New York: The John Day Company, 1964)

Butler, Eamonn, *Hayek* (London: Temple Smith, 1987)

Cain, Edward, *They'd Rather Be Right* (New York: The MacMillan Company, 1963)

Cannon, Lou, *Reagan* (New York: G.P.Putnam's Sons, 1982)

Carey, George W. (ed.), *Freedom and Virtue; the Conservative/Libertarian Debate* (Lanham: University Press of America, 1984)

Carter, Dan T., *The Politics of Rage; George Wallace, the Origins of the New Conservatism, and the Transformation of American Politics* (New York: Simon & Schuster, 1995)

Caute, David, *The Great Fear* (New York: Simon & Schuster, 1978)

Challener, Richard D. (ed.), *From Isolation to Containment, 1921-1952* (New York: St. Martin's Press, 1970)

Chamberlain, John, *A Life With the Printed Word* (Chicago: Regnery Gateway, 1982)

Chamberlin, William Henry, *The Evolution of a Conservative* (Chicago: Henry Regnery Company, 1959)

Chamberlin, William Henry, *America's Second Crusade* (Chicago: Henry Regnery Company, 1950)

Chambers, Whittaker, *Witness* (London: Andre Deutch, 1953)

Chambers, Whittaker, *Odyssey of a Friend* (New York: G.P. Putnam's Sons, 1969)

Chodorov, Frank, *Out of Step* (New York: The Devin-Adair Company, 1962)

Chodorov, Frank, *Fugitive Essays: Selected Writings of Frank Chodorov* (Indianapolis: Liberty Press, 1980).

Cole, Wayne S., *Roosevelt and the Isolationists, 1932-45* (Lincoln: University of Nebraska Press, 1983)

Coleman, Peter, *The Liberal Conspiracy* (New York: The Free Press, 1989)

Cooper, Barry, et.al (eds.), *The Resurgence of Conservatism in Anglo-American Democracies* (Durham and London: Duke University Press, 1988)

Cosman, Bernard, *Five States for Goldwater* (University, Alabama: University of Alabama Press, 1966)

Cosman, Bernard & Robert J. Huckshorn (eds.), *Republican Politics: The 1964 Campaign and Its Aftermath For the Party* (New York: Frederick A. Praeger, 1968)

Crawford, Alan, *Thunder on the Right: The "New Right" and the Politics of Resentment* (New York: Pantheon Books, 1980)

Crosby, Donald F., *God, Church, and Flag* (Chapell Hill: The University of North Carolina Press, 1978)

Crunden, Robert M., *The Mind and Art of Albert Jay Nock* (Chicago: Regnery Books, 1964)

Cummings, Milton C. (ed.), *The National Election of 1964* (Washington, D.C.: The Brookings Institution, 1965)

Curry, Richard O. & T. Brown, *Conspiracy; The Fear of Subversion in American History* (New York: Holt, Rinehart and Winston, 1972)

Dale, Edwin L., *Conservatives in Power; A Study in Frustration* (New York: Doubleday & Co., 1960)

Davis, David Brion (ed.), *The Fear of Conspiracy* (Itchaca: Cornell University Press, 1971)

De Toledano, Ralph, *Lament for a Generation* (New York: Farrar, Straus and Cudahy, 1960)

DeConde, Alexander (ed.), *Isolation and Security* (Durham, N.C.: Duke University Press, 1957)

Deutsch, Kenneth L. and John A. Murley (eds.) *Leo Strauss, the Straussians, and the American Regime* (Lanham, MD: Rowman and Littlefield, 1999)

Diamond, Sara, *Roads to Dominion; Right-Wing Movements and Political Power in the United States* (New York: The Guilford Press, 1995)

Diggins, John P., *Up From Communism* (New York: Harper & Row, 1975)

Dionne, Jr., E.J., *Why Americans Hate Politics* (New York: Simon and Schuster, 1991)

Dionne, E. J., *They Only Look Dead: Why Progressives Will Dominate the Next Political Era* (New York: Simon & Schuster, 1996).

Doenecke, Justus, *Not to the Swift* (Lewisburg: Bucknell University Press, 1979)

Doenecke, Justus D., *Anti-Intervention; A Bibliographical Introduction.*(New York: Garland Publishing, Inc., 1987)

Doenecke, Justus D., *The Literature of Isolationism* (Colorado Springs: Ralph Myles, 1972)

Doenecke, Justus D. (ed.), *In Danger Undaunted: The Anti-interventionist Movement of 1940-1941 as revealed in the papers of the America First Committee* (Stanford: Hoover Institution Press, 1990)

Domhoff, G. William, *The Higher Circles* (New York: Random House, 1970)

Drury, Shadia B., *Leo Strauss and the American Right* (London: MacMillan Press, 1997)

Dudman, Richard, *Men of the Far Right* (New York: Pyramid Books, 1962)

Dunn, Charles W. & J. David Woodard, *American Conservatism From Burke to Bush* (Lanham: Madison Books, 1991)

East, John P., *The American Conservative Movement; the Philosophical Founders* (Chicago: Regnery Books, 1986)

Eastman, Max, *Reflections on the Failure of Socialism* (New York: The Devin-Adair Company, 1955)

Eatwell, Roger (ed.), *The Nature of the Right; Themes in Right-Wing Ideology and Politics* (London: Printer Publishers, 1989)

Edsall, Thomas Byrne & Mary D. Edsall, *Chain Reaction; The Impact of Race, Rights, and Taxes on American Politics* (New York: W.W. Norton & Company, 1992)

Edwards, Lee & Anne, *You Can Make the Difference* (New Rochelle, N.Y.: Arlington House, 1968)

Edwards, Lee, *Goldwater* (Washington, D.C.: Regnery Publishing Inc., 1995)

Ellsworth, Ralph E. & Sarah M. Harris, *The American Right Wing; A report to the Fund for the Republic* (Washington, D.C: Public Affairs Press, 1962)

Epstein, Benjamin R & Arnold Forster, *Danger on the Right* (New York: Random House, 1964)

Epstein, Benjamin & Arnold. Forster, *The Radical Right; Report on the John Birch Society and Its Allies'* (New York: Random House, 1967)

Evans, M. Stanton, *Revolt on the Campus* (Chicago: Henry Regnery Company, 1961)

Evans, M. Stanton, *The Future of Conservatism* (New York: Holt, Rinehart and Winston, 1968)

Evans, M. Stanton, *The Liberal Establishment* (New York: The Devin-Adair Company, 1965)

Evans, M. Stanton, *The American Revolution: a study in conservatism* (Philadelphia: Intercollegiate Society of Individualists, 1962)

Evans, Medford, *The Assassination of Joe McCarthy* (Boston: Western Islands (John Birch Society), 1970)

Ewald, Jr., William Bragg, *McCarthyism and Consensus* (Lanham: University Press of America, 1986)

Ferguson, Thomas & Joel Rogers, *Right Turn* (New York: Hill and Wang, 1986)

Filler, Louis, *Dictionary of American Conservatism* (New York: Philosophic Library, 1987)

Finer, Herman, *Road to Reaction* (Boston: Little, Brown and Company, 1946)

Flynn, John T., *While You Slept; Our tragedy in Asia and who made it* (New York: Devin-Adair, 1951)

Flynn, John T., *The Roosevelt Myth* (New York: Devin-Adair, 1948)

Foley, Michael, *American Political Ideas; Traditions and Usages* (Manchester: Manchester University Press, 1991)

Francis, Samuel T., *Power and History: The Political Thought of James Burnham* (Lanham, Md.: University Press of America, 1984)

Francis, Samuel T., *Beautiful Losers: Essays On the Failure Of American Conservatism* (Columbia: University of Missouri Press, 1993).

Francis, Samuel T., *Revolution from the Middle* (Raleigh: Middle American Press, 1997)

Fraser, Steve & Gary Gerstle, *The Rise and Fall of the New Deal Order, 1930-1980* (Princeton, N.J.: Princeton University Press, 1989)

Freeland, Richard, *The Truman Doctrine and the Origins of McCarthyism* (New York: Alfred Knopf, 1972)

Fried, Richard M., *Nightmare in Red; The McCarthy Era in Perspective* (New York: Oxford University Press, 1990)

Fried, Richard M., *Men Against McCarthy* (New York: Columbia University Press, 1976)

Frum, David, *Dead Right* (New York: BasicBooks, 1994)

Genovese, Eugene, *The Southern Tradition: The Achievement and Limitations of an American Conservatism (Cambridge: Harvard University Press, 1994)*

Gerson, Louis L., *The Hyphenate in Recent American Politics and Diplomacy* (Lawrence: The University of Kansas Press, 1964)

Giddens, Anthony, *Beyond Left and Right; The Future of Radical Politics* (Cambridge: Polity Press, 1994)

Gies, Joseph, *The Colonel of Chicago* (New York: E.P. Dutton, 1979)

Goldberg, Robert A., *Goldwater* (New Haven: Yale University Press, 1995)

Goldwater, Barry M., *With No Apologies* (New York: William Morrow and Company, Inc., 1979)

Goldwater, Barry M., *The Conscience of a Conservative* (New York: Manor Books Inc., 1974 [1960])

Goldwater, Barry M., *Goldwater* (New York: Doubleday, 1988)

Goldwin, Robert A. (ed.), *Left, Right,and Center* (Chicago: Rand McNally & Company, 1965)

Gottfried, Paul, *The Search for Historical Meaning: Hegel and the Postwar American Right* (DeKalb: Northern Illinois University Press, 1986)

Gottfried, Paul & T Fleming, *The Conservative Movement* (Boston: Twayne Publishers, 1988)

Grantham, Dewey W., *The Life and Death of the Solid South; New Perspectives on the South* (Lexington: The University Press of Kentucky, 1988)

Grantham, Dewey W., *The South In Modern America; A Region at Odds* (New York: HarperCollins Publishers, 1994)

Griffith, Robert & Athan Theoharis, *The Specter; Original Essays on the Cold War* (New York: New Viewpoints, 1974)

Grove, Gene, *Inside the John Birch Society* (Greenwich, Conn.: Fawcett Publications, Inc., 1961)

Hamby, Alonzo S., *Beyond the New Deal* (New York: Columbia University Press, 1973)

Hamby, Alonzo S., *Liberalism And Its Challengers* (New York: Oxford University Press, 1985)

Hart, Jeffrey, *The American Dissent; A Decade of Modern Conservatism* (New York: Doubleday & Company, Inc., 1966)

Hartz, Louis, *The Liberal Tradition in America* (New York: Harcourt Brace Jovanovich, 1955)

Hayek, F.A., *The Road to Serfdom* (London: George Routledge & Sons Ltd., 1944)

Heale, M.J., *American Anticommunism* (Baltimore: The Johns Hopkins University Press, 1990)

Herberg, Will, *Protestant – Catholic – Jew* (New York: Doubleday & Company, Inc., 1956)

Hess, Karl, *In a Cause That Will Triumph* (New York: Doubleday & Company, Inc., 1967)

Hess, Stephen & David Broder, *The Republican Establishment* (New York: Harper & Row, 1967)

Higgs, Robert, *Crisis and Leviathan* (New York: Oxford University Press, 1987)

Himmelstein, Jerome L., *To The Right; The Transformation of American Conservatism* (Berkeley: University of California Press, 1989)

Hixson, Jr., William B., *Search For the American Right Wing; An Analysis Of the Social Science Record, 1955-1987* (Princeton: Princeton University Press, 1992)

Hodgson, Godfrey, *The World Turned Right Side Up: A History of the Conservative Ascendancy in America* (Boston: Houghton Mifflin Company, 1996)

Hoeveler, Jr., J. David, *Watch on the Right* (Madison: The University of Wisconsin Press, 1991)

Hofstadter, Richard, *The Paranoid Style in American Politics* (Chicago: The University of Chicago Press, 1979 (1965))

Holmes, Stephen, *The Anatomy of Antiliberalism* (Cambridge: Harvard University Press, 1993)

Horowitz, David (ed.), *Corporations and the Cold War* (New York: Monthly Review Press, 1969)

Human Events (ed.), *The Intelligent Conservative's Reference Manual* (Washington, D.C.: Human Events,1982)

Hunt, R.N. Carew, *The Theory & Practice of Communism* (London: Geoffrey Bles, 1950)

Jamieson, Kathleen Hall, *Packaging the Presidency; A History and Criticism of Presidential Campaign Advertising* (New York: Oxford University Press, 1984)

Janson, Donald & B. Eismann, *The Far Right* (New York: McGraw-Hill Book Company, Inc., 1963)

Jeansonne, Glen, *Gerald L.K. Smith Minister of Hate* (New Haven: Yale University Press, 1988)

Judis, John B., *William F. Buckley, Jr.; Patron Saint of the Conservatives* (New York: Simon and Schuster, 1988)

Kahn, E.J., Jr., *The China Hands* (New York: Viking, 1972)

Kelley, Joseph, *The China Lobby Man* (New Rochelle, N.Y.: Arlington House, 1969)

Kendall, Willmoore, *The Conservative Affirmation* (Chicago: Henry Regnery Company, 1963)

Kessel, John H., *The Goldwater Coalition* (New York: The Bobbs-Merrill Company, Inc., 1968)

Kilpatrick, James J., *The Sovereign States* (Chicago: Henry Regnery Company, 1957)

Kirk, Russell, *The Political Principles of Robert A. Taft* (New York: Fleet Press Corporation, 1967)

Kirk, Russell, *A Program for Conservatives* (Chicago: Henry Regnery Company, 1954)

Kirk, Russell, *The Conservative Mind* (Chicago: Henry Regnery Company, 1953)

Kirk, Russell, *Academic Freedom* (Chicago: Henry Regnery Company, 1955)

Klatch, Rebecca E., *A Generation Divided; The New Left, the New Right, and the 1960s* (Berkeley: University of California Press, 1999)

Richard Kleindienst, *Justice: the memoirs of Attorney General Richard Kleindienst* (Ottawa, Ill.: Jameson Books, 1985)

Koen, Ross Y., *The China Lobby in American Politics* (New York: Harper & Row, 1974)

Kolkey, Jonathan Martin, *The New Right, 1960-1968 With Epilogue, 1969-1980* (Washington, D.C.: University Press of America, 1983)

Kramer, Michael & Sam Roberts, *I Never Wanted to Be Vice- President of Anything!", An Investigative Biography of Nelson Rockefeller* (New York: Basic Books, 1976).

Lamis, Alexander P., *The Two-Party South* (New York: Oxford University Press, 1984)

Latham, Earl (ed.), *The Meaning of McCarthyism* (Lexington, Mass.: D.C. Heath and Company, 1973 [1965])

Lens, Sidney, *The Futile Crusade; Anti-Communism as American Credo* (Chicago, 1964)

Leuchtenburg, William E., *In the Shadow of FDR* (Ithaca: Cornell University Press, 1983)

Liebman, Marvin, *Coming Out Conservative; An Autobiography* (San Francisco: Chronicle Books, 1992)

Lipset, Seymour & Earl Raab, *The Politics of Unreason* (New York: Harper & Row, 1970)

Lipset, Seymour M. (ed.), *Student Politics* (New York: Basic Books, 1967)

Lokos, Lionel, *Hysteria 1964; the Fear Campaign Against Barry Goldwater* (New Rochelle, N.Y.: Arlington House, 1965)

Lora, Ronald, *Conservative Minds in America* (Chicago: Rand McNally & Company, 1971)

Lowi, Theodore J., *The End of Liberalism* (New York: W. W. Norton & Company, 1979)

Lowi, Theodore J., *The End of the Republican Era* (Norman: University of Oklahoma Press, 1995)

Lubell, Samuel, *The Future of American Politics* (New York: Harper & Row, Publishers, 1965)

Machlup, Fritz (ed.), *Essays on Hayek* (New York: New York University Press, 1976)

MacNeil, Neil, *Dirksen: Portrait of a Public Man* (New York: The World Publishing Company, 1970)

Mattar, Edward Paul III, *Barry Goldwater; A Political Indictment* (Riverdale, MD: Century Twenty One Limited, 1964)

Matusow, Allen (ed.), *Joseph R. McCarthy* (Englewood Cliffs: Prentice-Hall, 1970)

May, Lary (ed.), *Recasting America* (Chicago: The University of Chicago Press, 1989)

Mayer, George H., *The Republican Party, 1854-1966* (New York: Oxford University Press, 1967)

McAllister, Ted V., *Revolt Against Modernity: Leo Strauss, Eric Voegelin, and the Search for a Postliberal Order* (Lawrence: University of Kansas Press, 1996)

McEvoy III, James, *Radicals or Conservatives?* (Chicago: Rand McNally & Company, 1971)

McGirr, Lisa, *Suburban Warriors; The Origins of the New American Right* (Princeton: Princeton University Press, 2001)

McKenna, George, *American Populism* (New York, 1974)

McQuaid, Kim, *Uneasy Partners; Big Business in American Politics 1945-1990* (Baltimore: The Johns Hopkins University Press, 1994)

Meyer, Frank, *In Defense of Freedom: A Conservative Credo* (Chicago: Henry Regnery Company, 1962)

Meyer, Frank S., *What is Conservatism?* (New York: Holt, Rinehart and Winston, 1964)

Meyer, Frank S., *The Conservative Mainstrea* (New Rochelle, N.Y.: Arlington House, 1969)

Meyer, Karl E., *The New America* (New York: Basic Books, Inc., 1961)

Miles, Michael, *The Odyssey of the American Right* (New York: Oxford University Press, 1980)

Mintz, Frank P., *The Liberty Lobby and the American Right* (Westport, Conn.: Greenwood Press, 1985)

Moley, Raymond, *The Republican Opportunity* (New York: Duell, Sloan and Pearce, 1962)

Morley, Felix, *For the record* (South Bend, IN: Regnery/Gateway, Inc., 1979)

Nash, George H., *The Conservative Intellectual Movement in America Since 1945* (New York: Basic Books, Inc., 1976)

Navasky, Victor, *Naming Names* (New York: Viking, 1980)

Neal, Alfred C., *Business Power and Public Policy* (New York: Praeger, 1981)

Newman, Stephen L., *Liberalism at Wits' End* (Itchaca: Cornell University Press, 1984)

Nisbet, Robert, *The Quest for Community* (Oxford: Oxford University Press, 1953)

Nisbet, Robert, *Conservatism Dream and Reality* (Minneapolis: University of Minnesota Press, 1988)

Nixon, Richard M., *The Memoirs of Richard Nixon* (New York: Grosset & Dunlap, 1978)

Nock, Albert J., *Memoirs of a Superflous Man* South Bend, IN: Gateway, 1964)

Novak, Robert D., *The Agony of the G.O.P. 1964* (New York: The MacMillan Company, 1965)

Oakeshott, Michael, *Rationalism in politics and other essays* (Indiana: LibertyPress, 1991)

O'Neill, William L., *A Better World; Stalinism and the American Intellectuals* (New Brunswick: Transaction Publishers, 1990)

Ortega Y Gasset, Jose, *The Revolt of the Masses* (London: Unwin Books, 1932)

Oshinsky, David M., *A Conspiracy So Immense* (New York: The Free Press, 1983)

Overstreet, Harry and Bonaro, *The Strange Tactics of Extremism* (New York: W.W. Norton and Company, 1964)

Patterson, James T., *Congressional Conservatism and the New Deal* (Lexington: University of Kentucky Press, 1967)

Patterson, James T., *Mr. Republican; A Biography of Robert A. Taft* (Boston: Houghton Mifflin Company, 1972)

Perlstein, Rick, *Before the Storm; Barry Goldwater and the Unmaking of the American Consensus* (New York: Hill and Wang, 2001)

Peterson, Theodore, *Magazines in the Twentieth Century* (Urbana: The University of Illinois Press, 1956)

Phillips, Kevin, *The Emerging Republican Majority* (New Rochelle, N.Y.: Arlington House, 1969)

Phillips, William (ed.), *The Partisan Review Anthology* (New York: Holt, Rinehart and Winston, 1962)

Pickett, William B., *Eisenhower Decides to Run; Presidential Politics and Cold War Strategy* (Chicago: Ivan R. Dee, 2000)

Powers, Richard Gid, *Not Without Honor; The History of American Anticommunism* (New York: The Free Press, 1995)

Radosh, Ronald, *Prophets on the Right* (New York: Simon and Schuster, 1975)

Radosh, Ronald & M. Rothbard, *A New History of Leviathan* (New York: E. P. Dutton & Co., Inc., 1972)

Rae, Nicol C., *The Decline and Fall of the Liberal Republicans* (New York: Oxford University Press, 1989)

Raimondo, Justin, *Reclaiming the American Right: The Lost Legacy of the Conservative Movement* (Burlingame: Center for Libertarian Studies, 1993)

Reagan, Ronald, *An American Life* (New York: Simon and Schuster, 1990)

Redekop, John Harold, *The American Far Right* (Grand Rapids: W.B. Eerdmans Pub. Co., 1968)

Reeves, Thomas, *The Life and Times of Joe McCarthy; A Biography* (New York: Stein and Day, 1982)

Regnery, Henry, *Memoirs of a Dissident Publisher* (New York: Hartcourt Brace Jovanovich, 1979)

Reinhard, David W., *The Republican Right Since 1945* (Lexington: The University Press of Kentucky, 1983)

Ribuffo, Leo, *The Old Christian Right; the Protestant Far Right* (Philadelphia: Temple University Press, 1983)

Roberts, James C., *The Conservative Decade* (Westport, Conn.: Arlington House Publishers,1980)

Roepke, Wilhelm, *A Humane Economy* (Chicago: Henry Regnery Company, 1960)

Rogin, Michael Paul, *The Intellectuals and McCarthy: The Radical Specter* (Cambridge: The M.I.T. Press, 1967)

Rogin, Michael Paul, *Ronald Reagan, the Movie* (Berkeley: University of California Press, 1987)

Rossiter, Clinton, *Conservatism in America; The Thankless Persuasion* (New York: Vintage Books, 1962)

Rovere, Richard, *The Goldwater Caper* (London: Methuen, 1966)

Rovere, Richard H., *The American Establishment* (New York: Harcourt, Brace & World, Inc., 1962)

Rovere, Richard H., *Senator Joe McCarthy* (New York: Harper & Row, 1959)

Rozell, Mark J. & James F. Pontuso (eds.), *American Conservative Opinion Leaders* (Boulder: Westview Press, 1990)

Rusher, William A., *The Rise of the Right* (New York: William Morrow and Co., 1984)

Saloma, John S., *Ominous Politics: The New Conservative Labyrinth* (New York: Hill & Wang, 1984)

Schacht, John N. (ed.), *Three faces of Midwestern isolationism: Gerald P. Nye, Robert E. Wood, John L. Lewis* (Iowa: Center for the Study of the Recent History of the United States, 1981).

Schapsmeier, Edward L., *Political Parties and Civic Action Groups* (Westport, Conn.: Greenwood Press, 1981)

Schlafly, Phyllis, *A Choice Not an Echo* (Alton, Ill.: Pere Marquette Press, 1964)

Schlesinger, Jr., Arthur M., *The Vital Center* (Boston: Houghton Mifflin Company, 1949)

Schlesinger, Jr., Arthur M., *The Politics of Hope* (Boston: Houghton Mifflin Company, 1963)

Schoenberger, Robert A. (ed), *The American Right Wing; Readings in Political Behaviour* (New York: Holt, Rinehart and Winston, Inc., 1969)

Schriftgiesser, Karl, *Business Comes of Age* (New York: Harper and Brothers Publishers, 1960)

Shadegg, Stephen, *What Happened to Goldwater?* (New York: Holt, Rinehart and Winston, 1965)

Sherwin, Mark, *The Extremists* (New York: St Martin's Press, 1963)

Shils, Edward, *The Torment of Secrecy* (London: Heinemann, 1956)

Siegel, Frederick F., *Troubled Journey; From Pearl Harbor to Ronald Reagan* (New York: Hill & Wang, 1984)

Silk, Mark, *Spiritual Politics; Religion and America Since World War II* (New York: Simon and Schuster, 1988)

Singleton, M.K., *H.L. Mencken and the American Mercury Adventure* (Durham, N.C.: Duke University Press, 1962)

Smant, Kevin J., *How Great the Triumph; James Burnham, Anticommunism and the Conservative Movement* (Lanham: University Press of America, 1992)

Smith, James Allen, *The Idea Brokers* (New York: The Free Press, 1991)

Sperry, Baxter, *Senator Joe McCarthy, Martyr* (Galt, CA: Covenant Publ., 1968)

Stein, Herbert, *Presidential Economics* (New York: Simon and Schuster, 1984)

Stromer, Marvin E., *The Making of a Political Leader; Kenneth S. Wherry* (Lincoln: University of Nebraska Press, 1969)

Sundquist, James L., *Dynamics of the Party System; Alignment and Realignment of Political Parties in the United States* (Washington, D.C.: The Brookings Institution, 1983 [1973])

Taft, Robert, *A Foreign Policy For Americans* (New York: Doubleday & Company, Inc., 1951)

Tanenhaus, Sam, *Whittaker Chambers; A Biography* (New York: Random House, 1997)

Theoharis, Athan G., *The Yalta Myths* (Columbia: University of Missouri Press, 1970)

Thorne, Melvin J., *American Conservative Thought Since World War Two* (New York: Greenwood Press, 1990)

Tower, John G., *Consequences; A Personal and Political Memoir* (Boston: Little, Brown and Company, 1991)

Trilling, Lionel, *The Liberal Imagination* (New York: The Viking Press, 1950)

Tyrrell, R. Emmett, *The Conservative Crack-Up* (New York: Simon & Schuster, 1992)

Urofsky, Melvin I & Martha May. (eds.), *The New Christian Right; Political and Social Issues* (New York: Garland Publishing, Inc., 1996)

Vance, Mary, *Conservatism: Monographs, 1980-1987* (Monticello, Ill.: Vance Bibliographies,1988)

Viereck, Peter, *Shame and Glory of the Intellectuals* (Boston: The Beacon Press, 1953)

Viereck, Peter, *The Unadjusted Man* (Boston: The Beacon Press, 1956)

Viereck, Peter, *Conservatism Revisited* (New York: Collier Books, 1962)

Viguerie, Richard A., *The Establishment vs. The People* (Chicago, Ill.: Regnery Gateway, Inc., 1983)

Voegelin, Eric, *The New Science of Politics* (Chicago: The University of Chicago Press, 1952)

Vogel, David, *Fluctuating Fortunes, The Political Power of Business* (New York: Basic Books, Inc., 1989)

Watson, Justin, *The Christian Coalition; Dreams of Restoration, Demands for Recognition* (London: MacMillan Press, 1999)

Waxman, Chaim I. (ed), *The End of Ideology Debate* (New York: Funk & Wagnalls, 1968)

Weaver, Richard M., *Ideas Have Consequences* (Chicago: University of Chicago Press, 1948)

Wedemeyer, Albert C, *Wedemeyer Reports!* (New York: Henry Holt and Co., 1958)

Weinstein, Allen, *Percury: The Hiss-Chambers Case (New York: Vintage Books, 1979)*

Whitaker, Robert W., *The New Right Papers* (New York: St. Martin's Press, 1982)

White, F. Clifton, *Suite 3505; The Story of the Draft Goldwater Movement* (New Rochelle, N.Y.: Arlington House, 1967)

White, F. Clifton & W.J. Gill, *Why Reagan Won; A Narrative History of the Conservative Movement* (Chicago: Regnery Gateway, 1981)

White, Theodore, *The Making of the President 1960* (New York: Atheneum Publishers, 1961)

White, Theodore, *The Making of the President 1964* (New York: Atheneum Publishers, 1965)

Whitfield, Stephen J., *The Culture of the Cold War* (Baltimore: the Johns Hopkins University Press, 1991)

Wilcox, Clyde, *Onward Christian Soldiers?* (Boulder: WestviewPress, 1996)

Wilcox, Laird, *Guide to the American Right: Directory and Bibliography* (Olathe, Kansas: Laird Editorial Research Service, 1989)

Will, George, *Statecraft as Soulcraft* (New York: Simon & Schuster, 1983)

Wills, Garry, *Politics and Catholic Freedom* (Chicago: Henry Regnery Company, 1964)

Wills, Garry, *Confessions of a Conservative* (Garden City, N.Y.: Doubleday & Co, Inc., 1979)

Wolfe, Gregory, *Right Minds; A Sourcebook of American Conservative Thought* (Chicago: Regnery Books, 1985)

Wolfinger, Raymond E., *America's Radical Right* (Ann Arbor: ICPR, 1962)

Wolfskill, George, *The Revolt of the Conservatives* (Boston: Houghton Mifflin Company, 1962)

Young, Fred Douglas, *Richard M. Weaver, 1910-1963: A Life Of the Mind* (Columbia: University of Missouri Press, 1995).

Articles

Annunziata, Frank, "The Political Thought of John Chamberlain: Continuity and Conversion," *The South Atlantic Quarterly* (Vol. 74, Winter 1975), pp. 53-73.

Arendt, Hannah, "The Ex-Communists", *The Commonweal* (March 20, 1953), pp. 595-599

Ascoli, Max & Phillip Horton, "The China Lobby," *The Reporter* (April 15, 1952)

Ashbee, Edward, "Politics of Paleoconservatism." *Society*, Vol. 37, No. 3 (March/April, 2000), pp. 75-84.

Auerbach, M. Morton, "Do-It-Yourself Conservatism?" *National Review* (January 30, 1962), pp. 57-58

Barth, Alan, "Report on the Rampageous Right," *New York Times Magazine* (November 29, 1961)

Beck, Paul Allen, Partisan Dealignment in the Postwar South *American Political Science Review*, Vol. 71, 1977, pp. 477-496.

Berger, Brigitte & Peter L. Berger, "Our Conservatism and Theirs," *Commentary* (October, 1986), pp. 62-67.

Bernstein, Burton, "AuH$_2$O," *The New Yorker* (April 25, 1988)

Brandon, Donald, "Conservatives, and the Lost and the Silent Generations," *Modern Age*, Vol. 3 (Winter 1958-1959), pp. 2-8.

Braungart, Richard G., "Family Status, Socialization, and Student Politics", *American Journal of Sociology*, Vol.77, pp. 108-130.

Braungart, Margaret M. & Richard G. Braungart, "The Effects of the 1960s Political Generation on Former Left- and Right-Wing Youth Activist Leaders," *Social Problems*, Vol. 38, No. 3, August 1991, pp. 297-315.

Brinkley, Alan, "The Problem of American Conservatism," *American Historical Review* (April, 1994), pp. 409-429.

Broyles, J. Allen, "The John Birch Society: A Movement of Social Protest of the Radical Right," *The Journal of Social Issues*, Vol. XIX, No. 2, April 1963, pp. 51-63.

Buchanan, Patrick J., "The Future of the GOP; How History Passed Us By," *National Review* (September 16, 1988), p. 34 ff.

Buckley, William F., "Toward a Definition of Conservatism," *National Review*, Vol. 44 (August 17, 1992), pp. 17-18.

Calhoon, Robert M., "Watergate and American Conservatism," *South Atlantic Quarterly*, Vol. 83, No. 2 (1984), pp. 127-137.

Castle, David S., "Goldwater's Presidential Candidacy and Political Realignment," *Presidential Studies Quarterly*, Vol. 20, No. 1 (1990), pp. 103-110.

Chamberlain, John, "American Conservatism and the World Crisis; A Policy for Conservatives," *The Yale Review,* Vol.40, No. 2 1951, pp. 400-411.

Chambers, Whittaker, "Big Sister is Watching You", *National Review*, Vol.4 (December 28, 1957), pp. 594-596.

Chodorov, Frank, "Lest It Be Forgotten," *Human Events*, Vol. XII, No. 344 (August 20, 1955)

Church, Frank, "The Future of the Radical Right," *Harper's,* Vol. CCXXX (February, 1965)

Cohen, Warren, "Who's Afraid of Alfred Kohlberg?," *Reviews in American History* (March, 1975)

Conover, Pamela Johnston, "The Mobilization of the New Right: A Test of Various Explanations," *The Western Political Quarterly*, Vol. 36, No. 4 (December 1983), pp. 632-649.

Converse, Philip E. et. al., "Electoral Myth and Reality: The 1964 Election," *The American Political Science Review*, Vol. LIX, No. 2 (June, 1965), pp. 321-336.

Danzig, David, "Conservatism After Goldwater," *Commentary*, March 1965

Danzig, David, "The Radical Right & the Rise of the Fundamentalist Minority", *Commentary* (April, 1962), p. 291 ff.

De Santis, Vincent P., "American Catholics and McCarthyism", *The Catholic Historical Review*, Vol.51, No. 1 (April, 1965), pp.1-30.

Dennis, William C., "Kirk, Rossiter, Hartz, and the Conservative Tradition in America," *Modern Age*, Vol. 24 (Spring, 1980), pp. 161-167.

DeVoto, Bernard, "The Ex-Communists," *The Atlantic Monthly* (February, 1951)

Doenecke, Justus, "Conservatism the Impassioned Sentiment: A Review Essay" *American Quarterly 23* (Spring 1977), pp. 601-19

Dunphee, William, "The YAFs Are Coming," *Commonweal* (April 14, 1961).

Eastman, Max, "Buckley Versus Yale," *The American Mercury* (December, 1951).#

English, Raymond, "Conservatism: The Forbidden Faith," *The American Scholar*, Vol. 21, No. 4 (1953)), pp. 393-412.

Evans, Rowland & Robert Novak, "The Men Around Goldwater", *The Saturday Evening Post*, Vol. 237, No. 37 (October 24, 1964), pp. 32-36.

Freund, Ludwig, "American and Continental Conservatism: Some Comparisons", *Modern Age*, Vol. 3 (Winter 1958-1959), pp.40-49.

Friedman, Milton, "The Goldwater View of Economics," *New York Times Magazine*, October 11, 1964)

Glasner, David, "Hayek and the Conservatives," *Commentary* (October, 1992), p. 48 ff.

Gottfried, Paul, "Toward a New Fusionism? The Old Right Makes New Alliances," *Policy Review* (Fall, 1987), pp. 64-70.

Green, Barbara, Katryn Turner, Dante Geronimo, "Responsible and Irresponsible Right-Wing Groups; A Problem in Analysis," *The Journal of Social Issues*, Vol. XIX, No. 2 (April, 1963), pp.3-17.

Griffith, Robert, "The General and the Senator," *Wisconsin Magazine of History* (Autumm, 1970)

Group Research, Inc., "Barry Goldwater and the Organized Right Wing," *Group Research Special Report*, 17 (October 12, 1964).

Hartley, Anthony, "Eisenhower and After: U. S. Conservatism Since the 1950's," *Encounter*, Vol. 64, No. 4 (1985), pp. 61-66.

Huntington, Samuel P., "Conservatism as an Ideology," *American Political Science Review*, Vol. 51 (June, 1957), pp. 454-473.

Judis, John B., "The Two Faces of Whittaker Chambers," *The New Republic* (April 16, 1984), pp. 25-32.

Judis, John B., "The Conservative Wars," *the New Republic* (August 11 & 18, 1986), pp. 15-18.

Judis, John B., "Conservatives Stumble Into the Future," *Dissent* (Summer, 1988), pp. 327-340.

Judis, John B., "The End of Conservatism," *The New Republic* Vol. 207 (August 31, 1992), pp. 28-31.

Kaiser, Robert G. & Ira Chinoy, "How Scaife's Money Powered a Movement" Washington *Post* (May 2, 1999), p. A01.

Kendall, Willmoore, "Do We Want an 'Open Society'?", *National Review*, Vol.6 (January 31, 1959)

Kendall, Willmoore, "Quo Vadis, Barry?," *National Review*, (February 25, 1961)

Kendall, Willmoore, "What Goldwaterism Is All About," *The New Guard* (October, 1964), p. 8 ff.

Kilpatrick, James J., "The Right to Interpose," *Human Events*, Vol. XII, No. 52 (December 24, 1955).

Kitchel, Denison, "Explaining Things To Ike," *National Review*, April 30, 1976

Kraditor, Aileen S., "On the Relationship between Conservatism and American Social History," *Continuity* (Spring/Fall, 1982), pp.127-149.

Kristol, William, "A Conservative Looks at Liberalism," *Commentary*, Vol. 96 (September, 1993), pp. 33-36.

Liggio, Leonard P., "Felix Morley and the Commonwealthman Tradition," *The Journal of Libertarian Studies*, Vol.2, No.3 (Fall, 1978), pp.279-286.

Lippmann, Walter, "The Goldwater Movement," *Newsweek,* (August 5, 1963).

Lukacs, John, "The American Conservatives", *Harper's*,Vol. 268 (January, 1984), pp. 44-49.

Macdonald, Dwight, "Scrambled Eggheads on the Right," *Commentary* (April, 1956)

Macdonald, Dwight, "McCarthy and His Apologists," *Partisan Review* (Spring, 1954)

Macdonald, Dwight, "God and Buckley at Yale," *The Reporter* (May 27, 1952)

Machan, Tibor, "Libertarianism and Conservatives," *Modern Age*, Vol. 24, No. 1 (Winter 1980), pp. 21-33.

Malsberger, John W., "The Transformation of Republican Conservatism: The U.S. Senate, 1938-1952," *Congress & The Presidency*, Vol. 14, No. 1 (Spring, 1987)

McClosky, Herbert, "Conservatism and Personality," *American Political Science Review*, Vol. 52 (March, 1958), pp. 27-45.

McKitrick, Eric L., "Conservatism Today," *The American Scholar*, Vol. 27 (Winter, 1957-58), pp. 49-61.

Meyer, Frank S., "What Next for Conservatism,? *National Review*, (December 1, 1964)

Jeremy D. Mayer, "LBJ Fights the White Backlash; The Racial Politics of the 1964 Presidential Campaign" *Prologue: Quarterly of the National Archives and Records Administration* (Spring 2001), vol. 33, no. 1 (www.nara.gov/publications/prologue/lbj1964a.html#f55)

Miller, Warren E., "Electoral Myth and Reality: the 1964 Election," *American Political Science Review*, Vol. 59 (1965), pp. 321-336.

Moore, Leonard J., "Good Old-Fashioned New Social History and the Twentieth-Century American Right," *Reviews in American History*, Vol. 24, No. 4 (December 1996), pp. 555-573.

Morley, Felix, "The Early Days of Human Events,"*Human Events* (April 27, 1974), p. 26 ff.

Morley, Felix, "American Republic or American Empire?," *Modern Age* (Summer, 1957), p. 20 ff.

Nash, George H., "Willmoore Kendall: Conservative Iconoclast," *Modern Age* (Spring, 1975).

Neuchterlein, James, "William F. Buckley, Jr. and American Conservatism," *Commentary*, Vol. 85 (June, 1988), pp. 31-41.

Nisbeth, Robert, "The Conservative Renaissance in Perspective," *The Public Interest* (No. 81, Fall 1985), pp. 128-141.

Nock, Albert J., "A Little Conserva-tive,"*The Atlantic Monthly*, Vol.158 (October, 1936), pp. 481-489.

Nolan, Cathal J., "The Last Hurrah of Conservative Isolationism: Eisenhower, Congress, and the Bricker Amendment," *Presidential Studies Quarterly* (Spring, 1992), pp. 337-349.

Preece, Rod, "The Anglo-Saxon Conservative Tradition," Canadian Journal of Political Science, Vol. XIII, No. 1 (March, 1980), p. 3 ff.

Proshansky, Harold M., "The Radical Right; A Threat to the Behavorial Sciences," *The Journal of Social Issues*, Vol. XIX (April, 1963).

Reeves, Thomas C., "McCarthyism: Interpretations Since Hofstadter," *Wisconsin Magazine of History* (Autumn, 1976), pp. 42-54.

Ribuffo, Leo, "Why Is There So Much Conservatism in the United States and Why Do So Few Historians Know Anything about It?" *American Historical Review* (April, 1994), pp. 438-449.

Rothbard, Murray N., "Myth and Truth about Libertarianism," *Modern Age*, Vol. 24 (Winter, 1980), pp. 9-15.

Rothbard, Murray N., "The Foreign Policy of the Old Right," *Journal of Libertarian Studies*, Vol.2, No. 1 (1978), pp. 85-96.

Rothbard, Murray N., "A Strategy for the Right; Presidential Address to the Randolph Club, Herndon, Virginia, January 18, 1992, *Rothbard-Rockwell Report* (http://www.lewrockwell.com/rothbard/ir/Ch1.html)

Rovere, Richard, "The Conservative Mindlessness," *Commentary*, Vol. 39 (March, 1965), p. 38 ff.

Rovere, Richard, "Senator McCarthy's Eggheads," *The Reporter* (May 11, 1954).

Schiff, Lawrence F., "The Obedient Rebels: A Study of College Conversions to Conservatism," *Journal of Social Issues*, Vol. 20 (October, 1964), p. 91 ff.

Schlesinger, Jr., Arthur M., "The New Isolationism," *The Atlantic Monthly* (May, 1952), pp. 34-38.

Schlesinger, Jr., Arthur M., "The Threat of the Radical Right," *New York Times Magazine* (June 17, 1962).

Schuparra, Kurt, "Freedom vs. Tyranny: The 1958 California Election and the Origins of the State's Conservative Movement," *Pacific Historical Review*, Vol. 63 (November 4, 1994), pp. 537-560.

Shaffer, Helen B., "Future of Conservatism," *Editorial Research Reports*, Vol. 1 (January 4, 1974), pp. 1-20.

Stromberg, Joseph R., "Felix Morley: An Old Fashioned Republican Critic of Statism and Interventionism," *The Journal of Libertarian Studies*, Vol. 2, No. 3 (Fall, 1978), pp. 269-279.

Sugrue, Thomas J., "Crabgrass-Roots Politics: Race, Rights, and the Reaction against Liberalism in the Urban North, 1940-1964," The Journal of American History (September, 1995), pp. 551-565.

Tobin, James, "Barry's Economic Crusade," *The New Republic* (October 24, 1964), p. 13 ff.

Urban, Whitaker, "China Lobby's New Gambit," *The Nation* (October 7, 1961), pp. 225-228.

Villey, Daniel, "Catholics and the Market Economy," *Modern Age*, Vol.3 (Summer, 1959), pp. 250-261.

Weaver, Richard M., "Up From Liberalism," *Modern Age*, Vol. 3 (Winter, 1958-1959), pp. 21-32.

Weyrich, Paul M., "The Reagan Revolution That Wasn't," *Policy Review* (Summer, 1987), pp. 50-53.

Wilcox, Clyde, "Popular Backing For the Old Christian Right: Explaining Support For the Christian Anti-Communism Crusade," *Journal of Social History* (Fall, 1987), pp. 117-132.

Wilcox, Clyde, "The Christian Right in Twentieth Century America: Continuity and Change," *Review of Politics*, Vol. 50, No. 4 (1988), pp. 659-681.

Wilcox, Walther, "The Press of the Radical Right; an Exploratory Analysis", *Journalism Quaterly*, Vol. XXXIX (Spring, 1962).

Will, George F., "Goldwater: A Man Who Won the Future," Washington *Post*, (March 27, 1994)

Wolfe, Alan, "The Revolution that Never Was," *The New Republic* (June 7, 1999), pp. 42-47.

Yohn, Susan M., "Will the Real Conservative Please Stand Up? or, The Pitfalls Involved in Examining Ideological Sympathies: A Comments on Alan Brinkley's 'Problem of American Conservatism,'" *American Historical Review* (April, 1994), pp. 430-437.

Index

American Conservative Union 144, 207, 288
American Council of Christian Churches (ACCC) 190
American Enterprise Institute 13, 227, 243, 298-299
American Enterprise Institute 13, 227, 243, 299
American Liberty League 17, 105
American Mercury 91, 102-104, 116, 118-119, 124, 126, 203, 321, 324
Americans for Constitutional Action (ACA) 13, 289
analysis 118
anticommunism 39, 57, 69-70, 76, 117-118, 135, 190, 306, 316, 319, 321
Ashbrook, John 138, 169, 216, 288, 302
Babitt, Irvin 49
Baroody, Jr, William J. 205, 237, 243, 247-249, 273-274,
Bauman, Carol 182-183, 279, 288
Bauman, Robert 183, 207, 288
Bentley, Elizabeth 68
Bliss, Ray 255, 287
Bork, Robert 264
Bozell, L. Brent 62, 66, 119, 127, 129, 137, 167, 169, 174, 196, 211, 216, 248, 268, 288, 312
Bricker Amendment 100-101, 326
Bricker, John 56, 74, 100
Brown vs. Board of Education in Topeka 131
Bruce, Donald C. 169, 288
Buchanan, Pat 183, 292
Buckley, James 102, 160
Buckley, Jr, William F. 8, 14, 19, 31, 34-37, 44, 59-63, 66-68, 77, 80, 102-103, 115-117, 119-120, 124-125, 128-130, 134-136, 139, 143, 145-146, 154, 160, 163, 166-168, 171-173, 179-180, 189, 203, 205-207, 248-250, 285-287, 301, 309, 311, 317, 326
Burch, Dean 8, 234, 247, 249, 255, 287
Burnham, James 21, 30, 32, 59-60, 64, 97, 102, 116-117, 120, 123-125, 127, 133, 135-136, 143, 250, 309, 312, 314, 321
Bush, George 214, 278
Caddy, Douglas 155, 168-169, 178-180
Cardinal Mindszenty, Joseph 70
Chamberlain, John 31, 80, 104, 106-107, 109-110, 112-113, 116, 118-119, 143, 169, 288, 309, 312, 323-324
Chamberlin, William Henry 28, 68, 99, 312
Chambers, Whittaker 28, 30, 36-37, 49, 59, 71, 104, 119, 125, 127, 143, 204, 312, 321, 324-325
Chicago Tribune 79, 85, 169, 288
China Lobby 105, 109, 143, 310, 317, 323, 327
Chodorov, Frank 25, 40, 94, 99, 101, 113, 118-119, 125-126, 166, 169, 312, 324
Christian Anti-Communism Crusade 172, 200, 328
Christian Crusade 16, 126, 172, 175, 190, 200-201, 328
Church League of America 190
Civil Rights Act of 1964 266, 296
Clinton, Bill 14-15, 40, 49, 67, 307-308, 320
Committee of One Million 143, 174, 179, 310
Compact of Fifth Avenue 148-149, 211
Crane, Jasper 105, 113
Crane, Phillip 183
Davis, Forrest 28, 106-107, 109, 113, 119
De Toledano, Ralph 59, 102-103, 132, 309, 313
Decter, Midge 307
Democratic Party 18, 56, 72, 101, 146, 156, 188, 214, 256, 293-295

Dole, Bob 261, 291
Draft Goldwater movement 20, 75, 111, 137-138, 143-144, 183, 209, 215-216, 218, 228, 247, 322
Eastland, James O. 131
Eastman, Max 59-60, 102, 104, 107, 119, 125-127, 143, 314, 324
Edwards, Lee 168-169, 171, 176, 182, 211, 264, 271, 314
Eisenhower, Dwight D. 106-108, 110-113, 121, 193, 206, 210, 214, 236, 242-43, 249, 252-53, 256, 258, 262, 269, 274, 292
Engle v Vitale 152, 275, 297
Evans, M. Stanton 47, 100, 164-165, 167, 169-170, 173, 175, 282, 289, 314
extremism 20, 185, 197, 202, 250, 254-255, 257-258, 269, 319
Fellers, Bonner 101, 191
Flynn, John T. 85-86, 90, 96-97, 101, 104, 314
For America 63, 81, 101, 142, 308
Ford, Gerald 91, 255, 303-304
Foundation for Economic Education 105, 113, 167, 172
Franke, David 100, 151, 168
Free Society Association) 289
Friedman, Milton 28, 244-245, 324
fusionism 43, 45-46, 54, 124, 171, 325
Galbraith, John Kenneth 277
Goldwater, Barry M. 20, 58, 74, 130, 132, 137, 141, 147, 149-150, 155-156, 158, 169, 174-175, 181-183, 195, 210-203, 205, 209ff., 233ff., 261ff., 291ff.
Great Society 210, 270, 291, 296
Grenier, John 215, 224, 246, 287
Hanighen, Frank C. 82, 86, 93-94
Hargis, Billy James 190
Hart, Jeffrey 80, 127, 136, 139, 309, 316
Hart, Merwin K. 126, 191
Hayek, F.A. 25-26, 40, 50-51, 65, 95, 104, 120, 167, 316
Hazlitt, Henry 28, 104, 106, 112-113, 169
Herberg, Will 60, 316
Heritage Foundation 34, 173, 184, 261, 298, 303

Hess, Karl 54, 119, 217, 219, 237, 243, 289, 316
Hiss, Alger 28, 36, 57, 71, 98
Hofstadter, Richard 122, 199, 210, 276, 291, 316
Hook, Sidney 66, 117, 143
Hoover Institution 8, 13, 150, 159, 167, 195, 225, 243, 253, 259, 298-299, 309, 313
Hoover, Herbert 8, 22, 27, 83, 91, 105-106, 113, 175, 280, 309
Human Events 13, 19, 81-83, 86-87, 89, 91, 94-95, 98-100, 106, 115, 118, 166-168, 172, 227, 316, 324-326
Hunt, H.L. 189
Huston, Tom 134, 177-178, 183, 292
Intercollegiate Society of Individualists 165-166, 170, 314
isolationism 19, 79, 82, 87-90, 92, 96-97, 101-102, 109, 123, 313, 320, 326-327
Javits, Jacob K. 146, 159
Jenner, William 56, 58, 74, 189
Johnson, Lyndon B. 8, 20, 159, 210, 218, 220, 230, 262-263, 266, 277-278, 280, 284, 292, 294, 309
Keating, Kenneth 157, 159
Kendall, Willmoore 44, 64-67, 116, 127, 163, 169, 209, 317, 325-326
Kennedy, John F. 8, 91, 105, 136, 164, 188-189, 230, 284, 309
Kilpatrick, James J. 131-132, 215, 317, 325
King, Jr., Martin Luther 163
Kirk, Russell 11, 39-41, 44-45, 49, 51-52, 66, 95, 113, 115, 119-120, 124-125, 127, 167, 169, 173, 181, 193, 205, 212, 317
Kitchel, Denison 195, 201, 225-229, 233-234, 242-243, 246, 253, 259, 264, 279, 289, 309, 325
Knowland, William 56, 122, 143, 189, 239, 246
Kohlberg, Alfred 103, 105-106, 169, 191, 324
La Follette, Suzanne 104, 106, 112, 119, 125
Laird, Melvin 254

Landon, Alf M. 26
LeMay, Curtis 186
Libertarianism 16, 40-41, 43-45, 50, 52-54, 103-104, 123, 125, 326-327
Liberty Lobby 16, 126, 318
Lichenstein, Charles 243, 304
Liebman, Marvin 143, 150, 152, 159, 168-169, 171, 174, 177, 179-180, 196, 256, 288, 309, 317
Life-Line Foundation 189
Lindbergh, Charles A. 85-86, 91
Lodge, Henry Cabot 108-109, 149, 220, 235, 242, 261
Luce, Claire Boothe 105, 157-158
Mahoney, J. Daniel 143, 145, 169
Manion, Clarence 101, 142, 163, 166-167, 169, 189, 211, 263, 268, 309
McCarthy, Joseph 55-57, 66, 97, 105, 194, 318
McCarthyism 5, 19, 55, 57, 59-67, 69, 71, 73-75, 77, 79, 105, 123, 198, 206, 314-315, 317, 324, 327
McCormick, Robert C. 85-86, 110
Mencken, H.L. 102-104, 321
Meyer, Frank S. 14, 16, 41-42, 45-48, 119, 125, 143, 154, 167, 219, 225, 318, 326
Miller, William E. 156, 182, 256
Milliken, Roger 167, 175, 191, 205, 216, 221
Mises, Ludwig Von 26, 28, 104-105, 169, 175
Moley, Raymond 23, 104, 145-146, 273, 318
Mont Pelerin Society 27, 167
Moore, Paul Elmer 49
Morgenthau Plan 94
Morley, Felix 28, 82-83, 86-87, 91, 93-94, 98-99, 112, 282, 309, 318, 325-327
Moyers, Bill 266, 277-278, 309
National Association of Manufacturers 105, 191, 222
National Draft Goldwater Committee 226
National Review 5, 11, 13, 19, 36-37, 44, 54, 60, 64-65, 68-69, 74-75, 80, 91, 104, 106, 115-139, 143, 155, 163, 167-168, 171, 178-180, 195, 203-207, 215, 225, 242, 248-251, 283, 285, 301, 323-326

National Student Association (NSA) 13, 134, 177-178, 224
National Young Republicans 223, 250
NATO 109, 193, 196, 204, 236, 267
Neoconservatism 298
Neoconservatives 37, 298-299, 305
New Deal 12, 16-18, 21-24, 26-27, 29, 32, 36, 39-40, 47-48, 54-56, 58, 60, 67, 72, 76, 80, 84, 89-91, 96-98, 100, 102, 109, 121, 210, 242, 263, 266, 276, 291, 299, 303, 308, 311, 315-316, 319
New Guard 134, 143, 155, 168, 172-173, 176-178, 182, 204, 209, 224, 278-279, 286, 325
New Right 12-13, 16, 49, 60, 75-76, 97-99, 116, 122, 130, 138, 152, 165, 168, 181, 183, 185, 198-199, 204, 210, 217, 238, 248, 261, 275-276, 295, 298-301, 304-305, 311-325, 327
New Right 12-13, 16, 49, 60, 75-76, 97-99, 116, 122, 130, 138, 152, 165, 168, 181, 183, 185, 198-199, 204, 210, 217, 238, 248, 261, 275-276, 295, 298-301, 304-305, 311-325, 327
New York Conservative Party 5, 13, 137, 141-144, 146, 153, 155-156, 159, 178, 256
Niemeyer, Gerhardt 119, 127, 134, 169, 270
Nisbet, Robert 14, 39, 319
Nixon, Richard M. 74, 98, 109, 192, 258-259, 300, 319
Nock, Albert J. 26, 35, 65, 91, 103, 319, 313, 326
Nye, Gerald P. 85-86, 320
NAACP 101, 176, 264, 275
O'Doherty, Kieran 143, 145, 153, 159
O'Donnell, Peter 215-216, 224, 227, 234, 247, 288, 292
Ortega Y Gasset, Jose 35, 319
Paleoconservatism 305, 323
Paleoconservatives 37, 305
Paolucci, Henry 158, 160
Passos, John Dos 104, 107, 119, 125, 143, 169, 175, 283, 288
Pew, Howard 34, 105, 113, 172, 191
Phillips, Howard 177, 183, 292, 300

Phillips, Kevin 300-301, 319
Plain Talk 103, 106, 118
public orthodoxy 5, 55, 63-66, 129
racial segregation 132, 176, 213
Radical Right 16, 20, 49, 60, 67, 185-186, 189-190, 192, 197-198, 201, 203-204, 207, 240, 251, 269-270, 311, 314, 323-324, 327-328
Rand, Ayn 25, 203-204
Read, Leonard 105, 113, 167, 172
Reagan, Reagan 13, 23, 169, 183, 199, 210, 239, 249, 273-274, 289, 295-296, 300, 302-304, 320-321
Red Scare 56, 69, 97, 102
Regnery; Henry 40, 44, 46, 49, 62, 66, 83-84, 86-87, 89, 93-95, 99, 113, 118, 128, 131, 164, 167, 169, 191, 309, 311-312, 314, 317-318, 320, 322
Rehnquist, William H. 264
Republican National Committee 8, 17, 108, 182, 255, 278, 280, 309
Republican Party 12, 18-20, 22, 33, 57, 72-73, 86, 106-107, 110, 138, 141-142, 144-146, 148-149, 153-161, 178, 183, 192, 196, 201, 214-215, 218, 220, 223, 229, 234, 242, 247, 251-252, 261, 274-275, 279-280, 283-284, 286, 289, 291, 293, 304, 306, 308, 318
Richard Kleindienst 234, 240, 255, 292, 317
Richberg, Donald R. 23-24, 189
Rockefeller, Nelson 16, 146, 159, 202, 211, 217, 220-221, 223-224, 240, 251-252, 257, 287, 317
Roe v Wade 297
Romney, George 220, 241, 255, 261
Roosevelt, Franklin Delano 17, 24, 84, 160, 280
Rothbard, Murray S. 22
Rousselot, John H. 169
Rusher, William A. 8, 75, 137-139, 143, 169, 172, 174, 179-180, 196, 206-207, 215-217, 221, 223, 225, 234, 250-251, 285, 288, 300, 309, 320
Ryskind, Morrie 126, 169, 205
Santayana, George 49

Schlafly, Phyllis 33, 239, 320
Schlamm, Willi 36, 75, 104, 107, 118-119, 125-126, 205
Schlesinger, Jr., Arthur M. 31, 45, 48, 60, 79, 320-321, 327
Schwarz, Fred C. 172, 200
Scranton, William 202, 220, 230
Shadegg, Stephen 149, 212, 216-217, 222, 236, 239, 246, 248, 253, 259, 280, 310, 321
Sharon Statement 170-171, 178
Simon, William 297-298
Smith, Gerald L.K. 76, 87, 126, 203, 317
Social Security 58, 148, 159, 204, 236-237, 242, 245, 269, 272, 274
Sokolsky, George 104, 145, 173
Southern strategy 263, 265, 300
Spengler, Oswald 35
Stanley, Scott 179-180
States Rights 131-132, 170, 176, 193, 213, 215, 234, 264, 266
Strauss, Leo 64, 129, 313, 318
Students for a Democratic Society 54, 164-165, 170
Taft, Robert A. 83, 90, 92, 107, 111-112, 122, 267, 310, 317, 319, 321
The Draft Goldwater Committee 215-216, 224, 226, 233
The Freeman 19, 28, 31, 35, 80, 91, 100, 102-107, 109-113, 118-119, 124, 126, 143
The John Birch Society 16, 20, 70, 75-76, 167, 175, 185, 187, 190-196, 200-203, 205-206, 238, 254-255, 258, 270, 274, 311, 314-315, 323
The Knights of Columbus 70
Thomas, Norman 31, 90-91, 94, 104
Thurmond, Strom 169, 175, 188, 214
Tower, John G. 169, 214, 283, 321
Traditionalism 16, 40, 44-45, 50, 54, 123, 125
Truman, Harry S. 24
Utley, Freda 68, 91, 93-94, 107, 119
Vandenberg, Arthur M. 85
Vietnam 54, 79, 92, 129, 160, 181, 184, 220, 242, 270-272, 296

Viguerie, Richard 13, 180, 183, 279, 305, 322
Walker, Edwin A. 175, 186-188, 191
Wallace, George C. 256, 263, 300
Wallace, Henry 23, 81, 143
Warren, Earl 193, 196, 205, 238
Weaver, Richard 29, 36, 40, 119, 124, 131, 167, 169, 175, 322-323, 328
Wedemeyer, A.C. 191
Welch, Robert 190, 192-193, 195-196, 201, 203, 205-206, 258, 269
Wheeler, Burton K. 85, 189
White, F. Clifton 8, 111, 138, 156, 180, 183, 210, 216-217, 221, 223-225, 227-228, 235, 237, 241, 247, 252, 256-259, 273, 287, 310, 322
Wills, Garry 45, 119, 127-128, 204, 322
Wood, Robert E. 85-86, 101, 320
Young Americans for Freedom (YAF) 13, 19, 76, 100, 137, 151, 164-165, 168-170, 185, 189, 285-286, 310
Young Republican National Federation 138, 168, 178, 182